AMERICAN SERIAL KILLERS

ALSO BY PETER VRONSKY

Serial Killers
Female Serial Killers
Sons of Cain

AMERICAN
SERIAL
KILLERS

The Deadliest Years
1950–2000

PETER VRONSKY

BERKLEY
New York

For my beautiful wife, Anna Zinato,
for all the years of her love and coffee

BERKLEY
An imprint of Penguin Random House LLC
penguinrandomhouse.com

Copyright © 2021 by Peter Vronsky

BERKLEY and the BERKLEY & B colophon are registered trademarks of Penguin Random House LLC.

Berkley trade paperback ISBN: 9780593198957

The Library of Congress has catalogued the Berkley hardcover edition of this book as follows:

Names: Vronsky, Peter, author.
Title: American serial killers : the epidemic years 1950-2000 / Peter Vronsky.
Description: New York : Berkley, [2020]
Identifiers: LCCN 2020022004 (print) | LCCN 2020022005 (ebook) |
ISBN 9780593198810 (hardcover) | ISBN 9780593198827 (ebook)
Subjects: LCSH: Serial murder—United States—History—20th century. |
Serial murderers—United States—History—20th century.
Classification: LCC HV6515 .V75 2004 (print) | LCC HV6515 (ebook) |
DDC 364.152/32092273—dc23
LC record available at https://lccn.loc.gov/2020022004
LC ebook record available at https://lccn.loc.gov/2020022005

Berkley hardcover edition / February 2021
Berkley trade paperback edition / November 2021

Cover images: Top: Three sketches of the Golden State Killer, Wikipedia; Middle right: The Cannibal news article courtesy Mirrorpix / Reach Licensing; Bottom left: Zodiac Killer article, *New York Daily News*, © 1990, Getty Images; Wanted sign of Ted Bundy, Getty Images

Printed in the United States of America
1st Printing

Contents

An Arrest in Milwaukee

Cops can go for days, weeks and sometimes even years working routine shifts in which nothing extraordinary happens. They work a grind of calls to domestic disputes, medical distress, unruly customers, parking complaints and petty burglaries. A few go their entire career never once chasing a fleeing suspect, kicking in a door or unholstering their weapon. But all that can change in an instant.

On the evening of July 22, 1991, Milwaukee police officers Robert Rauth and Rolf Mueller were coming to the end of one of those routine shifts. They were assigned to District 3 in the Avenues West, a neighborhood that had seen better days. The Pabst beer family mansion stood there as did the campus of Marquette University and the Milwaukee High School of the Arts. But some parts of the neighborhood were rough and troubled, especially around the blocks at North 25th Street where the elegant old Victorian houses had been converted to rooming houses or torn down to make way for anonymous two- and three-story apartment buildings. The area was predominately populated by poor minorities, especially African Americans and recently arrived Southeast Asians.

It was 11:30 p.m., and it had been a quiet evening. Rauth and Mueller were hoping that nothing would come up in the next thirty minutes to delay them from ending their shift at midnight and going home. But just as they turned onto 25th Street from Kilbourn Avenue, the headlights of their patrol car came upon a shirtless black man running toward them. He had a pair of handcuffs dangling from his left wrist, and his face was contorted in panic and fear.

Rauth and Mueller had no idea what they had just driven into as they exited their vehicle to calm the hysterical man down. Thirty-two-year-old Tracy Edwards told the officers some "freak" had handcuffed him and begged them to get the handcuffs off his wrist. Rauth tried using his handcuff key, but it did not fit the brand of cuffs around Edwards's wrist. Had they been able to remove the handcuffs in the street, perhaps that would have been the end of it, and we would not have heard anything more of this story, at least not that July.

Edwards told them that he had been forcibly restrained for several hours in the Oxford Apartments just up the street. The officers accompanied Edwards to a shabby three-story apartment building at 924 North 25th Street. Their plan was to get the key, remove the handcuffs and hopefully "clear the matter up" quickly without having to arrest anyone, transport them and do a whole bunch of paperwork till God knows when.

Edwards led Rauth and Mueller to the door of apartment 213. The first thing they noted was that it had its own electronic alarm system and high-grade armored locks, unusual for a low-income apartment building in that neighborhood. Knocking on the door, they noticed a second thing: a distinct odor of death and decay wafting from the other side, a smell most cops are familiar with and never forget once they have experienced it.

The door was opened by a tall, slightly disheveled white male in his early thirties. He identified himself as Jeffrey Dahmer and showed them his employee identification card from the Ambrosia Chocolate factory, where he said he worked as a mixer. He was calm and polite and invited the officers and Edwards to step into his apartment.

Upon entering the small one-bedroom apartment, Rauth and Mueller almost gagged on the thick smell of human decay mixed with the perfumed scent of room deodorant and disinfectant.

At first glance, the apartment appeared to be completely normal. It was relatively well furnished with a couch and armchair, carpeting, floor and table lamps, cared-for plants and a large lit aquarium on a black table, its electric filter quietly humming and gurgling as fish lazily circled behind its glass. Thick blue curtains hung on the windows. The white walls were decorated with framed abstract posters and gay erotica, which by the 1990s wouldn't even raise a cop's eyebrow.

Immediately to the left of the front door was the kitchen area with a sink, counter, stove and fridge. A small upright floor freezer stood next to a kitchen table cluttered with tools and beer cans. The apartment was moderately littered—like after a small party—with empty beer cans, tissue boxes and spray cans of air freshener. There were several small plastic chemical containers and a stack of bright red boxes of Soilax, a floor and wall cleaner sold in hardware stores. The only *really* unusual thing about the apartment—other than the smell—was a big surveillance camera mounted high in a corner of the room.

Dahmer readily admitted that he had handcuffed Edwards but offered no explanation or showed any anxiety. His attitude was "I do this all the time. So what?"

Edwards got a sense that the two police officers did not appear particularly alert or interested in his complaint. Now Edwards added that Dahmer had threatened him with a knife and had told him he was going to "eat his heart." Rauth and Mueller rolled their eyes. They thought they knew where this was going. This was a "gay drama thing"—a domestic quarrel that got out of hand—and now wild accusations were flying. They radioed in a check on Dahmer, and the response came back that he was on probation for a felony sexual assault on a minor. Now Rauth and Mueller became alert.

Mueller demanded the handcuff key, and Dahmer told him that it was on the bedside table. When Mueller headed toward the bedroom, Dahmer suddenly became agitated and attempted to push ahead of him. Rauth held Dahmer back.

Mueller entered Dahmer's bedroom alone and stood there in the dim light. The first thing that caught his eye was a huge blue plastic chemical drum in the corner of the bedroom. There were a TV and a VCR on a dresser facing the bed. A two-drawer black metal filing cabinet. His attention was drawn to what looked like crusty bloodstains on the bedsheets and faded smears of blood on the wall around the bed, as if someone had been sponging the walls but couldn't quite get the stains out. The bedroom, like the living room, was decorated with erotic posters, and the window was draped in the same dark blue curtains.

As Mueller approached the bedside table to look for the handcuff key, his eye was drawn to a stack of Polaroid photos in a partly open drawer. It took Mueller a few seconds to process what he was seeing: severed heads and penises, dismembered bodies. In one photo he saw a severed head spray-painted gold, cupped in two severed hands, perched on a pile of ice in a kitchen sink, next to it a bottle of Dawn dish detergent and a sponge. There was a series of photos of unconscious or dead black men with their wrists handcuffed behind them. A photo of a corpse in a bathtub, gutted and skinned to the rib cage. Another series of photos featured a corpse bent over backward like an arching bridge on the mattress. Mueller immediately recognized in many of the Polaroids the decor of the apartment he was standing in—but he couldn't quite believe it.

When Dahmer saw Mueller come out of the bedroom, his face ashen and the Polaroids in his hands, he began struggling and had to be wrestled to the floor by the two officers and handcuffed. By now Mueller knew he would not be ending his shift on time that evening.

As Rauth held Dahmer to the floor, Mueller, almost in a daze, began trying to find the source of the awful smell. He walked into the kitchen past a pile of pans with a dark brown sticky material pooled in them. Mueller instinctively reached for the fridge door and opened it. As the light blinked on, Mueller gazed past a plastic squeeze bottle of honey and containers of mustard and relish, down into the face of a black man looking back at him from inside a cardboard box on the bottom shelf. Next to it stood an open container of Arm & Hammer baking soda to absorb the stench.

Inside the freezer compartment, Mueller came upon plastic bags with some kind of meat and a decaying head without a face, its empty skull sockets staring out through the frosty opaque plastic bag. As Mueller backed away from the fridge in horror, he heard Dahmer moan, "For what I did I should be dead." Over the next few days, as the homicide investigators and forensic technicians took over, Milwaukee police recovered an array of butchered human remains, including a heart from the freezer and three torsos floating in a brine of chemicals in the fifty-seven-gallon drum. In the floor-standing freezer they found three severed heads, a torso and other assorted cuts of human flesh. There were plastic-wrapped "patties" of human flesh stuck in a frozen pool of bodily fluids accumulated at the bottom of the freezer, which had to be defrosted to remove. In a cardboard box that once contained Dahmer's computer, they found two skulls and an album with more Polaroid photos of victims. The top drawer of the black filing cabinet near Dahmer's bed revealed three more skulls, while the bottom drawer was filled with a jumble of human bones from a complete skeleton. There were a couple of pots on the top shelf of the bedroom closet; one contained two heads, while the other had severed male genitals and a pair of hands. In the end, Milwaukee PD cataloged the remains of eleven victims in Dahmer's small one-bedroom apartment.

By July 1991 when Dahmer was arrested, the United States had experienced a surge of some 1,500 serial killer cases in the previous thirty years. Americans had almost become used to it. Some even followed serial killers' victim numbers like sports scores. Serial killer trading cards were just on the horizon. This was the era of Ted Bundy; John Wayne Gacy; David Berkowitz, "the Son of Sam"; and Richard Ramirez, "the Night Stalker," all celebrity serial killers and household names. There had been so many serial killers by the beginning of the 1990s that a high number of victims often no longer impressed the media; there had to be a twist. And the Dahmer case obviously had the twist.

Dahmer eventually confessed to seventeen murders committed between 1978 and 1991 and pleaded guilty in 1992. His insanity hearing was televised, and Dahmer took his place in the pantheon of recent celebrity serial killers like Ted Bundy and John Wayne Gacy.

His era, which we have come to characterize as the "serial killer epidemic" years, coincidentally began just a two-hour drive away from Milwaukee, in the small town of Plainfield, Wisconsin. That's where in 1957, Ed Gein, the inspiration for the killer in *Psycho*, ushered in a new age of serial murder. Just like the Dahmer case, the Gein murders also featured grotesque mutilations of corpses and the harvesting of body parts, which brought the case to national prominence. It is one of those strange twists of fate that both the beginning and the end of the epidemic years of American serial murder unfolded in Wisconsin.

What nobody knew, as all eyes turned to Jeffrey Dahmer, was that he was going to be the last of this wave of "celebrity" serial killers. There would be many more serial killers to come, but none garnered the kind of focus and attention that Dahmer's generation of serial killers received and still receives to this day. The question *why* is one of the subjects of this book exploring this epidemic era of serial murder.

INTRODUCTION

The "Golden Age" of Serial Murderers

"The golden age of serial murderers" is an ironic term coined by Harold Schechter, the American author and historian of nineteenth-century and early-twentieth-century serial killers. In Greek mythology, the Golden Age described a primordial era of peace, stability, harmony and prosperity, akin to a biblical paradise; the best of times. Today the term is applied to all sorts of things: golden age of jazz, golden age of sailing, golden age of radio, golden age of comics, golden age of television, golden age of Hollywood, and even golden age of piracy, golden age of organized crime and golden age of porn. The term is bestowed retroactively after the age passed and is often used nostalgically to describe an era that represented the best of something, the most innovative, exciting or groundbreaking.

In a 2011 article in *Slate* magazine entitled "Blood Loss: The Decline of the Serial Killer," Christopher Beam quotes Schechter as saying, "It does seem the golden age of serial murderers is probably past."[1] What Schechter meant tongue in cheek is that today there is no longer a wide-eyed, "breaking news" fascination with "celebrity" serial killers, in the way there once was in the decades of the 1950s through the 1990s. In its own time, however, when it was happening, this surge of serial murderers in the United States was referred to as a "serial killer epidemic."

The passing of this era—the age of Ted Bundy, Edmund Kemper, John Wayne Gacy, the Son of Sam and Jeffrey Dahmer—was followed by a dramatic statistical decline in the number of serial killers apprehended in the 2000s and 2010s compared to the previous three decades of the 1970s, 1980s and 1990s. There wasn't just a decline in the number of serial killers; there was also a huge decline in the number of victims each serial killer accrued. From 1970 to 1980, the average hovered at 10 to 13 victims per serial killer. By the 2000s, the number had declined significantly to between 3 and 4 victims, and there have not been any recent cases in the United States of "big-number" serial killers of the scale of "golden agers" like Juan Corona (25), Dean Corll (28), Ted Bundy (35), John Wayne Gacy (33), Gary Ridgway (49) or Samuel Little, who recently has been linked to as many as 50 to 93 serial murders from 1970 to 2005.[2]

As serial homicide expert Eric Hickey concluded in 2016, "Between 2000 and 2014 serial killers have emerged more slowly and quietly. In fact, over the past 15 years there has been a dearth of headline-grabbing killers like the Dahmers, Gacys, Kempers, Raders. . . . Many serial killers have emerged in recent years who receive little media attention. Part of the reason is that most of the new cases do not carry the social drama, social class, or high body counts to be of serious public interest."[3]

While there had been numerous small surges of serial killing in the past, their scope and number were not comparable to the surge from the 1950s to the 1990s. Of 2,604 identified serial killers in the United States during the twentieth century, an astonishing 89.5 percent (2,331) made their appearance between 1950 and 1999, with 88 percent of those appearing in just the three decades from 1970 to 1999—the "epidemic" peak years. The numbers speak for themselves.

Serial Killers in the US by Decade (1900–2016)[4]	
1900	49
1910	52
1920	62
1930	55
1940	55
1950	72
1960	217
1970	605
1980	768

**Serial Killers in the US by Decade
(1900–2016)[4]**

1990	669
2000	371
2010	117

It was in the middle of the "golden age" that the term "serial killer" was coined, creating an entirely new identifiable phenomenon in our political, social, psychological, forensic and cultural discourse, even though it had existed without the label since the beginning of human history. Prior to being named, serial killings were perceived as unconnected, inexplicable, individual, monstrous acts of personal aberration. But once labeled, they became a part of something bigger than an aberrant individual perpetrator. Serial killers emerged as a specifically defined *species of perpetrator*, with categorized subspecies, or "profiles," each with precise characteristics, motives and a psychopathological system of recognized, described and cataloged ranges of behaviors and "signatures" that could be identified by profilers.

As the number of serial killers began to multiply exponentially, so did the media accounts of their respective body counts, in a kind of macabre race to the top to see which serial killer would dominate headlines in what bizarre new way and with what shocking number of victims. Serial killers became front-page news.

From the late 1960s through the 1990s, just as there was an increase in the number of serial killers, those serial killers became much more famous: killers such as Jerry Brudos, Edmund Kemper, Charles Manson, Ted Bundy, John Wayne Gacy, David Berkowitz, Randy Kraft, Leonard Lake, Charles Ng, Kenneth Bianchi, Angelo Buono, Arthur Shawcross, Richard Ramirez and Henry Lee Lucas comprised a pantheon of "superstar" serial killers who captured our imaginations as if they were movie stars or athletes. With that came the emergence of serial killer trading cards, calendars, lunch boxes, action figures and coloring books, and ancillary industries like the trafficking of serial killer artifacts, artworks and autographs in the form of *murderabilia*.

In the 1980s, the FBI identified serial killers as an "epidemic" threat distinct from other killers and offered a response in the form of (a) specialized "criminal profilers" at the FBI's Behavioral Science Unit (BSU) and (b) a centralized database intended to link individual murders across the US to specific perpetrators: ViCAP (Violent Criminal Apprehension Program). Serial killers were now categorized and labeled by type and behavior, like species of insects.

Once we had the terms "serial killer" and "profiler," a host of movies, books and television shows fed a massive entertainment industry focused on tales (both fictional and "true") of serial killers and their apprehension, with *The Silence of the Lambs* as perhaps the breakthrough novel and film of the genre.

Serial Killer: The Current Definition

While primarily focused on sexual serial murder, for statistical and historical purposes this book uses the current definition of serial murder revised and adopted at the San Antonio Serial Murder Symposium in 2005, sponsored by the FBI's National Center for the Analysis of Violent Crime (NCAVC) Behavioral Analysis Unit (BAU), which defined serial murder as "the unlawful killing of *two or more* victims by the same offender(s) in separate events" *for any reason*, including "anger, thrill, financial gain, and attention seeking."[5] (my emphasis)

In the past, a serial killer had been traditionally defined as somebody who murders *three or more* victims in separate sexual fantasy–driven murders with a "cooling off" period in between. The FBI eventually realized the "three victims" definition presented all sorts of statistical and conceptual problems. It excluded murderers who have an obvious, identifiable serial killer psychopathology but are apprehended after their first or second murder, before they can commit the requisite third. It did not account for serial offenders with only two *convictions* despite having killed more, thus excluding on a technicality some notorious historic serial killers, like Albert Fish, Ed Gein, Albert DeSalvo ("the Boston Strangler") and Wayne Williams, who were all convicted of only one or two homicides, notwithstanding persuasive suspicions of many more victims.

Female predatory serial killers, profit killers, genocidal killers, contract and gangland killers, and missionary-type serial killers such as terrorists or those who might target abortion doctors or interracial couples are included under the FBI's broad umbrella defining what constitutes a serial killer today: anybody who kills two or more people in distinctly separate incidents.

For the purposes of this book, however, I focus on male sexual serial killers, the Ted Bundy types that we most often associate with the term "serial killer" and who make up a majority of serial killers.*

This book focuses on the so-called "golden age" epidemic years, describing some of its most consequential cases, the response from law enforcement and the forensic psychiatric communities, and the historical, sociological and cultural context. In this way, I attempt to account for this unprecedented surge in serial killing, and perhaps also explain its more recent (and hopefully, permanent) decline.

---

*Female serial killers or profit-motivated materialist serial killers are often included in gross statistics gathered on serial killers, as for example in the Radford University/ FGCU (Florida Gulf Coast University) Serial Killer Database, which I often cite.

CHAPTER 1

Sons of Cain:
A Brief History of Serial Murder
from the Stone Age to 1930

I am sorry that I am unable to murder the whole damned human race.

Carl Panzram, serial killer

Serial killers have existed since the beginning of humankind, except we did not call them that. Before civilization, humans were an animalistic, murderous, cannibalistic species, driven by a set of instinctual behaviors necessary to survival for hundreds of thousands of years; perhaps for as long as over a million years, depending on how one defines a "human."[1]

There were at least two distinct species of humans cohabiting the European continent as late as forty thousand years ago: *Homo sapiens* and Neanderthals (*Homo neanderthalensis*). Then, in a short span of five thousand years, the Neanderthals suddenly vanished, most likely in a genocidal war of extermination and conquest waged by *Homo sapiens* in which we wantonly slaughtered the Neanderthal males and raped their women.[2]

One explanation for our success in the slaughter is that *Homo sapiens* developed inhibitions against aggression toward members of our own species while the Neanderthals did not.[3] There is archaeological evidence that Neanderthals killed one another and cannibalized one another at a higher rate than *Homo sapiens* did, and in the war between the two species, *that* gave us the advantage, despite the fact that Neanderthals were physically more powerful and as capable as we were in fashioning stone tools and weapons.[4]

One scholar, the biblical historian Robert Eisler, argued that humans were at one time a docile vegetarian species, but that the onset of the last Ice Age reduced the availability of edible vegetation in northern regions, and that humans became carnivores out of necessity. At some point even animal prey became scarce, and northern humans clad in animal furs migrated south, attacking, killing, raping and cannibalizing more gentle vegetarian humans dwelling in the temperate climates.[5] In his 1951 book *Man into Wolf: An Anthropological Interpretation of Sadism, Masochism, and Lycanthropy*, Eisler argued that this was both the origin of our werewolf myths and the behavioral roots of modern serial killers. In fact, it is in Eisler's book that the term "serial murder" makes one of its earliest appearances in the English language.[6]

For over a million years, we were hardwired with a set of reptilian instincts essential to the survival of any species: the "Four-F" evolutionary complex—an unencumbered capacity to fight or flee, feed and fuck. We were all psychopaths, because we had to be. But there is evidence that at the height of our slaughter of the Neanderthals some forty thousand years ago, before we could turn all that aggression on ourselves, we developed an instinctual fear of our own dead—necrophobia. This fear, which was directed particularly toward those closest to us, was a fear that if they were not treated well by us in life, they would rise up from their graves after death and take revenge against us. The evidence is in so-called prehistoric "deviant burials" or "vampire graves" uncovered by archaeologists in which the body was somehow disabled, secured, pinned or mutilated, to prevent it from rising from the dead. The argument is that necrophobia required us to care for the elderly, the sick and the weak rather than abandon them as most species tend to do, which required a degree of social organization and order, a key to future civilizations.[7]

Then, with the emergence of agriculture some fifteen thousand years ago, we became enclosed by "civilization," and unbridled killing, rape and cannibalism were condemned by newly emergent religious tenets and by secular laws to enforce the instinctual necrophobic prerogative. To ensure an ordered society, humans began to develop social inhibitions against those behaviors. But those inhibitions were artificial. Fifteen thousand years of civilization are hardly enough to extinguish five hundred thousand years of deeply seated murderous instinct in an animal as freethinking and evolved as a human.

Indeed there is no species of human less necrophobic than a serial killer. They not only routinely handle and manipulate corpses with no fear or disgust but can even go into the opposite of necrophobia: necrophilia, a sexual predilection for a corpse. The subject is so taboo that often it is understated in news reporting and true-crime accounts. We forget that notorious serial killers like Jack the Ripper, Ted Bundy and Gary Ridgway were primarily necrophiliacs. Its exact frequency in serial murder cases remains somewhat controversial to this day. On the high end, the *Sexual Homicide* study by the FBI in the 1980s concluded that "a sexual act" was committed after a victim's death in 42 percent of the 92 victims they studied. In one case, for example, the perpetrator had ejaculated into the knife wound he had made in the victim.[8] On the low end, the FBI's Behavioral Analysis Unit concluded in 2014 that "postmortem sexual activity" was present in 11.2 percent of the 329 cases of sexual serial murder perpetrated by a sample of 64 offenders.[9] And even in non-serial-murder cases, "opportunistic" acts of necrophilia with a still-warm corpse have been reported often enough.[10] It is so taboo that even many serial killers who freely admit and describe their acts of torture, rape, mutilation and cannibalism will hesitate at admitting acts of necrophilia. Thus the wide ranging statistics of its prevalence.

Today we have all sorts of scientific, sociological and psychological terms to describe people with faulty inhibitions on primitive instincts: from simple criminality to more complex notions of psychopathy, sociopathy and antisocial personality disorder. Until very recently, however, we used to describe humans without inhibitions on these instincts as "monsters."

Monstrum: Organized Vampires and Disorganized Werewolves

The word "monster" is derived from the Latin *monstrum* meaning "an omen or warning of the will of the gods."[11] In the premodern past, serial killers were imagined to be supernatural monsters like vampires, werewolves, zombies and ghouls. Even the two primary monsters of Western imagination, the undead vampire and the diabolically transformed werewolf, correspond roughly to the *organized/disorganized* classification of serial killers used by FBI behaviorists and profilers for decades until it was deprecated by the FBI in 2004.

Like a vampire, the *organized* serial killer carefully chooses and stalks his victims, charms and seduces them, deceives and persuades them to invite him into their house (as per vampire lore). He is sometimes attractive and takes on a seductive human form. He takes control of the victims' bodies and drains them of their blood in a form of necrophilic intercourse and cold lust. The victims are *preserved*, not mutilated; the violence is typically measured and coldly controlled.

The *disorganized* serial killer "blitz" attacks with destructive brute force, like a werewolf. His victim is chosen at random, on impulse. There is no stalking or planning. These killers are repulsively animalistic. They kill and overkill, rape, mutilate, sometimes eat and destroy their victim in an unthinking hot rage and sexual lust. There is no preservation and control of the victim's body, only its destruction or physical consumption.

Five hundred years ago in Europe, serial killers who raped, killed, mutilated and sometimes cannibalized their victims were frequently formally charged as werewolves (lycanthropes) in both criminal and ecclesiastical court proceedings, the records of which survive to this day. Between 1450 and 1650, approximately three hundred werewolf serial killers were executed in Europe, a rate comparable to the nineteenth century and first half of the twentieth.[12]

Some historians of crime have argued that before the beginning of industrialization around 1750, sexual serial murder of any kind was virtually unknown on the theory that sex crime is a "leisure activity" requiring free time to develop and dwell on sexual fantasies and free movement to act upon them. Prior to the industrial age, anyone other than a wealthy aristocrat was just too busy trying to survive to fantasize about sex and killing, the argument went. Most people were desperately trying to feed themselves and survive invading armies, bandits, revolts and plagues.

But then industrialization drove the dispossessed and impoverished masses into rapidly growing cities, where they became part of a dense pool of anonymous victims to be hunted and killed, like the prostitutes that Jack the Ripper targeted in London's Whitechapel district in 1888. The argument was that before the existence of big cities, tightly knit communities where everybody knew one another policed themselves. A serial killer would be readily identified in such a community, while a migratory stranger would stand out and quickly attract suspicion and attention, in a way they would not in a dense modern city.

We now know, however, that serial killers did exist prior to industrialization, and they appeared in rural communities as often as they did in dense urban environments.

These murders were frequently investigated by ecclesiastical authorities and witch-hunter inquisitors, until the mid-nineteenth century, when policemen, criminologists and forensic psychiatrists supplanted priests, demonologists and church inquisitors in assessing the nature of criminal behavior and madness. We began to recognize serial killers as mortal, not supernatural, but we still did not use the term "serial killer." Individuals charged with offenses like repeated murder, rape, cannibalism and necrophilia were still called monsters, werewolves and vampires by the popular press but were now examined and described by "alienists," as psychiatrists were called back then. They were said to be suffering from monomania, defined as a singular pathological preoccupation or obsession in an otherwise sound mind.

Two schools of criminology emerged. The Italian school, led by Cesare Lombroso (1835–1909), argued that criminals, including serial murderers, were born criminals, "throwbacks" to primitive humans who could be recognized by their brutish, apelike physical features (physiognomy). The rival French school of Alexandre Lacassagne (1843–1924) argued that criminals were not born but made by their environment and upbringing. It was Lacassagne who proclaimed, "Society has the criminals it deserves" (famously paraphrased by Robert F. Kennedy when he was US attorney general). Lacassagne's "environmental" school of criminology prevailed over Lombroso's school when some notorious criminals were found to have refined, gentlemanly features. Unfortunately, in a kind of "throwing the baby out with the bathwater," Lombroso's theory of atavistic return to primitive instincts was thrown out along with his theory of physiognomy. In my previous book, *Sons of Cain*, I argue for revisiting the theory that serial killer behavior is partly linked to "short-circuited" prehistoric human "Four-F" survival instincts.

Forensic Psychiatry

In 1886, Austrian psychiatrist Richard von Krafft-Ebing (1840–1902) published *Psychopathia Sexualis: eine Klinisch-Forensische Studie* (*Sexual Psychopathy: A Clinical-Forensic Study*). In this book he cataloged and categorized a wide range of sexual crimes and disorders reported by psychiatrists. Krafft-Ebing identified a series of paraphilias (literally, "unusual loves"), more commonly known as "sexual deviations" or "perversions," that often motivated and characterized serial sexual murders. One of the most well-known is sexual pleasure in causing pain, for which Krafft-Ebing coined the term "sadism," inspired by the French libertine Marquis de Sade (1740–1814), author of the sexually violent novel *The One Hundred Twenty Days of Sodom*.

Found almost exclusively in males, a paraphilia is an obsessive predilection for a very particular and statistically unusual type of sex, without which the person cannot be aroused. Paraphilias include specific fantasy scenarios, an erotic fixation on a particular nongenital part of the anatomy (partialism), the sexualization of inanimate objects (fetishes) and a substitution of another act for the sexual one. There are dozens of different paraphilias, some of which are benign if engaged in with a consensual partner, such as:

- altocalciphilia (a fetish for high-heeled shoes);
- coprophilia (arousal from feces or from being defecated upon by or defecating on a willing partner);
- hyphephilia (arousal at the touch of certain things, such as feathers, or a particular textile, such as leather);
- masochism (arousal from being dominated, restrained or hurt);
- raptophilia (simulated rape with a consenting partner);
- trichophilia (fetish for hair).

Other paraphilias are more blatantly transgressive, dangerous and often criminal because their very premise is coercive or destructive:

- amokoscisia (desire to slash or mutilate females);
- anthropophagy (cannibalism);
- erotophonophilia ("lust murder" accompanied by mutilation of the victim before or after death);
- flagellationism (sexual satisfaction from whipping or beating a person);
- hybristophilia (a desire in a female to partner with a male serial killer, one of the few female paraphilias);
- necrophilia (sex with a corpse);
- sadism (sexual arousal from dominating, humiliating or causing pain to an unwilling subject).

American Nineteenth-Century Serial Killers

In the United States it has been recently claimed that Herman Webster Mudgett (aka H. H. Holmes), the killer who prowled the 1893 World's Fair in Chicago, was "America's first serial killer."[13] He was nothing of the sort.

First, there were many female serial poisoners, like Lydia Sherman, "the American Borgia" (10 victims: 1864–71); Sarah Jane Robinson, "the Poison Fiend" (8 victims: 1881–86); and Jane Toppan, "Jolly Jane" (31 victims: 1885–1901). And there were outlaw profit serial killers preying on frontier settlers and travelers, like the notorious Harpe Brothers in Tennessee in the 1790s or the Bloody Benders and their "murder inn" in Kansas, from 1869 to 1872.

There were also numerous "classic" sexual serial killers pre–H. H. Holmes:

- Jesse Pomeroy was arguably America's first known sexual serial killer (1874), and very likely the youngest, at fourteen years old.[14] Pomeroy had already been confined in a juvenile facility for a series of nonfatal assaults on young boys, but after his early release he went on to torture and kill two children in separate incidents. Pomeroy was sentenced to life in prison and died in 1932 at the age of seventy-two in the fifty-sixth year of his sentence.

- Joseph LaPage, a serial killer who ambushed and mutilated two women in Vermont and New Hampshire in 1874.

- Thomas W. Piper murdered two women and a little girl in 1873, battering them to death and engaging in necrophiliac sex acts. A sexton in a Boston church, Piper lured a five-year-old girl into the belfry where he bludgeoned her into unconsciousness with a cricket bat as her family desperately searched for her in the church below. He had planned on keeping her body there to abuse later, but the girl was found and brought home, where she died of her head wounds. Piper was convicted in two of the murders and executed.

- The Servant-Girl Annihilator in Austin, Texas, was an unidentified serial killer who murdered, mutilated and posed his victims' corpses with sharp objects inserted into their ears. He killed at least seven women (five African American and two white) between 1884 and 1885.

All these cases occurred prior to both Jack the Ripper in England and H. H. Holmes in Chicago. Moreover, while Holmes was a serial killer, he was only convicted in the murder of an insurance fraud accomplice and his three children. Holmes was paid by a newspaper to make a "confession" in its pages to many other murders, none of which were confirmed. While it is true that he owned and operated a hotel and boardinghouse in Chicago, there was no evidence that it was especially designed as a kill house with gas chambers and corpse chutes or that he even murdered anybody in it.[15]

Meanwhile, the seminal Jack the Ripper murders suddenly ended in November 1888. But serial killers continued to appear with the same regularity after Jack the Ripper as they had before him in what remained of the nineteenth century. For example:

- Dr. Thomas Neill Cream compulsively poisoned at least five women in London between 1881 and 1892 before he was apprehended, tried and hanged.

- Joseph Vacher in France was apprehended in 1897 for eleven necrophiliac murders of young boys, girls and women, some working as shepherds in the remote countryside. A migratory serial killer, Vacher opportunistically ambushed his victims as he tramped through multiple police jurisdictions.

- Theodore "Theo" Durrant in San Francisco was arrested in 1885 in the necrophiliac murder of two women whose corpses he stashed in a church where he was a sexton.

Serial Murder Around the World: 1900-1950

The Radford University/FGCU (Florida Gulf Coast University) Serial Killer Database is one of the most comprehensive statistical surveys of serial murder cases reported around the world.

According to the database, between 1900 and 1950, 5 to 6 new serial killers were reported in the United States each year, an average of 55 per decade for a total of 273.[16]

The number of serial killers outside the US during the same period, primarily in Europe, was roughly half the number, approximately 25 new serial killers per decade. The Radford/FGCU database is incomplete, as it often relies on news reports of past serial murders, and thus non-European regions where archived news reports might be more obscure and inaccessible to researchers are inevitably underrepresented. But the Radford/FGCU database is the best we currently have and at least represents the history of serial killing as it appeared primarily in the pages of contemporary newspapers.

European serial killers continued to make sporadic appearances in the first half of the twentieth century, with a "hot spot" in the chaos and degradation of post–World War I Germany.

- Fritz Haarmann, one of the earliest twentieth-century gay serial killers on record, raped and murdered twenty-seven young men in Hanover between 1918 and 1924. Haarmann, who was a police agent and private investigator, lured school-boys or drifters from the Hanover railway station back to his apartment. There he attacked his victims and killed them by chewing through their throats. It was rumored he sold their flesh to local butcher shops and restaurants claiming it was pork. (The selling of the victim's flesh was a frequent and unproven rumor in European serial killer cases.)

- Peter Kürten, "the Vampire of Düsseldorf," stabbed, stran-gled and battered at least nine and maybe as many as thirty victims between 1913 and 1930. Sometimes Kürten's victims went willingly with him to have sex, during which he would suddenly attack them with a knife. At other times, Kürten ambushed his victims, frequently children, on the streets and in parks. Kürten was executed in 1931.

- Georg Karl Grossman is believed to have killed as many as fifty people between 1913 and 1920 and sold their flesh at a hot dog stand he kept at the railway station in Berlin. He ap-parently found his victims in the same station where he sold their remains to hungry passengers. He committed suicide, however, when he was arrested, and thus his crimes remain obscured in myth and gossip.

- Karl Denke, an innkeeper in Silesia, was arrested in 1924 after attempting to murder a vagrant, and committed suicide in his cell. When police searched his inn, they found the dis-membered remains of at least thirty men and women.

Serial murders in Germany, Italy and France are as well-documented as in Britain and America; but one can only imagine how many still-undigitized eastern European and Scandinavian newspapers contain yet-to-be-discovered reports. Then there is serial homicide in Africa, Asia or South and Central America, where there is no reason to believe rates of serial killing were less than Europe's. Take, for example, this striking case in Morocco.

In April 1906, Hadj Mohammed Mesfewi was charged with murdering thirty-six young women and girls. Mesfewi was an elderly cobbler and letter writer for illiterate customers.[17] After parents of a missing girl lodged a complaint with authorities, search parties found twenty-six girls buried beneath the floor of his workshop, beheaded and mutilated with a knife, while another ten were buried in an adjoining yard. The girls came to dictate letters, were offered drugged tea and then were beheaded and dismembered, all apparently for their meager property. Mesfewi's seventy-year-old wife, Annah, confessed under torture (from which she died) to being his accomplice.

Mesfewi was sentenced to daily flogging in the Marrakesh market square.

After about three weeks, when it appeared that Mesfewi was on the brink of death, he was treated and restored for his final sentence, execution on Monday, June 11, the market day.

Masons had earlier excavated a six-by-two-foot-deep space in the massive Marrakesh city wall that flanks the market. After the crowds had gathered to watch, Mesfewi was led to the space in the wall. Chains were installed in wall recesses in order that Mesfewi remained erect and would not slump out of view of the crowd. Mesfewi shrieked and screamed as he was chained into position. For several hours, the crowd was allowed to view him, shout insults and curses, and pelt him with excrement and animal offal. Then the masons, with great ceremony, laid down rows of stones until only Mesfewi's head was visible, and after the jailer fed him a final ration of bread and water, the last stones were thrust into place, entombing Mesfewi completely except for a small slit for air; nobody wanted Mesfewi to die too quickly.

The crowd could hear Mesfewi screaming from inside his tomb and shouted back. On Tuesday, the crowds gathered again to listen to Mesfewi scream and beg to be put to a quick death. On Wednesday morning, only moans could be heard, and by the end of the day, he was dead, cursed by the crowds for dying too soon.

The story of Hadj Mohammed Mesfewi made world news from May to July 1906, and then was forgotten almost forever. There are probably hundreds of such stories of serial killing in the Baltics, Russia, central Asia, China, the Pacific islands, the African continent, Amazonian South America, Central America, and into the backwashes of the American frontier, its melting-pot cities, and the Great White North of Canada. Hundreds probably, all forgotten today, never microfilmed, perhaps only reported in the pages of some small local newspaper, now a yellowed scrap crumbling to dust behind an old attic ceiling or in some obscure archive waiting to be purged and pulped.

Serial Murder in the United States: 1900–1950

In the first fifty years of the twentieth century, the incidence of serial murder in the United States was low. If we include female serial killers and profit killers, a total of 273 serial killers made their appearance over the span of those fifty years, an average of 5.4 new serial killers every year.[18]

According to historian Philip Jenkins, the serial killer "epidemic" of the 1970s was preceded by two smaller serial killer "epidemics" during which there were unusually high rates of serial homicides in the United States: 1911 to 1915 and 1935 to 1941.[19]

The First Serial Killer Epidemic

Looking through the *New York Times*, Jenkins was able to find reports of at least seventeen serial killers in the five years between 1911 and 1915.

Henry Lee Moore, for example, was eventually linked to the murders of more than twenty-five people in 1911 and 1912—sometimes entire families. But little is known about him; he is a mere footnote in history.

In September 1911, thirty-seven-year-old Moore is said to have killed six victims in Colorado Springs—a man, two women and four children; in October, three people in Monmouth, Illinois; and then a family of five in Ellsworth, Kansas, in the same month. In June 1912, he is suspected in the murder of a couple in Paola, Kansas, and several days later, an entire family of eight, including four children, in Villisca, Iowa.

Moore then returned home to Columbia, Missouri, where in December 1912 he murdered his mother and grandmother in order to take possession of their house and marry a fifteen-year-old teenager he had been corresponding with. At this point, he was arrested and sentenced to life imprisonment. Moore was not immediately linked to the previous crimes until a federal agent investigating the Villisca homicides was informed by the agent's father, a warden of the Leavenworth Penitentiary with contacts throughout the prison system, of Henry Lee Moore's crimes in Missouri. The suspicions about Moore's twenty-five additional murders were avidly covered in the newspapers at the time, but there was insufficient evidence to charge him.

Moore was released on July 30, 1956, at the age of eighty-two, and was last reported living at a Salvation Army center in St. Louis before vanishing from the historical record.

An unidentified Atlanta serial killer between May 1911 and May 1912 is suspected in the murder and Jack-the-Ripper-style mutilations of twenty biracial or light-skinned African American women. Between May 20 and July 1, 1911, the unknown killer murdered the first seven victims, one every Saturday night like clockwork.

A Denver and Colorado Springs serial killer in 1911 and 1912 bludgeoned seven women to death with the perpetrator caught.

A Texas and Louisiana serial killer between January 1911 and April 1912 killed forty-nine victims in a series of unsolved axe murders. Very similar to the Moore murders, entire families were wiped out: a mother and her three children hacked to death in their beds in Rayne, Louisiana, in January 1911; ten miles away in Crowley, Louisiana, three members of the Byers family in February 1911; two weeks later, a family of four in Lafayette. In April, the killer struck in San Antonio, Texas, killing a family of five. In November 1911, the killer returned to Lafayette and killed a family of six; in January 1912, a woman and her three children were killed in Crowley. Two days later, at Lake Charles, a family of five was killed, and a note was left behind: "When He maketh the Inquisition for Blood, He forgetteth not the cry of the humble—human five." In February 1912, the killer murdered a woman and her three children in Beaumont, Texas. In March, a man and a woman and her four children were hacked to death in Glidden, Texas. In April, a family of five was killed in San Antonio again, and two nights later, three were killed in Hempstead, Texas. The murders were never solved, and the case has only recently been explored at length by Todd C. Elliott, in *Axes of Evil: The True Story of the Ax-Man Murders*.

In New York City, on March 19, 1915, the East Side Ripper killed and mutilated Lenora Cohn, a five-year-old girl sent by her mother on an errand inside her apartment building on the Lower East Side. On May 3, he killed and mutilated four-year-old Charles Murray, who was playing in a hallway of his First Avenue tenement, and stuffed his body under a staircase. He sent taunting letters to the victim's mother and the police, signing himself "H. B. Richmond, Jack-the-Ripper" and threatening to kill again. The offender was never identified but might have been the notorious Albert Fish (see below).

Again in New York City in 1915, the corpses of fifteen newborn infants were recovered, suspected to be linked to some sort of "baby farm" operation. That same year, six bodies with their skulls crushed were found hidden in a farmhouse being demolished in Niagara, North Dakota. The victims, who were dropped into the basement through a clever trapdoor, were all farmhands who had been employed by the homeowner. There were numerous hospital and nursing home serial murders and female poisoners rounding out the number of serial killers in this period.

These murders were all spectacular crimes, some widely reported in their time, others not, but all mostly forgotten today. Jack the Ripper with his five or six victims is immortalized, but the Louisiana-Texas axe murderer with forty-nine victims is entirely forgotten. The primary difference is that London in 1888 was the center of a huge global English-language newspaper industry, while North Dakota, Louisiana and Texas were not. The story of Jack the Ripper was retold endlessly and entered popular myth and literature—while the Louisiana-Texas axe murderer faded from public consciousness. Like real estate, serial murder "epidemics" are all about location, location, location, more so than they are about the number of victims.

The 1916–1934 Serial Killer Interlude

Once the United States went to war in Europe in 1917, there appeared to be a lull in reports of sexual serial killing at home. After World War I, the affluent "Roaring Twenties" was a Jazz Age of celebrity gangsters, spates of kidnappings, lynch mob race rioting and wanton thrill killing like the infamous Leopold and Loeb murder in Chicago in 1924.

Overall murder in the United States increased by 77 percent between 1920 and 1933.[20] Oddly, sexual serial killing still went on at the same rate as before, but it was now relegated to page six in the newspapers, even while it was becoming pathologically weirder, with increasing reports of necrophilia and bizarre fetishes creeping into the murders. Paradoxically, it was during this "interlude" period between the two surges that some of the more infamous historical cases of serial homicide occurred.

Earle Leonard Nelson, "Dark Strangler" or "Gorilla Killer," United States and Canada, 1926–1927

Born to parents who both died of syphilis by the time he was two, Earle Nelson was raised by a severe Pentecostal grandmother. Typical of some serial killers, Nelson suffered a major head injury when at the age of ten he was hit by a streetcar. After that his behavior was said to have changed. What that might mean in serial killer psychopathology we are only now beginning to understand.

Reports of serial killers having childhood head injuries followed by dramatic behavioral change are frequent. But it was only in the 2000s that we began to better understand the relationship between injury to the frontal lobe paralimbic nodes in the brain and behavioral disorders like psychopathy. Forensic psychologist Kent A. Kiehl, after developing deep MRI scanning software and scanning the brains of more than ten thousand incarcerated psychopaths over a fifteen-year period, concluded,

> If you damage a part of the paralimbic system, you can acquire a psychopathic personality. As a group, paralimbic brain damaged patients are characterized by problems with aggression, motivation, empathy, planning and organization, impulsivity, irresponsibility, poor insight, and lack of behavioral controls. In some cases, paralimbic brain damaged patients may become prone to grandiosity and confabulation.
>
> These are all symptoms that we see in psychopaths. Damage to some areas of the paralimbic system are not that uncommon. For example, when the brain is slammed forward against the front part of the skull, it can rub against the bony ridge that exists right above the eyes. This rubbing can damage the orbital frontal cortex of the brain. This is the type of injury that can occur in football players who suffer repeated concussions. Whether due to a single event or to the cumulative impact of multiple head traumas, individuals who damage their orbital frontal cortex can end up developing problems. . . . It is this reality that is just beginning to be recognized by former National Football League players as a potential occupational risk to their sport.[21]

Kiehl claims he can recognize psychopaths by merely looking at images of their brain scans. He does not go all the way in claiming that psychopathy is a completely physiological condition but concludes that psychopathic behavioral traits or "pseudo-psychopathy" or "acquired sociopathic personality" can mimic psychopathy as a result of damage in the paralimbic system, and may explain why so many serial killers report childhood head injuries, or don't have a "classic" background history of family dysfunction or abusive trauma in their childhood.[22]

Back to the young Earle Nelson, who became increasingly obsessed with sex and the Bible to the point that he began scaring his own family. Nelson was institutionalized numerous times in psychiatric facilities because of his erratic behavior, including an attempt to molest a twelve-year-old girl when he was twenty-four.[23]

In another statistic typical of serial killers, Nelson committed his first murder at the age of twenty-eight; on February 20, 1926, he murdered sixty-two-year-old Clara Newman, a San Francisco boarding-house landlady. Nelson apparently saw a "Rooms to Let" sign in her window and knocked on the door, asking to be shown the room. The house was filled with people, but that did not stop Nelson. Newman was found dead seated on a toilet with her dress pulled up around her waist. She had been strangled and then raped. Two weeks later, Nelson killed his second victim, and from there went on a killing spree of landladies from San Francisco to Portland. Nelson would come to the door inquiring about an advertised room with a Bible in hand, quoting biblical verse to assure the elderly landladies of his good character. He would then strangle them, have sex with the corpse and stuff their bodies under a bed. Eventually, he made his way up into Canada, where police finally arrested him for the murder of a landlady in Winnipeg, Manitoba, in June 1927. By then Nelson had murdered an extraordinary twenty-two women, a victim count unparalleled in the United States until the serial killers of the 1970s.

Nelson was a migratory predator trolling through the pages of newspaper classified ads for rooms to let. Today he would have been on Craigslist or Kijiji trolling for victims on the Internet. Nelson was executed, despite his insanity plea.

Carl Panzram, United States, 1920–1930

Carl Panzram was a tightly wired, vicious killing machine, confessing to one thousand male rapes and twenty-one murders, the last of which he perpetrated in prison, where on his arrival he warned, "I'll kill the first man that bothers me." Shortly afterward, he beat to death his foreman in the prison laundry with an iron bar. For that murder he was sentenced to death and executed in 1930 at the age of thirty-nine.

Panzram was born in East Grand Forks, Minnesota, in 1892. In his autobiographical papers he writes, "All of my family are as the average human beings are. They are honest and hard working people. All except myself. I have been a human animal ever since I was born."[24]

When Panzram was eleven, he was arrested for burglary and sent to a reformatory where he was beaten by the administrators and raped by fellow inmates. He wrote, "I had learned that a boy's penus [sic] could be used for something besides to urinate with and that a rectum would be used for other purposes than crepitating. Oh yes, I had learned a hell of a lot from my expert instructors furnished to me free of charge by society in general and the State of Minnesota in particular."

Panzram was a highly migratory serial killer, traveling throughout the United States and eventually sailing to Europe, South America and Africa. He raped and murdered numerous victims, mostly male, along with committing burglaries and arsons and other criminal acts. At one point, he even acquired a yacht on which he killed victims. He admitted to twenty-one murders, including seven boys of age ten or eleven, some in the country of Angola, some in the US. Near the end of his life, Panzram wrote, "In my lifetime I have murdered 21 human beings. . . . I am sorry for only two things. . . . I am sorry that I have mistreated some few animals in my lifetime and I am sorry that I am unable to murder the whole damned human race."

At his execution in Leavenworth, Kansas, he reportedly spat at the executioner, and when asked if he had any final words, he allegedly said, "Yes, hurry it up, you Hoosier bastard! I could kill a dozen men while you're screwing around!"

Gordon Northcott, "Wineville Chicken Coop Murders," California, 1928

Nineteen-year-old chicken farmer Gordon Northcott, originally from Canada, abducted, raped, axe-murdered and dismembered at least three little boys: two brothers aged ten and twelve and a Mexican migrant who was never identified. Northcott had brought his fifteen-year-old nephew, Sanford Clark, to work on the farm and ended up using him as a sex slave and forced him to help with the disposal of the bodies. Sanford's older sister, Jessie, visited from Canada, and when they were out of Northcott's sight, Sanford revealed what was happening. Jessie fled back to Canada and reported the matter to the US consulate, which then contacted the Los Angeles Police Department.

When police descended on his chicken farm, Northcott escaped to Canada with his mother, Sarah Louise Northcott, but both were extradited back to California. His mother confessed to the killings and was sentenced to life imprisonment, even though she retracted her confession. Gordon confessed to five murders, stood trial and was executed in 1930. Sarah was paroled in 1940 and died in 1944.

Albert Fish, "The Werewolf of Wisteria" or "The Grey Man," New York, 1928–1935

The most shocking case of this era is that of serial killer Albert Fish. Even by today's standards, his was a tale of true horror.[25]

Albert Fish came from a family with a history of mental illness and was brought up in foster homes where he apparently was horrifically abused. He was a self-flagellant, consumed his own urine and excrement, and tortured himself by inserting needles, pins and nails into his groin, dozens of which showed up on X-rays taken after his arrest. He enjoyed putting cotton swabs soaked in kerosene up his anus and setting them on fire. He had a collection of self-torture devices, including nail-studded paddles with which he would beat himself bloody while masturbating. He was a Tasmanian devil of paraphilias, a whirlwind of perversions, a "polymorphous pervert" according to one psychiatrist who believed that Fish might have raped as many as one hundred children.

Fish was a serial killer inspired not by pornography or erotica but by the Bible. He was probably clinically insane, suffering from visionary psychosis, with hallucinations of God instructing him to mutilate and murder children, as in Genesis 22 when God instructs Abraham to kill and sacrifice his son.

In June 1928, Fish was fifty-eight but prematurely aged when he spotted a classified ad placed by the family of Edward Budd, a teenager in New York City seeking summer employment. Fish contacted the family, introducing himself as Frank Howard, a farmer with a large farm in New Jersey. His plan, he later confessed, was to lure the boy away and kill him by cutting off his penis and letting him slowly bleed to death and then eat him.

On a visit to the family home, he impressed the Budds with his well-dressed, kind and grandfatherly demeanor and the opportunity for their son to spend a summer gainfully employed in the fresh air away from their crowded New York City tenement. He agreed to return on Sunday for lunch and afterward bring Edward back to the "farm" with him.

On Sunday afternoon, June 3, Fish arrived at the Budds' apartment bearing a gift of pot cheese and fresh strawberries. He was introduced to their ten-year-old daughter, Grace, and, Fish later confessed, instantly made up his mind to kill and eat her instead. Fish now told the parents that he needed to postpone the trip to his farm until later that evening because his sister was throwing a birthday party for his niece. There would be lots of children, games and cake at the party, and would little Grace like to go with him that afternoon? The combination of the era's naivete, Fish's grandfatherly persona and the Budds' reluctance to offend the kindly farmer offering their son a summer job led the parents to allow their child to leave with a complete stranger. (Of course they asked where the sister lived, and Fish told them Columbus Avenue and 137th Street. Who knows how many New Yorkers even today know that Columbus Avenue ends at 110th Street?)

Grace never returned, and her abduction remained a highly publicized mystery for four years, until Fish mailed a letter to the girl's mother describing in excruciating detail how he murdered and ate the girl. In it Fish infamously fantasized about cases of cannibalism in famine times in China, and then wrote:

On Sunday June the 3–1928 I called on you at 406 W 15 St. Brought you pot cheese—strawberries. We had lunch. Grace sat in my lap and kissed me. I made up my mind to eat her, on the pretense of taking her to a party. You said Yes she could go. I took her to an empty house in Westchester I had already picked out. When we got there, I told her to remain outside. She picked wild flowers. I went upstairs and stripped all my clothes off. I knew if I did not I would get her blood on them. When all was ready I went to the window and called her. Then I hid in a closet until she was in the room. When she saw me all naked she began to cry and tried to run down stairs. I grabbed her and she said she would tell her mama. First I stripped her naked. How she did kick—bite and scratch. I choked her to death then cut her in small pieces so I could take my meat to my rooms, cook and eat it. How sweet and tender her little ass was roasted in the oven. It took me 9 days to eat her entire body. I did not fuck her tho I could of had I wished. She died a virgin.

Police managed to trace the letter to Fish from the stationery logo on the envelope. After his arrest, Fish confessed that he'd planned to take Edward Budd to Irvington, a town in Westchester County just north of New York where he had briefly lived. Fish knew there was an abandoned house there known as "Wisteria House" on Mountain Road. Before he went up to the Budds' apartment, he had left a package of knives wrapped in paper at a local newsstand for safekeeping. Now with Grace in tow, he picked up the knives from the newsstand, took the subway to a commuter railway station and rode out to Irvington with Grace. He bought a round-trip ticket for himself and a one-way ticket for the little girl. He told police that when they got off the train, little Grace pointed out to him that he had forgotten the package, and she ran back to the train car to retrieve the parcel of knives.

He then walked her to the abandoned house and strangled her as he described in the letter, dismembered her, bringing her body parts back to New York to stew and roast and eat as "leftovers" over a span of nine days. Fish insisted he did not rape the little girl but admitted to ejaculating twice as he strangled her. Police recovered some of Grace's skeletal remains from a hillside behind Wisteria House. (The house still stands today, looking pretty much as it did in the 1920s but upscale and restored. It was recently listed for sale.)[26]

Psychiatrists were divided on Fish's sanity. While he might have been delusional, he nonetheless carefully planned and executed the murder. The issue for the jury was not so much whether Fish was insane, but whether he should be put to death even if he was. Surely in the jury members' minds was a recent "thrill" killing of a fourteen-year-old boy in Chicago perpetrated by two wealthy youths, Nathan Leopold and Richard Loeb. Their attorney, Clarence Darrow, entered a guilty plea and argued successfully before a judge without a jury that although the boys were "legally sane" they were immature and disturbed and their lives should be spared. The judge sentenced Leopold and Loeb to life imprisonment. Loeb was murdered in prison, but Leopold was released in 1958 and retired to a comfortable life in Puerto Rico until his death in 1971.

The Albert Fish case, on the other hand, went to trial with an insanity defense, but the jury did not care whether he was insane or not; he was sentenced to death and executed at Sing Sing in 1936.

Before his execution, Fish confessed to dozens of murders, but only two were persuasively connected to him: the mutilation murder of eight-year-old Francis McDonnell in 1924 as he played by a pond in a wooded area in Staten Island, and four-year-old Billy Gaffney kidnapped from his apartment hallway in Brooklyn in 1927. A further six victims are plausibly attributed to Fish but without conclusive evidence, including the "East Side Ripper" murders of two children in 1915.

Approximately two hundred serial killers would make their appearance in the United States in the first four decades of the twentieth century; except for a handful like Earle Nelson, Albert Fish and Carl Panzram, they are forgotten, relegated to obscure local newspaper accounts, their stories never fully told or explored. American newspapers had reported more extensively on serial killings overseas than at home, sometimes preferring to depict serial murder as something foreign to the American experience.

CHAPTER 2

American *Monstrum*:
The Rise of Sexual Signature Killers
1930–1945

For heavens sake catch me before I kill more.

William Heirens, serial killer

By the mid-1930s, despite the relative scarcity of serial murder, the American public was familiar with the phenomenon without the term "serial killer" itself having been used. The "multiple murderer" or "mass murderer," as he was called in those days, was emerging as a stereotypical character in popular culture.

Arsenic and Old Lace, a 1939 play by Joseph Kesselring, is a black comedy about a kooky family of serial killers. One of the earliest crime novels with the theme of serial murder also appeared in 1939, Agatha Christie's *And Then There Were None*.

Real-life serial killers, or suspected serial killers, continued to appear in the US at a steady rate of approximately five new serial killers every two years. When confronted with multiple unsolved murders, newspapers began noting similarities between cases, describing them sometimes as "pattern murders" or "signature killings," suggesting that some perpetrators of multiple murders either deliberately or subconsciously left their imprint or "signature" at a crime scene. These terms would be used right into the early 1980s, when the term "serial murder" was universally adopted.

The 1930s and 1940s saw notorious serial killers like:

- The Kingsbury Run Butcher or Cleveland Torso Murderer, who perpetrated twelve mutilation killings between 1934 and 1938, victims' torsos, heads and limbs dumped in Kingsbury Run, a city creek bed that runs from East 90th Street and Kinsman Road to the Cuyahoga River. The victims were Depression-era drifters, migratory workers, homeless and prostitutes, the typical victim that serial killers frequently target. The former "Untouchable," Special Agent Elliot Ness, was Cleveland's recently appointed safety director, but even he was unable to solve this series of murders.

- Jake Bird, "Axeman of Tacoma," a migratory African American serial killer who claimed he killed as many as forty-six white female victims between 1930 and 1947 in Florida, Illinois, Iowa, Kansas, Kentucky, Michigan, Nebraska, Ohio, Oklahoma, South Dakota and Wisconsin. He was arrested, quickly tried and sentenced to death in 1947 for a double axe murder of a mother and her teenage daughter in their home in Tacoma, Washington. His execution was delayed when he confessed to an additional forty-four murders, although the police were able to substantiate only eleven of them.

- Joe Ball, "Alligator Man" or "Butcher of Elmendorf," was suspected in the murder of six to twenty women whose bodies he allegedly fed to captive alligators behind his Texas roadhouse from 1936 to 1938, although the number of victims has been significantly mythologized.[1]

- The San Diego Girl Murderer, a serial killer suspected in the press to be behind a string of six unsolved murders of women between 1929 and 1936 (see below).

- The Dupont Circle Murderer, a serial killer suspected in eleven murders in Washington, DC, from 1929 to 1941 (see below).

The Serial Murder Script

Rapes, strangulations and mutilations of both children and women were ubiquitous throughout history, but by the 1930s, many sexual murders (both single and serial) were exhibiting more complex and extreme fetishistic elements. The necrophilic anatomical mutilations perpetrated by Jack the Ripper or Joseph Vacher were "organic" in their nature, primarily committed outdoors, and were primordial, feral and werewolf-like, rarely incorporating manufactured or social fetishes and fantasies. But in the twentieth century, we began to increasingly see episodes of highly "scripted" extreme pathological and paraphilic serial murder that would characterize the upcoming surge of serial killing. The scripting—"what to do and in what way"—for these murders seemed to originate less from the deep instinctual recesses of the primitive corners of the perpetrators' brains and more from the social, cultural and historical cues from the society they lived in, from what both popular and transgressive culture celebrated in literature, newspapers and the newly emerged medium of cinema. These social-cultural phenomena of the era did not "create" serial killers, any more than they do today, but they inspired and facilitated the scripting of their primitive impulses to extend beyond the instinctual into the realm of fantasy and imagination. The path they took was often illuminated by transgressive cultural artifacts like, for example, pornography or works on the scale of the Marquis de Sade's *One Hundred Twenty Days of Sodom*, and buttressed by contemporary social mores and values.

The late author Colin Wilson described, for example, how emergent Victorian-era puritanism changed the erotic imagination and nature of pornography in Britain. Earlier, pornography, like John Cleland's notorious 1748 novel *Fanny Hill, or Memoirs of a Woman of Pleasure*, had portrayed women as lustfully indulging in sexual pleasure as much as males, seducing the male as frequently as the other way around. But in the Victorian age, female celibacy and virginity became a primary pillar of social order and class values. Britain introduced the Obscene Publications Act in 1857 outlawing the publishing and distribution of erotic literature portraying women willfully indulging in sex, classifying it as obscenity subject to criminal penalties and confiscation. As pornography went underground in the new puritanical age, women were no longer portrayed as willfully pursuing sex with a lustful appetite but instead as victims forced to breach their Victorian chastity.

They became, in other words, sex "objects." Increasingly, pornography, and popular literature, portrayed unmarried women having sex only if they were forced into it, bound, battered and raped. (While married women only did it out of duty, gritting their teeth.) In this new emerging pornography, sex became something women experienced only against their will and often as children. Sex, seduction, bondage, force and pain became interconnected. It introduced narratives of abduction, bondage, enslavement and flagellation, and the more chaste the girl or woman subjected to forcible sex, the more unwilling she was, the more attractive she was as the "sex object" of the pornographic fantasy.[2] The cultural abolition of female sexual desire was the first step in transforming women into "pure" objects of male desire, including that of serial killers.

Those early pathological sex murderers who were making their appearance were often apprehended after their first killing or two, before they got a chance to serially repeat their offenses over a longer period. (Like the infamous murder and dismemberment of eight-year-old Fanny Adams in Britain in 1867 by Frederick Baker, who was apprehended the same day after making a journal entry "Killed a young girl. It was fine and hot"; or the two mutilation murders by Joseph LaPage in 1875.) Only a handful went on to become prolonged serial Rippers. The psychopathology of these offenders and the nature of their acts would be very similar to those of future serial killers, except they were being apprehended relatively quickly. They were like homicidal baby birds learning to fly, able to wing out of their nest of fantasies but unable to stay aloft the distance. They either lacked imagination and sophistication to continually get away with their crimes, or somehow their mental "scripting" did not include the possibility of living a double life as a serial murderer, or maybe they did not have enough role models. Also, society was less anonymous and murderers were quickly exposed by attracting attention to themselves in a pretelevision era, when people were out congregating in public, going to the theater and later movies, sitting on their front porch or stoop, flocking to parks, saloons and diners, visible, easily identified by neighbors in a simpler world with fewer people in it. But individual occurrences of extreme sex murders would essentially set the bedrock for future serial murders; the only thing left was for the pathological murder to be repeated serially. From Jesse Pomeroy's torture of child victims in Boston, reported to have been inspired by dime novel tales of "Indian torture," to the mutilation cannibal murders by Albert Fish in New York "facilitated" (as the FBI terms it) by popular tales of South Pacific cannibalism and biblical passages, a new breed of sexual murderers was emerging: some serial, some not, and all feeding on new ideas, themes and fetishes, new ways of thinking and new ways of moving around through new social customs and mores.

In the US during the 1930s, California would incubate a string of notorious extreme sexual homicide cases that would eventually set the framework and "script" for many of the serial killers to come. There is no exact answer as to why a rash of these murders occurred in California in particular. Serial murders at different points in time sometimes cluster in regions—the Pacific Northwest, Florida, Nevada, Louisiana and Alaska, for example, had periods when there were disproportionate increases in serial killers compared to other regions. Maybe California in the 1930s had its surge because at the time it was almost as puritanical as Victorian Britain, at least compared to a more cosmopolitan New York. But that alone would not explain why California would become a hot spot again in the 1970s and 1980s when it was the mecca of the new age of progressive freethinking. Overall, with more than seventy serial killers cataloged by Eric Hickey between 1800 and 2011, California remains the leading state for the number of serial killers.[3]

"San Diego Girl Murders" or "The Modern Girl Murders," San Diego, 1929–1938

Some newspapers speculated that these six unsolved sexual murders were perpetrated by the same killer, although in the end this was never conclusively determined. Some of the girls were independent and dated freely and were dubbed "modern girls" by the press, seeking to link their "immorality" to their deaths (even though the youngest was ten years old and the oldest of the "girls" was forty-three). Looking at the cases today, I consider it unlikely that the same perpetrator committed them all. The third murder, however, was notable for the bizarre, fetishistic crime scene.

Seventeen-year-old Louise Teuber was a store clerk living at home. The press described her as a "butterfly," a girl who dated a variety of men. On Saturday, April 18, 1931, Louise quit her job, telling her employer she "was going away" without specifying where or with whom. A letter to her father would arrive by special delivery on Monday, in which the girl wrote, "Dear Dad, I have tried for a long time to be satisfied with the way you are running the house and I can stand it no longer. I am leaving home tonight and I am not coming back." It was postmarked at 7:00 p.m. Saturday. By the time the letter arrived, Louise was already dead.

Her body was found by picnickers in Black Mountain Park. Louise was naked except for a pair of gray silk stockings and black pumps. She was hanging at the end of a rope thrown over an oak tree branch and secured to a large bush, in a semi-seated position, her buttocks suspended about a foot above the ground and her legs extended forward, her heels resting on the ground. The rope around her neck was secured with a sailor's double half hitch knot. Her clothes were found neatly folded nearby on an Army blanket, along with a package containing a bra and a pair of hose purchased Saturday evening. When found Sunday, Louise was estimated to have been dead for about eight hours.

There was no evidence of penetrative rape, but skin was found under her fingernails, indicating she had fought with her murderer. She had also sustained a severe blow to her head.

In her diary, Louise described dating some fifteen men, including a married commercial photographer who shot suggestive photographs of her. None of them could be conclusively connected to her murder, and it remains unsolved.

The other "San Diego Girl Murders" were:

- Virginia Brooks, ten, who disappeared on her way to school on February 11, 1931. Her dismembered body was discovered on March 10 in a burlap bag under a clump of sagebrush, clutching several strands of blond hair in her hand. Police could not determine the exact cause of death due to the dismemberment but believed it was a blow to the head.

- Dolly Bibbens, forty-three, was found four days after Louise Teuber, on April 23, 1931, in her apartment, strangled with a towel, beaten and her throat slashed. Although a diamond ring had been viciously torn off her finger, the rest of her jewelry had not been taken, ruling out robbery as the motive.

- Hazel Bradshaw, twenty-two, was found May 3, 1931, by Boy Scouts at Indian Village in Balboa Park, stabbed and slashed seventeen times (seven knife wounds were defensive wounds on her hands). A boyfriend was charged with her murder but acquitted in a jury trial.

- Celia Cota, sixteen, was reported missing by her father after going out for a short walk on the evening of August 17, 1934. Her body was found the following morning in the backyard of her home clutching strands of gray hair in her hands. She had been strangled and raped.

- Ruth Muir, thirty-five years old, a YMCA worker from Riverside, California, was found near a beachside bench, raped and battered to death, on September 1, 1936.

Albert Dyer, "Inglewood Babes Murders," Los Angeles, 1937

Up to now, most serial murder profiling was undertaken by the newspaper reporters trying to link unsolved murders with similar characteristics. The first apparent attempt by American police to psychologically profile an unknown subject in a sexual homicide case took place in 1937, with the rape-murders of three little girls aged six, eight, and nine found strangled in the Baldwin Hills ravine in Inglewood, Los Angeles. Their shoes were neatly set out by each corpse and became an iconic image for the press of a world beginning to go mad.

Inglewood by the mid-1930s was considered a "utopian paradise" for the working class, with Centinela Park and its swimming pool and playgrounds a safe haven for local children to play in. This was still an innocent era when parents had no trouble letting their children leave their eyesight, despite the occasional reports of child abductions and murders.

The three girls had been seen Saturday morning in a nearby park playing there as they often did. Shortly before they vanished, they told a swimming pool attendant they were going to go look for "bunny rabbits" with somebody. Their bodies would be found two days later by search parties in a ravine about two miles from the park.

New Orleans–born psychiatrist Dr. J. Paul de River was employed by the Los Angeles probation department assessing parolees when the LAPD asked him to view the crime scene and offer any insight into the character and possible identity of the unknown child rapist-murderer. De River ventured the following profile:

> Look for one man, probably in his twenties, a pedophile who might have been arrested before for annoying children. He is a sadist with a super-abundance of curiosity. He is very meticulous and probably now remorseful, as most sadists are very apt to be masochistic after expressing sadism. The slayer might have a religious streak and even become prayerful. Moreover, he is a spectacular type and has done this thing, not on sudden impulse, but as a deliberately planned affair. I am of the opinion that he had obtained the confidence of these little girls. I believe they knew the man and trusted him.[4]

A number of the "usual suspects," that is, bachelor men and Mexican migrants, were brought in for questioning but cleared. Then a week after the murders, thirty-two-year-old Albert Dyer, a uniformed crossing guard, came into the Inglewood Police Station ranting and raving about being harassed by the police for the murders.

Police had indeed questioned Dyer when a witness reported seeing him lurking around Centinela Park, but he was cleared after he claimed to have been gardening at home on the day the girls disappeared. When the bodies of the girls were discovered, Dyer showed up at the crime scene in the ravine, wearing his crossing guard uniform and badge, trying to give instructions on how to move the girls' bodies and haranguing bystanders who were smoking near the scene for being disrespectful to the victims. All week long he had been making a nuisance of himself, bringing in tips on possible suspects and inquiring frequently on the progress of the investigation.

Now police gave Dyer a second look and brought him in for another round of questioning. Before long, he confessed, telling police that he had been fantasizing for years about having sex with a young girl, that he had always wanted "something tight and young" but that he "would rather they be dead so that he would not hurt them." Dyer staked out the park, where he saw children frequently playing and prepared his rope. The familiar, friendly crossing guard then approached the three girls and invited them to meet him later in the afternoon and go with him to "look for bunnies" in the Baldwin Hills. After strangling the girls one by one, he vaginally raped their three corpses and anally raped two of them. Dyer then arranged the girls' shoes neatly by their bodies, in order that whoever found them, according to his confession, would "think that the children had been orderly to the last." Then, just as de River had estimated in his profile, Dyer knelt next to each dead girl and said a prayer: "God please save the soul of this child, and save my soul, and forgive me for what I have done."[5]

Albert Dyer was convicted and executed by hanging in September 1938.

In 2018, lawyer and former journalist Pamela Everett, the niece of two of the victims, wrote a new account of the case, *Little Shoes: The Sensational Depression-Era Murders That Became My Family's Secret*, in which she presents very compelling—but inconclusive—arguments that Dyer might have been innocent. For example, Dyer did not own a car, and Everett is skeptical that the little girls would have walked two miles to a place they had never been before, even in a quest for "bunny rabbits."

Otto Wilson, "Walking Dead Murders," Los Angeles, 1944

On Tuesday, November 15, 1944, police responded to the report of a mutilated female body found by staff at the seedy Barclay Hotel on the corner of West 4th and South Main Streets in downtown Los Angeles. The hotel stood on the fringe of the burgeoning skid row that had first risen up in the Depression east of Main Street where it still festers today, hard up tight against the once-elegant Victorian-era Romanesque office buildings, storefronts and movie palaces of early downtown Los Angeles. When it opened in 1897 (as the Van Nuys Hotel), it had been a premier hotel, the first in the city to offer electricity and telephones in all its rooms. But the Barclay had fallen through the hard times of the 1930s into a dollar-a-night fleabag by the 1940s.

The victim, twenty-six-year-old Virginia "Virgie" Lee Griffin, was a five-dollars-a-trick sex worker, so desperate that she was working at eight o'clock in the morning in a Main Street bar, when according to witnesses she was picked up by a handsome, well-dressed young man with a neatly trimmed mustache who resembled the movie star Robert Taylor. The two checked into the Barclay at 9:00 a.m. as "Mr. and Mrs. O. S. Wilson from Steubenville, Indiana." At around noon, the man left the hotel alone, on the way out tipping the maid a dollar "to not disturb his wife." But another maid went in to clean the room, and she would never be the same after what she saw; even some of the hardened cops arriving at the scene later would never get over it.

The victim was lying naked on the floor of the bathroom, limbs askew and broken, like a puppet cut from its strings. Her torso was vertically cleaved and "cracked" open literally in two, all the way from her left shoulder down to her crotch, which was itself, along with the genitals, entirely excised. The mutilation had been performed with a butcher knife left lying next to her. Her intestines and internal organs had been scooped out in a slimy pumpkin "pulp"-like mass and tossed between her legs—or where "between her legs" would have once been, because one of her legs had been completely severed and flung aside while the other had been hacked deeply just above the knee and folded up almost underneath itself. One of her severed breasts was discarded next to her bent leg. Both of her arms were completely separated from her shoulders but remained in place, connected by a loose strip of flesh and fatty tissue strapped around her back. Her throat was deeply cut, her face and head battered and her torso slashed and stabbed numerous times, her breasts mutilated and severed. It was one of the worst mutilation cases that the LAPD had seen, and is still infamously extreme even by today's standards.

Griffin's killer was thirty-four-year-old Otto Stephen Wilson, a discharged Navy pharmacist's mate. Wilson had been abandoned by his single mother and raised in an orphanage where his childhood was steeped in rape and abuse. He married but was bisexual. He admitted engaging in rough sex with his wife, biting her and hurting her. Fearing his escalating violence and becoming wary of his fetish for razors and knives, his bruised and bitten wife reported his bisexuality to the Navy, and as a result he was medically discharged in 1941. They separated. Wilson ended up working dead-end jobs as a dishwasher while flopping in skid row rooming houses on East 5th Street in downtown LA. He later confessed that he began developing a rage toward women and cannibalistic sexual fantasies. In 1943, he attacked a woman entering her apartment house and attempted to strangle her in the stairwell, but she managed to escape. His offense was pleaded down to battery, and he served a six-month sentence. Once released, the urge overtook him again.

That November morning in 1944, after a two-day drinking binge, Wilson armed himself with his favorite shaving razor, went to a local hardware store and purchased a butcher knife, then went trolling through downtown bars for a victim. At 8:00 a.m. he came across the hapless skid row denizen "Virgie" Griffin, so desperate for a drink that she willingly went to a hotel room with him for the price of five dollars and a few shots of whiskey.

Once in the room, Wilson set the knife on the dresser out of her sight and the two of them downed two glasses of whiskey each. Wilson stripped naked and folded up his clothing neatly on a chair. He later told police that Virginia suddenly raised her price from five to twenty dollars and that he punched her and strangled her in a rage until she was unconscious or dead. He then slashed her throat and stabbed her in the chest and torso. He bit her around the neck and shoulders and performed cunnilingus on her and bit her between her legs. Afterward, he dragged her body off the bed to the washroom and carved her up into pieces, leaving the knife and its bloodstained wrapping paper and towels crumpled up among the chunks of fatty flesh and slippery intestines spewed out on the floor. After an hour of "playing" with the human pulp, Wilson washed up in the washroom sink, put on his jacket and left.

Wilson then went to a movie theater around the corner, where he watched *The Walking Dead*, in which Boris Karloff plays a zombie, a man wrongly executed for murder who is scientifically restored to take vengeance on those responsible for his death. Stepping out at the end of the movie into the bright afternoon light, Wilson was now aglow and feeling mentally disconnected between the fantasy death he'd just watched and the one he had just hours ago perpetrated in reality, far more grotesque than that portrayed in the Karloff zombie movie.

At around 2:00 p.m., the same time that Virginia Griffin's body was being discovered, Wilson dived into a nearby bar and targeted another prostitute, thirty-eight-year-old Lillian Johnson, who went with him to a room a few blocks away at the decrepit Joyce Hotel on 310 South Hill Street, near the bottom of the Angels Flight funicular railway. The "couple" asked for a wake-up call at 3:30 p.m., probably Johnson's way of timing her tricks. Once she was naked except for her shoes and ankle socks, he punched and strangled her on the bed. He beat and bit her in such a frenzy that he bit off and swallowed one of her nipples. He had left his butcher knife at the Barclay, but he still had his razor. He slashed into her body with the razor, attempting to excise her genitals with a circular cut, accidentally cutting his own hand in the process. Almost spent, he forced the razor into the center of her chest and sawed away, opening a deep vertical gash through her torso, abdomen and down her left leg, almost severing the left third of her body clean off. Wilson then went to the washroom in the hallway to wash up but discovered that he had locked himself out of the room. After coolly getting housekeeping to open his door, he slipped in, got his jacket and left the hotel. He didn't go very far. He walked over to a bar a few doors away on South Hill Street and began trolling for a third victim.

In the meantime, back at the Joyce Hotel, when nobody responded to the 3:30 wake-up call, staff entered the room and found Lillian Johnson's body on the bed. With two mutilated women found in downtown hotel rooms within a span of a few hours and matching descriptions of a suspect with a Robert Taylor–like mustache, police now fanned out through downtown bars and dives. At 5:30 p.m., LAPD officer Harry E. Donlan entered a bar a few doors down from the Joyce Hotel and observed a man matching the description seated with a glass of wine talking with a woman. On approaching the couple, the officer noted that the man had traces of dried crusted blood in his mustache and cuts on his hand. A cursory search of the man turned up an empty matchbox from the Barclay Hotel in his pocket. Otto Wilson was brought in for questioning and eventually confessed to both murders.

Wilson had little insight into his crimes and described himself going through the motions of killing and mutilating his victims as mindlessly as a zombie. Despite having admitted to bringing a butcher knife to the scene, Wilson claimed the first murder had been triggered by Griffin's demand for more money, but quickly added, "Of course, that is not a very good excuse, but I don't know." Wilson basically explained, "I was just out of my mind and I am trying to recall as much as I can."

LAPD's forensic psychiatrist Dr. J. Paul de River interviewed Wilson and concluded that he was sane and aware of his actions but did not feel anything that would enable him to explain his actions. He was a psychopath, and according to de River, the women were

> the victims of a playful, sadistic dissectionist, the objects of the caprices of a butcher. He was not a rapist. He was highly perverted with a lust for murder. . . . This display of cruelty which is closely associated with the digestive processes, is quite indicative of sadism. This order of associations may be traced in the lower animals where one has to kill if one is hungry, and

here we see this same desire, this craving for voluptuous sensations of slaughter, and if we follow this, we see how killing and slaughter become interwoven with the nutritive instinct, and in the sadomasochist complex such as in this subject's case, we frequently find cannibalistic tendencies which may be likened to the sadistic buccal stage of childhood. During this stage the child finds pleasure and gratification in biting and sucking. This hunger concept may reach the extreme in the desire to incorporate—to swallow—to possess as one's very own. . . . He was a necrophiliac and cannibalistic.[6]

De River attributed Wilson's disorder and hate for females to his childhood abandonment by his mother and the abusive institutional foster upbringing that left him traumatized and cannibalistic and necrophiliac—a mindless "werewolf" zombie killer.

"Black Dahlia" Murder, Los Angeles, 1947

The "Walking Dead Murders" would be dramatically supplanted in the public's memory three years later by the sensational unsolved murder of twenty-two-year-old Elizabeth Short, who was found in an empty lot at South Norton Avenue between 39th and Coliseum, naked and completely sawn in half at her waist, her body having been drained elsewhere of blood and meticulously bathed and groomed, her torso and breasts and legs slashed and a "Joker" smiley face carved into her cheeks from the edges of her mouth to her ears. Her face and head showed signs of battery. Her intestines were found tucked under her buttocks. Traces of ligature marks were found on her wrists and ankles; it was clear she had been held prisoner and tortured. (Short was last seen six days before her body was found.) Like the Jack the Ripper case, the Black Dahlia (the origin of the nickname is in dispute) to this day obsesses a legion of researchers and amateur investigators seeking a solution as to who so horribly murdered Elizabeth Short.

The New Serial Killers, 1930–1949

American serial killers in the 1920s like Earle Nelson and Albert Fish mostly arrived at a victim's door on foot or they ambushed their victims on lonely paths or streets, dragging them away like spiders to a nearby dark alley, coal yard or deep woods where they would rape, kill and mutilate them. Many were driven by overt family madness, biblical passages or pulp adventure literature, laudanum addiction, incest child rape, and outhouse and attic room Gothic secrets. They were often odd and twitchy, Scripture-quoting, rootless, migratory, shabby outsiders; sick refugee flagellant drifters with indiscernible specks of dried blood on the cuffs of their soiled shabby pants. They did not fit into a community of neighbors and looked like the sick monsters they were. They rode the rails, they hitchhiked or they just compulsively tramped on foot from kill to kill.

But in 1941 when serial killer Jarvis Roosevelt Catoe was identified and apprehended, he would prove to be a *monstrum* in its classic meaning: an omen of everything that was to come three decades later.

Jarvis Theodore Roosevelt Catoe, "The Dupont Circle Killer," Washington, DC, and New York, 1929–1941

Women were murdered in Washington, DC, at an alarming rate beginning in 1929. The first in the long series to come was twenty-two-year-old Virginia McPherson, a nurse. She had recently separated from her husband, Robert, a bank clerk. On September 14, 1929, after she failed to respond to his telephone calls, her estranged husband visited her second-floor apartment near the corner of I Street and Pennsylvania Avenue in Northwest Washington. He found Virginia on the floor of the bedroom, clad only in a silk pajama top. A pajama cord was tightly wrapped five times around her throat and secured in place with a surgeon's knot.

A coroner's jury quickly declared Virginia's death a suicide, but a rookie police officer with connections in the Senate managed to get the case reopened, claiming a cover-up and that there were witnesses who saw a suspect escaping out of the rear window of the apartment onto a low roof. Several senior police officials were suspended, but the case remained unsolved.

The second victim was twenty-eight-year-old Mary Baker, a clerk with the Navy Department, on April 11, 1930. A witness saw Baker near the Washington Monument in a car with a man at the wheel who apparently struck her several times with his fist before driving the two of them away. The witness scribbled down the license plate number and reported it to the police that same evening. The license belonged to Mary's car, which was found on a remote road on the fringe of Arlington National Cemetery the following morning. Police found Mary's body nearby, face-up in the shallow water of a culvert. Her underwear had been torn away, and she had been scratched, strangled, beaten severely enough to dislodge several teeth and shot three times with a .25 caliber handgun in the throat, back and left side. The case remained unsolved.

On May 24, 1934, sixty-five-year-old retired schoolteacher Mary E. Sheads was found in her Northwest Washington apartment at 2000 16th Street, the third victim. She had been punched in the eye, raped and strangled. Her killer had apparently entered her apartment from a fire escape abutting her windows. From under her fingernails police scraped skin samples allegedly belonging to a "light-skinned" African American. No further leads were uncovered.

On November 9, 1935, twenty-six-year-old Corinna Loring was found in a lovers' lane a few blocks away from her home in Mount Rainier, just outside Washington, DC, in Maryland. Loring was a Sunday school teacher with an impeccable reputation, scheduled to be married in two days. There were two bone-deep lacerations over her right eye and an inexplicable burn, almost like a brand, on her forehead. She had been strangled with a five-foot length of twine tightly wrapped around and embedded in her throat. A whiskey bottle with a pocket-sized edition of the Bible stuffed through its neck was found nearby. Police suspected several former suitors and even her fiancé's ex-girlfriend. Corinna was buried in her wedding gown, and the case remained unsolved.

The national press kept count of the unsolved murders. "ONE

MORE IN THE CHAIN OF WASHINGTON'S BAFFLING MURDER MYSTERIES," the *Dayton Daily News* reported in 1936. Although the concept of a serial killer had not yet been precisely articulated, the newspaper hinted that the murders were interconnected. "The national capital is stirred by the strangling of beautiful Corinna Loring, the fourth time in six years that a pretty girl has met mysterious and violent death under circumstances strangely similar."[7]

The *Herald-Press* in Michigan reported, "Washington, Home of the 'Best' Detective Brains, Cannot Solve Murders of Four Young Women . . . Four murders all bearing the same resemblance . . . and yet all different. In each case a beautiful young woman was slain by a hand which left no trace."[8] The *Minneapolis Tribune* described some of the murders as "motiveless."[9]

Police in Washington, DC, could not imagine or comprehend the notion of a single multiple murderer, despite the precedents. It was not something in their realm of experience or language yet, nor would it be until well into the 1970s.

On December 31, 1935, nineteen-year-old Beulah Limerick was found dead in her bed in her 19th Street apartment in Southeast Washington. An inexperienced doctor at the scene certified her death as natural due to "internal hemorrhage," and her body was released to a funeral home. As the undertaker began preparing the corpse, he uncovered a small .25 caliber gunshot wound in the nape of her neck, cleverly stuffed with her hair and combed over by the killer, who also washed away the blood and applied rouge to the dead girl's face.

The case immediately attracted avid press attention. Beulah was the "secretary" of a former prohibition-era drinking club, the Sky High Whoopee Club, and since the age of fifteen had had a string of lovers and admirers she described in a diary that was found in her apartment. Eventually, a Washington Metropolitan PD police officer was charged in her murder but was acquitted at trial. The Limerick murder was the subject of gossip and speculation for years to come.

After the death of Beulah Limerick, the murders appeared to abruptly cease—but only because the newspapers were no longer reporting them. The killing went on; at least six more women were murdered, primarily in the Northwest section of Washington, DC, most raped, strangled and battered. But they were all African American. The press was not interested in reporting *these* crimes. Even today we only have a sparse and sketchy grasp of these murders of black women:

- Florence Dancy, 65, April 12, 1935, murdered in her home on 2139 L Street NW;
- Josephine Robinson, 34, December 1, 1939, Blagden Court NW, with no further details;
- Lucy Kidwell, 62, September 28, 1940, a landlady strangled in her home at 307 Virginia Avenue SE;
- Mattie Steward, 48, November 28, 1940, a landlady strangled in her home at 1432 Swann Street NW;
- Ada Puller, 22, January 22, 1941, strangled in her basement apartment at 1442 Corcoran Street NW;
- Mabel Everett, 16, June 30, 1941, found battered to death in an apartment building basement locker at 3032 14th Street NW.

Dupont Circle Murders

Then in 1941, a white woman was raped and strangled in her own apartment, and the press suddenly woke up and threw itself at this new murder in a series that was eventually dubbed the "Dupont Circle Murders."

Twenty-five-year-old Rose Abramowitz had been married to her husband, Barney, for exactly a month on March 8, 1941. They lived in a small upscale apartment building at 1901 16th Street NW, up the road from Dupont Circle. She was a secretary, while Barney worked at the Social Security agency as a staff lawyer. To celebrate their one-month anniversary, they were having some of Barney's friends from work over in the evening. That Saturday morning, Rose stayed home to supervise a janitor who was going to wax the floors before the guests arrived, while Barney went in for a half day's work at the office.

Barney returned home at around 1:30 p.m. to find Rose, lying on her side, one hand resting on her chest and the other beside her. She was clad only in her housecoat, and her slippers were neatly placed at the foot of the bed.[10] The medical examiner determined that she had been raped and manually strangled. Once again, the case remained unsolved.

On Sunday, June 15, twenty-two-year-old Jessie Elizabeth "Betty" Strieff was expecting her fiancé for dinner. She lived with a coworker in a small apartment on 19th Street NW near Dupont Circle, about four blocks away from where Rose Abramowitz had been murdered three months earlier.

Betty was a spirited, independent girl from Iowa with everything going for her. Exuberant and pretty, she was a graduate of Drake University and held a private pilot's license. Employed in the Ordnance Division of the War Department, she had top secret clearance and had been recently promoted to chief clerk.

It was around 2:30 p.m., in the middle of a Sunday afternoon, just starting to rain heavily, when Betty realized she didn't have enough butter for the lemon pie she was planning to bake. She quickly donned a transparent hooded rain cape over a skimpy blue-and-white-striped "playsuit" with a wraparound skirt she had been wearing with sports socks and saddle shoes, grabbed her roommate's umbrella of translucent oiled silk printed with white polka dots and quarter moons, and dashed out to a store three blocks away to buy a stick of butter. She must have looked as if she stepped straight out of the pages of *Vanity Fair* or *Harper's Bazaar* in her jaunty single-girl Sunday afternoon outfit, accessorized with the gay silk umbrella.

She'd be back in five minutes, she told her roommate.

Betty never returned.

A clerk at the store later told police that she had arrived in a black car that remained double-parked outside while she made her purchase. The clerk could not make out the driver's face through the pouring rain and back-and-forth swish of the windshield wipers.

Betty's body, naked except for her wet shoes and socks, was discovered the next morning eight blocks away from her apartment at the end of a trail of blood leading through an alley into a two-car garage behind a retired professor's house on 1717 Q Street NW. She had been beaten up, stripped naked, brutally raped and garroted with a belt or rope. Her blue playsuit and underwear were missing along with her raincoat and umbrella. Once again, Washington PD was helpless in solving the case.

The newspaper headlines blared, "GIRL'S MURDER IS 7TH FOR D.C. IN 8 YEARS."[11] Many of the murders had occurred on streets in Northwest Washington radiating from Dupont Circle, and were now dubbed the "Dupont Circle Murders."

District of Columbia, a federal territory, was administrated by a congressional committee. Representative Felix Edward Hébert, a Democratic congressman from Louisiana who served on the committee, used Strieff's murder as an opportunity to conduct a federal investigation into the Washington Metropolitan Police Department. As Hébert argued, "There is no excuse for the failure of the department to check crime and solve a murder occasionally."

Serial Murder and the Politics of Race

The committee hearings focused entirely on the Washington PD's failure to solve the murders of white women and completely ignored the string of unpublicized murders of black women.

As historian Mary-Elizabeth B. Murphy recounts:

> An unknown perpetrator began to attack black women in the nation's capital. Four black women—Josephine Robinson, Lucy Kidwell, Mattie Steward, and Ada Puller—were raped and murdered. . . . The white press did not cover these deaths when they occurred, and police officers conducted minimal investigations to locate the culprit. While these murders did not occur at the hands of the police, the police department's apathetic response signaled an institutional culture of racialized negligence around black women's safety in the city, which was itself a form of brutality. This profound indifference toward black women was thrown into sharp relief in June 1941 when Jessie Elizabeth "Betty" Strieff, a twenty-two-year-old

white clerk from Iowa, was raped and murdered. News of Strieff's murder made local and national headlines.[12]

The *Baltimore Afro-American* newspaper asked, "How thorough an investigation did the police make when they found Mrs. Kidwell murdered? Mrs. Florence Dancy ravished? Mrs. Ada Puller mutilated?"

Murphy points out, "At several points during the hearings, Representative Hébert justified the use of police brutality against black Washingtonians based on their alleged rates of crime by arguing, 'Force begets force.' He contended that black citizens were lawless and suggested that Washington police officers needed to locate 'a way to handle those fellows.'"[13]

Murphy's is not the bleating of a white-guilt politically correct academic historian. Newspaper accounts from the era sustain Murphy's assessment of the racial dynamics plaguing Washington's murders. After Strieff's disappearance, both police and newspapers pointed the finger at the black janitor in her apartment building, but police "were unable to break down his alibi for the day."[14] Representative Hébert's home state newspaper, the *Times* in Shreveport, Louisiana, reported that the recent unsolved murders of white women "were in the same general section of Washington . . . on the edge of a district heavily populated by negroes."[15]

On the other hand, black newspapers like the *Afro-American* did not appear to cover the murders of Josephine Robinson, Lucy Kidwell, Mattie Steward and Ada Puller any more than the "white press" did.[16]

Serial Killer Caught

In the end, Washington's serial murders would be solved by the NYPD. On August 4, 1941, the body of a young white woman with brunette hair was found near a sidewalk curb at a vacant dirt lot on Jerome Avenue, between Burnside Avenue and 181st Street in the Bronx. The victim had been strangled but apparently not raped (not uncommon in serial homicides; sexual assault can take many subsidiary forms other than penetrative rape). The victim was eventually identified as twenty-six-year-old

Evelyn Anderson. Evelyn was a waitress at the White Top Restaurant at 167th Street and Southern Boulevard, but she hadn't shown up at work the previous morning. When she did not return from work that evening, her husband, Erhardt, assumed she stayed over with friends in the Bronx as she sometimes did rather than return late at night to their West 92nd Street apartment in Manhattan.

Erhardt told police that some of the jewelry Evelyn wore, including a wristwatch, was missing. Erhardt had recently pawned the watch and then redeemed it shortly afterward, and police were able to recover a description and serial number from the pawnbroker. Two thousand police circulars with the watch's details were circulated to pawnshops around the city.

On August 27, a pawnshop on Eighth Avenue reported that the watch had been pawned for four dollars by an African American giving the name Charles Wolfolk, living at 6 East 133rd Street. When police interviewed Wolfolk, he stated that the watch had been presented to him by his niece, Hazel Johnson. Hazel told the police she'd been given the watch by an admirer, Jarvis Roosevelt Catoe of Washington, DC. He had given her the watch on August 3—the day of the murder—and warned her not to pawn it as it might get him "into trouble." Hazel also said that Catoe gave another girl a pocketbook, remarking, "I promised you a pocketbook, and I'm sorry I couldn't get you a new one, but here is a nice second-hand one."

He was described as a slim but powerfully built light-skinned African American, five feet nine inches tall, about 165 pounds, with extremely large, strong hands. He had arrived in July from Washington, DC, driving a black 1937 Pontiac with white sidewall tires. He had gotten a job as a busboy in a cafeteria but had been fired for making advances to a white waitress.

His landlady complained, "He went back to Washington on August 5 without paying $12 rent he owed me for the month he had roomed here. He was shiftless, no good, liked the women, and was always polishing up his car. You could never get any sense out of him, and when he'd take us for a ride we'd always have to buy gas for his car."

Conveniently, she had his address in Washington: 1730 U Street

NW, smack-dab in the middle of the Dupont Circle Murders. You didn't have to be a forensic geoprofiler to see the significance, but the NYPD was focused on one murder, in the Bronx.

NYPD detectives flew to Washington, and accompanied by DC officers, they called at the address only to discover that Catoe and his girlfriend had recently moved. Nonetheless, in an age when automobiles were still relatively scarce, Catoe's Pontiac was quickly located parked a few blocks away at another rooming house, at 1704 Swann Street. The detectives disabled the car's ignition, waited until Catoe appeared and took the thirty-six-year-old suspect into custody.

Catoe was polite and cooperative. On questioning, he eventually admitted to giving Hazel the watch but spun a ridiculous story of witnessing the murder and robbery of Evelyn by two thugs who gave him her watch and handbag to buy his silence. He claimed they forced him to get rid of her body and that he did not see her face because they had wrapped it in a cloth of some kind.

Catoe was shown a picture of Evelyn Anderson and asked, "Is that the woman?"

"She sure is."

"You're sure?"

"Sure as sure."

"How can you tell whether this is the woman if you never saw her face?"

Once Catoe's story began to come apart, it took police about five hours to get his full confession:

> That morning, I saw this woman at 92nd Street near Broadway. (She had actually been at the corner of Amsterdam and 90th Street, waiting for a bus.) I drive up beside her and asked her the way to some address in Harlem. She pointed where I should go, and I offered her a lift. She refused, but I told her, "Why not get in?" She finally did.
>
> She told me where she worked, and I told her I'd drive her up that way. It was then 6:30. I went to a lonely spot (an alley near the restaurant) and tried to make an appointment with

her. But she said she was happy with her husband and refused. So, I choked her and assaulted her.

I saw she was dead. I put her body in the back seat, put a slip cover over it, and drove to 113th Street and Seventh Avenue near where I was living. I parked the car and left it there all day. That night, after I'd had a good sleep, I drove to Jerome Avenue and dumped the body at the place where it was found.[17]

Evelyn's husband doubted the story, insisting that she was extremely afraid of ride-offering strangers and would never have entered a car willingly. She must have been forced, he insisted, but in the end it made no difference.

Once Catoe finished confessing to the murder of Evelyn Anderson in the Bronx, he proceeded to confess to another ten murders of both white and black women, including the so-called Dupont Circle Murders, most of which occurred within blocks of his flat. He also confessed to over a dozen rapes in which the victims survived. Typically, many of the rapes had not even been reported to the police.

Catoe stated he "had spells" in which he would rape and kill after drinking wine and "reading detective stories about rape cases and looking at pictures of nude women."

Catoe claimed, "I didn't mean to kill them but some of them fought so that I had to choke them hard. They just kicked off."

Time magazine reported that when asked how many women he had killed, "Chocolate-colored Jarvis Theodore Roosevelt Catoe held up his long sinewy fingers and counted off. 'About ten,' he finally said."[18] A press photographer snapped a photo of Catoe holding up his huge hands. It became the iconic image of Catoe—the Paganini of serial killer stranglers.

Catoe explained, "I didn't squeeze their throats with my fingers. I'd put my left hand on the back of their neck and then I'd push their throats in front with my right hand. I'd just put the palm of my right hand against them, with their throat between my thumb and fingers. That way I didn't leave any marks."

Catoe now took police through his murders. It was often unclear whether Catoe raped the women before they were strangled or after they were dead or both.

Catoe described how on June 15 he was driving down 19th Street during a heavy rainstorm when a girl in a transparent raincoat wearing a blue playsuit mistook his car for a taxicab and hailed him. Catoe offered to give her a ride just the same, which the exuberant woman accepted. He waited for her to purchase a stick of butter. When she got back into the car to be driven back to her apartment, Catoe either threatened or battered her into submission. He then drove her through the rain to a garage he was familiar with at 1509 S Street NW, owned by Dr. Laura Killingsworth, and raped and killed Strieff in it, strangling her with the cloth belt of her playsuit. Killingsworth would later tell police, "He used to come to my place to do odd jobs. He cleaned my car and of course knew the garage. I never locked the garage during the day and Catoe knew that too."[19]

Catoe then loaded Strieff's naked body back into his car, threw her clothes into a nearby trash can and drove the body to an alley behind Q Street. He dragged her body through the alley, leaving a bloody trail until he found an unlocked garage behind 1717 Q Street, where Strieff's body would be found the next morning. It all happened within a half hour, he said.

Catoe kept the pretty umbrella with the polka dots and quarter moons Strieff had left in his car and gave it as a gift to his girlfriend. Police later recovered the umbrella from the girlfriend's house, and Strieff's roommate identified it as hers. In his girlfriend's apartment, they also found several pairs of women's shoes and articles of female attire that he had presented to her as gifts.

Police were not unfamiliar with the phenomenon of false confessions, and Catoe was taken to the vicinity of the various crime scenes and asked to lead the investigators through the murders. He noted correctly that the garage where he left Strieff had been painted a new color and its doors changed since he left the body there. When brought to the apartment building where he killed Rose Abramowitz in March, he led police to the correct apartment and to the spot inside where he had left her body.

Catoe described how he was walking on 16th Street on March 8, when Abramowitz appeared in front of her apartment dressed in a housecoat and slippers, anxiously looking for the caretaker who failed to arrive on time to wax her apartment floor. Turning to the first black man she saw on the street, she demanded if he knew where the caretaker was. When Catoe politely replied he had no idea who or where the caretaker was, she offered him the job to wax her floor. On an impulse, he accepted the job and followed her up the stairs into the apartment and strangled her into unconsciousness, carried her to the daybed and raped her. When she began returning to consciousness, he strangled her to death, smoothed out her housecoat and left her slippers neatly arranged at her feet. He said he took twenty dollars from her pocketbook before leaving, a fact police had withheld from the press.

This satisfied the police as to the murder of the white women. The murder of the black women would be described in a more cursory manner.

Catoe stated he visited a series of black landladies, on the pretext either of renting rooms or doing handyman work. He would insist that they show him all the rooms, to ensure that nobody else was home, then strangle them.

On April 12, 1935, he strangled sixty-five-year-old Florence Dancy. Catoe could not furnish many details of the murder or the exact address—he said he was very drunk at the time—but accurately remembered the layout of the apartment. The Dancy case was particularly touchy for the police and courts, as another black man had been convicted of the murder and sentenced to life: James Matthew Smith.

On September 28, 1940, Catoe killed sixty-two-year-old Lucy Kidwell. He lured her into the basement by telling her he was a mechanic and wanted to store his tools there. He strangled her, raped her and then carried her body upstairs. Before leaving he stole forty-two dollars. On November 28, 1940, he strangled and raped forty-eight-year-old Mattie Steward. He said, "She kicked out in my hands." While the police were escorting Catoe to the scene of the murder on Swann Street, he gave friendly waves and greetings to several women they passed. "I used to make love to them," he explained.

On January 22, 1941, he picked up twenty-two-year-old Ada Puller on the street and took her to a basement apartment. When she demanded money for sex, he became infuriated and choked her. He said, "She came to before I could attack her, so I choked her good."

The exact number of murders that Catoe confessed to became blurred somewhere between seven and ten. The murder of Florence Dancy was batted back and forth while the court reviewed the conviction of James Smith.

Who Was Jarvis Theodore Roosevelt Catoe?

Jarvis Theodore Roosevelt Catoe was born October 6, 1905, in Kershaw, South Carolina, the eldest of eight children of former slaves. Catoe attended school until the fifth grade and then went to work as an undertaker's assistant in Rock Hill. After the death of his parents in 1919, he lived on an uncle's farm.

In 1925, Catoe suffered a fractured skull when he was thrown from a vehicle during an accident. The injury was so severe that he was not expected to live. But he did. Here again is a frequent theme in serial killer histories: a head injury followed by radical changes in behavior. As soon as Catoe recovered consciousness, his behavior had changed, his brother recalled: "When he was in the hospital in Charlotte he would often get out of hand and choke the nurses and doctors. When he finally left the hospital, he had occasional spells and acted sort of queer. We could not do anything with him so I brought him to Washington in 1929."

Catoe worked for the police as an informant in prohibition violation cases, as a busboy in the Social Security Board cafeteria, as a garageman, houseman and handyman. In February 1932, he obtained a taxi license, listing himself as a former police employee. In 1937, he acquired a brand-new black Pontiac sedan.

Between November 16, 1931, and May 3, 1941, he had accrued seventeen traffic violations and his license was suspended, but he was allowed to continue driving pending an appeal.

As is typical of serial killers, Catoe also had a record for minor sexual offenses. He was sentenced to 135 days in jail on May 7, 1935, for two counts of indecent exposure, and then again in December he was sentenced to 180 days and released on May 5, 1936.

Esther Hall, the girlfriend to whom Catoe had given Betty Strieff's umbrella, loyally came to visit him in jail, accompanied by three other female friends of his. They all came out after the visit amazed by Catoe's confessions, one of them remarking, "I never would have believed it of Jarvis."

Catoe's brother would later say, "It was a great shock to me when I saw my brother's picture in the paper. I could hardly believe that he was the one who had killed those poor girls. Yet, now, after thinking it all over, I can understand how it could have happened.

"He told me not to worry. He said to tell all our folks not to worry. Just pray for him. He said we shouldn't spend any money on lawyers. I just can't believe he meant to do all this. He never was right ever since that accident. His own wife wouldn't live with him because he would have these spells."

Catoe had married a girl in North Carolina, but they separated. His brother John had brought her to Washington in the hope of reconciling his brother with his wife, but it didn't work out. Catoe would sometimes disappear for a week at a time. Sometimes he would sleep in his car and wouldn't come into the house. Finally, his wife went home.

Women who knew Catoe described him as a "smooth" talker who had a way of striking up a conversation and keeping it going. The day after the murder of Betty Strieff, Carrie Jackson, the landlady of his rooming house at 1730 U Street, was sitting on the front steps of the house. She later told reporters, "Catoe came downstairs and sat on the steps beside me. I was reading about the murder. He asked me, 'What are you reading in the paper? What's the big story?'

"I told him that a girl had been raped and killed and that she lived just around the corner on Nineteenth Street. He didn't seem nervous or act unusual. I told him that she had been raped and that it was a terrible thing. He then said: 'Yes, it sure is. The man must have been crazy to do a thing like that! Do you think they'll ever catch him?'

"Whenever I did see Catoe, he would ask me if there were anything new in the murder case. He always said the police wouldn't solve it."

Jarvis Catoe went on trial in October 1941 for the murder of Rose Abramowitz. By then he was claiming he had been coerced into a confession. Police, however, had ensured that his confessions were not the only evidence mustered against him by having him take them to the scenes of his murders and walk them through them. Catoe was sentenced to death for the murder of Abramowitz.

Although indicted for the other murders, Catoe never stood trial for any of them.

The review of James Matthew Smith's conviction for the murder of Florence Dancy in 1935 dragged on for years. Smith had been fighting his conviction long before Catoe was arrested. Smith was so vehement about his innocence that at one point he was transferred to a psychiatric facility for a period of two years.

Catoe's confession, which was so detailed that police stated they were persuaded he had committed the murder, did not lead to Smith's release.[20] On the eve of Catoe's scheduled execution in 1943, he was supposed to testify on Smith's behalf. Instead, Catoe broke out of a line in prison and climbed up sixty-five feet onto a railing, where he perched for the next three hours, threatening to jump as prison guards, firemen and inmates tried to coax him down. Eventually, Catoe came down and gave his testimony—he recanted his confession, condemning Smith to remain in prison.[21] All further news of James Matthew Smith's fate promptly vanished from the public record.

On January 15, 1943, Jarvis Theodore Roosevelt Catoe was executed in the electric chair.

The press had been right that there was a serial killer on the loose in Washington, DC. But they were wrong about which victims he had killed. The murders of Virginia McPherson, Mary Baker, Mary E. Sheads, Corinna Loring and Beulah Limerick were never solved.

The Monstrum *Catoe*

Catoe was indeed in many ways a harbinger—a *monstrum*—of the kind of serial killers to come in the 1970s:

- a serial killer operating in a perceivable geographic territory;
- a public awareness of his existence in a community he is targeting;

- the use of an automobile to lure victims and transport their bodies;
- a "forensic awareness" (perpetrator uses a strangling technique intended according to him "not to leave any marks" and avoids leaving fingerprints);
- the claim of a behavior-changing head injury;
- the assertion that true-detective magazines and erotic imagery inspired the rapes and murders;
- the collection of trophies from the victims and their presentation as gifts to girlfriends;
- witnesses recalling a marginally odd but otherwise harmless neighbor, a seemingly hardworking individual who had no problems attracting girlfriends and female admirers;
- a pervasive double standard where the murders of black women are less thoroughly investigated and less reported on by the media.

Perhaps the most foretelling of serial murder to come was the challenge for investigators to recognize and connect multiple murders committed by the same perpetrator, especially in interjurisdictional cases, a phenomenon known as "linkage blindness." It became a dramatic problem in the 1970s in the wake of the Ted Bundy murders across multiple states and has not been conclusively solved to this day.

The 1941 congressional management committee review of policing in Washington, DC, found, as an example, that the murder of Mary Baker on a road next to Arlington National Cemetery, fell across five jurisdictions. Baker was last seen in Washington, DC, and that brought the Washington Metro PD into the investigation; she was a Naval Office employee, and that brought the police section (today Naval Criminal Investigative Service [NCIS]) of the Office of Naval Intelligence (ONI) into the case; as Arlington Cemetery is military property, it also brought in the military police; and since military property is federal property, it brought in the US Justice Department; and finally, the property was geographically located in Arlington County, Virginia, whose police were also in on the investigation.

Washington itself was not only policed by the Metropolitan Police, but also by the White House Police covering the White House grounds and its vicinity, the Capitol Police covering the Senate and House territories and the Park Police covering the vast number of parks in the city. There were too many chefs in the kitchen.

And finally, just as in the 1970s, there was a call to bring in the FBI to coordinate murder investigations between the various jurisdictions in Washington, DC.[22] It wouldn't be until the 1980s that the FBI would indeed become a quasi-"clearinghouse" agency and "authority" on US serial murders, although the primary investigation of serial murders to this day remains with local jurisdictions with few exceptions.

Jarvis Theodore Roosevelt Catoe represented almost everything to come in the world of serial murder, except perhaps his race. When the "epidemic" would hit in the 1970s, the serial killers would be primarily, although not exclusively, white males.

William Heirens, "The Lipstick Signature Killer," Chicago, 1946

As the slaughter of World War II was winding down in the Pacific in the summer of 1945, police in Chicago were stymied by a series of three murders:

- Josephine Ross, forty-three, was found on June 3, 1945, in her fifth-floor apartment bedroom at 4108 North Kenmore Avenue. Somebody had entered through an unlocked door in the late morning while Ross was still in bed, stabbed her in the throat and face and slit her jugular vein, killing her. The murderer then carried her into the bathroom, washed the blood off her body in the bathtub, which police found half-filled with bloodied water, her pajamas and two towels floating in it, and bandaged her wounds. He carried her washed body to the blood-soaked bed and wrapped a skirt around her head and throat with a nylon stocking. The victim was not sexually penetrated. Despite her body being washed, a few strands of coarse dark hairs were found clutched in her hand. The apartment was completely wiped clean of fingerprints. The coroner determined that the bandages were placed on her body about ninety minutes after her death; her killer had lingered that long in her apartment, yet took no valuables.

- Frances Brown, thirty-one, was found December 10, 1945, in the residential Pine Crest Hotel at 3941 North Pine Grove Avenue, six blocks from the Ross murder scene. The victim was found nude from the waist down, kneeling over the edge of a bathtub, her head hanging into the tub. Several bloodied towels lay on the floor near the bathtub. Her pajama top was pulled up and wrapped around her throat and head. When police removed the garment, they found a bread knife driven through her neck from one side out the other. She had been shot once in the right side of her head and once in her right arm. A deep defensive cut was found between her right thumb and index finger. The killer had soaped and bathed her body and taped her wounds after her death but did not sexually penetrate her.[23] The perpetrator had gained entry through a window by making an acrobatic leap from a fire escape down to a narrow ledge. A message was scrawled on her living room wall in bright red lipstick, starting about six feet from the floor:

For heavens
SAKe catch me
Before I Kill more
I cannot control myself

The killer had wiped down the apartment but missed one bloody partially rolled fingerprint left on a doorjamb between the living room and bathroom.

During the night of January 6–7, 1946, about two and a half miles away from the scene of the Frances Brown and Josephine Ross murders, six-year-old Suzanne Degnan was abducted from her bed at 5943 North Kenmore Avenue. The intruder entered through her bedroom window by placing a ladder beneath the window ledge. A ransom note written on a grimy, oily scrap of paper was found on the floor. It read, "Get $20,000 Reddy & wAITe foR WoRd. do NoT NoTify FBI oR Police. Bills IN 5's & 10's. BuRN This FoR heR SAfTY." A partial fingerprint was lifted from the note despite the oil.

The next day while conducting an area search for the missing girl police looked down a street sewer catch basin. At first, officers couldn't wrap their minds around what they were seeing. It looked like a pink doll's head with shiny golden hair floating in the black murk of the sewer water. It was Suzanne's severed head, found about a block away from where she lived. Her right leg was found in another nearby sewer and her left leg in yet another. Her torso was recovered from a storm drain at a third location, and a month later both her arms would be found in a fourth location. The body parts had apparently all been washed clean of blood. Police determined that the dismemberment had been carried out in an apartment building basement laundry tub facing the alley where her head was found. Beneath an alley stairway, police found a wire noose with a strand of the victim's blond hair clinging to it. They concluded the killer left the girl's body there while searching for a location to dismember it.

The first two murders were similar enough and close enough in proximity to be easily connected, but the murder and dismemberment of Suzanne Degnan wasn't as obviously related. Yet it shared some striking similarities: the perpetrator surreptitiously entered into the victim's premises, and the body and body parts had been washed clean of blood.

In the same period, police were also investigating a series of attacks in which women survived.

On October 1, 1945, nineteen-year-old Veronica Hudzinski was writing a letter at her desk in her first-floor apartment at 5722 North Winthrop Avenue when she was shot in the arm through the window. The .38 caliber bullet was similar to the one that Frances Brown had been murdered with, but because the bullet that wounded Hudzinski was damaged, a conclusive ballistic match could not be made.

Four days later, October 5, Evelyn Peterson was struck unconscious from behind and her skull fractured by a prowler who dropped through a skylight into her penthouse apartment on 6020 Drexel Avenue, which she shared with her sister. He tied her up with a lamp cord, and after ransacking the apartment, left, locking the door behind him. Peterson's sister returned around lunchtime and found the apartment locked. She did not have her keys and assumed her sister had stepped out. She encountered a helpful teenage boy in the hallway who promised to look for the superintendent while she went to see if she could find her sister. In the meantime, Evelyn regained consciousness at the sound of somebody knocking on her apartment door. When she stumbled to the door and managed to open it with her hands still tied, she found a teenager in the hallway who asked her if she was all right and helped her back into the apartment to a chair but did not untie her. He then went down to the superintendent and told him that a tenant upstairs was "not well" and needed help and departed before leaving his name. Peterson was found conscious but dazed and was taken to the hospital. Police discovered that the intruder had defecated outside the skylight window.

On December 5, 1945, while Marion Caldwell was seated in the kitchen of her home on 1209 Sherwin Avenue, a .22 caliber bullet entered through her window and grazed her arm. Police determined that the shot was fired from a roof across the street. This shooting occurred five days before the "lipstick murder."

A Suspect Arrested

The Degnan child murder and dismemberment in January shocked not only Chicago but the nation. It was closely followed by the press, and there was tremendous pressure on the police to solve the case. Despite several confessions to the Degnan murder, the police found them to be false, and the case dragged on without much progress.

Six months later, on June 26, 1946, a caretaker in an apartment house plagued by burglaries confronted a teenage male prowling the building. The teen threatened the caretaker with a handgun and fled. Arriving police officers caught sight of him near 1320 Farwell Avenue, and as they approached him, he drew the handgun and attempted to shoot one of them. The gun misfired twice before the officer tackled him. (It was later determined that the stolen handgun had been kept loaded in a desk drawer for many years, and the cartridges became inert over time.) The police officer found it difficult to control the slippery and athletic suspect, who succeeded in twisting out of his grip and disarming the officer. As the struggle became dangerously desperate, another officer jumped in to the rescue and attempted to knock the boy unconscious by breaking a heavy clay flowerpot over his head. The boy seemed impervious to pain. The officer had to smash three clay pots over his head before he went limp.

The prisoner was identified as seventeen-year-old William "Bill" Heirens, a University of Chicago student who had a notable juvenile record of pathological compulsive burglaries, or "neurotic burglaries" as they had been described at the time. Back in 1942, on the day Heirens was to graduate from eighth grade at the age of thirteen, he made the Chicago newspapers when he was arrested and charged in eleven burglaries and suspected in another fifty. Papers described him as a one-boy crime wave. Bill Heirens was a student at St. Mary's of the Lake parochial school, and the charges came as a surprise to his teachers and fellow students, who remembered him as a friendly, intelligent and well-behaved boy. To help support his family, he worked several after-school jobs, while police reported that his burglaries had netted him some $3,500 in furs, clothing, jewelry, guns, old coins and cash (equivalent to $52,000 in 2020). Many of Heirens's burglaries had occurred on Pine Grove Avenue near the site of the later Ross and Brown murders and a few blocks away from where he lived at the time of his arrest on 714 West Grace Street.

The thirteen-year-old Heirens was sentenced to reform school where, after a failed escape attempt shortly after his arrival, he eventually adjusted well and was considered a model student in its academic program. Shortly after he was paroled home, he was caught burglarizing another apartment complex and charged with burglary again. By then the family had moved to 1020 Loyola Street, a mile away from the Degnan home.

Heirens was again put on probation and boarded in a Catholic school outside of Chicago, away from temptation, except that he would return home on weekends. In an attempt to further stymie Bill's proclivities for apartment house burglaries, the family moved to Lincolnwood, a more rural residential suburb, about a twelve-mile bus and train ride into downtown Chicago.

On January 19, 1945, Bill Heirens was released from probation for a second time. Over the winter, spring and summer Bill lived in Lincolnwood, went to high school and commuted to his summer job as a laborer on the Central Railroad in downtown Chicago. On the morning of June 3, the day Josephine Ross was murdered, Heirens had gone into Chicago for work but never showed up at his jobsite that day. Ross lived 450 yards from a station on the same El Line that Heirens took to his jobsite.

Heirens had done so well at school in the meantime that in September 1945 he was admitted to the University of Chicago without having to complete high school. He moved into a dorm rather than make the twenty-four-mile round trip to his parents' home in Lincolnwood. Heirens was a popular, well-liked and sociable student, a member of a number of clubs, including the university gun club, and a popular date with some of the female students, although apparently the dates remained platonic. His grades, however, were poor.

Now Heirens was under arrest a third time for burglary. After being knocked unconscious by the police, he remained in what appeared to be a catatonic state, handcuffed in a hospital bed. He seemed unable to answer any questions put to him by police, staring off into space instead. The doctors thought he was feigning.

When police searched Heirens's dorm room (without a search warrant), they found two suitcases crammed with handguns, jewelry, wristwatches and other stolen items, including a set of pictures of prominent Nazi leaders (which became a significant circumstantial link to one of the murders) and $1,800 ($24,000 in 2020) in negotiable war bonds. Later, Heirens directed police to a locker in the Howard Street El station where they found an additional $7,355 ($101,500 in 2020) in war bonds. When in the end police totaled up the value of cash and property seized from Heirens's campus room, his parents' home and the station locker, it came to $80,000 ($1.1 million in 2020). Heirens had not attempted to sell any of the loot—his burglaries were purely pathological.

Heirens had been described as a "human fly" for some of his acrobatic burglaries, and the fact that the murderer of Frances Brown had made a precarious leap from a fire escape to a narrow window ledge to gain entry to her apartment aroused suspicions. Police wondered if there was more to him than just burglaries. Why would a juvenile burglar (or any other kind of burglar) be so desperate as to attempt to shoot a police officer? It did not make sense. Now his prints were sent down to the identification bureau to see if they matched any crime scenes.

Confession

Sergeant Thomas A. Laffey was Chicago PD's fingerprint expert, and over the past six months he had compared more than seven hundred sets of suspect prints attempting to find a match to the print on the Degnan ransom note. By now, Laffey knew the ransom note fingerprint by heart, its every swirl and loop as intimately familiar to him as those of his own hand. When Heirens's fingerprints arrived at his desk, Laffey immediately recognized the match he'd been searching for. Heirens's little finger matched the print left on the ransom note in fifteen points of similarity. Police would also match Heirens's print to the bloodied rolled print left at the "lipstick murder" scene and a print found at the Evelyn Peterson bludgeoning scene.

The .22 bullet that wounded Marion Caldwell was ballistically matched to one of the handguns found in his dorm room. The handgun's serial number was traced to a handgun stolen in a burglary two days prior to her shooting.

The photos of the Nazis came from an album stolen the night before Suzanne Degnan's murder, from an apartment at 5959 North Kenmore Avenue overlooking her bedroom.

Even though the Ross and Brown murders were several miles from the Degnan murder, Heirens had lived in both neighborhoods near the murder scenes, and the shooting scenes, and property from burglaries in the vicinity of all the crime scenes was found in Heirens's possession.

Numerous witnesses identified him, including Evelyn Peterson, her sister and their superintendent, who recognized him as the concerned teenager at the scene. Heirens burglarized one building so frequently that the caretaker had assumed he lived there and readily identified him.

But Heirens wasn't talking. He just lay strapped in his bed, staring blankly into space. Frustrated, Chicago police allegedly roughed up the teen, slamming his bandaged head into a wall, in the hope that would help his memory. It didn't.[24]

When the beating did not get a response, they pumped him up on sodium pentothal, believed in those days to be a "truth serum," and for good measure gave him a spinal tap without an anesthetic, and kept him awake for long hours. All this without an attorney present. Of course, this being 1946, Heirens's parents were not present either and he was not read a Miranda warning (that would not be introduced until 1966). For six days, the Chicago Police probed, pricked, drugged and battered Heirens.

At first, the most Heirens would admit to was that he had an accomplice, "George Murman," who had killed Suzanne Degnan. For a while, police believed that George actually existed, as they found in Heirens's pocket a typed letter signed by "George" referring to burglaries "they" had committed together and, in his dorm room, a letter from Heirens to "George." Eventually, police realized that the signature on the letter from George was Heirens's; "George Murman" (for "Murder Man," as some argue) was his alter ego, his Mr. Hyde. George Murman did not exist other than in Heirens's imagination. (George was also his father's first name and Heirens's middle name.)

By now Heirens had a defense attorney. Police had Heirens do a writing sample test. They read the text of the ransom note. Heirens misspelled "ready" and "wait" exactly as they were misspelled in the ransom note: "reddy" and "waite." Heirens would later claim that police had him copy the original note. Police insist that the text was dictated to him.

When confronted with the misspellings, Heirens first went silent, but then made a confession when he and his lawyer were promised that the prosecution would not seek a death penalty. The prosecutors called a press conference and brought out Heirens before a roomful of reporters to make his confession public. Instead, Heirens claimed he couldn't remember anything. Embarrassed and enraged, the prosecution put the death penalty back on the table.

Over the next few days, Heirens repeatedly confessed and retracted those confessions, until finally the prosecutor, his own lawyer and his mother wore him down into making a cohesive written confession, the death penalty again taken off the table. The Chicago press, especially the *Chicago Tribune*, threw themselves on Heirens like a pack of dogs. A child killer is always a focus of lurid reporting, and Heirens became the subject of months of vitriolic coverage, false accusatory information and fabricated versions of confessions that he had never made. There was no way an impartial jury was going to be found in Chicago or anywhere in the state of Illinois for that matter.

Rather than going to trial, at the advice of his counsel, Heirens pleaded guilty in the three murder cases and a string of assault and burglary charges, and received a life sentence.

Innocent or "Kill-Crazed Animal"?

After his imprisonment, Heirens withdrew his confession yet again, and over the next six decades filed a series of appeals that were rebuffed by the courts. In 1972, he became the first inmate in Illinois to earn a Bachelor of Arts (BA) degree. He later took postgraduate courses in various languages, analytical geometry and data processing. He managed a prison garment factory for five years, overseeing 350 inmates, and when transferred to another facility, he set up their entire educational program. Always the polite charmer, the likable Heirens cultivated a legion of supporters who believed in his innocence. The older and more educated he became, the more harmless, gentle and vulnerable his persona became. Over the decades, he and his supporters argued that Heirens was a victim of a police "conspiracy" to frame him for the murders. The appeals courts condemned police and prosecutorial misconduct but upheld the conviction on the basis of the actual evidence (even if unconstitutionally acquired) and the fact that Heirens had confessed.

When Heirens became eligible for parole in 1983, Illinois attorney general Neil Hartigan pronounced, "Only God and Heirens know how many other women he murdered. Now a bleeding-heart do-gooder decides that Heirens is rehabilitated and should go free. . . . I'm going to make sure that kill-crazed animal stays where he is." Heirens was turned down for parole.[25]

Chicago-area high school students and college kids were particularly touched by Heirens's tender age at the time of his conviction and formed Free Bill Heirens clubs dedicated to his release. After my book *Serial Killers* came out in 2004, I occasionally received e-mails from Chicago students asking me to endorse their campaign to free Heirens. A class in "social justice" visited him in the minimum-security facility he had been transferred to, and saw him as a sweet old man, an unjustly incarcerated grandpa to a generation of kids, some of whose parents hadn't even been born when six-year-old Suzanne Degnan was snatched from her warm bed in the middle of the night, strangled, decapitated and dismembered in a basement laundry tub, her severed body parts dumped into sewers.

In the 1990s, attorneys made a concerted effort to discredit the evidence cited in Heirens's conviction. Pro- and anti-Heirens websites went up, characterized by virulent rancor and accusations of "conspiracy" from both sides. Again, Heirens's advocates failed to persuade the state of Illinois to give Heirens a new trial.

In April 2002, Lawrence C. Marshall, a Northwestern University School of Law professor and cofounder of the Center on Wrongful Convictions, and Steven A. Drizin of the Children and Family Justice Center formally took up his case, filing a petition with the governor of the state of Illinois and Illinois Prisoner Review Board to grant Heirens clemency without a new trial. The petition was rejected 14–0 by the Prisoner Review Board. Thomas Johnson, a member of the parole board, said to Heirens, "God will forgive you, but the state won't." Heirens was going to be kept locked up to the bitter end.

What escaped many of Heirens's supporters was that "unfairly convicted" is not the same as "wrongly convicted." Indeed, Marshall and Drizin's appeal began with the declaration, "This petition—presented by Northwestern University School of Law's Center on Wrongful Convictions (CWC) and Children and Family Justice Center (CFJC)—will not argue the issue of innocence."[26] The petition stated:

> We believe that, irrespective of Heirens's guilt or innocence, his case stands out as one of the grossest miscarriages of justice in the history of the United States. His conviction is contaminated by more sources of error—prosecutorial misconduct, police misconduct, incompetent defense counsel, unprecedented prejudicial pre-trial publicity (orchestrated by police and prosecutors), junk science, probable false confessions—than any other case we have studied. Any one of these factors alone would be enough to have wrongfully convicted an innocent man, but the combination of all of them in a single case leaves us, as it should leave the Governor and Prisoner Review Board, with no confidence in the result.[27]

When Heirens began his appeals in the 1950s, the courts ruled against him on precisely the same issue, deciding that it was not the procedural breaches and irregularities, the fundamental breaches of fairness, that resulted in Heirens's conviction, but his confessions and the evidence, however illegally obtained. Nothing had changed by the 2000s.

Preponderance for Guilt

The most compelling piece of evidence for Heirens's guilt, in my opinion, was his revelation of something the police *did not know*. In his written confession, drafted with the help of his lawyers and his mother, Heirens stated that he had cut up Suzanne Degnan's body with a hunting knife he had acquired in a burglary and that he had disposed of the knife by tossing it up onto El tracks from the alley behind Winthrop Avenue as he walked to the Granville El station three blocks away from the Degnan home. The police, who had not found the knife in their extensive search of the neighborhood, had not searched elevated tracks.

Upon investigation, it was discovered that a track maintenance man had indeed found a knife on the tracks in that area shortly after the murder and had kept it in his tool locker in the storage room at the Granville El station. It was the knife reported stolen by Guy Rodrick of 5000 South Cornell Avenue, the same Guy Rodrick who owned the .22 revolver found in Heirens's dorm room. Rodrick identified the knife as his. (In later years, Heirens would change his story and claim that he was riding home to Lincolnwood on the El one day and did not want his mother to see the knife, so he tossed it from the El train and it *just happened* to land near the Degnan home.)[28]

But the available evidence, his numerous *confirmed* points of geographic and chorological proximity to *all* of the murder scenes and the assault scenes, appears to be beyond the realm of a mathematical anomaly: just *too much* a coincidence.

Yes, inconsistencies between his confession about times, places and dates and the facts of the crime can indeed be "signature elements of a false confession" as argued in the petition. They can also be errors of memory. Murderers don't always remember with precise accuracy the details of their crimes; they often get dates, times and locations wrong. While some serial murderers remember and record with relish every minuscule detail of their murders, others commit them in a fugue state, in an alcohol- or drug-induced stupor, or a blind rage or hazy impulse. They don't remember the details because they are in a state of chaos or robotic compulsion. As one impulse-driven serial killer explained to me, "It was like I was in fast-forward on my own remote control. It was fast and chaotic. . . . Afterwards, I didn't dwell on it. I had no fantasies because I was living in my fantasies, doing whatever I *wanted* to do *whenever* I felt like I could get away with it. I didn't have to think about it or fantasize about it, before or afterwards. I enjoyed the *doing* it. Afterwards I didn't think about it, ruminate on it, or look it up in the newspapers or collect clippings."

One can even argue that a perfect recollection of a crime scene is just as much "a signature element of a false confession," suggesting that police had fed details of the crime to the suspect in order to "help" his memory along. The minor contradictions between known facts and Heirens's confessions are evidence of nothing but Heirens's imperfect memory.

William Heirens is interesting because he was one of the first serial killers to be psychologically assessed shortly after the 1941 publication of *The Mask of Sanity: An Attempt to Clarify Some Issues About the So-Called Psychopathic Personality* by Hervey M. Cleckley. His groundbreaking text laid the foundation for the modern concept of psychopathy, but not yet its inner mechanics and minutiae of accompanying physiological characteristics. The psychiatrists also deep focused entirely on his childhood and teenage years; there was nowhere else for them to go with a seventeen-year-old subject.

Much had been made by Heirens's advocates of his gentle and friendly demeanor, his intelligence and charm, affability and boyishly vulnerable persona, the apparently nonviolent nature of his juvenile burglaries, and his unusually young age (twenty-seven to twenty-eight years old is the statistical average age for a first serial murder). Those notions are undermined by the pathological nature of his burglaries as he described them to psychiatrists, and his childhood history. His childhood had many of the typical markers of a budding serial killer, as eventually cataloged by FBI behaviorists. But in the mid-1940s, serial killers were still too rare to establish any kind of comparative statistical norms. Psychiatrists recorded factors in Heirens's history that seemed unimportant at the time but were very telling about Heirens's personality and his potential for violence when assessed from a later vantage point.

Who Was William Heirens?

William George Heirens was born in Evanston, Illinois, on November 15, 1928. Both his mother, Margaret, and his father, George, were American-born Luxembourgers and devout Catholics. Three years later, his brother, Gerald "Jere" Heirens, was born. The two brothers reportedly lived and played together without any issues between them.

George grew greenhouse flowers and operated a florist shop, but both enterprises failed during the Great Depression. George apparently did not despair and quickly found a series of jobs, eventually landing a position in the Carnegie Steel Company police, rising up to the rank of special investigator with sufficiently lucrative pay for the family of four to afford middle-class housing. The family *appears* to have been functional and harmonious, with none of the alcohol-fueled Sturm und Drang so often reported in serial killer childhood histories. On the other hand, one can easily imagine the sense of insecurity and anxiety of having two family businesses fail during an age of mass unemployment, soup kitchens and homelessness; everyone in the family must have suffered the anxiety of the Great Depression. Margaret had two paralytic nervous breakdowns while raising her boys.

Parental interviews were contradictory on whether Heirens was a lonely asocial child or whether he happily played with his peers.

William had a spotty health record but nothing dramatic: he was a difficult forceps birth; Margaret had painful breastfeeding issues; his tummy was upset as a baby; his tonsils took longer to heal; he had measles and chicken pox; when brought to kindergarten, he had hysterical separation issues from his mother; when his brother contracted measles, Margaret kept William at home for the remainder of the kindergarten year. But millions of kids experienced similar things without becoming serial killers.

Inside a Serial Killer's Mind: Psychopathia Sexualis

There were a few items in Heirens's history, though, that are typical of serial killer childhood histories. For example, a head injury (or several) to the frontal lobe. His mother reported that when the infant Billy (the future "human fly") was seven months old, he grabbed and twisted and pitched himself out of his baby pram over a stairwell railing, flying headfirst twelve feet down to a concrete landing. Apparently, the baby did not lose consciousness, and after the grotesque grapefruit-sized swelling on the front of his head subsided, he seemed recovered. Then at age twelve, Billy tumbled off the concrete steps of his school. It was reported that this time he lost consciousness and had "cut his head over his eye" (at the frontal lobe). After that, Heirens began suffering from frequent headaches.[29]

Like Earle Nelson and multiple serial killers to come, we have a childhood head injury—two, in fact.

Then there were the fetish burglaries. Sexual serial killers frequently stole, as children, the objects of their fetishes. Moreover, what are sometimes dismissed as "nonviolent" crimes, such as voyeurism, exhibitionism or burglary, are actually compulsive fetishistic sexual expressions of sadistic anger and lust for control. Serial offenders sometimes start young, breaking into premises while the occupant, often female, is sleeping. They stand over the sleeping subject, enjoying the control they have over the unaware victim, masturbate and leave without disturbing the victim. Eventually, either a victim wakes up and is murdered in a panic, or the fantasy escalates to that on its own, depending on the psychopathology of the particular perpetrator.

Heirens told court-appointed psychiatrists that since the age of nine, he had been obsessed with stealing and wearing women's panties, that the feel of them aroused him. Heirens described a cardboard box he stashed in his grandmother's attic when he was thirteen, which they then located. Inside were forty pairs of bright pink or blue rayon panties. At first, William stole the objects of his fetish from clotheslines and apartment house laundry rooms, but later he would go through people's opened doors into their premises and eventually climb through their windows.

Heirens described the transmutation of his sexual obsessions from the *object*—the female underwear—to the *process*—the act of acquiring it. He became primarily aroused by the thrill of the surreptitious and illicit act of entering an apartment, occasionally even ejaculating as he slipped through an open window into someone's private place. He would linger inside, sometimes not bothering to steal anything, and leave, having sexually satiated himself for the moment. Other times, he would proceed through the burglary in a state of arousal, remaining inside for hours, gathering up not only female garments, but also jewelry, firearms, books, cash and other loot, until he ejaculated or simply lost his erection. He sometimes compulsively defecated and urinated on the floor or bed or into drawers or jewelry boxes and set small fires. Once he reached a climax, he would sometimes leave the loot behind, but more often he took it with him and stashed it in various hidden locations.

Heirens was a frustrated, perhaps angry, sexually wound-up boy but developed an abhorrence to the idea of actual sex with women and sublimated it with a shifting range of fetishes and compulsions. While Heirens dated in college, he found the idea of sex repulsive. Sex, burglary and murder were all equally "dirty" to him, and when he gave in to his various compulsions in the worst way—murder—he afterward soaped and washed their corpses clean and taped their wounds closed, in his own version of a Catholic-inspired penitence.

Among the books Heirens had in his campus dorm room, many of them stolen, was a well-thumbed copy of Richard von Krafft-Ebing's *Psychopathia Sexualis*, the pioneering study of abnormal and criminal sexuality and fetishes associated with it. The book featured a number of cases of mutilation murders of children and women. Heirens must have been trying to understand his own compulsions and fantasies. *Dr. Jekyll and Mr. Hyde*, he said, had been his favorite movie, and probably inspired his homicidal alter ego "George Murman," a fantasy so real to him that for a while he convinced police that George actually existed.

Heirens claimed that he would "black out" when he was aroused and only regain consciousness after ejaculation. He described how he would "come to" and find his victims already washed and laid out where they'd be found by police. In the case of Degnan, at first he claimed he regained consciousness in the basement laundry room, finding its tub and his knife covered in blood, with no memory of dismembering his victim. Later, he recalled lifting sewer tops and throwing body parts into the water. He stated that he wrote the ransom note in the laundry room and then returned to toss it through the girl's bedroom window in order to give her parents "hope" that their child was still alive. He said that he had strangled the girl in the bedroom, either with his hands or the length of wire that was later found a few blocks away, and that he had carried her corpse through the open window down the ladder.

When asked if he felt any remorse, he said no. In 1946, this would have been a confounding thing, but today we easily understand it as just old-fashioned psychopathy. After murdering and dismembering Suzanne Degnan, Heirens went for a hearty breakfast and then returned to his dorm room to study a little before attending morning lectures, just like on any other day that semester.

Heirens was both interviewed and physically examined by a Cook County panel of psychiatrist MDs. Had he been in their hands three hundred years earlier, he would have been pronounced a witch or werewolf. But now it was 1946, and the doctors reported that Heirens had

> a remarkable reduction to the perception of pin pricks, however strong, as "pain." This was present all over the body with the exception of the glans penis. Sharp pin pricks inside the nose on the mucous membrane and the soles of the feet was denied as being painful and no motion of withdrawal was made there or elsewhere. This was also true as regard the mucous membranes of the lip and the scrotum and body of the penis. A sharp needle could be pressed more than four millimeters under the nails without inducing pain or defense withdrawal movements. As the sensory examination proceeded, the "analgesic cloak" deepened. . . . He became unable to feel pin prick[s] as other than "not blunt." The corneal reflexes at first were greatly reduced, and at the close of the examination had disappeared so that it became possible to tap the eyeballs with a closed safety pin without his winking or giving any motor sign of sensation. Deep pain produced by pressure on calf muscles and Achilles tendons and the testes was also reduced. The perception of vibration and the other forms of sensation were normal. The visual fields were found to narrow progressively as the test continued, so that they became finally almost pin-point. This phenomenon is known as a "spiral" or "helicoid" visual field, and is positive objective indication of profound hysteria.[30]

The psychiatrists concluded all this was "clear proof of the patient's hysterical personality." Today the psychiatric wind blows the other way. What psychiatrists in 1946 described as "hysterical personality" today is described as psychopathy.

In 2014, a study at Université Laval in Quebec resulted in a report entitled "Feeling but Not Caring: Empathic Alteration in Narcissistic Men with High Psychopathic Traits." It measured and compared both the muscular and brain wave responses to viewing others in pain and experiencing pain itself, comparing a group of non-incarcerated ("out-patient") diagnosed psychopath narcissists with a group of normatives—that is, "normal" people. An electric probe to the forearm was used to measure cold/heat pain, while pressure pain was measured with a gradual crushing force on the thumbnail of the subject. Reaction to the pain of others was elicited through projected images of people in pain, as measured by electroencephalograph (EEG)—to record brain activity—and electromyograph (EMG)—muscular activity.

According to the report, when feeling their own pain, both groups had the same response to heat-induced pain, but the psychopath narcissists scored "a significantly higher pressure-pain threshold."[31]

As for viewing others in pain, it was an infinite universe of pleasure for the psychopaths: their muscles and brain waves sparkled and purred like happy kittens.

Psychopaths, including the serial killing kind, not only have a low level of remorse and empathy but also anxiety, fear and their own pain; they suffer less because they feel less! That's why they constantly feed on stimulation, excitement, risk and other people's fear and pain. As one diagnosed psychopath explained:

> People think we have no emotion, which is absolutely not true. We just feel them way turned down. If most people feel an emotion between seven and eight on a dial of ten, I feel it between zero and two. Negative emotions are background noise. We can't tune into that frequency because our brains just don't process enough information for them to ever be loud

enough to feel or direct behavior. We enjoy things, get excited
about things, like adrenaline—that's great. I laugh with people,
I enjoy intellectual discussions.[32]

Since the age of nine, and probably earlier, Heirens was a spinning
wheel of escalating paraphilic transgressive addictions. He began with
a tactile sexual fetish for female undergarments and progressed to the
sexual thrill of stealing them, then to breaking into homes, where he
stayed for hours in a state of sexual arousal. His first murder might have
been as accidental as perhaps his first pantie theft. He was prowling
around Josephine Ross's apartment, not realizing she was there; when
she awoke she either interrupted his sexual ecstasy and he stabbed her
in a rage, or she startled him and he killed her in a panic to silence her.
He tried to "fix her" by washing her blood away and taping her wounds.

Now he was addicted to a new thrill that stimulated his emotional
state numbed by psychopathy. Just as the act of burglary replaced his
pantie fetish, murder would now replace the stimulus of burglary. He
would continue burglarizing, but it was no longer as exciting as that
moment when he killed his first victim. He resisted the temptation for
several months before he shot nineteen-year-old Veronica Hudzinski
through a window from the exterior of her apartment. It wasn't as sat-
isfying as hands-on murder.

A few days later, he entered Evelyn Peterson's apartment through the
skylight, perhaps again being surprised by her when she was awakened.
He bludgeoned her into unconsciousness, bound her and slipped out of
her apartment, locking the door behind him. We know Heirens was
very forensically aware, systematically wiping his fingerprints away. In
his study of Heirens's case, Colin Wilson speculates that the reason
Heirens returned to Peterson's apartment was a compulsion to double-
check if he'd left any evidence behind.[33]

Between the ballistic match to a handgun found in his dorm room
and witness IDs, there is no doubt that Heirens was at least capable of
shooting and wounding women and perpetrating violence. Today Heirens is, clearly, if not a murderer, then at least a psychopath, although

that in itself does not absolve nor condemn him, but in the overall circumstantial matrix, leans toward a circumstantially inculpatory conclusion and understanding of his possible motive.

William Heirens may have been convicted in a procedurally *unfair* process, but it's doubtful he was *wrongly* convicted. He was a raging bundle of pathological compulsions and confessed to the murders with sufficient accuracy in the details for the confessions to be believable.

William Heirens died unrepentant on March 5, 2012, at the age of eighty-three, after serving sixty-five years in prison, currently the seventh-longest sentence to be served by an inmate in US history.[34]

CHAPTER 3

American Noir:
Raising Cain Through the
Trauma Years 1930–1950

These are the things that you at home need not even try to understand.

Ernie Pyle, war correspondent

Between the abduction and cannibal-mutilation murder of Grace Budd by Albert Fish in 1928 and the unsolved murder of Elizabeth Short, "the Black Dahlia," in 1947, a generation of future "epidemic era" serial killers was born, including Juan Corona (1934), Angelo Buono (1934), Charles Manson* (1934), Joseph Kallinger (1935), Henry Lee Lucas (1936), Carroll Edward Cole (1938), Jerry Brudos (1939), Dean Corll (1939), Patrick Kearney (1939), Robert Hansen (1939), Lawrence Bittaker (1940), John Wayne Gacy (1942), Rodney Alcala (1943), Gary Heidnik (1943), Arthur Shawcross (1945), Dennis Rader (1945), Robert Rhoades (1945), Chris Wilder (1945), Randy Kraft (1945), Manuel Moore (1945), Paul Knowles (1946), Ted Bundy (1946), Richard Cottingham (1946), Gerald Gallego (1946), Gerard Schaefer (1946), William Bonin (1947), Ottis Toole (1947), John N. Collins (1947), Herbert Baumeister (1947) and Herbert Mullin (1947).

They were followed by the births of Edmund Kemper (1948), Douglas Clark (1948), Gary Ridgway (1949), Robert Berdella (1949), Richard Chase (1950), William Suff (1950), Randy Woodfield (1950), Joseph Franklin (1950), Gerald Stano (1951), Kenneth Bianchi (1951), Gary Schaefer (1951), Robert Yates (1952), David Berkowitz (1953), Carl Eugene Watts (1953), Robin Gecht (1953), David Gore (1953), Bobby Joe Long

---

*If we accept Manson as a "missionary-cult"-type serial killer, inspiring his followers to murder.

(1953), Danny Rolling (1954), Keith Jesperson (1955), Alton Coleman (1955), Wayne Williams (1958), Joel Rifkin (1959), Anthony Sowell (1959), Richard Ramirez (1960), Charles Ng (1960) and Jeffrey Dahmer (1960).

The vast majority of these children would not begin their serial killing until they were in their late twenties or early thirties in the 1970s and 1980s, with the exception of Edmund Kemper, who first killed in 1964, Patrick Kearney who began killing in 1965, John N. Collins in 1967, Richard Cottingham in 1967 (perhaps even as early as 1963) and Jerry Brudos in 1968.

In trying to explain the surge of serial murders from the 1970s to the 1990s, we often invoke the epoch in which the serial killings happened.[1] From the cultural and sexual revolutions of the 1960s and the wanton hedonism of the 1970s to the cruel Reaganomics callousness of the 1980s and the rapacious greed of the 1990s, we argued that somehow serial killing was a product of the violent times in which the killing happened. But that was only half the story.

Psychopathology is first shaped in childhood, so to understand surge-era serial killers of the 1970s and 1980s, we actually need to look back some twenty or thirty years earlier, to the eras in which they were steeped *as children* in the 1940s and 1950s. I've already described the process of basic "scripting" of transgressive fantasies. The direction these "scripts" take and how people are chosen for the role of victim in them has a complex structure pinning it all together.

Diabolus in Cultura and the "Less-Dead"

In *Sons of Cain*, I threw myself at the term *diabolus in cultura* in an attempt to describe the range of phenomena that could lead to a surge of children who grew up to be serial killers. The term was coined by anthropologist Simon Harrison, in his study of soldiers who brought home necrophilic collections of body parts as war trophies. Invoking the discordant tritone musical chords forbidden in the medieval era, known as *diabolus in musica* ("Satan in music"), he wrote there are also discordant tones in culture, a type of "*diabolus in cultura*—a forbidden conjunction of cultural themes, each unexceptionable in itself, but highly disturbing when brought together."[2] This notion best describes "scripting" in a serial killer culture, or serial killing "ecology," as I sometimes call it, when charting the ebbs and surges of serial killing at various points in history.

These "discordant tones" consist of not only cultural but also historical, social and economic phenomena that align in a "perfect storm" of a cocktail that triggers serial killer surges and has to do primarily with a serial killer's preference for certain types of victims and their availability.

In explaining surges of serial murder, criminologist Steven Egger argues, it was not that there were *more serial killers* but that there were *more available victims* whose worth was discounted and devalued by society. Egger maintains that society perceives certain categories of murder victims as "less-dead" than others, such as sex workers, homeless transients, drug addicts, the mentally ill, runaway youths, senior citizens, minorities, Indigenous women and the inner-city poor; these victims are all perceived as less-dead than, say, a white college girl from a middle-class suburb or an innocent fair-haired child. Sometimes the disappearance of these victims is not even reported. Criminologists label them the "missing missing."

Egger writes:

> The victims of serial killers, viewed when alive as a devalued strata of humanity, become "less-dead" (since for many they were less-alive before their death and now they become the "never-were") and their demise becomes the elimination of sores or blemishes cleansed by those who dare to wash away these undesirable elements.[3]

We popularly regard serial killers as disconnected outcasts, as those who reject societal norms, but more often the opposite is true. In killing prostitutes, Jack the Ripper, for example, was targeting the women that Victorian society chose for its most vehement disdain and scorn. Gary Ridgway, "the Green River Killer," who was convicted for the murder of forty-nine women, mostly sex workers, said he thought he was doing the police a favor, because they themselves could not deal with the problem of prostitution. As Angus McLaren observed in his study of Victorian-era serial killer Dr. Thomas Neill Cream, who murdered at least five victims (prostitutes and unmarried women coming to him seeking abortions), Cream's murders "were determined largely by the society that produced them."[4]

The serial killer, according to McLaren, rather than being an outcast, is "likely best understood not so much as an 'outlaw' as an 'over-socialized' individual who saw himself simply carrying out sentences that society at large leveled." Social critic Mark Seltzer suggests that serial killers today are fed and nurtured by a "wound culture," "the public fascination with torn and open bodies and opened persons, a collective gathering around shock, trauma, and the wound," to which serial killers respond with their own homicidal contributions in a process that Seltzer calls "mimetic compulsion."[5]

Or, as the late Robert Kennedy once put it more simply, "Every society gets the kind of criminal it deserves."[6]

Serial killers, in other words, partly take their cue from society as it is filtered through a combination of history, popular discourse, mainstream media, culture and subcultures.

To try to understand why there was this surge of serial killers in the 1970s through the 1990s, we need to look at the American *diabolus in cultura* of the 1920s through the 1950s and the generation of the parents who were raising the children who would become the future "epidemic era" serial killers.

Breakdown of the American Dream, 1919–1940

Prior to the First World War (1914–1918), American society was relatively disciplined and cohesively structured between the upper, middle and working classes, between rural and urban, and between white and people of color. The privileges and burdens, the rights and responsibilities of each class of Americans, aside from that of industrial labor, were rarely challenged, questioned or crossed before the Great War. In the way that medieval Europeans with passive Christian forbearance lived their place in society from birth to death as divine destiny, Americans settled into their place in the social hierarchy on the basis of Horatio Alger's "rags-to-riches" promise that with hard work and prayer, anyone can rise in the American class hierarchy to something spectacularly better than what they were born into. Most Americans quietly settled for moderately better, and did so, and that was what made America great.

World War I and its aftermath changed all that. It challenged the notion that duty and sacrifice would be rewarded with real change. A "Lost Generation" of disillusioned and shell-shocked American men returned from the horrors of a "war to end all wars" that did nothing of the sort. In the spring of 1919, as the Allies sat down at Paris and Versailles to draft a peace settlement to create a better world, the United States instead was subsumed in a rising surge of terror, murder and race war.

In late April 1919, thirty-six dynamite bombs were mailed to prominent politicians and appointees by a shadowy anarchist group. One bomb just missed killing the future president Franklin D. Roosevelt and his wife, Eleanor, who lived across the street from the targeted house of US attorney general A. Mitchell Palmer and had passed on their way home just minutes prior to detonation.[7] On June 2, nine large bombs exploded nearly simultaneously in eight cities: Philadelphia; Cleveland; Boston; Pittsburgh; New York; Washington, DC; Paterson, New Jersey; and Newton, Massachusetts. A night watchman in New York was killed by one of the blasts. The bombs were accompanied with the following message:

> War, Class war, and you were the first to wage it under the cover of the powerful institutions you call order, in the darkness of your laws. There will have to be bloodshed; we will not dodge; there will have to be murder: we will kill, because it is necessary; there will have to be destruction; we will destroy to rid the world of your tyrannical institutions.[8]

The bombings culminated with the Wall Street Bombing on September 16, 1920, that killed 38 people and seriously injured 143. The time bomb set for noon had been left behind in a horse-drawn carriage near the New York Stock Exchange and has been described as history's "first car bomb."[9] The culprits were never conclusively identified but are believed to have been Italian American anarchists. Blaming the bombings on Italian, eastern European and Jewish immigration, the United States closed its doors to immigrants from anywhere except the UK and Nordic countries. Immigration to the US for all others would now be stymied to a trickle until after World War II.

At the same time, the 350,000 African Americans who had served in the war "defending democracy" came home to a segregated America to be told, even when in uniform, to give their seats up for whites on streetcars and where they might walk, sit, eat or sleep or whom they might date or marry. W. E. B. Du Bois, the editor of the NAACP's monthly magazine, wrote:

> We *return*.
> We *return from fighting*.
> We return *fighting*.[10]

Already in 1917, a "Buffalo Soldier" regiment of black infantrymen (many from the North, where segregation was not enforced by law) stationed in Houston went to battle with Houston police over the issue of segregation and harassment in town. Eleven civilians and five policemen were killed by rioting soldiers. After a quick drumhead court-martial, thirteen black soldiers were summarily hanged without appeal, executed simultaneously on thirteen gallows in the largest single mass execution in American history on December 11, 1917. Altogether, nineteen would eventually be put to death.

The "Red Summer" of 1919 saw over a thousand African Americans hanged, stoned, shot, burned and battered to death in race riots across the nation. Some sixty cities that year from north to south saw violent race riots. Over two days in rural Elaine, Arkansas, roaming white mobs killed at random an estimated 100 to 237 African Americans, many of them migrant sharecroppers.[11]

Then on January 17, 1920, when the National Prohibition Act (Volstead Act) went into effect, millions of law-abiding Americans were turned into outlaws overnight for doing something they had been doing forever: drinking alcohol. It was perhaps the most profound break of faith between Americans and their government since the Civil War. As serial killing gangsters with tommy guns began to seize control of the lucrative illicit alcohol trade, murder rates soared.[12] In the growing affluence and ennui of the "Roaring Twenties," anybody who could make a buck made it. Wealth, time and leisure spawned the beginning of a "youth culture" and a narcissistic "speakeasy" anything-goes attitude.

In October 1929, it all crashed on Wall Street, wiping out billions of dollars of wealth in what became known as the Great Depression. By 1933, the unemployment rate in the United States was an astonishing 25 percent.[13] Making matters worse in the Midwest, an environmental disaster in the form of the Dust Bowl uprooted millions of families from their homes and farms. All this without a "social safety net" of welfare, food stamps or public housing. Men raised and socialized for generations into their role as family patriarchs and breadwinners suddenly found themselves helpless and broken, shivering in a soup kitchen line just to eat.

Families came apart under these strains, like the family of Joseph Lee Brenner III, born in Philadelphia in 1935. By 1937, Joseph's father had abandoned the family, and his mother could not keep going. Little Joseph was put into foster care and eventually adopted by a crazily sadistic religious couple, Stephen and Anna Kallinger, who subjected Joseph to a range of mental and physical tortures. When Joseph grew up, he had six children of his own, whom he abused and tortured in the same way he was as a child. By 1974, this child of the Depression became a serial killer, taking on as a partner his own thirteen-year-old son in a series of rapes and murders in Pennsylvania, Maryland and New Jersey.

While some families, like William Heirens's, survived in a neurotic state of stress and anxiety, others just broke apart, but they all left a generation of hardened and traumatized children and teenagers, some of whom would be old enough to be thrown into the next horrible thing to come along and fuck them up even more: World War II.

The "Last Good War" and the "Greatest Generation": 1941–1945

That battered generation of young men who matured over the 1930s was now sent into what was going to be history's most lethal and brutal war, sometimes referred to as the "last good war" because of the unambiguous evil of the enemy we fought.

In December 1941, Japan bombed Pearl Harbor and Nazi Germany declared war on the United States, dragging it into World War II. Some 16.5 million men (61 percent of American males between the ages of eighteen and thirty-six) were mobilized into the military and deployed in Europe, the Pacific or on wartime duty at home. Their average age was twenty-six.

About 990,000 of them would see combat, and 405,000 were killed. Nothing in their experience at home prepared them for what they were going to see in this war, a primitive war of total kill-or-be-killed annihilation culminating with two thermonuclear detonations that in several nanoseconds incinerated 120,000 men, women and children. Winston Churchill said it best: "The latest refinements of science are linked with the cruelties of the Stone Age."[14]

Things That Warriors Have Always Done

In *Sons of Cain*, I described in detail not only what American GIs endured on the battlefields of Europe and the Pacific, but what some of them perpetrated as well. They did things that warriors have always done. Northern Kentucky University's criminal sociologist J. Robert Lilly reported, for example, that American GI "liberators" raped fourteen thousand to seventeen thousand women between 1942 and 1945 in Britain, France and Germany, while German historian Miriam Gebhardt argues that American GIs raped 190,000 women in Germany.[15]

American GIs were not immune to the primordial primitive state that all warriors descend into to do what they have to do, especially so in a kill-them-all war of the kind World War II was. As Lt. Col. Dave Grossman writes in *On Killing: The Psychological Cost of Learning to Kill in War and Society*:

> The linkage between sex and killing becomes unpleasantly apparent when we enter the realm of warfare. Many societies have long recognized the existence of this twisted region in which

battle, like sex, is a milestone in adolescent masculinity. Yet the sexual aspects of killing continue beyond the region in which both are thought to be rites of manhood and into the area in which killing becomes like sex and sex like killing.[16]

A baby boom generation of future serial killers were about to be raised by a generation of fathers initiated in that "twisted region" of sex and battle in many different ways. And more.

In the Pacific, so many American soldiers engaged in wanton acts of trophy taking, collecting teeth and body parts and boiling and curing the skulls of severed Japanese heads, that US Customs inspectors were alerted to search the bags of homeward-bound GIs and confiscated all human-body-part trophies.[17]

Yes. The Nazis and the Imperial Japanese troops did all the same things, more wantonly and frequently and perversely than we ever did. But we did our part.

To be clear, the majority of American GIs did not perpetrate any of these acts; but most witnessed others among their "band of brothers" committing them. War is horror, and warriors are called upon to do horrific things, no matter how noble the cause for which they kill and are killed. When it was over, some could not find their way back.

Kill Crazy

The familiar term "PTSD"—post-traumatic stress disorder—would appear only in the 1980s in the wake of the Vietnam War, but during World War II the terms "combat stress reaction" (CSR), "battle fatigue" or "battle neurosis" were rolled up into a general statistical term: "neuropsychiatric casualty." Of American ground combat troops deployed in World War II, an astonishing 37 percent were discharged and sent home as neuropsychiatric casualties.[18] It just wasn't often reported or talked about. America preferred to see their sons coming home less a leg or arm than "crazy in the head." Hometown newspapers would euphemistically report on returning "wounded" or "casualty" figures without specifying the nature of the "wound" or "casualty."

A 2013 RAND Corporation study of World War II casualities reported that after the war:

> The neuropsychiatrically impaired, 454,699 veterans, accounted for 30 percent of all service-connected active disability awards in 1946. Of this group . . . the largest category, with about 66 percent of the cases, included those diagnosed with a "functional nervous disorder or psychoneurosis," a category that includes what is called PTSD today.[19]

Combat psychoneurosis was something new and very much unlike the physically disabling concussive "shell shock" from World War I. The annual American Psychiatric Association meeting in 1943 heard from Naval physician Edwin Smith about a new disorder labeled at the time as "Guadalcanal Neurosis." According to a May 24, 1943, *Time* magazine article, Smith described

> a group neurosis that has not been seen before and may never be seen again that occurred after prolonged warfare on Guadalcanal. He had treated over five hundred Marines from that killing island and he described their physical and mental strain as combining the "best of Edgar Allan Poe and Buck Rogers. . . . Rain, heat, insects, dysentery, malaria all contributed—but the end result was not bloodstream infection nor gastrointestinal disease, but a disturbance of the whole organism, a disorder of thinking and living, of even wanting to live." Symptoms displayed by these hard-bitten Marines were "headaches, sensitivity to sharp noises, periods of amnesia, tendency to get panicky, tense muscles, tremors, hands that shook when they tried to do anything. They were frequently close to tears or very short-tempered." Smith felt that it was doubtful these men could go back to the type of combat they had been exposed to on Guadalcanal.[20]

Returning World War II veterans did not have the current diagnosis of PTSD to take comfort in. "Combat psychoneurosis" sounded shamefully "psycho," and most wanted to just go home and forget about everything they had seen and endured. Our returning soldiers were patted on the back and told they did their duty in a just cause, were given medals and a parade and tossed a GI Bill and then sent home to suck it up in sullen silence in the privacy of their own trauma. They couldn't even talk to their families about it. Nobody wanted to hear it . . . at least not the truth. Our traumatized fathers and grandfathers were forever trapped in silence, like prehistoric life preserved in transparent amber, as "the greatest generation any society has ever produced," a term journalist Tom Brokaw coined in his 1998 book, *The Greatest Generation*.[21]

When after the war politicians and civilians who had never experienced it began talking about "the next war," one combat veteran wrote bitterly in the *Atlantic Monthly*:

> Probably I shall be tagged as a psychoneurotic veteran of too much bloodshed when I say that I get alternately fighting mad and cold sick inside whenever I hear people talk about the next war. . . . What kind of war do civilians suppose we fought, anyway? We shot prisoners in cold blood, wiped out hospitals, strafed lifeboats, killed or mistreated enemy civilians, finished off the enemy wounded, tossed the dying into a hole with the dead, and in the Pacific boiled the flesh off enemy skulls to make table ornaments for our sweethearts, or carved their bones into letter openers. We topped off our saturation bombing and burning of enemy civilians by dropping atomic bombs on two nearly defenseless cities, thereby setting an all-time record for instantaneous mass slaughter.[22]

Mostly, however, the popular media remained focused on the atrocities and war crimes perpetrated by the enemy.

When the American war correspondent Ernie Pyle was killed on a small island just off the coast of Okinawa in April 1945, he was writing an article that read, in part:

Death and misery is a spouse that tolerates no divorce. Such companionship finally becomes a part of one's soul, and it cannot be obliterated. . . . There are many of the living who have had burned into their brains forever the unnatural sight of cold dead men scattered over the hillsides and in the ditches along the high rows of hedge throughout the world.

Dead men by mass production—in one country after another—month after month and year after year. Dead men in winter and dead men in summer.

Dead men in such familiar promiscuity that they become monotonous.

Dead men in such monstrous infinity that you come almost to hate them.

These are the things that you at home need not even try to understand. . . .[23]

Who was coming back the same from that? You had to be crazy not to be crazy.

The Women, 1930–1945

It wasn't just the men and children who were battered out of shape by the Great Depression and World War II. The women had to take it twice as hard, once for themselves and then again for their children. It was easier for the men to just turn their back and make a go of it alone. During the Depression, some men gave up and drifted away from their families, abandoning them, but most of the women hung in there, found work or some way to make a living and raise their children. In the 1940s, as the men went to war, women were thrust into munition factories and other realms traditionally occupied by men.

Millions of women found opportunity in a booming war industry at home, as men went away into military service. When it ended, women were expected to give up those lifesaving jobs and stand aside for the returning men. With the Great Depression a distant memory, the war secure in victory, the postwar years were supposed to be a re-birth of everything America thought it was before the Dirty Thirties killed it; "as the clever hopes expire of a low dishonest decade" is the way W. H. Auden described it in his poem "September 1, 1939."

War Bride Clarnell

Clarnell Stage from Great Falls, Montana, would be the subject of some seventy society-page newspaper articles before her death in Santa Cruz, California, at age fifty-two in 1973. She wasn't an obvious candidate. Clarnell's father was a pipe fitter, but her mother, Nellie, had ambitions to a "better" class. The newspaper articles in its "society" pages began in 1931 on Clarnell's tenth birthday, when the *Great Falls Tribune* de-scribed the extravagant party her mother threw for her. Over the next ten years, the paper reported on Clarnell's progress in the Girl Scouts, her appearances at social events and the parties and events she orga-nized and clubs she led. She chaired the Great Falls Junior Women's Club at the YMCA and organized charity events for underprivileged children on Christmas.

When Clarnell graduated high school, the newspaper featured a quarter-page studio portrait of the stern and bucktoothed, hatchet-faced girl with a determined and commanding look on her face. The caption extolled her membership in the Quill and Scroll, the Young Authors club, the school orchestra, the Little Symphony and the Rainbow Girls Assem-bly. Not only was Clarnell smart and ambitious; she was six feet tall, tow-ering over most boys and men in Great Falls. Her height, her determined jawline, her brilliance and drive were surely a one-way ticket to a busy social life devoid of a romantic, personal, private one.

After graduating, Clarnell went to work as a collector for the Inter-nal Revenue Service in Helena, Montana, where she ruthlessly pursued tax debtors. Very quickly, the hard-nosed and efficient Clarnell rose to the rank of deputy collector, and she was elected president of the local branch of the National Federation of Federal Employees. Clarnell ruled with a stern hand both members and nonmember federal employees in

Helena, admonishing nonmembers to toe the Federation line.[24] As the war began and the men went away, Clarnell's power and ambition grew.

In 1942, twenty-one-year-old Clarnell met the man of her dreams: twenty-three-year-old US Army staff sergeant Edmund Emil Kemper Jr. of North Hollywood, California, stationed at Fort Harrison near Helena. At six feet eight, a man towered over her for once, and not just any man, but a handsome, dashing Special Forces commando with an aristocratic pencil-thin mustache and shiny paratrooper wings on the left breast of his crisp uniform. And Edmund wasn't just a muscle-head staff sergeant; he was future executive officer material, in her opinion, as smart and ambitious as she was. She immediately saw themselves as a power couple.

Like Clarnell, her beau came from a blue-collar family striving for better things. Edmund Emil Kemper Sr. worked as a mechanic for the California Department of Highways, while Edmund's mother, Maude Hughey Kemper, was an ambitious painter and a published author of boys' adventure stories, appearing in the social pages of Los Angeles papers. Maude founded and chaired a writers' club in North Hollywood and was a precinct organizer for the Democratic Party there.[25] Clarnell could see somebody just like that for a future mother-in-law as clearly as she could see the palm trees and coconuts of sunny California as she shivered in the cold of backwoods Montana.

After completing high school, Edmund had enlisted in an Army engineering battalion in 1939. When the US entered the war in 1941, he was recruited into a newly formed 1,400-man elite airborne commando unit, the legendary First Special Service Force (FSSF)—which would become known as the Devil's Brigade. Recruits were drawn from among experienced soldiers in the US and Canadian armies with backgrounds as rangers, lumberjacks, north woodsmen, hunters, prospectors, explorers and game wardens. Edmund must have had something special and was quickly promoted to staff sergeant. The FSSF was sent to Fort Harrison, Montana, to train for future forest and mountain special operations in Europe.

Clarnell and Edmund were married in a Methodist ceremony at her parents' home in Great Falls on Thanksgiving Day, November 26, 1942.

On April 15, 1943, Edmund and the FSSF left Montana and began a series of deployments: to the East Coast of the US, to the Aleutian Islands in Alaska, and to Morocco, from where they would launch toward Italy.

Back home, on November 8, 1943, the first of their three children was born, Susan Hughey.

By then, Edmund was deployed in Italy with the FSSF's Second Regiment, Second Battalion. On the night of December 1, Edmund's regiment of 418 commandos was ordered to scale a thousand-foot cliff to the top of Monte La Difensa in Campania, between Rome and Naples. Their mission—a suicide mission for all intents and purposes—was to take out the German panzer-grenadiers of the elite Hermann Göring Division dug in on a series of mountaintops.

From December 2 to January 8, 1944, in fierce mountain fighting, the FSSF suffered 77 percent casualties: 91 dead, 9 missing, 313 wounded and 116 neuropsychiatric casualties.[26]

Edmund was one of the 23 percent to survive. After just a three-week regroup, the Devil's Brigade was thrown back into combat on February 1, 1944, in the Battle of Anzio, south of Rome.

Operating clandestinely behind the German lines, the FSSF terrorized the Nazis by silently killing sentries or cutting the throats of sleeping soldiers in foxholes, leaving one alive to spread the news on awakening. The Germans nicknamed the FSSF the "Black Devils" because of their night camouflage. The FSSF left cards on German dead whom they had ambushed in the night. The cards showed the unit's insignia, a bloodred stone-flint arrowhead, with text in German: "*Das dicke Ende kommt noch*," roughly translating to "The worst is yet to come."

The FSSF would see ninety-nine continuous days of combat before they were relieved early in May 1944. By August, they were in combat again, this time in Southern France in Operation Dragoon, attacking German island fortifications. By the end of the war, the Devil's Brigade had killed or wounded some 12,000 Germans, captured 7,000 prisoners and sustained in return a final casualty rate of over 600 percent.

Film director Quentin Tarantino would later say that the commandos in his 2009 movie *Inglourious Basterds* were based on the Devil's Brigade.[27]

Edmund finally came home from the Army in 1946 and took Clarnell and Susan home with him to sunny California, to live the postwar dream.

After the war, Clarnell's hometown newspaper, reporting on her visit home, casually mentioned that her husband had been "wounded during combat [at] Anzio."[28] The nature of Edmund's wound, whether physical or otherwise, is obscured. Nobody talked about it. But when Edmund returned home, he no longer was the same. Who would be?

To Clarnell, used to running things on her own since she was a Girl Scout, her husband now appeared listless, depressed, lacking the former vigor and ambition of the handsome young commando she had met and married.

Clarnell hated his choice to work as an electrician while she stayed at home with their daughter, Susan. As a single woman, Clarnell had been on the way up: an empowered female, federal employee and community leader. She wanted a power husband for her power marriage. She wanted her killer commando back, in a suit-and-tie uniform. Instead, she got this tired, burned-out husk from the war. A blue-collar slob. Like her father had been. Like his father had been.

Clarnell pushed the twenty-seven-year-old Edmund to go to college and better himself. She would later complain, "The war never ceased. Upon his return he tried college under the G.I. Bill, couldn't get back into studying, argued like a staff sergeant with the instructors, dropped out, and worked rapidly into the electrical business."[29]

Edmund would later say that his wife "affected me as a grown man more than three hundred ninety-six days and nights of fighting on the front did. I became confused and I was not certain of anything for quite a time."

By 1948 their daughter, Susan, would soon be away at school during the days. With a little help from the in-laws, Clarnell would have some time for herself to get back into the social scene, do some volunteer work, maybe even get a part-time job. She could see the light getting brighter at the end of the tunnel. But then she got pregnant again.

On December 18, 1948, their second child was born, Edmund Emil Kemper III, one of the most notorious serial killers of the 1970s.

Roy Shawcross's Homecoming

Twenty-one-year-old US Marine corporal Roy Shawcross from the scrublands of Jefferson County near Watertown, New York, would become one of those "Guadalcanal Neurosis" cases. In the 1930s, Roy had dropped out of school after eighth grade and was lucky enough to find work with his father for the county road maintenance department. After the Japanese bombed Pearl Harbor, he enlisted in the Marines, and in August 1942, at the age of nineteen, Roy was deployed with the First Marine Division at Guadalcanal in the first major offensive against the Japanese in the Pacific. It was a brutal campaign, in which some 7,100 Americans would be killed over six months.

Roy barely survived being buried alive under tons of coral sand after being hit by a Japanese shell. His buddy next to him suffocated to death as Roy prayed for rescue. Lucky to be dug out by fellow Marines, Roy and his unit ended up cut off in the jungle, separated from US forces for four months, surviving on abandoned maggot-ridden Japanese rice rations. Roy would later say they never picked the maggots out because there'd be nothing left to eat.

Roy earned four battle stars but was never the same after Guadalcanal and was evacuated to Australia as a neuropsychiatric casualty in February 1943, rather than being redeployed in the next campaign in the Pacific.

While recuperating, Roy met an Australian girl, Thelma June, and promptly married her on June 14, 1943. They had one child, Hartley Roy Shawcross. But after Roy was shipped back to the United States in July 1944, he didn't send for Thelma or Hartley. He seemed to forget all about them.

Roy had been either posted to or hospitalized at the Portsmouth Naval Hospital in New Hampshire. Shortly after his arrival there, Roy met Elizabeth "Betty" Yerakes from Somersworth, an eighteen-year-old assistant pipe fitter working in the naval yards. Betty was a petite five feet two but tough as nails; a "Rosie the Riveter" war teen. Betty's parents were factory workers; her dad was Greek, her mom maybe the same, or Italian, or Mediterranean French.[30]

Betty and Roy were married on November 24, 1944, despite the fact that Roy apparently did not file for divorce from his first wife nor tell Betty he had a son and wife in Australia.

On June 6, 1945, their first son was born two months premature in a US Naval hospital in Kittery, Maine: Arthur John Shawcross, the future necrophile cannibal serial killer, the Genesee River Killer, who would kill the first of his thirteen victims in 1972.

And so it went.

Dennis Rader, "the BTK Killer," born in 1945, would tell his biographer Katherine Ramsland, "My dad, William Elvin Rader, a Marine, was still in the Pacific when I was born, on Midway Island."[31] "Golden Age" serial killers Douglas Clark, Richard Cottingham, Herbert Mullin, Carl Eugene Watts and Chris Wilder all had fathers serving in World War II. John Wayne Gacy's father, a shell-shocked World War I veteran, brutalized him.

Mostly, however, the biographies of the fathers of serial killers are sketchy and vague. Often they were just not there. Gone. The FBI "mindhunter" study of serial killers conducted in the late 1970s and early 1980s concluded that 66 percent of serial killers reported their mother as the dominant parent, and 47 percent reported their father gone before they reached the age of fourteen.[32]

Indeed, during 1945 and 1946, the divorce rate doubled from what it was in 1939 to an average of thirty-one divorces for every hundred marriages, the highest rate in the world. And the divorce rate among veterans was twice that of civilians. Some 53 percent of marriages in Los Angeles County in 1944 landed in divorce court by 1945.[33]

The 454,699 neuropsychiatrically impaired veterans did not include those who had been too crazy to send into war. At the height of the recruitment drive in 1942 and 1943, 1.25 million young American men were rejected "because of mental and emotional abnormalities."[34] This included men like Otto Wilson, "the Walking Dead Killer," who disemboweled two women in Los Angeles.

These men rejected by the Army were just too crazy to kill or be killed and were left behind at home. Some of them too went on to father kids; some even tried to raise them.

Postwar Fevers, Red Meat Movies and the Pulp Sweats

It wasn't just the war over there that affected people. There was a seismic shift in popular culture at home that took a darker and more paranoid turn. In his disturbing study of postwar America, *The Noir Forties: The American People from Victory to Cold War*, historian Richard Lingeman describes an era of anxiety and dread rather than the optimistic Norman Rockwell impression that we have of happy-to-be-home soldiers and optimistic baby-boom years. After describing the mass arrivals in 1947 of hundreds of thousands of coffins from Europe and the Pacific (the war dead had been temporarily interred overseas, and families had the option to leave them there in military cemeteries or have them shipped home for reburial), Lingemen describes how Hollywood launched a new genre of brutally violent and cynical crime movies, the so-called red meat movies that French film critics would later dub "film noir." Lingemen writes that the typical film noir was "peopled with recognizable contemporary American types who spoke of death in callous, calculating language and shot with dark chiaroscuro lighting, told an unedifying tabloid-style story of greed, lust, and murder. . . ."[35]

It was something the *New York Times* pondered in the last days of the war, describing a crop of "homicidal films" either just released or in production, like *Double Indemnity, Murder, My Sweet, Conflict, Laura, The Postman Always Rings Twice, The Lady in the Lake, Blue Dahlia, Serenade* and *The Big Sleep*.

> Hollywood says the moviegoer is getting this type of story because he likes it, and psychologists explain that he likes it because it serves as a violent escape in tune with the violence of the times, a cathartic for pent-up emotions. . . . The average moviegoer has become calloused to death, hardened to homicide and more capable of understanding a murderer's motive. After watching a newsreel showing the horrors of a German concentration camp, the movie fan, they say, feels no shock, no remorse, no moral repugnance when the screen villain puts a

bullet through his wife's head or shoves her off a cliff and runs away with his voluptuous next-door neighbor.[36]

The femme fatale was now raised to iconic heights, starring in the film noir as a greedy, narcissistic, bored, oversexed female often plotting to do away with her poor husband. An article in the *New York Times* in 1946 entitled "The American Woman? Not for This GI" gave voice to the thousands of frustrated veterans coming home to find women transformed:

> Being nice is almost a lost art among American women. They elbow their way through crowds, swipe your seat at bars and bump and push their way around regardless. Their idea of equality is to enjoy all the rights men are supposed to have with none of the responsibilities. . . . The business amazon would not fit into the feminine pattern in France or Italy. . . . They are mainly interested in the rather fundamental business of getting married, having children and making the best homes their means or condition will allow. They feel that they can best attain their goals by being easy on the eyes and nerves of their menfolk. . . . Despite the terrible beating many women in Europe have taken, I heard few complaints from them and rarely met one, either young or old, whose courtesy and desire to please left anything wanting.[37]

The *diabolus in cultura* of postwar America is evidenced most dramatically in the pages of popular men's magazines directed at returning veterans and at their young sons growing up in the years that followed the war. If there was ever a discernible homicidal-rape "mimetic compulsion," a popular cultural phenomenon extolling vengeful woman-hunting, rape, torture, cannibalism, mutilation and killing, then it was garishly celebrated in the pages of true-detective and men's adventure magazines with monthly circulations in the millions. They were sold openly on newsstands and in supermarkets everywhere from the late 1940s until the end of the 1970s. And it was an ugly thing to behold.

Where did it ever come from, what dark and ugly part of the American male psyche?

Cave drawings, myths, popular lore, folktales and fairy tales, fables and literature often reflect the hidden, unspoken yearnings and deep, dark fears and hates in a society, as well as its traumas and triumphs. In the limited three-TV-channel-plus-Hollywood-movies world of postwar American popular culture, without cable and satellite TV, without video, without video games, DVDs, the Internet or Netflix, guys read mainstream magazines, comics and paperbacks for entertainment. Other than movies, radio and later TV, there wasn't much of anything else in the way of popular narrative entertainment.

What entertained and came to obsess some boys of Ted Bundy's and John Wayne Gacy's generation, and their fathers, were dozens of men's adventure magazines like *Argosy, Saga, True, Stag, Male, Man's Adventure, True Adventure, Man's Action* and *True Men*.

From the 1940s to the 1970s, these magazines often presented salaciously exaggerated accounts of wartime Nazi rape atrocities. The magazine covers featured garish images of bound and battered women with headlines like SOFT NUDES FOR THE NAZIS' DOKTOR HORROR; HITLER'S HIDEOUS HAREM OF AGONY; GRISLY RITES OF HITLER'S MONSTER FLESH STRIPPER; HOW THE NAZIS FED TANYA SEX DRUGS; CRYPT IN HELL FOR HITLER'S PASSION SLAVES.[38]

Even today, more than seventy-five years after the war, the Nazis and their psychosexual sadistic cruelty remain a major theme in our popular culture and imagination, from *Ilsa, She Wolf of the SS, The Night Porter* and *Seven Beauties* to the more recent *Inglourious Basterds* and *The Reader*.

The adventure magazines were known as the "sweats" for the luridly colored cover illustrations of male torturers and female victims glistening with sweat, an effect enhanced by casein paints and acrylics used by the cover artists. These magazines featured not only a gamut of Nazi and Japanese atrocities but sweaty cannibal stories based in the South Seas and Africa; Middle East harem rape scenarios; and eventually Cold War, Korean War and Vietnam War vice and torture themes.[39]

Parallel to the "sweats" was a genre of grotesque crime tabloids like the *National Enquirer* (before it turned to celebrity gossip) and titles like *Midnight, Exploiter, Globe, Flash* and *Examiner* and true-detective magazines that mixed staged bondage photos with horrific crime scene photos and tales of sex, death and mutilation, with headlines like 39 STAB WOUNDS WAS ALL THE NAKED STRIPPER WORE; HE KILLED HER MOTHER AND THEN FORCED HER TO COMMIT UNNATURAL SEX ACTS; I LIKE TO SEE NUDE WOMEN LYING IN BLOOD; SEX MONSTERS! THE SLUT HITCHHIKER'S LAST RIDE TO DOOM; RAPE ME BUT DON'T KILL ME.

All these hundreds of magazines had one thing in common: their covers featured a photograph of a professional model posing as a bound victim (detective magazines) or a lurid painted illustration of a bound victim (men's adventure magazines). Either way, she was inevitably scantily clad or her dress was in disarray or tatters, her skirt hiked up to expose her thighs or stockings, her breasts straining under the thin material of her torn clothing, her bronzed flesh glowing with a fine sheen of perspiration, often with bound legs or legs spread open, tied up in a torture chamber, in a basement, on the floor, on a bed, on the ground outside; tied to a chair, a table, a rack, a sacrificial pole; in a cage or suspended from a dungeon ceiling next to red-hot pokers and branding irons heating on glowing coals, turning on a roasting spit to be cooked by lusty cannibals, strapped spread-eagle on surgical tables for mad Nazi scientists to probe and mutilate. The woman's face is contorted in fear and submission, sometimes gazing out from the magazine cover toward the male reader, as if she was the reader's victim, his personal slave who could be possessed for the price of the magazine.[40]

Norm Eastman, one of the cover artists for those magazines in the 1950s, recalled in 2003, "I often wondered why they stuck with the torture themes so much. That must have been where they were heavy with sales. I really was kind of ashamed of painting them, though I am not sure they did any harm. It did seem like a weird thing to do."[41]

Women in these blatantly misogynistic publications were portrayed in only two biblically paraphilic ways: either as captives bound and forced into sex against their will or as sexually aggressive, bare-shouldered women with a cigarette dangling from their lips, subject to punishment or death for their evil-minded sexuality. In this paraphilic world of the "sweats," women were either a sacred Madonna defiled or a profligate whore punished; there were no other options available.

These magazines were not squirreled away behind counters or in adult bookstores or limited to some subculture; they were as mainstream as apple pie. Some had monthly circulations of over two million copies at their height and were openly sold *everywhere*: on newsstands; in grocery stores, candy stores, supermarkets; on drugstore magazine racks, right next to *Time*, *Life*, *National Geographic*, *Popular Mechanics* and *Ladies' Home Journal*.[42] They would be found lying around anywhere and everywhere men and their sons gathered, in workshops, barbershops, auto shop waiting rooms, mail rooms, locker rooms and factory lunchrooms. At their peak, there were over a hundred monthly adventure and true-detective magazine titles, available to all ages.

All this in a country where it is still taboo to show even a glimpse of a bare female breast or buttock on television.

In a colorless world, where photographs, movies and television were mostly black-and-white, I remember in the late 1950s and the early 1960s going to the local supermarket with my mom and waiting for her by the magazine and comic book racks, facing row after row of these magazines with their candy-colored covers of bound women in distress, offered up for the taking. "GIRLS PRICED TO SELL," as one headline advertised.

I was five or six years old and had no notion of sex, but I remember that those images stirred some kind of powerful primordial male reptilian euphoria. I recognize it today as entirely a sexual stirring for dominance and possession of my prim and bossy older-sister humans, from babysitters and nurses to female store clerks and teachers towering over me, under whose supervision and authority I constantly found myself as a male child. These magazine images of prostrate females drew me into a fantasy world in which women were tipped over into a powerless and vulnerably disheveled state.

I was one of those lucky kids given no reason to be hurt, traumatized or angry, and I was encouraged and raised to be independent and autonomous by both the men and women in my young life. I had a trauma-free childhood with no episodes of abuse or head injury. But I can only imagine now, if some severe abuse, humiliation or trauma had been fused with that powerful, primitive, reptilian sensation I describe, what might have happened and to what dark place I potentially could have taken those impulses stirred by this constant imagery had I been angry at women, or desperately craved control, revenge or even redemption, as psychiatrist John Money described sexual paraphilia: "tragedy or trauma turned into triumph."

These men's magazines, along with true-detective magazines, would increasingly be cited as favorite childhood and adolescent reading by "golden age" serial killers.

Already in 1941, Jarvis Theodore Roosevelt Catoe claimed he was aroused by stories of rape and murder in true-detective magazines.

John Joubert, "the Nebraska Boy Snatcher," a serial killer who murdered three young boys from 1982 to 1983, stated that when he was eleven or twelve he had seen true-detective magazines in the local grocery store and become aroused by the depiction of bound women on the covers. He began acquiring these magazines and masturbating to the images, eventually superimposing the fantasy of bound young boys over the images of the women. He could not recall whether these images brought on the masturbation or the masturbation brought on the fantasies.[43]

Serial killer Dennis Rader, "the BTK Killer," in his recent interviews with forensic psychologist Katherine Ramsland, described his adolescent obsession with illustrations of bound women. Rader said, "I was soon addicted to them and was always looking for 'strung-up' models in distress."

Rader described fantasizing about attacking women: "She became a 'True Detective Horror Magazine' hit and fantasy. Her bedroom appeared to be in the center east. I was planning on tying her up on the bed, either half naked or totally. Then I would either strangle her or suffocate her. Her hands would be bound in front and tied to her neck—like a True Detective Magazine model I had seen. I used to fantasize about women on the cover, showing terror in their eyes, bound hand up near her neck, a man with a threatening knife overhead."

Rader said, "I quit buying detective magazines when they dropped the B/D women from the covers. I still read books about serial killers if they related to the style I was into. I always cut photos out of ads from places like Dillard's and J. C. Penney's."[44]

By the 1980s, these magazines were labeled by FBI behaviorists as "pornography for sexual sadists" and would eventually be driven off the newsstands both by the failing economics of monthly magazine publishing and by a popular social revulsion to "rape culture" imbued in that sector of mainstream media.[45]

Why had the Greatest Generation and their sons fed on this sadistically depraved popular literature and imagery after the war? Why did this material even exist? What really happened to our fathers and grandfathers in that war? What dark secrets were encoded in this literature and its imagery? What made the men and their sons so angry with women?

It was only fifty years later, in the early 2000s, as most of the war generation started to pass away, that we began gathering the courage to ask those unaskable questions about what it meant for them to fight a primitive war to utterly exterminate an enemy. We did not like the answers coming back to us.

It's never one thing but a combination of things in the *diabolus in cultura*. The fathers in the 1930s and 1940s laid the road, but now as America lurched forward into the fear and loathing of the Cold War and the chaos and death of the sixties, their serial killing sons would be marching down it.

The New Serial *Sadist Raffiné* (Genteel Sadist): "Everything a Girl Could Wish For"

In this new complex social chemistry of broken-pride males, war-traumatized husbands and fathers, recently unfettered women reluctantly prodded back into their social cage by postwar readjustment and mainstream celebration of the bondage, torture, rape and murder of women, a new species of sexual serial murderers began to emerge. They were cognizant of the new assertive and independent woman who could no longer be easily led into ambush by an old-school chauvinist male—

she needed to be seduced by what appeared to be a "new" man respectful of the new woman. This was the same old wolfish predator but now disguised as a lamb, the refined "nice guy" torturer and necrophile, the *sadist raffiné*.

The concept was introduced by Dr. J. Paul de River, who in 1939 became the first forensic psychiatrist to be permanently hired by a law enforcement agency in the United States when the LAPD assigned him to the Sex Offense Bureau. His function was to assist police in profiling unknown suspects and to prepare prosecutorial psychiatric assessments to preempt any potential insanity defense. In 1949, de River published *The Sexual Criminal: A Psychoanalytical Study* in which he revised and expanded the psychiatric terminology, including the concept of the psychopath's "mask of sanity" as described at the time by Hervey M. Cleckley.

De River did away with the notions of vulgar, crude, quirky werewolf "monster" serial killers and introduced a new typology of offender that we recognize today in many serial killers. De River labeled them as the *sadist raffiné* (genteel sadist). He described them as

> the genteel "nice boy" type, whose suave manner and smooth tongue ingratiates him in the favor of his victim. He may be studious and pedantic and often strives to give one the impression of being very religious. His genteel manner and fastidious appearance, together with a winning personality, dimpled chin, wavy hair, usually offset by dreamy, neuropathic eyes, are very often everything a girl could wish for.[46]

De River could have been describing the sadistic necrophile serial killer Ted Bundy when he wrote those lines in his 1949 book, except Ted Bundy was only three years old at the time. That in itself is of great significance, because Bundy was part of an incoming generation of "golden age" serial killers to come, and the age he was now growing up in would have much, if not everything, to do with the murders he would perpetrate as an adult in the 1970s.

CHAPTER 4

Pulp True Horror:
The Rise of the New Serial Killers
1950–1969

I like killing people because it is so much fun.
Zodiac Killer, unidentified serial killer

In the second half of the 1940s, Americans were awakened from the twelve years of financial degradation and the four years of apocalyptic warfare that followed. The birth rate had declined. America had been an Edward Hopper painting—redbrick tenements, smoky skies, gloomy diners, lonely souls and war-wrecked males. Gasoline, rubber and metal had been rationed for the war effort, so Detroit stopped producing cars for consumers and retooled its factories for war production. After 1942, no new car models were produced.

In May 1945, as the war ended in Europe, the US War Production Board authorized a restart of manufacturing of 200,000 automobiles for the domestic market, mostly "warmed up" 1942 models.

In 1946, there were 8,000 television sets in American homes. By 1956, there were 37 million television sets in American households. Americans were watching *Alfred Hitchcock Presents, I Love Lucy, Gunsmoke, The Mickey Mouse Club, Roy Rogers, Captain Kangaroo, Dragnet,* and *Adventures of Superman.* Some television shows were broadcast in color, and Elvis Presley made his first television appearances in that year.

There were 54 million cars and 10 million trucks. A national interstate freeway system was beginning to rip through inner-city neighborhoods, connecting outward to a rapidly growing suburban sprawl with its clean new schools and shopping malls, into which a new generation of serial killers would be injected. American families that put off having children during the Great Depression and the war now started families. The war years were followed by a resurgent booming economy, partly fueled by the Marshall Plan, which funneled US dollars into the war-torn European nations on the condition they spend the dollars on American-made products. It prevented a depression that typically follows a war. Between 1941 and 1961, 65 million children were born in the United States in what became known as the baby boom.

The years of fear and loathing, blacklisting and inquisitorial House Un-American Activities Committee (HUAC) hearings and Senator Joe McCarthy's paranoid rantings had come to an end midway through the 1950s. McCarthy had been censured and condemned in 1954 by the Senate, and by 1957 he'd be dead.

After Joe McCarthy's decline, the 1950s saw the beginning of an age of sweet innocence that would last until its abrupt end in November 1963 when JFK was assassinated. One doesn't need to describe the loss of innocence here, as it has been nostalgically celebrated in movies like *Grease* and *American Graffiti*, the *Happy Days* TV series (1974–1984) and scores of "golden oldies" radio stations and revival shows.

But as always there remained in popular culture a craving for the dark side. Nuclear test mishaps inspired a slew of science fiction monster movies and radiation-created comic book superheroes. The true-detective magazines and the men's adventure "sweats" were in their heyday, with the "sweats" primarily focused on Nazi sexploitation themes of rape, bondage, torture, mutilation and murder while the true detectives reported on the same thing at home. Both featured photo-realistic imagery—sometimes with posed models, sometimes authentic forensic evidence photos.

There was a creeping rise in violent crime, but the country was more alarmed by a rise in juvenile delinquency (although it remained unclear whether there was more juvenile delinquency or simply more juveniles!). The generation born in the 1940s, as they were entering their adolescence in the 1950s, was "acting up" now at an unusually higher frequency than before. The future serial killers among them were only starting to test their compulsions and fantasies, not yet mature enough to follow through all the way to murder.

In response to this rise in juvenile crime, the Comics Code Authority (CCA) was introduced in 1954 to police the depiction of crime, violence and horror in comic books. But the true-detective magazines and "sweats" were as easily available as comic books for readers of all ages. One only had to go to a barbershop for a haircut to paw through dozens of garishly illustrated magazines depicting abduction, bondage, rape and murder.

The serial killers of the 1950s and early 1960s like Ed Gein and Albert DeSalvo were primarily the older brothers or uncles of the "golden agers" to come. They were steeped in the Great Depression, in the psyche of serial killers like Albert Fish, Earle Nelson, Jarvis Roosevelt Catoe and William Heirens, the creepy brain-injured necro-psychos who acted more on deviant impulses than compulsively masturbated paraphilic fantasies.

Some of those cases resonated on multiple levels and are today part of serial killer lore and popular culture.

Edward Gein, "The Plainfield Ghoul" or "Original Psycho," Plainfield, Wisconsin, 1954–1957

Ed Gein looked like a farm elf with his flannel hat and checkered shirt buttoned to the neck. He was fifty-one, just 140 pounds, a good-natured semi-recluse with neatly groomed gray hair who lived alone on a farm after his mother and brother died. He was well-known in the community as slightly odd but otherwise harmless. He did not farm his land but earned a meager living working occasionally on county highway projects, doing odd jobs for local farmers and babysitting the locals' kids. Nobody knew he had been robbing graves of freshly buried corpses since the late 1940s after his mother died. Then on December 8, 1954, in the late-afternoon winter dusk, he killed fifty-four-year-old tavern keeper Mary Hogan in her bar and hauled her body on a sled back to his farm. Nobody saw him or at least took notice of the wrapped cargo he was sledding home.

Her disappearance remained unsolved for three years.

On November 16, 1957, Bernice Worden, fifty-eight, disappeared from her hardware store in the middle of the day. Somebody remembered seeing Gein on the premises earlier. The local police detained him that evening and proceeded to his farm to search it. Upon entering his shedlike summer kitchen, they came upon the headless and quartered corpse of Worden hanging from the rafters by hooks driven through her heel bones, dressed out and washed like a freshly killed deer carcass.

Searching Gein's dingy, cluttered farmhouse, police found a horror show: Worden's freshly severed head in a burlap sack; a box with another mummified female head, perhaps Mary Hogan; a human heart in a pan on the stove; human entrails in the refrigerator; a shoebox with nine vulvas in it; another box containing four noses; a pair of stockings made from human skin; a soup bowl fashioned out of a skull; a wearable vest with breasts made from the skin of a female torso; skulls mounted on bedposts; nine masks made out of the flesh of female faces, some hanging on the walls as decoration; a human scalp in a cereal box; a drum fashioned out of human skin; four chairs whose upholstery was made of human skin caked in dripping fat; various pieces of jewelry fashioned out of body parts; and ten decomposed female heads. Many of the artifacts had been rubbed down with oil to retain their luster; the human masks were made up with lipstick; a red ribbon was tied through one of the vulvas.

Four days after his arrest, an unidentified investigator summed up the case in what remains the essential core of the Gein historical narrative:

> Gein had been extremely close to his mother throughout his life, so close, in fact, that he apparently acquired a feminine complex. After the death of his father, George, about 20 years ago he became more attached to his mother, with whom he lived, along with his older brother, Henry, who died in 1944. [Mysteriously, in a brush fire on the farm.]
>
> Before her death in 1945, his mother had two paralytic strokes during which her devoted son Ed nursed her, further strengthening their relationship. Gein associated little with girls. He was too shy and had little interest in them. He said he never had any sex contact with them.

Some years ago, at the height of his mother devotion, he wished he had been a woman instead of a man. He bought medical books and studied anatomy. He wondered whether it would be possible to change his sex. He considered inquiring about an operation to change him to a woman, and even thought of trying to operate upon himself, but did nothing about such plans.

After his mother's death, he brooded for a long time. From this disconsolate mood emerged the compulsion to visit cemeteries. After a few nocturnal trips to graveyards, he began digging into fresh graves.

He said he took the bodies to his home and cut them up. He kept only the heads, the skin, and some other parts. He insisted he disposed of the remainder of the bodies by burning them in small pieces in his kitchen cook stove.

Gein said he kept all of the faces of his victims. He was particularly intrigued by the women's hair. He removed the skin of some of them and used it for making belts, a drum fashioned by stretching skin over the ends of a large tin can, and other items. He stripped the skin from the entire upper part of one woman's body and made a vest.

He gave particular attention to the women's faces which he stripped off the skulls leaving a human mask. He said he preserved these by curing them with oil and keeping them as cold as possible. He rubbed oil on the faces whenever they became stiff.

On occasions, he said, he would don one of the masks, slip into the torso skin vest, and attach to himself other parts he had removed from a woman's body and parade around by himself in his lonely farm house. He said this gave him great satisfaction.[1]

Ed Gein had no compulsion to kill—what he wanted was the female skin. When, during the hard winter months, he could no longer dig into the frozen earth to uncover fresh graves, he began killing to refresh his supply of female body parts.

Other than that, he was considered a nice guy by the folks and neighbors.

One of his neighbors remarked, "Good old Ed. Kind of a loner and maybe a little bit odd with that sense of humor of his, but just the guy to call in to sit with the kiddies when me and the old lady want to go to the show." For years, children who visited Gein's house had been reporting to their parents that Gein had a collection of "shrunken heads" and strange masks hanging on the walls, but the parents dismissed the stories as imagination. None of the children ever reported Gein's behavior toward them as threatening or unusual in any way.

The Gein murders inspired a Christmas poem recited by Wisconsin schoolchildren that year:

> T was [*sic*] the night before Christmas
> And all through the school
> Not a creature was stirring,
> Nor even a mule
> The teachers were hung
> from the ceiling with care
> In hope that Ed Gein
> Soon would be there.

There were even Gein jokes:

> Someone asked Gein how his folks were. He replied,
>   "Delicious."
> Gein Beer: lots of body but no head.
> What was Gein's telephone number? O-I-C-U-8-1-2.
> There were no mice at Gein's house because there were too
>   many pussies.
> What did Gein have in his sewing box? Belly buttons.
> What did Gein say to the Sheriff when he arrested him? Have
>   a heart.
> They say Gein was popular with the ladies. There were always
>   a lot of women hanging around his place.

> You had to keep the heat on in Gein's house or else the
> furniture got goose-bumps.
> Why did his girlfriend stop going out with him? Because he
> was such a cut-up.
> What did Gein say when a hearse went by? "Dig you later
> Baby."[2]

Gein's fetish for human skulls, mummified female nipple belts and vaginal labia necklaces, he confessed, was partly inspired by the pulp men's adventure magazine stories and illustrations of Japanese atrocities against female captives. The other component of his inspiration came from the true wartime accounts of necrophilic trophy taking by GIs in the Pacific that were ingrained in the American *diabolus in cultura* of the 1940s.*

After Gein's arrest, *Life* magazine, the same magazine that in 1944 proudly ran the infamous photo of a young woman with a skull captioned "Arizona war worker writes her Navy boyfriend a thank-you note for the Jap skull he sent her,"[3] now published photos of the squalid interior of Gein's house, cluttered with stacks of true-detective and adventure pulp magazines.[4] Gein was a carnival sideshow freak of a serial killer—the rare serial killer who was truly too insane to be put on trial. He went straight into the psychiatric wing, and nobody blinked an eye about it.

Ed Gein grew in stature with time, not so much as himself as for the myths spun around him. Gein became the inspiration for the Alfred Hitchcock movie *Psycho* based on Robert Bloch's novel, and Gein was later incorporated into the composite character of Buffalo Bill, the fictional serial killer who skinned his victims in the *The Silence of the Lambs*, and Leatherface in *The Texas Chainsaw Massacre*. But Gein himself, with two confirmed murders, until recently was not even considered "officially" a serial killer by those insisting on the traditional "three or more" victims defining serial murder.

Edward Gein died on July 26, 1984, at the age of seventy-seven, a

---

*See *Sons of Cain* for a more detailed description of this phenomenon.

quiet, model inmate-patient at the Mendota Mental Health Institute in Madison, Wisconsin.

Two serial killer contemporaries of Ed Gein were much more indicative of the evolution of serial killers to come, yet somehow they remain mostly footnotes in the history of serial homicide. Their cases are worth delving into, however, because in many ways they are the direct precursors of things to come when the 1970s hit.

Harvey Murray Glatman, "The Glamor Girl Slayer," Los Angeles, 1957–1958

By the 1950s, the village-like structure of Los Angeles had amalgamated into the United States' third-largest city, a massive megalopolis. Hollywood was the movie mecca, and it drew hundreds of thousands of worshippers, adherents and disciples seeking fame and fortune. The movie industry was centralized in several large factorylike studio lots serviced by thousands of independent subcontractors, service providers and casual laborers. Television had taken a bite out of national movie attendance: it dropped dramatically from its heyday of 96 million a week to 46 million by 1956. The response from the movie studios was not a cutback in production but an escalation of big, spectacular widescreen Technicolor movies, drawing even more pilgrims seeking fame and employment in the Hollywood dream factory.

Young beautiful women were (and still are) the currency of Hollywood, and thousands flocked to Los Angeles to try their luck. Their hope was to be "discovered" and raised to Lana Turner or Liz Taylor star status, but even getting steady employment in bit speaking parts was a victory over the odds. Most girls ended up doing other work: waitressing, clerking in stores or performing in lounges if they had any talent.

Some struggling young women carved out a niche in the "glamor girl modeling" business, which ranged from legitimate modeling for catalogs, calendars or local advertising to the seedy gray market of "art photography," where women self-advertised their availability for hourly rate "art modeling" and "figure studies" either in an improvised "studio" or in their own home or a client's premises. Some girls even had cameras and film to loan out to the "photographer" if they did not have their own equipment. Many of the photos taken never made it to print.

The "modeling" ranged from posing for amateur photographers and struggling wannabe professionals to seminude lingerie shoots, artistic nudies, "cheesecake pinups" and sometimes even outright porn if the girl was willing to go that far. Sometimes "modeling" included prostitution, especially if the model and client hit it off.

Judith Ann "Judy" Van Horn Dull was one of those models, working under the name Judy Van Horn. Judy had just turned nineteen in June 1957, was the mother of a fourteenth-month-old girl and had recently separated from her twenty-two-year-old husband, Robert L. Dull, a newspaper printing room worker.

Judy was beautiful in all the right ways for Hollywood: she was shapely, baby-doll wide-eyed and golden blond. She looked like a younger, softer and fresher teenage version of Marilyn Monroe. And like Monroe, Judy was willing to pose nude—most pinup models were. Her husband, Robert, did not approve, and one day he scooped up their daughter, Susan (or Suzanne), while she was at work and refused to return her. Judy was now in a bitter and expensive custody battle.

Judy lived in an apartment in the landmark El Mirador building on the corner of North Sweetzer and Fountain Avenues in West Hollywood. The "bombshell blonde" Jean Harlow had lived there in the 1930s, and up-and-comers in the movie business still lived there. Judy shared the place with two other pinup models, eighteen-year-old Betty Ruth Carver, who had just arrived from Florida, and twenty-two-year-old Lynn Lykels, who had been around the modeling business for a while. All three were very busy and looked out for one another's clients and bookings.

"Johnny Glynn"

On the evening of July 30, 1957, Betty Carver was alone at home with a male friend, a photographer, when an unexpected visitor knocked at the door. Standing there was a young, squirrel-faced nebbish with jug-handle ears and huge horn-rimmed glasses. She would later describe him as about twenty-nine, five feet nine, 150 pounds. Scrawny. Loser. Creepy odd but harmless.

He introduced himself as Johnny Glynn ["Glenn" in some sources], a commercial photographer seeking her roommate, Lynn, for an "urgent" shooting assignment. He said he had worked with her before. Betty explained that Lynn was away on a shoot. He really should call first before coming by.

Johnny was apologetic, but could he look at Lynn's portfolio, just to confirm that she was the best for the assignment? With her male friend there, Betty didn't hesitate to let the guy into the apartment. When Betty returned with the portfolio, Johnny pointed to one of the models' photos displayed in the living room: "Do you have a portfolio for *her*?"

"That's Judy Van Horn. She's not here either, but I'll bring you her book."

His owllike eyes lit up as he went through Judy's photos. She was exactly what he wanted for the shoot, he said.

Johnny called the next day, Wednesday, but Judy was away on a shoot.

Thursday, August 1, 1957, was a busy day for Judy. She had three appointments in the late afternoon and evening: a commercial photo shoot, a meeting with her estranged husband about their daughter, and dinner with her boyfriend.

Johnny Glynn called at lunchtime, wanting to book her for an urgent afternoon shoot. He didn't have a studio, so he'd like to shoot it at her apartment. Twenty dollars an hour for two hours—how could she say no?

Glynn arrived a little early for their 2:00 p.m. appointment. Now he told her he'd managed to secure a studio. It was only a ten-minute drive away. When they finished, he would give her a ride to her next job. Judy and Lynn exchanged glances. Lynn did not remember shooting with Johnny Glynn, but she had heard his name at the studio where she worked, and he looked familiar—the big ears and glasses. He was legit, she nodded to Judy.

Judy reluctantly agreed. As she gathered up her clothing changes, including the one for her next shoot, she asked Glynn to give her roommate his phone number where she could be reached. Lynn jotted down the phone number as he and Judy went out the door.

That was the last time anybody saw Judy alive.

After she failed to appear at her appointments, calls flooded in to the number Johnny Glynn had left: it was a pay phone in a parking garage. The next day, California newspapers were reporting on their front pages: "Pinup model missing in L.A." with a huge studio headshot of Judy. Had Judy been able to return from this, having her photo out there like that might have been a huge career break. But she wasn't returning. She was dead.

Her bones were found four months later, 120 miles away, in the desert between Thousand Palms and Indio, so bleached and animal ravaged that nobody recognized her. The local pathologist estimated the victim to be in her mid-thirties and the bones at least a year old. Judy's name was removed from the list of victims possibly linked to the bones.

Two more women were going to die before Judy's killer was apprehended.

"Johnny Glynn" was really twenty-nine-year-old Harvey Murray Glatman of Denver, Colorado, an ex-con who had served time for abductions and assault. Glatman was still a virgin on the afternoon he abducted Judy Dull, despite his record of assaulting women. On the Tuesday night when he first appeared at the girls' door, he had planned on ridding himself of his virginity by raping Lynn Lykels in her apartment, but he did not count on her having roommates. Once he saw Judy's portfolio, all his desire and attention shifted to her.

The Squirrel

Harvey Glatman was born on December 10, 1927, in New York to Albert and Ophelia Glatman, both employees in the garment business. Ophelia was thirty-nine years old when she had Harvey but reported no unusual problems in the birth. Harvey had the usual childhood illnesses, including a bout of whooping cough and a tonsillectomy. Albert in the meantime attempted to establish a stationery store in New York, but it failed in the Depression years, and in 1937, the Glatmans closed out the business and moved to Denver, where Ophelia's sister lived. They settled into a modest bungalow in the Montclair district, 1123 Kearney Street. Albert went to work driving a taxicab.[5]

None of the typical childhood traumas or abuse frequently reported by serial killers were evident in Harvey's childhood, but Albert was said to be a strict and often disapproving father, while Ophelia was highly protective and always indulgent of her son. She would remain so to the bitter end.

Ophelia did later report one unusual and alarming thing about their boy: he was obsessed with rope and genital play and masturbation. Harvey was three or four years old when she caught him tying a string around his penis to a door handle. His parents would both admonish him about his frequent masturbation. By the time Harvey was twelve, he had developed a dangerous compulsion to combine masturbation with autoerotic asphyxiation—popularly known as "gasping" (or "strangubation," "head rushing," "chokey strokey," and "scarfing"). It is not an exceptionally unusual practice in adolescents both male and female.* Harvey would draw a warm bath, get into the tub and tie a noose to the faucets slowly choking off his oxygen supply to bring himself into a euphoric state as he masturbated. One day his parents noticed a deep rope burn around Harvey's neck and became alarmed enough to take him for professional help. The physician told them he'd grow out of it. He never did.

According to former FBI profiler Roy Hazelwood, Glatman continued the practice of autoerotic asphyxiation into adulthood, combining it with self-bondage and transvestism.[6] The combination of these paraphilias is not unusual.

Harvey was intelligent and did well at school, but he was painfully shy. Although he was not subjected to bullying, his nicknames at school were "squirrel" and "weasel." There would be no dating for Harvey; his mother described him as "girl-shy," reporting that he would cross the street rather than walk by a girl. Otherwise, Harvey appeared on the

---

*Looking through the Toronto Police files on a series of child strangulations in the 1950s, I noted reports from schools at the time that children and adolescents were sometimes strangling one another into unconsciousness as a game during recess in the schoolyard.

surface to be a well-adjusted teen, going on Boy Scout outings and holding a string of after-school jobs.

Harvey would later confess to a secret thrill-seeking life that he started to engage in at the age of seventeen. Like William Heirens, Glatman began prowling and breaking into apartments of single women. He suddenly became unusually aggressive and hostile toward girls in school. He acquired a handgun in one of his burglaries and escalated to accosting women in the street.

On the night of May 4, 1945, in Denver, seventeen-year-old Harvey Glatman committed his first known assault, on seventeen-year-old Eula Jo Hand. She was returning home on the bus from the movies, and Glatman was riding on the same bus. When she got off at her stop about half a block from her home, Glatman followed behind her. He thrust a handgun into her back and forced her into a backyard where he tied her up and gagged her. He struck her hard on the head with the handle of the handgun and stole the money she had in her purse. He took off Hand's jacket and fondled her. When somebody appeared, Glatman ran off. Although she did not know his name, Eula recognized Glatman as a student at the high school she used to attend.

Two weeks later, on May 18, Glatman was arrested and charged with armed robbery. Police had reports of several similar assaults and robberies but could not conclusively link them to Glatman. Ophelia posted a two-thousand-dollar bail bond and took him home.

On July 15, while out on bail, Glatman took a forty-five-minute bus ride north to Boulder. Twenty-four-year-old Norene Laurel, a mother of two, was returning from the movies when Glatman forced her at gunpoint into a dark alley. He bound and gagged her and then walked her miles outside of Boulder's city limits into the foothills. He kept her there all night, fondled her, but did not rape her. In the morning he took her money, hailed a cab and instructed the driver to drop him off at the bus depot and take Laurel home. He was arrested two days later in Denver and brought back to Boulder and charged with armed robbery. Again, Ophelia paid his bail, this time five thousand dollars, but as soon as Glatman was released, he ran away from her. A few days later, a court

ordered Glatman to be confined for evaluation in a psychiatric facility.
A psychiatric evaluation from Dr. J. P. Hilton reported:

> Harvey Glatman first came to see me in August of 1945 at
> the age of seventeen. At that time he had a history of having
> bruised his neck by tying a rope around it. He was sullen, mo-
> rose and very disrespectful and for several years had felt that
> everyone was against him including his parents. He had been
> shy with girls prior to the past year when his attitude changed
> completely, and he became aggressive with women.[7]

Eula Jo Hand, Glatman's first victim, married shortly after the assault, and when it came time to bring him to trial, her mother-in-law
demanded she refuse to testify as it would be "embarrassing" to the
family. Glatman in the meantime was arrested a third time in September, again for accosting and binding women.[8]

Glatman finally stood trial in December and was sentenced to a one-
to-five-year prison term for robbery but paroled after eight months in
July 1946, judged to be a young, compliant and cooperative "model inmate." Ophelia would later claim that psychiatrists recommended a trip
out of state and dancing lessons to increase his confidence with girls.
While Albert remained in Denver, Ophelia took Harvey to Yonkers,
New York, where Harvey immediately purchased a knife and a realistic-
looking toy pistol.

On August 17, 1946, Glatman confronted a woman walking on the
street without realizing her boyfriend was coming up behind her. In the
confrontation, Glatman slashed the boyfriend with his knife and escaped.

Glatman immediately left Yonkers for Albany, New York, where in
a two-day spree he accosted three women in the street and robbed them
of their purses. He was apprehended on August 27. Because the youthful Glatman presented a mild-mannered, geekish persona, charges of
first-degree robbery were reduced to larceny. The district attorney commented that Glatman showed potential to be rehabilitated. In October

1946, Glatman pleaded guilty and was sentenced to a term of five to ten years in the New York State correctional system.

Glatman earned positive reports on his conduct and progress as an inmate and was enrolled in a radio and television repair program. On April 16, 1951, after serving five years, he was paroled and subject to supervision until September 1956. He returned to Denver to live with his parents.

In 1952, Albert passed away and left him his 1961 black Dodge Coronet sedan, the one that would become a key instrument in his murders. He continued taking courses in television repair while working at a string of casual jobs. In 1954, he moved into his own apartment after unspecified difficulties with his mother. His mother would help him with the rent if his part-time work was insufficient.

Bizarre *Magazine*

Harvey seemed to be staying out of trouble. But secretly, Glatman was scripting his fantasies and compulsions through his consumption of a postwar boom of new sexual paraphernalia in the form of mail-order fetish bondage comics, photos and stories, 8 mm film loops and magazines, produced by artists like John Willie, the editor of *Bizarre* magazine, and publisher Irving Klaw of Nutrix. Bettie Page became and remains to this day the queen star of these publications.

Intended for mail-order distribution, there were no nudes or explicit depictions of sex to draw the ire of postal inspectors. Models were featured wearing exaggerated "elegant" fetish lingerie, hosiery and footwear and were posed gagged and restrained in elaborately knotted rope bindings or custom-made leather restraints. Irving Klaw's Nutrix publications would advertise photo sets: "114 4x5 bondage photos for $42.00; 26 spanking photos for $9.50; 160 different Fight Girl photos divided into 3 different fights at the rate of 10 Fight photos for $2.50; 36 bound and gagged photos; 26 tied but not gagged; 40 different High Heel photos; 26 different specially posed knee-length laced boot photos of dominant Maria Stinger in shiny silver metallic threaded toreador pants (many holding whip in hand) . . ."

By the standards of the 1970s and 1980s, or today, the photos were naively erotic despite the bondage theme. Men were mostly absent from the photos. Just like in true-detective magazines, the models often looked off the page into the camera, meeting the viewer's gaze.

The Klaw bondage magazines featured two basic types of scenarios. There were the coy, playful bondage scenes where consent was implicit, set in living rooms and bedrooms, and the smiling model wore exaggerated sexual lingerie and ultra-high-heeled fetish footwear. The message was she came dressed to willingly play bondage fantasy "games" on her own accord. There was often a lesbian twist with another female dominating the submissive model in restraints.

The other type of scenario was a darker abduction theme: frightened-looking models gagged and bound also in intricately knotted cords and restraints, but in basements or warehouse storerooms, women often in formal office clothes and everyday shoes, thrown down onto a dirty warehouse floor, tied or shackled to a basement post, their garments in disarray, skirts raised above the welts of their nylon stockings, legs bare to the garter line.

Glatman purchased camera equipment and lights and began tentatively seeking out models to pose for his own bondage pictures. His first approach was to hire two models at the same time and have them tie each other up. That way, he calculated, the models would feel safe. Soon, Glatman began to realize that his demands were not all that bizarre or unusual in the models' experience, even in Denver, and that many had no objection to being gagged and bound. The only problem was, Glatman wasn't turned on by women *pretending* to be bound into submission; he wanted them to be in actual bondage, in a state of real fear and dread, under his complete and actual control.

On September 7, 1956, Harvey Glatman completed his term of parole and was now completely free of supervision. Noting a Los Angeles return address for many of the photos he was ordering by mail, Glatman headed out to Hollywood to start a new life.

In Los Angeles, Glatman found a bounty of pinup models, many quite ready and willing to be bound and gagged in staged poses. But Glatman wanted it *real*. And there was something else. Glatman was turning twenty-nine (near the average age at which male serial killers first kill), but he was still a virgin. He resolved to experience actual "sexual intercourse" (the only term he used in his police interview). And he was going to have it forcibly, in the kind of bondage scenario he was obsessing over.

That is how he ended up calling on Lynn Lykels and eventually settled on her roommate, Judy Dull, instead.

The Murder of Judy Dull

After picking up Judy, Glatman drove her to his "studio" in his apartment on Melrose Avenue, where he had set up his Rolleicord f/3.5 medium-format camera and some lights. Glatman's Rolleicord was a cheap consumer version of the higher-end professional Rolleiflex camera, but a lot of the models didn't know it (or care). Glatman had also learned how to develop and print his own photos, setting up a darkroom in his washroom. He wasn't going to risk taking his photos to the drugstore to be developed and printed.

Glatman told Judy he had an assignment to shoot a true-detective magazine cover. He would need to tie her up, gag her and pose her in various stages of disheveled clothing, gradually hiking her skirt up and over her waist, exposing her in her underwear, garters and stockings. He selected from Judy's wardrobe a pleated skirt and a cashmere sweater top, under which she was to wear a frilly slip, nylon stockings held up by a garter belt and open-toed pumps. He instructed her to pose with a look of fear and submission, like all the models on true-detective magazine covers.

After tying her hands behind her back and gagging her, he seated her in an armchair and shot a series of photos in which Judy feigned fear and distress. He bound her legs, at first just above the ankles. As he shot his sequence of photos, he pulled Judy's skirt higher and bound her legs with another cord just above her knees. He then pulled off her skirt, laid her facedown on the floor and took more pictures.

Judy was probably familiar with true-detective magazine covers and fetish bondage photos and perhaps even posed for them for other photographers. The photos that Glatman shot of Judy are often posted on the Internet with a set of harder abduction bondage photos of a blond model who resembles Judy Dull, posed in a storeroom setting and in a different wardrobe. One photo has her tied topless spread-eagle to an X-frame. The websites stupidly claim that the photos are among those that Glatman took of her. In fact, they were shot and published by fetish photographer John Willie in *Bizarre* magazine. The model, however, *maybe* was Judy. Her resemblance is striking, although the soft blond Marilyn look Judy cultivated was one that many girls chose in that epoch. But if Judy did indeed previously pose in John Willie bondage photos, it helps explain why she so readily allowed herself to be bound and restrained by a photographer she had only met an hour previously.

In his confession, Glatman recounted how after some time passed, Judy became increasingly uncomfortable, restless and anxious and how that excited him. When he began fondling her, he crossed the professional line between photographer and model. Now Judy became fearful that she might be in real peril.

Glatman had acquired a Browning .32 handgun, and he threatened her with it, telling her he was going to keep her for a while and have "some fun" with her. As Judy lay helpless, she motioned for him to take her gag off, then assured him that whatever he wanted, she would go along with. There was no need to hurt her; her worst fear was her husband finding out about this and making it an issue at the upcoming custody hearing. She assured him she would not tell anybody of this incident. But Glatman was only beginning.

Glatman kept her tied up on the floor. He went into the kitchen and ate an apple and drank a glass of water, relishing the sight of the bound woman struggling on the floor. Eventually, he untied her and ordered her to undress. Glatman then raped her twice on the couch, at long last losing his virginity. Glatman was still testing the limits of his fantasies. He was turned on by bound and gagged women, but he would untie them to complete the sex act, probably still testing and trying the transition between his fantasies and their realization into reality. Often that is the addictive cyclical nature of serial murder, a constant attempt to perfect and narrow the gap between fantasy and reality, between disappointment and fulfillment.

After being raped, Judy did her best to remain calm and collected, again reminding Glatman that the only thing she was concerned about was her husband finding out about this. If he let her go, she wouldn't breathe a word of what just happened, she told him repeatedly.

According to his confession, Glatman was undecided about what to do with her. Killing was not part of Glatman's fantasy; binding and gagging women and putting them under his absolute control were his fantasy. It was now approaching six o'clock, and Glatman knew that Judy had missed her appointments. People by now must have been calling the fake number he had left with Lynn Lykels. While he wanted to believe that Judy perhaps would keep her mouth shut, the same could not be said for the others. The one thing that Glatman feared the most was being arrested and sent back to prison, not so much for himself, as for what it would do to his trusting mother.

It is unclear exactly when Glatman decided he would coldly kill Judy. They now calmly sat together on the couch like a couple from 6:30 p.m. to 11:00 p.m., watching TV as Glatman waited for nightfall. We don't know what they watched, but that evening the TV shows on air in the Los Angeles area included *Sheena, Queen of the Jungle, Amos 'n' Andy, The Little Rascals, The Mickey Rooney Show, The Lone Ranger, The Best of Groucho, Dragnet* and the movies *Judge Hardy's Children* with Mickey Rooney, *Night Song* with Dana Andrews and *Conquest* starring Greta Garbo.

When it became dark, Glatman calmly told Judy that he was going to drive her out into the desert and leave her there with some bus fare while he made his escape. She was not thrilled at the premise but had no choice. He drove her out at random to the desert and parked on a remote dirt road. He gathered up a blanket and strands of rope and walked her into the desert with her hands bound behind her back, telling her he wanted to have sex one more time before he let her go.

He spread the blanket on the ground and laid her on it facedown. He tied her ankles together with one strand. He then took a five-foot length of cord, tied it around her pinioned ankles, pulled on it hard, bending her legs back at the knee, and then quickly wound the other end of the cord around her throat. The spring tension of her legs as they pulled to unbend tightened the line around her throat; the more she struggled, the more it tightened. As she weakened and stopped struggling, the tension in the bind slackened. Glatman drove his knee into Judy's back, pulling hard on the cord to finish her off. He later recalled it took about five to ten minutes before she stopped moving. He said he did not shoot her because it would have been "too messy" and he also worried about leaving ballistic evidence.

Once he thought Judy was dead, he undid all the rope ligatures and put them in his pocket so as not to leave evidence behind. Afterward, he scooped out a shallow grave with his hands and buried Judy Dull in the desert.

That's how twenty-nine-year-old Harvey Murray Glatman finally lost his virginity.

Now he wanted more.

The Murder of Shirley Bridgeford: "GIRLS—GIRLS—GIRLS"

Despite the immediate hue and cry in the media over Judy Dull's disappearance, nobody got a fix on the mysterious jug-eared "Johnny Glynn." Glatman was clever. Following the murder, he gave up his apartment and drove back to Denver to lie low for a few months at his mother's house before returning to Los Angeles. Although there was nothing he could do about his big bat ears, he changed his glasses and grew a mustache.

Glatman also changed his MO. He had noticed a classified advertisement for a "lonely hearts" dating service: "GIRLS, GIRLS, GIRLS— Call Patti Sullivan Club for introductions." Harvey now adopted a new name—George Williams—and appeared for the required personal interview at the Patti Sullivan Club office on South Vermont Avenue. He claimed to be a wealthy single plumber living in Pasadena. He gave them his fake name, a fake phone number and a fake address, paid a ten-dollar fee, and without confirming any of the information, the dating service obligingly handed him the names and phone numbers of two divorced women who had recently enrolled with them.

The first date Glatman called up was a disaster. She was a twenty-six-year-old Hollywood secretary with a son. She immediately fell for him, huge ears and all. She seated him on her couch, doted on him, brought him tea and cookies, coffee and cake, babbled and giggled flirtatiously and by the end of the evening she was ready to sweep Harvey Glatman off his feet into her bedroom. She told him she loved a smart man who was also good with his hands like a plumber. Glatman found her so intimidating that he must have rushed out of her apartment, coffee cup still in his hands. She was exactly what he *did not* want.

Later she said of her date with Glatman, "I found him to be very pleasant, and a perfect gentleman." She was a little miffed that he never called her again.

His second date was with twenty-four-year-old Shirley Ann Loy Bridgeford, a divorcée in Sun Valley with two young sons. Shirley had just enrolled in the dating service at her friend's urging. Glatman called and invited her to go square-dancing at the Sun Valley Rancho, an urban cowboy club and banquet hall, about a mile and half from where she lived. It sounded like fun. This was going to be Shirley's first date in over a year.

For the occasion, Shirley chose a blue-and-green dress cinched at the waist with a wide, big-buckled belt, seamed stockings and her favorite black suede heels. Being March, it was cool, and she borrowed her mother's long tan coat with big, flat buttons. From her sister she borrowed a pair of sexy bright red underwear.

Much would be made of the red underwear, which became key in the identification of Shirley's remains. It was a precursor to an attitude that many female victims would be subjected to in the decades to come in which their "sexual promiscuity" became the explanation for why they were raped, killed and mutilated.

On Saturday, March 8, 1958, Glatman rang the bell of Shirley's home on Tuxford Street, where she lived with her mother and sons. A house full of people was waiting there to give Harvey a look-over. There were her two sons, aged three and five; her mother babysitting them; her two sisters; and the husband of one of the sisters. They spoke with Glatman for about fifteen minutes while Shirley finished getting ready.

They described him as at least six feet tall with blue eyes, but Shirley's mother was later unable to recognize photos of Glatman. They commented that he seemed reserved but pleasant. He wore a blue jacket and gray pants, which one of the sisters remarked made him look a little shabby. They all agreed on one thing: he had enormous ears.

As she left with her date, Shirley asked her mother for a quarter for cigarettes.

That was the last time anybody saw her.

On this occasion, Glatman had packed some water and candy in his car, for the eventual trip into the desert. As soon as they got into his car, he asked Shirley if she'd mind skipping dancing and instead take a moonlit drive down the coast for dinner. She agreed. Glatman found her suitably compliant. In his confession, he said they stopped for dinner and then they necked and petted in his car in the restaurant parking lot. When he attempted to have sex with her, she demurred and asked him to drive her home. Without Shirley realizing it at first, Glatman instead drove them in the opposite direction, southeast into San Diego County. When she saw that he was not driving her home and began to protest, he pulled the car over to the side of the road and raped her at gunpoint in the back seat. Afterward, he drove out at random into the Anza-Borrego Desert State Park where he parked at a secluded spot, unloaded his camera equipment, blanket, and lengths of cord and gags, and walked Shirley out into the desert. He bound and molested her while waiting for dawn so that his photographs would be better lit. Shirley reminded him she had two children, and he assured her that he would not hurt her. As the sun rose, he set up his Rolleicord and photographed her in various stages of bondage. Then he tied her just as he did Judy Dull, attaching her pinioned ankles to a cord wrapped tightly around her throat, and watched her strangle to death in the desert dawn's early light.

Glatman would later state he felt "sorry for her" and regretted killing her because of her two children and because she wasn't as "pretty" as the other girls and did not "deserve" to die. But he wasn't going back to prison and therefore he "had to" kill her.

He rolled Shirley's body into her mother's tan coat and tore off its buttons, concerned he might have left fingerprints on them. He left her there under a Joshua tree but took the quarter her mother had given her.

After his arrest seven months later, Glatman was able to lead police to her body. After hiking through the desert, they came upon the tan coat and scattered bones, a shoe and scraps of blue and green dress material. There was little left of Shirley Bridgeford. When police lifted up the coat, they found the pair of red panties that her sister would later identify. Although he had admitted to abducting, binding, gagging, photographing, raping and murdering his victims, Glatman absolutely denied stripping off her panties. He insisted that they ended up under her coat "due to natural action or animals, or something that may have . . . I understand there are coyotes that are . . . whatever some of those kind of things in that area . . . and possibly they had picked at the body, or something like that."

Serial killers are touchy about odd things. Edmund Kemper, who confessed to abducting, murdering and decapitating female victims, said that he apologized to one of his victims *as he was stabbing her* when his hand accidentally brushed her breast. He told police that he never "touched inappropriately" any of his victims; at least, not while they were alive.

The Murder of Ruth Mercado: "She Was the One I Really Liked"

Ruth Rita Mercado, twenty-four, had made her way from New York to Los Angeles, seeking fame and fortune, but was surviving by stripping under the name Angela Rojas and advertising herself as a model with her own studio available for both professional and amateur photographers. She lived in a warren of apartments on 3714 West Pico Boulevard and had a back room that served as the "studio." Glatman saw her ad in the paper and called her. They made an appointment for the late evening of July 22. He packed bread, peanut butter, fruit, candy, water, rope and blankets and drove over to her place, but when Glatman appeared at her door, Mercado apologetically canceled the appointment, stating she was not feeling well. Glatman in the meantime took note of the apartment doors and the street.

On the next day, July 23, 1958, he returned, this time unannounced.

He parked his car several blocks away and walked over to Mercado's apartment with his handgun, some lengths of rope, a cloth gag and a pair of red rubber dishwashing gloves in his pocket. Glatman was, as they say, "forensically aware."

Mercado was surprised to see him but recognized him as a wannabe client from the night before and allowed him to enter. Glatman closed the door and locked it and then drew his handgun. He ordered Ruth Mercado into her bedroom and then gagged her and tied her hands and legs and fondled her for a while. Then he undid the rope binding and raped her on the bed (or at least he claimed to have removed it).

It was after 11:30 p.m. now. Glatman told Mercado he wanted to keep her a little longer and take her out on a drive for "a picnic" and more sex. He ordered her to get dressed in "street clothing," robbed her of about twenty dollars and then walked her out at gunpoint down deserted Pico Boulevard to his car, her hands bound behind her back but covered by a coat he draped over her shoulders. He drove in the same direction he took Shirley Bridgeford, toward Anza-Borrego Desert State Park. Along the way he stopped several times to eat a sandwich and fondle and rape his victim again.

He kept Mercado captive in the desert all of the next day. Eventually, he laid out his blanket, bound her like the others, took photographs of her and then strangled her in the same way. He made no attempt to conceal Mercado's body. He took her stockings, slip, wristwatch and identification as souvenirs and returned to Los Angeles in the early-morning hours with a fresh new batch of photographs. Glatman would later say, "She didn't suffer much. I really didn't want to kill her, she was the one I really liked. But she could have identified me."

It was the landlord who several days later noted Mercado's absence and reported it to the police. Since Mercado was living alone and worked independently as a striptease dancer and model, there were no leads or suspects in her disappearance. Because of her profession, her absence did not set off any alarms and her disappearance was noted but made a low priority. No mention of it was made in the newspapers in the way it was of Judy Dull's and Shirley Bridgeford's disappearances.

Captured

Calling himself "Frank Johnson," Glatman responded to an ad for Diane's Studio at 5353 Sunset Boulevard offering pinup models for private and professional photographers at hourly rates. He booked Diane herself for several sessions at $22.50 for the use of the studio plus $15.00 an hour for modeling.

Diane thought him harmless but creepy and was put off by his increasingly disheveled state and unpleasant body odor. When he appeared at her studio at around 8:00 p.m. on Monday, October 27, wanting to book a session with her, Diane didn't want to do it. She did, however, have a new model for him, and the studio was available if he wanted to shoot her. Glatman agreed.

Diane called twenty-eight-year-old Lorraine Vigil, a pretty, almond-eyed secretary who was looking to branch out into modeling. Was she interested in a modeling assignment at the studio that night? The photographer would come by her place and pick her up. Lorraine agreed. Before hanging up the phone, Diane warned her, "It may be nothing, but he's sort of creepy. Just watch yourself, all right?"

"Frank Johnson" soon appeared at her door. Lorraine asked to see his identification, but he told her he had left it at home. Not wanting to lose the fifteen dollars, she reluctantly agreed to accompany him to the studio. The man appeared rumpled, seedy and indeed creepy, with big glasses and protruding ears—but otherwise harmless. She asked for her fee up front. He rummaged around in his pockets and produced a ten-dollar bill, telling her he'd get change for the other five he owed her. Lorraine told her landlord that she was going for a photo session at Diane's Studio and gave the address, making sure that the photographer heard her. She thought it would be an "insurance policy."

Once they were on the road, he announced that Diane had double-booked the studio and that instead they would drive to another place in Anaheim, about forty minutes away. Even though Lorraine's intuition was warning her that something was off, she needed the fifteen dollars and did not want to disappoint the agency on her very first assignment. She reluctantly agreed.

As they drove on the Santa Ana Freeway south toward Anaheim, Glatman chatted about the photo assignment and how he hoped it would be a cover photo for a magazine. But once they passed the Anaheim turnoff, Glatman became menacingly silent. Lorraine now became alarmed. She began contemplating leaping from his car, but they were moving too fast. When they reached Tustin, Glatman took the off-ramp and pulled to the side of the road. He produced his handgun and threatened to kill Lorraine if she did not comply with his orders. When he attempted to tie her hands behind her back, she realized he had put the handgun down and began resisting. She tussled with him in the car as Glatman yanked at her wrist, grabbed her by the throat and punched her in the face. But he was unable to deliver a knockout blow. He picked up his handgun, but Lorraine began grappling for it. The pistol went off in the struggle, a single round penetrating Lorraine's skirt and grazing her thigh. Glatman was surprised by the gunshot, while Lorraine took the opportunity to throw the door open and began to run. Glatman quickly overtook her and tackled her to the shoulder of the road. Cars with their headlights blazing passed by the couple as they struggled on the ground. Nobody stopped, except for California Highway Patrol motorcycle officer Thomas Francis Mulligan on his way to the station at the end of his shift. The parked car with its opened door and dome light on caught his attention. As he rode by it, he spotted a man and woman struggling in the dirt. As Mulligan turned his bike around and pulled up behind the vehicle, the woman broke free and came running toward him.

It was over for Glatman. He was arrested at the scene.

Glatman was booked and turned over to Orange County Sherriff's Department detectives in Santa Ana to be questioned. The detectives determined that the abduction began in Los Angeles, so they notified the Los Angeles Sherriff's Department and the LAPD.

Lieutenant Marvin Jones in the LAPD noted Glatman's address and realized it was near that of the missing Ruth Mercado. On a hunch, he added the name of Shirley Bridgeford to the mix and sent two of his detectives to Santa Ana to question the arrested suspect. One of them was LAPD detective sergeant Pierce Brooks, and that was how he first became involved in the case of Harvey Glatman and the Glamor Girl Murders.

The Legend of Pierce Brooks and ViCAP

Accounts of the Glatman case often segue into the story of Pierce Brooks and his idea for what would become ViCAP—the Violent Criminal Apprehension Program—a national database of violent crime incidents and their case characteristics, intended to match and link similar cases across multiple jurisdictions to a single migratory perpetrator. The late Robert Ressler's account of his FBI career profiling serial killers (coauthored with Tom Shachtman), *Whoever Fights Monsters*, is probably where the legend comes from. Simplifying the story of Pierce Brooks, Ressler wrote, "Brooks was the man put in charge of the investigation of two seemingly unrelated murders of young women in the area." According to Ressler, Brooks had to go to a library and read through newspaper accounts of similar murders in different jurisdictions "to see whether other murders had been committed that matched the MO of the killer he believed he was chasing" and that this "eventually led to the conviction of Glatman, who when confronted with the evidence confessed to the murders."[9]

According to the story, in an age when nobody understood computers and what they can do, Brooks proposed a networked computer system linking various police jurisdictions on which individual crime characteristics could be compared and connected to one another, in order to overcome what is known as "linkage blindness"—a daunting problem for multiagency/multijurisdictional investigations. (A problem, as recent as 9/11, with a lack of comparative communications between the FBI and CIA.) Pierce's idea was dismissed by his old-school Luddite superiors and remained fallow for twenty-five years until the 1980s "serial killer epidemic," when Pierce got a Justice Department grant and partnered with the FBI's Behavioral Science Unit to create ViCAP. That, at least, is the legend.

There is this great line in the John Wayne and Jimmy Stewart Western *The Man Who Shot Liberty Valance*: "This is the West, sir. When the legend becomes fact, print the legend."

Ressler simplified the story into its legendary form, and even I printed it as I heard it from him in my first book on the history of serial homicide, *Serial Killers: The Method and Madness of Monsters*.

It's Michael Newton in his book *Rope: The Twisted Life and Crimes of Harvey Glatman* who points out that nobody was investigating any murders before Glatman's arrest. Nobody knew that Judy Dull, Shirley Bridgeford and Ruth Mercado were murdered until Glatman was arrested attempting to abduct Lorraine Vigil and subsequently confessed; they were all missing persons cases and did not involve Brooks as a homicide investigator.

When Brooks eventually did interview Glatman, it was about the abduction of Shirley Bridgeford; her murder was collateral to the abduction. Murders are prosecuted in the county where they are committed, and in Glatman's case that was in Riverside County in the murder of Judy Dull and San Diego County in the murders of Shirley Bridgeford and Ruth Mercado. Los Angeles County, where the abductions occurred, and Orange County, where Glatman was arrested, deferred to San Diego County to prosecute Glatman for the two murders there.[10] (Judy Dull's murder was never formally prosecuted once Glatman was convicted in San Diego.)

Newton suggests that Ressler may have been referring to a different set of "two seemingly unrelated murders of young women" that Brooks was investigating, or that the Glatman case later inspired Brooks to propose the information network. In any case, it is true that after Brooks's proposal was dismissed, he put it aside for nearly twenty-five years until it came to life in the 1980s when he secured a grant, partnered with the FBI and testified before Congress advocating for what would become ViCAP.

Photographic Confessional

After his arrest, Harvey Glatman confessed and described in excruciatingly helpful detail the murders of Dull, Bridgeford and Mercado. He led police to the exact site near Indio where unidentified bones were found the previous December, which finally led to the conclusive identification of Judy Dull. He also led police to the remains of Bridgeford and Mercado on the opposite ends of Anza-Borrego Desert State Park in San Diego County. He had to twice tell the police to look in a metal toolbox in the garage of his Norton Street apartment, before they found the twenty-two black-and-white photographs and color transparencies of his three victims that he had squirreled away.

After Glatman's arrest, dozens of inquiries came in from police departments regarding other possible homicides. Glatman responded, "Aren't three enough?" While confessing freely to the three murders, he steadfastly denied committing any others and even agreed to submit to polygraph examinations, which returned no evidence of deception.

Despite his mother's urging, Glatman refused to claim insanity and insisted on pleading guilty and accepting a death sentence. Police had kept quiet about the existence of his photos, but after he was sentenced to death on December 17, 1958, the San Diego County prosecutor released three of the photos to the press. Newspapers across the country ran the horrific photos of the bound women on their front pages; even sober *Time* magazine printed the photos. Nobody, other than other serial killers, had ever seen anything like it in the annals of murder. Eventually, several other photos of Glatman's victims leaked out, and all of them are salaciously circulated on the Internet today.

Justice moved fast in those days. On September 18, 1959, eleven months after his arrest, Glatman was put to death in San Quentin State Prison's gas chamber for the two murders he committed in San Diego County.

Hearing of his crimes, his mother, Ophelia, said, "Oh, my God in Heaven! Not my boy! He was always so good—so dependable! He never hurt anybody!" When she died in 1968, she left a $10,000 endowment to the University of Denver "to perpetuate the memory of my son Harvey": the Harvey M. Glatman Memorial Scholarship for accounting students. In 2006, after it was revealed the university was awarding a scholarship in the name of a serial killer, Denver University changed the name to the Ophelia Glatman Endowed Memorial Scholarship.[11]

Boulder Jane Doe: Dorothy Gay Howard

One piece of unfinished business from the Glatman case is the question of whether "Boulder Jane Doe," found murdered in Boulder Canyon on April 8, 1954, was one of his victims.

The young woman was found by hikers, stripped of all her belongings except for three hairpins. She had been so battered by her killer and ravaged by animals that she was unidentifiable, but it was estimated that her body had been there for at least a week. No precise cause of death could be determined other than a general finding of "shock"— but it was probably due to blunt force trauma. One of her wrists had a trace of a ligature mark. The Boulder community adopted the young victim and raised the money to bury her. She would be known as "Boulder Jane Doe" for the next fifty-five years.

Through brilliantly relentless research and interviews by Boulder historian Silvia Pettem and Boulder County Sheriff's Office investigator Steve Ainsworth, Boulder Jane Doe was, amazingly, identified in 2009—fifty-five years after the discovery of her remains—as eighteen-year-old Dorothy Gay Howard, a troubled, restless, twice-married teenager from Phoenix, Arizona. How and why she ended up in Boulder remains a mystery.

Having identified the victim, Pettem and Ainsworth, however, overreached when concluding Glatman murdered her. When Howard was exhumed in 2004 in a renewed attempt to identify her, she was discovered to have a knee fracture injury that was not in the original autopsy report. The account of how Lorraine Vigil had escaped Glatman's car with one wrist bound inspired Ainsworth to measure the height of the bumper on a 1951 Dodge Coronet (the model that Harvey drove) to the height of Howard's knee. It matched, although so did some other car models. Ainsworth and Pettem speculated that perhaps, like Vigil, the victim in Boulder had fled from Glatman's car and was run over by him. Further fueling this speculation was Glatman's strange response during his police interview in California when asked if any of the women he photographed in Colorado were dead. He said no, "unless they've been run over."

Pettem pointed out that when Glatman was driving his victims to the desert sites where he would kill them, he took great care to bind their hands behind their backs. Was this because back in 1954 Dorothy Howard managed to escape from his vehicle?

Glatman was indeed questioned and polygraphed on several unsolved cases including Boulder Jane Doe and two others from the Denver-Boulder area. While readily confessing to the three California murders, Glatman vehemently denied killing any other victims. He passed the polygraph. True, polygraphs can be unreliable, and true, serial killers sometimes have an incomprehensible scale of values as to what they will or will not confess to. It is possible that for the sake of his mother, Glatman did not want to confess to having murdered women while he lived with her.

But in the end, there is no hard evidence that Glatman murdered Dorothy Howard, and Pettem sometimes stretches the evidentiary links further than she should. For example, she claims in her otherwise excellent book *Someone's Daughter: In Search of Justice for Jane Doe* that "the ligature marks shown in the victim's morgue photographs are strikingly similar to the marks left on the three corpses of the women he later murdered in California."[12] Yet no ligature marks could have been discerned on Judy Dull's wrist; nothing was found of her but bones. Nor is a wrist ligature on a murdered abduction victim highly unusual. Moreover, Dorothy Howard was found without any of her clothing. Glatman's victims were all found with their clothes, which had been part of the signature fantasy that Glatman was engaged in. Nor was a cache of female attire found among Glatman's trophy collection after his arrest.

While it is entirely plausible that Glatman *could have* murdered Dorothy Howard in 1954, there is no conclusive evidence that he did.

Photographic Totems and Freeways of Death

In several ways, Glatman was a sign of things to come in the world of serial murder. Of generations of serial killers in the future who will take photographs, Polaroids and videos of their victims, alive and dead, "capturing" them forever for themselves, Glatman was the first.

Partly it was a technological factor; the ability to process and print photographs in home darkrooms became easier in the 1950s as amateur photographers embraced the hobby; and partly it was a cultural factor, the rise of mainstream true-detective and men's adventure magazines that featured the kind of photos Glatman felt compelled to shoot for himself.

There is nothing in Glatman's photos that could not be seen in the thousands of photos in true-detective and men's adventure magazines available at newsstands and supermarket racks. In fact, there were flaws in the narrative logic of the photos he took: the victims were gagged even though they were posed in a remote desert where nobody could hear them scream. The gagging was ritual. For Glatman it was not the photo itself as an object of his desire, but the knowledge that the victims in the photos had been *his*, that *he* was there standing behind the camera. These weren't just photos clipped from magazines taken by somebody else of somebody else. They were his darkest memories frozen on film. Glatman put himself a single quantum dimension away from *his* victims forever. He had captured the direct light reflected from his victims frozen to negative film with his own camera held in his own hands. He then printed the image himself from that negative to a positive first-generation print. I can imagine him all by himself, owl-eyed crazy in those horn-rimmed glasses, bathed in the red light of his improvised darkroom, immersing the exposed but still blank photo paper into the developer fluid, swishing and tapping it with his rubber-tipped bamboo photo tongs, coaxing out the image of his victims to its desired contrast and resolution, before putting it into the stop bath and fixer to be forever his. It was a metaphysical perpetuation of the capture and murder, more than just memory; it could be held in his hand, the captured light from his murders.

The other thing that characterizes Glatman's murders and those of serial killers to come is the role of his car and the interstate freeway system that began expanding after World War II at a cancerous rate. Glatman is among the first serial killers to routinely use the freeway system to quickly transport the victims he abducted in Los Angeles to different, distant and opposite locations, over a hundred miles away, where he would kill them and leave their bodies. As car ownership became ubiquitous, the car and the freeway became tools for serial killers to arrive at their victim's door, to troll for and transport them, and finally to move on as migratory predators, sometimes hunting for victims right on the freeways and their rest stops and towns along the way. When the FBI in 2009 launched its Highway Serial Killings Initiative, there were more than five hundred unsolved homicides linked to interstate freeways, appearing to confirm this sense of the US highway system as "circulating" serial killers like bad blood in the body of the American nation.

Essayist and environmentalist Ginger Strand argues that the freeways, because of the way they were built in the 1950s and 1960s—tearing through lower-income neighborhoods—contributed to rising serial murder, not by mobilizing killers, but by increasing the *less-dead* victim pool.[13] The freeways' construction destroyed unwanted ("blighted") inner-city, often minority, communities and scattered people into soulless and degrading public housing ghettos. Strand writes, "In its first decade [1956–1966], the interstate highway program destroyed some 330,000 urban housing units across the nation, the majority of them occupied by minorities and the poor. After that the pace picked up. No one knows the exact number, but estimates are that the highway program displaced around a million Americans."[14] This had dual consequences; the displacement of poor and minority communities created a pool of less-dead victims, while the chaos and degradation destabilized families and spawned serial killers.

Strand recounts how a thriving and prosperous Bronx was destroyed in the 1950s when vibrant low-income neighborhoods were razed to make way for the Cross Bronx Expressway and its dispossessed residents were packed into high-rise public housing complexes. In Atlanta too, the vital and prosperous Auburn Avenue neighborhood known as Sweet Auburn, pronounced by *Forbes* magazine in the 1950s "the richest negro street in the world," was ripped apart by an elevated interstate freeway in 1966. Vibrant African American–owned neighborhood businesses, cultural institutions, churches and family homes were destroyed, forcing low-income residents into bleak, anonymous, high-density public housing complexes.[15]

The expropriation and destruction of Sweet Auburn would give serial killer Wayne Williams his vast victim pool of vulnerable children a decade later. Strand writes, "I-20 would play a key role in Atlantans' understanding of why, in the late seventies, their children began to disappear."[16]

The destruction of families and communities wrought by the building of highways through the hearts of poor and minority communities in New York, Miami, New Orleans, Detroit, Chicago, Nashville, Boston, Atlanta, Los Angeles and other cities, along with the crack cocaine epidemic of the 1990s, took its toll and is still taking it. Devastated, broken and degraded families can produce serial killers.

The decades-long process of destroying inner-city minority communities and families has produced a new pool of both serial killers and victims. While in the past serial killers were believed to be predominately white males, Eric Hickey's survey shows that from 2004 to 2011, 57 percent of all serial killers were African Americans; while the Radford/FGCU Serial Killer Database indicates that in the 2010s, almost 60 percent of serial killers were African Americans (even though African Americans make up only 13.2 percent of the American population).

Way Out in Kansas: Little Dennis Rader

Dennis Rader, the future BTK serial killer of ten victims starting from the 1970s, was born in 1945 and grew up on a farm in Kansas. We do not know much about his Marine father, William Elvin Rader, who was twenty-five when he returned home from the war in the Pacific. He went to work with the Kansas Gas and Electric Company in 1948 and then somewhat mysteriously retired at the early age of forty-five in 1963. There is no record of his being employed after that.[17]

Dennis Rader recalled first being aroused at the age of four by the sight of his mother accidentally restrained when her wedding ring caught on a spring underneath the couch cushions. As she twisted about, trying to disengage her ring, her dress slid upward, revealing the lace trim of her slip. Rader eventually developed a fetish for his mother's white satin slip and would secretly fondle it and masturbate, making sure not to stain it. When his mother caught him masturbating, she beat him with a belt, telling him that God would kill him. Rader told forensic psychologist Katherine Ramsland that he would become aroused at the beating and later developed fantasies of restraining women dressed in slips or other types of underwear, particularly teachers he did not like. He developed a lifelong addiction to self-bondage combined with transvestism, often photographing himself bound and hanging while wearing female lingerie.

Eighteen years apart, Rader and Glatman had acquired similar obsessions and similar combinations of paraphilias, but nobody knows from where.

Rader was fourteen years old when he apparently came across a 1959 issue of *True Detective* magazine in his father's car. The issue featured a story about Harvey Glatman and ran the photos of his victims. Rader would recall:

> This was exactly the pictures and theme that I dreamed about. The old chicken house was near. I had ropes and hooks stashed away there, and some of Mom's feminine clothing. I secured a blanket. I read the article and masturbated into the clothes I had hid.
>
> The women in the photos knew they were going to die. Glatman liked to bind their bare legs over the knees and their hands behind them. He even placed a gag twisted into a rope over their mouths. One woman, wearing just a slinky white slip, lay on a blanket, bound at the ankles, knees, and hands, with a rope going around her across her midriff.
>
> The lady in the white slip in the desert, that triggered me off. Slips turn me on sexually. They are soft satin, and like the early ribbons I used to stroke in my Grandma's, Aunt's, or Mom's hair, it was the type of material I found in a special place in my Mom's bedroom, I assume for her and Dad. Glatman as a child also play [sic] or carry around string and rope and did self-gratification. . . .
>
> I put the magazine back where I found it, but it had a profound effect. The image of the woman staring, terrified, knowing death was coming, was frozen for me. It was part

of my SF [sexual fantasy] the rest of my life. The best gratification. . . . The *Action Men* magazine in the barber shop became popular for me to read. I recall that *Stag* was popular, and I never really bought any, but at the drugstore at the corner of 53rd Street North and Seneca, I would buy *Popular Science* or *Popular Mechanic*, and while thumbing through them, I would sneak a look at the recent *Stags* or detective magazines. Most had women in distress on the cover, a big Cookie Jar for me. I couldn't get enough of them.[18]

Rader recalled as a boy being aroused by scenes in the Dudley Do-Right animated cartoons on *The Rocky and Bullwinkle Show* when the villain Snidely Whiplash ties the cute young damsel in distress Nell Fenwick to railway tracks. Nell wears a knee-length blue dress with frills around the hem—or is that her slip showing? In one sequence, Snidely with rope in hand forces Nell spread-eagle across the tracks, her arms outstretched along the rail behind her shoulders, her legs spread open across the opposite rail, her dress sliding upward, exposing her calves. As Nell wiggles and struggles, he unties her spread legs, loops a rope around her ankles and pulls them tight together high in the air, exposing the back of her bare legs, her skirt sliding farther down as he restrains and gags her.[19]

Hundreds of thousands of horny boys would tune in to *The Rocky and Bullwinkle Show* to see Nell get bound and gagged before Dudley Do-Right rescues her and gets her kiss. Most boys wanted to be Dudley at the end of Nell's kiss, but there were some damaged ones who were feeling things from Snidely's point of view. I never went for freckled redheads with braids like Nell, but I'd tune in to *Rocky and Bullwinkle* for Natasha Fatale, the dark vamp Russian spy in a tight, slutty purple dress with lipstick and eyeliner color to match, for whom I'd get a little boy-boner every time.

Scripting Bondage: The Parsed Paraphilic Imagination
Would Glatman and Rader have killed if there were no true-detective magazines? Or *The Rocky and Bullwinkle Show*? Yes, of course they

would have. But *how* they would have; *how* they would express their sexual rage and through which rituals—the *scripting*—would have been something entirely else.

To most of us, the true-detective and men's adventure magazines all look alike: the covers show a woman in bondage. To the paraphilic serial killer, however, the literature was a stimulant for highly selective fantasies, very specific, parsed subplots that radiated out from his own imagination. It wasn't just the question of abduction and rape—there was a very narrow self-defined specificity to it. Some serial killers would paw through hundreds of these rape scenarios until they came upon just the right one that either reflected their own fantasy script or inspired a new additional twist to it that they had not imagined on their own. It is a constant and obsessive give-and-take process that consumes enormous blocks of time and energy in the serial killer's fantasy world. These are the brushstrokes in the "work" of the "artist" that profiler John Douglas referred to when he famously said of serial killers, "If you want to understand the artist, look at his work."

Glatman as a youth was inspired by his generation of true-detective covers from the 1940s, turned on by bound and frightened women in distress. The bindings, the ropes and cords, he already at an early age sexually ritualized as he engaged in autoerotic asphyxiation, which enhanced his pleasure as the lack of oxygen put him into a euphoric state of arousal. After he came out of prison in his mid-twenties, Glatman stumbled on the new postwar bondage fetish publications like those distributed by Irving Klaw. Unlike the improvised bindings on the disheveled true-detective models with their lingerie accidentally exposed, the Klaw women were carefully posed *in* their lingerie, while the ropes and cords restraining them were carefully and intricately, almost ritually, knotted and laced about their bodies in a way for their captor to move and pose them in different positions of submission, like gagged sex puppets on strings.

What Glatman wanted was a rape culture hybrid of his very own, an abducted, intricately bound Klaw lingerie model but inserted into a menacingly rougher, dirtier and darker true-detective scenario, and he was ready to murder for it. And that's what Glatman did with his victims: froze the realized fantasy on film, killed the models and left them in the desert to the animals and the baking heat. Afterward, he would return to the safety of his home with the pictures to compulsively masturbate in the *afterkill*. Many serial killers do not climax during the commission of their rape and murder. DNA of any kind, including from ejaculate when present, was found in only 29.2 percent of sexual serial homicides according to the recent FBI study.[20] After they have killed their victim, many serial killers remain in the same state of tension and arousal that they started off with until they return to a safe and secure location and finally achieve relief through masturbation, sometimes hours or days after the murder (the afterkill), before they "come down" into their cooling-off period and start working back up the cycle anew to the next murder. Totems and souvenirs from the victim are often taken to enhance the masturbatory experience once a serial killer has abandoned the body of his victim but is still in an aroused state.

Glatman's photos became the featured visual for every article recounting his crimes in the late 1950s. From daily newspapers and *Time* magazine to tabloids and true-detective magazines, all splashed across their pages the horrific photos of the intricately bound victims. The victims are still there fixed in their last minutes of life in a state of fear and dread on the Internet today, staring into their killer's lens, and beyond it, all the Internet creeps on the other end jerking off to real snuff sex and death.

The adolescent Rader was living on a farm in Kansas, masturbating into detective magazines in the barn with his mother's underwear and the chickens. He didn't have Glatman's sophistication or the means to order Irving Klaw publications by mail. He probably didn't even know that kind of bondage material existed. But he didn't need to. Glatman had done the mash-up for Rader, and the results were in every magazine in the drugstores of every little town and big booming city, all of Klaw's special knots and bindings on Glatman's victims. (Glatman bragged to police how he selected low-grain panchromatic film for his photos so that details could be enlarged.) Glatman added the final touch of his own: a cloth gag interwoven with a rope on several of his victims.

Rader got the second-generation Glatman-processed homicidal fetish fantasy, ready to go, and that would be where Rader would pick up in his script and take it in the 1970s to the third generation of homicidal crazy of his own as the Bind-Torture-Kill—BTK—Killer.

Melvin Davis Rees, "The Sex Beast" or "The Bebop Nietzsche Necrophile," Maryland and Virginia, 1956–1959

The "Sex Beast Killings" unfolded on the opposite side of the country from the desert freeways of California, on the wooded back roads of Virginia and Maryland. In many ways, the case mirrored the Harvey Glatman murders, yet it has been largely forgotten and not well-documented or reported. There is only one very recent book on the case, Katherine Ramsland's *The Sex Beast*.[21] Like the "Glamor Girl Murders," this case involved a car, a handgun, abductions, detective magazines, a more-intelligent-than-average perpetrator and deeply twisted sexual impulses. But while Harvey Glatman had been the organized vampire monster of his generation, wooing and luring his victims into his monstrous fantasies, Melvin Rees, the Sex Beast, was the disorganized werewolf, brutalizing and dragging his victims into his monstrous impulses.

Double Abduction of Mary Fellers and Shelby Venable

The case began with the disappearance of two teenage girls in Beltsville, Maryland, on June 1, 1956: Mary Elizabeth Fellers, eighteen, and her longtime friend Shelby Jean Venable, sixteen. The girls grew up in Tennessee originally, but their parents moved to Beltsville and North Laurel in Maryland, towns ten miles apart. The teens often traveled to visit each other by bus, perhaps even hitchhiked despite their parents' admonishments not to. They were "good girls," according to their parents, but they had a typical hidden teen girl flirtatious side to them that their parents might not have been fully aware of. Diaries left behind by the girls revealed that they sometimes dated soldiers from nearby Fort Meade and racetrack workers.[22] Ramsland reports that the girls were attracted to "bad boy rebel" James Dean types, beatniks, poets and bebop jazz musicians.

On June 1, the girls were waiting for a bus on US 1 to travel up to

North Laurel, where they planned to spend the night at Venable's house. Fellers's little brother, twelve-year-old Irwin Jr., caught a glimpse of his sister and Venable at the bus stop just as a light blue Ford sedan with a dented fender and a Virginia tag pulled up beside the girls. Irwin had the impression that they recognized the driver and readily climbed into the car. Then they got out to reverse positions before getting back in. Irwin described a white male with bushy eyebrows and thought he had a scar across his face. That was the last time the two girls were seen alive.

Nothing appeared in the media about the missing girls until June 10, when a newspaper in Tennessee reported that the police were on the lookout for the girls there in case they returned to the state where they grew up. When an adolescent or teenager disappeared, the assumption was that they had run away, unless there was some hard evidence that something more sinister had occurred. And it was only going to get worse once kids really started taking to the road on their own in the turbulent 1960s. It wouldn't be until the 1980s with the "serial killer epidemic" that missing children and youths would become an issue of national concern.

By the time the Tennessee papers reported the missing girls, police near Brunswick, Maryland, had pulled one of them from the Potomac River. She had been found nude, jammed by the river current against some rocks.

Nobody knew who she was at first, and her body was laid out at a funeral home for people with missing relatives to view. One newspaper reported, "B. Lee Feete, the Brunswick funeral director, said hundreds of persons had come to his establishment over the weekend to look at the body. He said he had no idea there were so many missing girls in this area."[23]

Mary Elizabeth Fellers's father arrived at the scene but was unable to positively identify his daughter. Based on the shade of her bright red painted toenails and her ear piercings, her older sister made the identification, later confirmed through dental records. Due to the water-logged condition of her body, no cause of death could be immediately determined.

On June 14, the nude body of Shelby Jean Venable was found facedown in six inches of water in the Catoctin Creek, a tributary of the Potomac near Wheatfield, Virginia, about nine miles from Brunswick. Because of the direction in which the waterways flow it was immediately evident that the two girls were put into the water at different points. Through stomach content analysis it was established that both girls died at approximately the same time and that Venable had been strangled. No final cause of death could be determined for Fellers, nor whether either girl had been raped.

Police in the meantime attempted to identify and interview some of the males named in the girls' diaries. According to Katherine Ramsland, the girls had told their parents about one musician in particular who played at dances they attended on Saturday nights, a versatile and talented young man they called Rees.[24] He was handsome and friendly, and quoted poetry and philosophy. Hundreds of interviews were conducted in the weeks following the girls' murders, but in the end police developed no leads.

Double murders like this one are relatively rare even today, but in Maryland, the abduction and killing of Fellers and Venable made headlines across the nation. And worse. This was the second double murder of teenage girls in that many years. In 1955, Nancy Marie Shomette, sixteen, and her friend Michael Ann Ryan, fourteen, took a short cut through Northwest Branch Park near the University of Maryland in College Park, in the middle of the day to pick up Nancy's report card from her high school. Their bodies were found several hours later by a girl walking her dog. Judging by the shell casings, the girls had been shot with a .22 rifle from a distance of about 150 yards in an ambush. Nancy was shot eleven times, while Michael was shot three times. The killer had walked up to the bodies and shot Nancy one more time in the forehead between the eyes. They did not appear to be sexually molested. Nobody knew what to make of the killings. The two pairs of murders were substantially different, but two pairs of teenage girls killed in the same Maryland region were troubling. Again, no useful leads were developed.

Margaret Harold Murder

On June 26, 1957, Margaret Virginia Harold, a thirty-six-year-old wife and mother of two teenagers working as a clerk at Fort Meade, wrapped up work early. She changed into a pair of tight black toreador pants and a sexy pink blouse. Waiting for her in his car was thirty-one-year-old Master Sergeant Roy Hudson, who had also changed into civilian clothing. Margaret threw her work clothes onto the back seat of Roy's car, and the two of them drove off the base. They headed south from Fort Meade through Gambrills, stopping along the way to have lunch and a few beers. Eventually, they took Route 424 south and turned east along Route 450 (Defense Highway), which took them into Mount Tabor, a remote stretch of forest and farming country that lay between the highway and Mount Tabor Road to the north. Today, some housing developments have crept into the area, but there are still spooky isolated farmhouses accessible only by hidden private roads. After about a mile along Defense Highway, Roy turned at random into a narrow country lane to find a secluded place for the couple. They passed what looked like an abandoned shack, and Roy noted there was a foam green car parked near it. He described to Anne Arundel County chief of police Wilbur Wade what happened after he parked with Margaret at the end of the road:

> Some twenty minutes later the man came up. Margaret saw him coming down the road first and said, "There comes a man." He was hollering at us. I got out of the car to see what he wanted and the man said, "What do you think this is, a national park?"
>
> I told him, "No, we're just sitting here." He asked if we were interested in buying a lot and I told him we weren't. He said he was the watchman of the area and we couldn't park here so I told him we would leave.
>
> The man said, "Let me bum a cigarette off you." I reached in the car and got a cigarette for both of us and the man said, "I guess there's no harm in just sitting here talking."

Then the man said, "Well, since I walked this far down how about giving me a ride back to the shack."

Margaret said, "We have some clothes on the back seat and don't have room for you."

Roy climbed back into his car intending to drive off, but the man opened the rear door and jumped into the back seat. Roy told police:

As he opened the door, I saw he had a snub-nosed blue steel revolver. He said, "Put your arms across the back of the front seat," which we did. I saw the man had an electric light cord in his hands. I told him, "I can't give you my billfold if you tie my hands. Put that gun away," and he said, "Don't worry about that, I'll get your money," and he shot and she slumped over.[25]

Margaret had been shot once in the back of the head, the bullet on impact and leaving wounds that police first thought were the result of two gunshots.

Roy was quick thinking enough to fling open his door, roll out of the car and dash into the bush. He ran through the woods and across a field until he came across a farmhouse and called the police.

Police rushing to the scene later recalled passing a light green car, but by the time they interviewed Roy and got a description of the suspect's car, it was long gone.

Police found Margaret stripped naked and lying in a pool of blood and brain matter in the front passenger compartment of Roy's car. She had been raped postmortem in a necrophilic act.

The electric cord that the murderer had attempted to tie Roy with was found at the scene near the car. A description of the suspect was published in all the newspapers the next day: about thirty-five years old, black hair combed straight back, bushy eyebrows, about six feet tall and 170 pounds. A truck driver reported that he helped a man of that description pull a car from a ditch where it had skidded into a tree not far from the crime scene. Police were now looking for a 1947 or 1948 foam green Chrysler sedan with Maryland tags and a dent on the front from hitting the tree.

Cinder Block Shack

Police searched the shack Roy said he passed and where he saw the car parked. The shack was dilapidated and abandoned, but they immediately found lengths of electrical cord like the one found at the crime scene. As the police officers shined their flashlights into the dank cinder block basement, they came upon a bizarre scene. The walls were completely covered with autopsy photographs of women and lurid bondage images cut from true-detective magazines and men's adventure periodicals.[26] In the middle of that, one image stood out: a formal portrait of a young woman that looked like it was cut out of a high school or university yearbook.

With the FBI's help, the photo was traced to a University of Maryland yearbook and the woman in the picture identified as Wanda Tipton from the graduating class of 1955. The June 1955 double shooting murder of Nancy Marie Shomette and Michael Ann Ryan in the proximity of the university and now this photo in the midst of some pervert's lair near the site of another woman's shooting immediately put the police on the trail of Wanda Tipton. Perhaps she knew who the bushy-eyebrowed man might be and why he would have her photo taped next to dozens of images of dead women. It was just too weird for words.

Lovers' Lane Attacks

Then it got weirder. Another couple stumbled into a police station, the woman barefoot and covered in mud and scratches, and gave a harrowing account of being accosted about six miles from the Margaret Harold murder site. Irwin Howard Adams, twenty-five, and Denise Eggelston, twenty-five, were parked in a wooded picnic area, looking up at the stars and listening to the radio, when another car drove up behind them and stopped with its headlights blinding them. A man got out of the car and slowly walked up on the driver's side and in a normal voice asked the couple what they were doing there.

Irwin told him that they were listening to the radio.

The man suddenly produced a .38 blue steel snub-nosed revolver and said he would kill them if they did not do what he told them. He ordered them out of the car and made them lie down on the ground and laid out precut lengths of cord. He bound Irwin's arms behind him. Then he hauled Irwin to his feet and walked him around to the back of the car and attempted to open the trunk. As the man fumbled with the keys, Irwin managed to work his arms loose and tackled him. Denise leapt up and ran away barefoot toward the road. Irwin then broke free from the man and followed Denise. They ran as fast as they could until they couldn't run any farther. Expecting him to come around the bend in his car any second, they bounded over a guardrail and rolled down a hill into the dark of a swamp and hid there until the next morning.

Finding Wanda Tipton, the college girl in the yearbook picture found in the porn lair of the cinder brick house cellar began to take on urgency. When police finally tracked her down, they were crestfallen when Wanda told them she had no idea why her picture was in the shack or who their suspect could possibly be. And after that police ran out of leads.

But Wanda was not telling the truth. She knew exactly who the man with the bushy eyebrows was. She had dated him. A handsome fellow student at the University of Maryland just out of the Army, a talented jazz musician, poet and philosopher. A gentleman intellectual with a cool cat, bebop nonconformist edge to him. But he was married, and she didn't want to cause him grief with his wife, so she told the police nothing.

Road Rage

On August 24, 1958, Frank Tuozzo and his wife, June, both thirty-six, were driving on a country road near Laurel, Maryland, at around 10:00 at night. Suddenly they saw the headlights of a car closing in on them from behind, weaving erratically. Eventually, the car overtook them and suddenly skidded to a halt, forcing them to stop. A man leapt out of the car and walked toward them with a handgun in his hand. The Tuozzos just sat there stunned, not knowing what to do.

The man ordered them out of their car and forced them to lie down in the road. After turning off Frank's car, the man then ordered Frank around to the back of his car, a blue Ford with Washington, DC, tags. Opening his trunk, the man ordered Frank to get in and closed it.

He then forced June into his car and ordered her to slide down to the cramped space on the passenger floor and drove off with Frank in the trunk. Eventually, the man stopped at a dark and secluded area. He ordered June to lift up her dress and take off her underwear. Then he tied her hands to the steering wheel and performed oral sex on her. After a while, he unzipped his pants and ordered her to fellate him. June made a half-hearted effort but then pulled away, refusing to continue, begging him not to kill her because she had two children.

The man suddenly freed her hands and said, "You're a good woman. You can get out of the car. I'm glad this wasn't any worse than it was."

He then climbed out and opened the trunk, letting Frank out. "Get out of here, both of you," he said. Frank and June took each other's hands and ran into the dark woods, expecting to be shot down. Instead, they heard the man start his car up and drive away. The description of their assailant matched the descriptions in the previous attacks—but nobody knew that. The previous attacks took place in Anne Arundel County, but this was in Prince George's County. Might as well have been in another country.

At the core of the serial killer problem always, to this day, is "linkage blindness," and it was at its most blind on the county level, the level at which states investigate and prosecute crimes. In those days, jurisdictions rarely exchanged information about or were aware of or even much interested in what took place in other counties. There was no pooling of information in which discernible patterns could be identified. And when murders occurred across state lines, they might as well have happened in another universe altogether. This would become a huge problem when the serial killer surge hit in the 1970s and serial killers like Ted Bundy, Henry Lee Lucas and the recently identified super serial killer Samuel Little got into their cars and hit the road, leaving dead women behind like bread crumbs. As we saw in earlier cases, it was mostly newspapers that speculated on "patterns" and "links" and gave monikers to possible multiple murderers or "strings" of related murders. But the abduction of the Tuozzos had been sparsely reported in just a few newspapers, and no connection to the Margaret Harold murder was made or speculated on, let alone the double strangulations of Mary Fellers and Shelby Venable the year before.

What was needed here was an investigative agency that worked across state lines: the Federal Bureau of Investigation—the FBI.

Jackson Family Abduction Murders

On Sunday, January 11, 1959, Carroll Vernon Jackson, twenty-nine, his wife, Mildred Jackson, twenty-six, and their two daughters, Susan Ann, five, and infant Janet, eighteen months, disappeared after visiting Mildred's parents in Buckner, Louisa County, Virginia.

The next morning, Mildred did not answer phone calls from her parents, which was unusual. By Monday afternoon, they were worried enough to drive out to Mildred's home, ten miles away. They traveled about two miles along Route 609, Buckner Road, before they came upon the Jackson family car sitting askew on the shoulder as if it had been forced off the road. The engine was turned off, keys in the ignition and doors closed. The rearview mirror was flipped upward as if to deflect headlight beams shining from behind. Mildred's purse with two dollars was in the front, while the back seat was scattered with diapers, dolls and toys, two pillows and a white wool child's cap among an assortment of other items a family would pack for a short road trip with two children. Volunteer search parties combed the countryside in the vicinity but found nothing.

As news of the mysterious disappearance spread, police received reports from two other people who stated that on the same night a vehicle came up behind them, flashing its high beams, and attempted to run them off the road. In one case their car was overtaken and forced to stop, and a young man with dark hair and bushy eyebrows emerged from his vehicle with a handgun in his hand and started to walk back toward them, but the driver reacted quickly and backed his car away, turned and escaped. Police dismissed the reports as unrelated.

In February, a newspaper article headlined "As if something swooped down in the night . . ." described theories involving witchcraft or UFOs behind the family's mysterious disappearance.[27]

On March 4, forty miles away in Spotsylvania County, Virginia, near Fredericksburg, farmers James Beach and John W. Scott were salvaging sawdust from the site of a former sawmill. Their truck got stuck in the mud, and as Beach began to gather branches to put under the wheels, he suddenly came face-to-face with a shoe, toe pointed into the ground, heel to the sky. It was a men's oxford shoe; as his eyes came to a socked ankle protruding from the shoe, he caught a glimpse of gray flesh, in turn protruding from a wool suit trouser leg emerging from beneath the tangled bush and sawdust refuse.

That's how they found Carroll Jackson.

When police cleared the foliage and branches, Carroll was found facedown on the soft ground, clad in his winter coat and suit, feet spread wide apart, hands bound tightly in front of him with his red tie.[28] His face and the top of his head were covered in lacerations from an apparent beating. He had been shot once; the large-caliber bullet entered his left temple at the eyebrow line and emerged above the right eyebrow.[29] Nearby, police would find Carroll's smashed eyeglasses and plastic grips from a .38 handgun, which must have broken off when the murderer beat Carroll about the face and head before shooting him. One of the grips had a hair adhered to it, but in pre-DNA days of forensics, it could not be conclusively matched to any of the Jacksons.

Before Jackson's body was raised and removed from the scene, an Associated Press photographer had farmer James Beach and Spotsylvania sheriff B. W. Davis Jr. squat down next to the corpse and look down at it pensively. He snapped a photo (which was duly splashed across front pages the next day).[30] Then they lifted Jackson's body.

That's how they found eighteen-month-old Janet.

The baby was also lying facedown but had no wounds or signs of blunt trauma. It was theorized that the child had been in Carroll's bound hands and he fell on her when he was shot. The coroner would later elaborate that with the head wound Carroll sustained, he might have lived for another three or four hours, his infant daughter squirming beneath him until she died from either suffocation or exposure.

The area around the site was intensively searched for the rest of the family, Mildred and her five-year-old daughter, Susan. After a day, it became sickeningly evident that the murderer had taken the mother and girl away for his own twisted purposes. A lot of cops that day must have prayed that when the two were found, it wouldn't be on their turf. The ones in Virginia got prayers answered.

On March 21, fourteen-year-old John Bolin and his friend John Paddy were hunting small game with their air rifle BB guns in the Mount Tabor region in Maryland. They were about a half mile away from where Margaret Harold had been murdered in 1957 and fifty feet away from an abandoned shack. (It's a subject of controversy whether this shack was the same one in which the bondage photos had been found taped to its basement walls following the Harold murder.)

The boys spotted a flash of what looked like a small squirrel or rat and fired their BB guns at it. It didn't move. As they approached, they began to make out what looked like golden strands of fur or hair. They had either shot the animal dead or it was a rat's nest. Bolin cautiously poked it with the barrel of his air gun, and when he pulled it back, the hair tangled around the front sight and came up with the barrel along with the head of a small girl. Two years later at trial, Bolin would testify, "I first thought it was a baby doll, then I saw it was a human."

Susan Jackson had been found.

When police dug the child out of the shallow grave, they found Mildred Jackson's body beneath her daughter's, lying on her back, her face badly beaten and with one of her stockings tied tightly around her neck. Her dress was pulled up over her head, but otherwise she was fully dressed except for her shoes, which were not found.

In the nearby shack, police found a red button torn from Mildred's coat. The Sex Beast, as he became known, had taken Mildred into the shack to do what he did to her. According to a later trial motion:

> Defendant took Mrs. Jackson into the house, where a button off her coat was later found. There or nearby he beat her brutally about the right side of her face and head, probably with his left fist (he is left handed), and forced her to her knees so hard that her knees were bruised. His purpose was to perform an abnormal sexual act on her and to try to persuade or force

her to perform an abnormal sexual act on him. The injuries about her head were so severe that she died of aspiration of blood into the lungs. A stocking had been tied around her neck so tight that it cut into her flesh, and it may also have been used to gag her. Most of the blood was aspirated while she was lying on her back either in or near the grave which defendant dug for her and Susan in the sandy soil. Susan had died from the effects of a very severe blow on the back of her head.[31]

The killer had probably tied the stocking around Mildred's neck to lead her around as if on a leash.

The FBI and the Capture of the Sex Beast

The discovery of Mildred and Susan Jackson brought the FBI into the case, perhaps for the first time in a sexual serial murder investigation. Since the 1980s, the FBI and its "mindhunters" at the National Center for the Analysis of Violent Crime (NCAVC)'s Behavioral Analysis Unit 4 have been regarded as the nation's "clearinghouse" on serial killers. Soon we will see how this was not only a *product* of the serial killer epidemic, but actually shaped the very notion of a serial killer epidemic.

If we set aside the serial murders committed by bank-robbing "public enemies" that the FBI pursued across state lines in the 1930s, the FBI had never, until the Sex Beast case, been involved in the investigation of serial murders beyond offering their laboratories to local police for evidence analysis. Former profiler Robert Ressler writes that when he began first focusing on serial killer behavioral patterns in the 1970s, "the FBI was almost completely uninterested in murderers, rapists, child molesters, and other criminals who prey on their fellowmen. Most of these violent-behavior cases fell entirely within the jurisdiction of local law-enforcement agencies and were not violations of the federal laws that the FBI was charged with enforcing."[32]

But when Mildred and Susan Jackson were taken across the state line from Virginia and murdered in Maryland, this brought the FBI into a sexual serial murder case for the first time in its history. Following the infamous Lindbergh baby kidnapping in 1932, Congress had passed the Federal Kidnapping Act, 18 U.S.C. § 1201(a)(1) (known as the Lindbergh Law) making it a federal crime to abduct and take a victim across state lines. As such, the abduction of Mildred and Susan fell into the jurisdiction of the FBI to investigate, although not that of her husband, Carroll, and daughter Janet, nor the murders of the four victims—those crimes remained local counties to investigate and prosecute.

The FBI, unfortunately, was no better at apprehending the murderer of the Jackson family than were the various Virginia and Maryland county sheriff's investigators. Yet on June 24, 1960, after two and half years of no apparent leads or progress, the FBI suddenly announced an arrest in the Margaret Harold murder.

Once again, the FBI had gotten involved on a technicality. The suspect had been arrested in West Memphis, Arkansas, on the charge of "unlawful interstate flight to avoid prosecution"—a federal crime within the jurisdiction of the FBI to investigate and enforce. The prosecution he was accused of fleeing was the case of Margaret Harold. The Jackson family murders were not mentioned at first.

The exact chain of events leading to the identification and arrest of Sex Beast serial killer Melvin Rees Jr. remains somewhat murky and convoluted to this day, as does his childhood history and biography.

After the bodies of the Jacksons had been found, the governor of Virginia and police in Virginia and Maryland received letters naming jazz musician Melvin Rees, a divorced father with a four-year-old son, as someone who should be investigated in the Jackson murders. When police appeared to fail to act on the information, the letter writer now personally went into the FBI office in Norfolk and introduced himself as Glenn Leroy Moser, a childhood friend of Rees and a graduate of the University of Maryland in criminology.

Moser stated that he and Rees had been roommates, along with two women, in a Norfolk beachfront cabin at the time of the Jackson murders. On the night of the Jackson family abduction, Moser claimed, Rees was scheduled to play in a club in Washington, DC, but left Norfolk too late to arrive on time. The FBI checked with the club, but the manager had insufficient records to determine whether Rees had appeared that night, nor could they find any band members who could conclusively recall if Rees had played on that occasion. Moser stated that Rees inexplicably did not return to the beach house for ten days after the murders.

Moser stated that Rees had strange "existential" ideas. "He would never say it was wrong to kill but believed that there are individual standards of right and wrong. It was an Existentialist theory. Anything he reads he likes to experience. He's a thrill-seeker, I suppose."

Moser's mother recalled that Rees had been since his childhood a frequent guest in her home and that in recent years she occasionally joined in the philosophical discussions that her son and Rees were engaged in. She recalled she disagreed with his existentialist argument that violence in some cases can be forgiven on the grounds that it is self-expression.

"But if you don't feel, you're dead," he replied, railing against "today's sick society."

Mrs. Moser reminded Rees that he had good health, good looks, a quick mind and an unmistakable talent in music. "With all that it seems as if you'd enjoy living."

"There are some things that I find pleasure in doing," Rees replied, without explaining what they were.[33]

Mrs. Moser was unconvinced by her son's suspicions. She admitted that Rees was somewhat erratic and passive-aggressive—he would cheat, for example, in a friendly game of Scrabble—but she could recall no occasion on which he had been involved in a violent act, not even a schoolyard fight.

Moser said Rees was obsessed with true-crime stories, Nazi atrocities and personalities, and existentialist philosophers such as Nietzsche and Schopenhauer. Rees also enjoyed reading the Marquis de Sade, according to Moser. Rees was addicted to the amphetamine Benzedrine (bennies) and was on a cough syrup "Benzedrine jag" the night before the Harold murder. Moser stated that he first became suspicious after the Harold murder when newspapers published a composite portrait of the suspect that resembled Rees. When Mildred Jackson and her daughter were found near the same location as the Harold murder, Moser became even more suspicious.

Moser described Rees as bright and talented, the son of a respectable family, "but he takes benzedrine and he has something wrong with him sexually. Why, in March 1955, about eight months after he got married to a nice Baltimore girl, he tried to drag a woman into his car at the Hyattsville bus stop. It was hushed up, but we all knew then there was something wrong."[34]

He stated that one day while driving with Rees he confronted him about the murders and that Rees became so nervous he drove the car off the road. Later, in the company of several fellow musicians, he again confronted Rees, urging him to contact the police and submit to an interview. Rees became terribly upset, and Moser never saw him again.

Why it took authorities so long to investigate the information provided by Moser has never been well explained in any sources. Rees certainly met the physical description of the suspect. He was tall, had relatively handsome chiseled features, dark black hair combed back and prominent dark bushy eyebrows. He drove a blue Ford like the one reported terrorizing other couples on the roads around the time of the Jackson abduction.

When exactly and which jurisdiction first reviewed Melvin Rees's criminal record is unclear, but they would have found only two items listed. The first was minor: on April 1953, Rees was fined $10 and $4.25 for throwing trash on a highway in Virginia.[35] The second was more troubling and exactly as Moser had described it: on March 25, 1955, Rees had been charged with assault when a woman said he attempted to drag her into his car while she was waiting for a bus. The unidentified woman refused to press charges and they were dismissed.

According to Katherine Ramsland, Rees had already come to the attention of the police in the 1956 murders of Mary Fellers and Shelby Venable. As one of the many males the girls were acquainted with, he was apparently interviewed and eliminated as a suspect. It is not unusual in serial murder cases for police to discover, when they finally make an arrest, that the accused was known to them and that they'd even been interviewed already, sometimes several times, as in the case of Gary Ridgway, the Green River Killer, or in Britain, Peter Sutcliffe, the Yorkshire Ripper.

Realizing that Rees had been a student at the University of Maryland, police returned to interview Wanda Tipton again, whose photo was found in the cinder block shack during the Margaret Harold murder investigation. Tipton now admitted to having dated Rees and that she had lied to them because she did not want to cause him problems with his wife. Now police had evidence that Rees was connected to the shack.

It wasn't until June 1960 that the FBI finally interviewed Rees in East Memphis. (Ramsland reports the FBI had difficulty finding him until Moser heard from Rees and furnished his new address to the FBI.) When questioned, Rees appeared unperturbed, polite and mild mannered. Sergeant Roy Hudson, Harold's companion on the day of her murder, was brought down to view a lineup and identified Rees as the man who had attacked the couple. That clinched it. Rees was arrested on June 24, 1960, and charged with unlawful flight from the prosecution of the Margaret Harold murder.

Shortly afterward, federal prosecutors added the charge of abducting across state lines Mildred and Susan Jackson, the only other crime that federal authorities had jurisdiction in.

Melvin D. Rees Jr.—The Sketchy Bio

Melvin Davis Rees Jr. was born in Washington, DC, on January 21, 1929, to telephone company employee Melvin Davis Rees and US Department of Interior office worker Virginia Elizabeth (Allen) Rees.[36] He was raised in Hyattsville, Maryland, in the vicinity of the murders, and frequently stayed there on and off with his parents throughout the 1950s. Nothing is known about his childhood other than there might have been behavioral problems and he was packed off to the Edwards Military Institute in Salemburg, North Carolina, where "the pupils often came from broken and single parent homes,"[37] but his father denied that. It does not appear that he graduated high school despite his apparent intelligence and good grades, a sign of trouble.

His parents described Melvin as a completely normal, clever, friendly boy who liked animals and was musically gifted. He could read and write music by the age of ten. When testifying about his son's visit the day after the Jacksons disappeared, his father said, "He has a kind and sympathetic nature and could not hurt any living thing. His little son adores him. He could not possibly have maintained his natural disposition and manner with us if he had this horrible thing on his mind."[38]

Rees joined the Army in October 1946 and later transferred to the Air Force. He was stationed for some time in Britain, where he played in a military band and attained the rank of corporal before leaving the service in 1953. While stationed in Britain, he enrolled in the overseas program of the University of Maryland. After his discharge, he continued studying economics at the University of Maryland on their College Park campus from 1953 to 1957 but never graduated, dropping out to pursue a full-time career as a jazz musician playing primarily in various clubs across Maryland and Virginia.

Fellow students remembered Rees as friendly, mild mannered, intelligent, and a very talented and versatile musician who could play saxophone, vibraphone, piano and accordion. He loved to cite poetry and was enamored with the more nihilist aspects of existentialism, as Moser had reported. He taught piano to young students and in fact on the days before and after the Jackson murders was giving lessons in Washington, DC.

In late 1954, Rees married Elaine Rachmaninoff, whom he had met at the university. They had a son, Philip. They separated in 1957 and divorced in 1959. His ex-wife testified that he did not beat her and denied any "unusual" sexual practices. She said she sued for divorce on the grounds of desertion.

In 1958, Rees met nineteen-year-old red-haired stripper Pat Routt, who was dancing under the name Vivian Storm. They moved in together, and she was living with Rees in West Memphis when he was arrested.

"The Mother and Daughter Were All Mine"

On the day Rees was arrested, the FBI showed up at his parents' home in Hyattsville with a search warrant. At first, they found nothing incriminating, but eventually they uncovered a small hidden compartment at the back of a closet in which they found a locked accordion case. Rees Sr. gave them permission to open it. In it police found two pieces of highly incriminating evidence.

First, there was a blue steel snub-nosed .38 revolver with traces of blood on it. Unfortunately, the bullets recovered from the crime scenes were too damaged to conduct a ballistic match test with the handgun, nor, in pre-DNA times, could the traces of blood be conclusively matched to any of the victims. But the grips found at the site of Carroll Jackson's murder would be matched through a broken screw and scratches from the metal burrs on the handgun handle frame.

The second piece of evidence was what became known as the "Death Diary." In it Rees described what he had done to the Jacksons. He wrote, "Caught on lonely road. After pulling them over leveled pistol and ordered them out and into car trunk was open for husband and both bound. Drove to select area and killed husband and baby. Now the mother and daughter were *all mine*" (emphasis in the original). A newspaper photo of Mildred was attached to the pages with a gag drawn over her mouth. Beneath the photo was a detailed account of what Rees had done to Mildred. Police withheld that passage from the public and court record, except for the ending of the last sentence: "then tied and gagged, led to her place of execution and hung her."[39]

Trials and Judgments

Melvin Rees was first tried in federal court in Baltimore in February and March 1961, charged with violation of the Lindbergh Law in the case of Mildred and Susan Jackson. He was convicted and sentenced to life imprisonment. Then he was sent over to Virginia to stand trial for the capital murder of Carroll Jackson in Spotsylvania County, a death penalty charge.

From the beginning, the defense attempted to exclude both the handgun and "Death Diary" on the grounds that neither the search warrant nor the parents' permission gave the FBI authority to open the locked accordion case, which belonged to Rees, not his parents. The court ruled that the diary was inadmissible as it violated Rees's Fifth

Amendment constitutional protection from self-incrimination; however, the handgun could be admitted into evidence.

The trials were a hell of a show.

All the Rees women took the stand in his defense, mom (he was kind to animals and affectionate), ex-wife (he never beat me and we only had "straight" sex), ex-girlfriend (he was romantic and handsome and could get any girl). They all wept and sang his praises. Yes, he had his quirks and failings, but there was absolutely nothing violent or kinky about Dave, as Rees liked to be called.

When Rees's ex-girlfriend, Pat Routt, stripper "Vivian Storm" took the stand, she was dressed for Instagram before there was Instagram. The papers reported, "The dark red-haired witness wore a two-piece black silk dress with high neckline and three-quarter sleeves. She had on large pearl earrings, white gloves and black patent leather pumps."[40]

"She spoke quietly in a voice that could be barely heard."

"She crossed her legs casually."

The courtroom spectator lines went around the block.

Asked by the prosecutor if she was "a strip teaser," she replied, "Not exactly, no, I'm a specialty dancer."

Routt insisted that she and Rees had "normal sexual relations." Asked if she had ever posed nude for Rees, she gamely replied, "I *never* posed in the nude," but, "Yes, he did take pictures" while she was in the bath.

It was dirty and salacious in an era of "I like Ike" clean-cut American Protestant simplicity and *Leave It to Beaver* conformative innocence. Routt was the *anti*–June Cleaver whore, the psychosexual right hand to Melvin Rees's sadistic left, which abducted, brutalized, murdered and necro-raped wholesome June Cleaver mothers like Margaret and Mildred.

It was the horniest of true-detective magazine fantasies—sex and death, killing Mother—and it appealed to the ancient stirrings of lycanthropic monstrosity: the serial killer as a dual mirror to humanity, the Dr. Jekyll and Mr. Hyde, the nice guy Lon Chaney Jr. and the werewolf monster into which he transforms.

Through the trials, Rees remained calm and stoic, dark and handsome in that chiseled Rock Hudson way. He even had a Madison Avenue executive suit on. Women swooned before the Sex Beast. But in May 1961, Rees was convicted in Virginia in the murder of Carroll Jackson and sentenced to death.

Once the trials were over, nobody really talked much about the Sex Beast and he was mostly forgotten in the post-JFK slaughter to come, and even today the case remains obscure.

Melvin Rees Postscripts

Pat Routt went on to earn a good measure of posttrial fame, becoming Pat Barrington, a 1960s B-movie star with roles in cult films like *Orgy of the Dead*, *Psychedelica Sexualis*, *The Agony of Love*, *Mondo Topless*, *The Girl with Hungry Eyes*, *The Satanist*, *The Acid Eaters*, *Hedonistic Pleasures* and *Sisters in Leather*. She continued stripping until the early 1990s, then became a telemarketer. She died in 2004.[41]

After Rees was convicted there were numerous appeals, which were sporadically reported in short newspaper blurbs. There were sanity reviews and more appeals. By 1967, Rees appeared to break down mentally. He became an unkempt, apathetic, drooling zombie. He waived his right to appeal and demanded to be executed. The Supreme Court questioned his mental competence to make such a decision and temporarily vacated his death sentence and waited for him to regain his competency for decades, until Rees died of heart problems at age sixty-six in a federal facility in Missouri on July 10, 1995.[42] The Rees death penalty suspension remained a citable case in Supreme Court deliberations as recently as 2013, when a unanimous ruling invalidated it as a future precedent.[43]

In 1985, ten years before his death, Rees gave a journalist from the *Richmond Times-Dispatch* an exclusive interview in which he confessed to abducting and strangling the teenage girls Mary Fellers and Shelby Venable; he claimed they were his first victims and denied any role in the 1955 ambush shooting of Nancy Shomette and Michael Ann Ryan. (In 2000, the *Washington Post* reported an alleged 1995 deathbed confession from a man in Florida, who grew up in the vicinity of the murders, claiming that when he was seventeen years old, he shot the girls with a squirrel rifle in a rage after one of them rudely rejected his invitation for a date.[44])

Rees explained that he had been addicted to Benzedrine for ten years and had not slept for four or five days prior to murdering the Jacksons. The shape and form of his sadistic fantasies, he said, came from his compulsive reading of true-detective magazines. He denied beating Mildred, claiming that he had attempted to hang her in the shack but that her nylon stocking couldn't hold her weight and she bruised her face when she fell to the floor. He said he completely forgot about the five-year-old Susan, having locked her in the trunk. When he let her out, she began screaming and he hit her with a two-by-four board and threw her on top of her mother in the shallow grave he had dug.

Clarnell's Boy: "Just Wondered How It Would Feel to Shoot Grandma"

As Ed Gein, Harvey Glatman and Melvin Rees acted out their long-gestated fantasies, the future "epidemic era" serial killers were entering into their formative childhoods. The 1950s was when the disappointed war bride Clarnell was abandoned by her broken war hero husband, E. E. Kemper, who insisted on pursuing his trade as an electrician despite her protests that it was "beneath his station." Eventually, he took a contract to work as an electrician on the nuclear bomb tests in the Pacific for several years. He would later say, "Suicide missions in wartime and the atomic bomb testings were nothing compared to living with her." In his absence, little Edmund became the go-to target of Clarnell's frustration and anger with her unmanageable husband. She enlisted Edmund's two sisters to torment little Edmund, making him the subject of their joint derision. In response Edmund severed the heads of one of his sisters' Barbie dolls. He lopped off the top of the family cat's skull and hid its carcass in his closet. He buried another one alive. He began nocturnal forays peeking into neighbors' windows with a knife in hand. When his sister teased him that he wanted to kiss her teacher, Edmund told her, "I would have to kill her first."

Edmund grew to be unusually tall for an adolescent: six feet four. (He reached six feet nine as an adult.) He was a sensitive child with a then tested high IQ of 136. For reasons known only to her, Clarnell became concerned that Edmund was going to molest his sisters. One day, Edmund returned from school and found his bedroom had been moved into the cellar.

E. E. Kemper eventually divorced Clarnell and settled in his home state of California. He remarried and started a new family. Clarnell married twice more, she claimed because her son "needed a father." The marriages did not work out any better than her first marriage. Clarnell was unable to find a man who could live up to her expectations, and she vented her frustrations on her son, Ed.

Edmund began his transformation into a serial killer unusually young, at the age of fifteen in the summer of 1964. He had begged to go live with his father and eventually ran away and showed up at his father's door in 1963. His dad took his new family and Edmund to visit his parents, seventy-two-year-old Edmund Emil Kemper Sr. and his wife, the artist and author of boys' stories, sixty-six-year-old Maude Hughey Kemper. They had retired to a seventeen-acre farm in North Fork, California. When the Christmas visit ended, Edmund's dad left Kemper with his grandparents to raise him.

At first, it seemed to work out. The grandparents bought Edmund a dog and a .22 rifle. Edmund proceeded to wipe out all the wildlife in the vicinity of the farm but otherwise was no trouble. (He did not kill livestock as alleged in some sources.) He was enrolled in the Sierra Joint Union High School in nearby Tollhouse, where he quietly earned average grades without attracting any attention to himself. But when the school year ended, he was sent back home to Clarnell for the summer. He suddenly returned two weeks later, completely transformed back to his disturbed self. He now became a problem for the grandparents, disobeying their demands that he stop shooting birds on the farm.

On August 27, 1964, his grandfather was in town purchasing groceries. As Maude sat at the kitchen table editing a recent manuscript for *Boys' Life*, the official magazine of the Boy Scouts, Edmund shot her twice in the back of the head with his rifle and then stabbed her three times in the back because he did not want her "to suffer," he said. He wrapped her head up in a dish towel and then carried her body into the bedroom. Then Edmund waited for his grandfather to return.

He didn't want his grandfather to see what he had done. When his grandfather came driving up the road with the groceries, Kemper went out to greet him. "Granddad was smiling at me," Kemper told police. "When he turned, I placed the rifle this far (indicating about 30 inches) from the back of his head and shot him."[45]

Kemper then called his mother and told her what he had done. When police arrived, Kemper had little to say in explanation other than that he was "mad at the world" and "I just wondered how it would feel to shoot Grandma."

Kemper was immediately packed off to the Atascadero maximum-security state psychiatric facility, where the intelligent and disarmingly charming youth became the favorite of the psychiatric staff. He was assigned to work in the psychology laboratory, where he became a crew leader in administrating and helping to score the results of inmate psychology tests. Psychologist Frank J. Vanasek was impressed with Kemper's performance, commenting, "He was a very good worker—and this is not typical of a sociopath. He really took pride in his work. Now, a sociopath would have been more likely to *use* his performance to achieve other ends." Kemper understood himself much better than the degreed psychologist Vanasek. Kemper later said, "I broke my butt. . . . I was the dynamic young man, and they began to say maybe we can let him out sooner than we had thought."[46]

Arthur Shawcross, "The Genesee River Killer," Part 1, Jefferson County, New York, 1972–1989

On the other side of the country, in upper New York State near Watertown, Arthur John Shawcross, the son of the tenth-grade dropout Elizabeth "Betty" Yerakes and traumatized Guadalcanal veteran Roy Shawcross was growing up through the 1950s and 1960s.

Although Betty would claim that Arthur was normal, healthy, and never gave her any trouble until the age of five, other relatives remember little Art as being "odd" even as an infant. One cousin recalled that Arthur had beautiful, big eyes but a blank, expressionless stare and he almost never cried. But when he did, he creepily cried from only one eye. He still talked baby talk when he was six. He suffered from nightmares and frequently wet his bed. He was absent from kindergarten for a total of thirty-three days, and when in first grade, he began running away from home—unusual for a child of that age. He enjoyed making other children cry and invented fantasy friends with which he carried on extensive conversations.

He was called "Oddie" by other children and became a frequent target of their derision. He always seemed to be left out. Many former students remember Shawcross as a boy at the edge of the playground, wanting to join in but never being invited. Early school reports note that he wandered away from his classroom and was found sitting in empty classrooms and "he brings an iron bar on the school bus and hits at the children."

In May 1953, at the age of eight, Shawcross was sent for a mental health evaluation. The report stated, "There seems to be a general feeling that one can't tell what he will do. . . . Harbors a fair amount of hostility especially toward his mother because of fear of punishment and rejection, and seems unable to find many legitimate outlets for it. Defenseless objects (and possibly younger children) seem to take the brunt. . . . His conscience does not seem to be strongly developed as yet, but some guilt feelings appear." In other words, little Arthur was on his way to becoming a psychopath.

The report concluded, "The mother appears to be rejecting (from Arthur's point of view) and punishing even where it is uncalled for. This has resulted in a great deal of confusion about what he should be like. He feels as if he is a bad boy a lot of the time and is hostile enough in a confused sort of way to want to remain 'bad.' Is unable to develop moral standards. Instead, he appears to be indulging in a considerable amount of fantasy in which he perceives himself as a new person with respect and dignity."

Shawcross would later claim that his mother beat him with a broomstick, inserted it into his anus and gave him forced enemas, that he had incestuous sex with his sister, his cousin or his aunt, and that he had sex with a male when he was fourteen, although none of these later claims could be confirmed. And Shawcross, as we will see, will tell a lot of tall tales.

When Arthur was nine, a letter arrived from Roy's wife in Australia and his hidden past was exposed. From then on, family life was hellish. Betty became permanently embittered, referring to all other women, whether in life or on television, as "whores." She berated her husband constantly, for the rest of their marriage. He now stayed away at work for long hours and became withdrawn and quiet. Arthur's father became a "nonperson" in the family.

Later, Shawcross would write:

> From that day forward my life turned upside down. Dad hung his head in shame. He couldn't look you in the eye and say it was not so! Mom took over and she made life hell in that house. Dad can't even watch TV without mom cursing or throwing something at him. Even where he worked he could of done better for himself, but now he started working in a gravel pit. I am ashamed of my father and now I am ashamed of myself. This same woman did it to both of us.[47]

Numerous episodes of cruelty to animals were later reported. A cousin remembers how Arthur liked to skin living fish to watch them suffer and see how long it took them to die. He snared rabbits and enjoyed snapping their necks, plucked feathers off baby birds, pinned frogs to his dartboard as targets and tied cats together. One friend remembers him throwing a kitten into a lake, over and over, until the animal drowned.

Shawcross also committed numerous acts of petty thievery, further filling in the typical serial killer's childhood profile, along with the many instances of arson. Firefighters were constantly being called out to extinguish brush fires near his house.

It was all there, all the classic symptoms in the childhood history of a gestating serial killer: bed-wetting, bullying of fellow children, arson, cruelty to animals and flights of fantasy as a means of retreat, and a dominating mother taking center stage. The hysterical dominating mother and a weak, ineffectual or totally absent father figure is a motif that runs through many a serial killer's childhood biography (Edmund Kemper, Jerry Brudos, Henry Lee Lucas, Kenneth Bianchi).

One of the common aspects of serial killer childhoods is rejection by peers, resulting in loneliness. It's hard to say whether childhood peers reject the child because of his weirdness, resulting in frustrated and violent behavior further alienating the child from his peers, or it's the violent behavior that leads childhood peers to reject their playmate, but regardless, the child feels rejected and in its loneliness begins to dwell on comforting fantasies of violent retribution in which they control and dominate everything around them, including the people who rejected them in the first place.

When Shawcross underwent a mental health assessment at the age of eight, the report stated, "Mother says he has no playmates. . . . Asked which of his brothers and sisters he liked best he said, 'Not any of them' because they wouldn't play with him."

"Crazy Boy"

One of his strangest quirks was an obsession with walking in a straight line, no matter what the obstacle—swamp, hills or barbed wire. His clothes would get torn, he'd get mired in the Watertown swamps, but he would not change direction. He called it "walking cross-lots."

As Shawcross became an adolescent, he grew stronger. Instead of ridiculing him, many began to fear him. When one girl called him "stupid," he attacked her with a baseball bat. He did not know the meaning of the term "uncle" when fighting. Once he began, there was no stopping him until somebody would pull him off. A male cousin recalled that Artie did not know how to express his anger other than to shout out comic book captions as he hit: "Bang . . . zap . . . pow." He hit a boy in the face with books, breaking his glasses; he broke his cousin's nose with the butt of a toy rifle.

A cousin recalled, "He made weird noises as he walked. . . . I'd run into him and he'd be saying, 'Die die *dee* die, die die *dee* die . . .'" Another cousin stated, "It came from his throat. . . . At first it sounded like a chant but later on we realized he was just saying 'die' over and over."

In school, he was having academic problems. He was left behind three times with the result that he was sixteen when he entered eighth grade. He excelled in sports but was uncontrollable. He was dismissed from the wrestling team when he used TV wrestling tactics like body slams and punches. In track and field, he assaulted his competitors. His nickname was "Crazy Boy."

From the age of nine, Shawcross also started to display undiagnosed blackouts and strange episodes of paralysis. At the age of ten, while picnicking with his family, he suddenly appeared to lose consciousness and slipped into the water. After his father pulled him out, Arthur claimed he could not move his legs. He spent six days in a hospital undergoing a battery of tests without any clear diagnosis. He was sent home and shortly afterward miraculously regained the use of his legs.

At school, Shawcross sustained the first of a long string of head injuries, also a frequent feature in the childhood histories of serial killers. He was hit in the head by a discus, resulting in a four-day hospitalization with hairline skull fractures. In the next few years, he would be knocked unconscious by a surge of electricity, a blow from a sledgehammer, a fall onto his head from a forty-foot ladder and a hit from a truck.

By the age of seventeen, Shawcross had dropped out of school and was employed in various temporary jobs. He matured into an attractive and strong youth with captivating green eyes and dark and handsome features, but his odd behavior still put many people off. He continued to "walk cross-lots" but now added a new twist to the obsession—he would speed up and slow down every twenty paces or so. Although he had a car given to him by his grandfather, he quickly wrecked it and preferred to use his bicycle, claiming that driving made him nervous. Whenever rising from a chair, he had a strange habit of grabbing his buttocks and "lifting himself up." At dances he displayed weird and spastic moves, twenty years ahead of Devo and Talking Heads. His few dates with girls ended with his inappropriate behavior; one girl remembers him suddenly violently grabbing at her crotch.

In December 1963, when Arthur was eighteen, he registered his first criminal conviction. Responding to a silent alarm late one night, police caught him inside a downtown department store. He had smashed through the front window. The judge sentenced him to eighteen months' probation as a youthful offender.

Despite his violent and disturbed behavior, some women found him attractive. Over the winter of 1964, Shawcross began steadily dating a girl a year older than him, and in September they were married. A year later, in October 1965, they had a baby boy. The couple lived in a trailer on property owned by his bride's parents. Shawcross worked a variety of jobs but often faked injuries to collect insurance and went through long periods of unemployment. He engaged in acts of petty thievery at work and was considered an unreliable worker. Shawcross was an unfaithful husband, explaining later that his wife refused to engage in oral sex. Shawcross discovered that he had an ability to attract women, despite his weirdness.

Little is known about this first marriage; his wife, Sarah Chatterton, and their son managed to successfully disappear into obscurity. Later, Sarah would say that she feared for their son's life around Arthur. A cousin remembers once coming over to the couple's trailer and Arthur telling him, "She's resting. I just got her. If you want to go in the back and get her, you can."

In the winter of 1965, Shawcross was driving a car when a boy threw a snowball at it. He slammed on the brakes and chased the boy to his house, broke down the door and, once inside, slapped him several times. Shawcross was charged, on a technicality, with second-degree burglary. He pleaded guilty to unlawful entry and was sentenced to six months' probation and a psychiatric evaluation. His wife left him and filed for divorce. After the divorce, Shawcross never saw his child again.

In 1966, Shawcross met Linda Neary, a bartender at a local square dance hall. Neary recalls that he was very quiet, never swore and disliked crowds. He was passionate about fishing. He hated to drive. He constantly complained about his mother, telling Neary that he felt she did not love him and that no matter what he did, his mother always thought it was wrong. Neary recalls that he seemed to be obsessive about his clothes, always insisting that his work clothes were superclean and pressed. Likewise, he was very one-track-minded, never deviating from an evening's plan, for example—not even to stop for a cup of coffee.

Sex was not a problem, Neary says, because they did not have any. She did not want to unless they were married, and Shawcross did not object.

Arthur Shawcross Goes to War

In April 1967, Shawcross was drafted into the Army, and in September, after his training was completed, he and Linda Neary got married. Early in October 1967, Private Arthur John Shawcross, serial number 52967041, was shipped out to Vietnam with the Fourth Infantry Division, where he was assigned to the Fourth Supply and Transport Company at Pleiku, the center for the defense of the central highland region in Vietnam.

Like their World War II fathers, many Vietnam war vets returned from the war with psychological demons. Vietnam war trauma was different in many ways from World War II and Korean War "combat stress reaction." Vietnam was a war like no other fought by American soldiers. At the age of twenty-two, Shawcross was older than the average soldier sent to Vietnam but still young compared to the average age of twenty-six in World War II. Once sent to Vietnam, the mostly teen soldiers were expected to survive a twelve-month tour of duty (thirteen for Marines). In World War II, soldiers did their tours as a unit, supporting one another as a "family" through the required combat period from arrival to departure; in Vietnam, soldiers were shipped out by birth date, arriving on his own personal, lonely one-year schedule known as DEROS (Date Eligible for Return from Overseas). Once "in-country," a soldier checked off on a calendar every day he escaped death or horrific injury, day by day, until his scheduled date of return to "the world." The wait for the DEROS, when life would return to what it was before, often built up unrealistic expectations in the young soldiers, and as he approached the final weeks of his tour and the possibility of escaping unharmed, the mental stress often became intolerable.[48]

And there was more to it. During World War II, American troops sometimes went months between combat campaigns; in Vietnam, troops were often ferried by helicopter into combat zones every day of their tour except for short, disorientating R & R ("Rest and Recreation") breaks. In other wars, the enemy wore distinct uniforms; in Vietnam, nobody knew where and who the enemy was. During other wars, soldiers gradually adapted to a wartime environment that was remote and different from their home. In Vietnam, they were constantly catapulted back and forth between homey air-conditioned facilities with steak dinners and television and the obscenity of the battlefield, resulting in a hallucinatory existence between the illusion of being safe at home and the reality of death in the field. And in the middle of all that, there were vacation leaves in Hawaii (halfway to home), so soldiers could reunite with their wives in hotel suites before returning to the deadly jungles and the rice paddies.

Readily available marijuana, heroin, amphetamines and LSD, consumed both on the battlefield and off, further heightened the hallucinatory experience. It was a rock and roll war with all the drugs and sex that came with it.

Vietnam was unprecedented in its brutality for American troops, with children and women frequently becoming accidental, collateral or deliberate targets. As the civilian population occupied combat zones and there was no way to tell friendly Vietnamese from hostile, and because young women and children sometimes took part in combat operations against the Americans, horrific battlefield atrocities transpired.

In the past, soldiers going home from war slowly "depressurized" on long ship journeys; and, once home, they were treated as heroes and praised and rewarded for their service no matter how horrible they might have been. Even the most primitive societies held rituals for their warriors cleansing them of sins committed on the battlefield and welcoming them back to the community. In Vietnam, a soldier completed his tour of duty, crawled out of the muck of the battlefield, showered, had a cold beer and within thirty-six hours, after a flight on a plane full of strangers, was suddenly back home. Alone. There he was reviled for having fought in an "immoral" war by those who stayed at home. Instead of "talking out" the traumas of battle, the Vietnam veteran bottled them up inside of him. The good life, the hero's welcome, a return to what was before, adulation from the people at home he supposedly was defending against the evil of communism, all the things he expected, never materialized.

The end result was that some Vietnam combat veterans began to display a matrix of emotional disturbances, ranging from nightmares, depression and social withdrawal, to outright violent outbursts and vivid hallucinations. The disturbance became known as the "flashback syndrome" or PTSD—post-traumatic stress disorder—which was recognized by the American Psychiatric Association as an "official" disorder in the mid-1980s. In some instances, the hallucinations came complete with the sights, sounds and smells of combat and were so acute that Vietnam veterans injured or killed those around them in the full belief that they were still engaged in battle. Increasingly, a small minority of Vietnam vets found themselves in court after having inexplicably committed violent crimes.

On the positive side, unlike World War II veterans, the Vietnam War vet's traumas were eventually acknowledged, understood, and became part of the political-cultural discourse. Therapeutic programs were implemented, bringing veterans together to support one another in a healing process.

"Boy, Did She Quiver When I Shot Her!"
Several weeks after Arthur Shawcross left for Vietnam, his mother and wife began to receive letters from him, in which he wrote that he was "made to kill" women and children. There were also horrifically vivid descriptions of battles, which upset his mother. At the same time, Shawcross never failed to send his wife and mother cards on their birthdays or on holidays.

Much later, after he was arrested for murder, this is how Shawcross would describe his experiences in Vietnam:

> I shot one woman who was hiding some ammo in a tree. She didn't die right off. I tied her up, gagged her, then searched the area. Found the hut with another girl inside; age about 16.

Knocked her out with the butt of the gun and carried her to where the other girl was. There was a lot of rice, ammo and other stuff in the hut. I tied the young girl to a tree, still gagged, tied her legs too. They didn't say anything to me at all. I had a machete that was very sharp. I cut that first girl's throat. Then I took off her head and placed it on a pole in front of that hut. . . .

That girl at the tree peed then fainted, I stripped her then. . . . First I gave her oral sex. She couldn't understand what I was doing but her body did! I untied her, then retied her to two other small trees. . . . She fainted several times. I cut her slightly from neck to crotch. She screamed and shit herself. I took my M-16, pulled on a nipple then put the gun to her forehead and pulled the trigger. Cut off her head and placed it on a pole where they got water. . . .

That was war! . . . All and all I know for a fact, I killed 39 people in Vietnam.

When I left Vietnam, I wasn't ready for the states. I was too keyed up, too hyper! I should have stayed another six months!

I left Vietnam and flew to Japan, Alaska, Washington State, Chicago, Detroit, Syracuse. Stayed overnight. The next morning people started calling me names, babykiller, etc. If I had a gun! I was home three days before I was asked if I was going to see Linda. I said, Linda who? I had forgotten that I was married.

Shawcross returned from Vietnam in September 1968. While some veterans lapsed into brooding silence upon their homecoming, Shawcross had no problem recounting stories of his war service. Several acquaintances recalled that he literally babbled about how a baby wired up with a grenade crawled into a crowd of soldiers, blowing them up; how he would smash the gold teeth out of corpses with his rifle butt afterward stringing them together into jewelry. He relished telling a story of how one Vietnamese prostitute hid a razor in her vagina and slit open a soldier's penis "like a banana."

One cousin remembers Shawcross telling him that he shot a Vietnamese prostitute as he was climaxing. He told the story in a goofy cartoon duck voice, saying, "Boy, did she quiver when I shot her!"

Shawcross was back from Vietnam, but he remained in the Army. After a few weeks' vacation, he and Linda Neary packed their things and moved into a small apartment in Lawton, Oklahoma, where Shawcross was assigned as a weapons repair specialist at nearby Fort Sill. Neary recalls that she had to drive Arthur from Lawton to the base every day because he seemed to "be afraid to drive." She testified that Shawcross read a lot: "war stories, history, sports, but mostly science fiction."

Neary stated, "We'd had okay sex before, but now he began having problems. He would be too fast or have trouble getting an erection. It bothered him because he felt he wasn't pleasing me. I just told him to relax: 'Slow down. You're not only supposed to please me, you're supposed to please yourself.'

"After that, things improved a little. If I talked to him, calmed him, he could perform, but he still had trouble getting an orgasm. I didn't know what to do."

Neary recalled that Shawcross became sullen and brooding and spent much of his free time off by himself somewhere. He would go on three-hour walks after supper. Neary said that Arthur was tormented by his combat experiences but couldn't express his grief. He told her that as a child he was forbidden by his mother to cry; she would tell him, "You're not much of a man if you cry."

Neary said, "He wanted me to hold him all the time. He was cuddly and easy to love, but he had no idea how to give it back."

Shawcross's torment appeared to intensify. Neary testified that one night he came home from one of his walks all shaking and sweaty. He told her he had been thinking about Vietnam.

"It took a long time to get it out of him. 'I had to kill her,' he said, and he started to cry.

"I said, 'Kill who?'

"He said, 'A kid. She was carrying bombs for the Vietcong. It was kill or be killed.' He told me that the My Lai incident was nothing compared to what he'd seen. It tore him up. I figured he identified with kids because he'd been a hurt kid himself."

Linda Neary also recalled that Shawcross began to reveal to her a fascination with fire during this period. He would sit in their apartment, focused trancelike on lighting books of matches. One night he confessed that he had started a big bushfire near the barracks. He became increasingly erratic, with violent mood swings. One day, their dog nipped Shawcross on the hand. He flew into a rage and snapped the dog's neck. Afterward, Neary said that he wept over the dead dog.

Arthur Shawcross's behavior did not go unnoticed by the military. He was ordered to report to a psychiatrist but seemed to be able to avoid most of his appointments. His military career came to an end when Shawcross attempted suicide. His wife found him overdosed in the middle of the day on their bathroom floor, wearing his full dress uniform with ribbons. Army medics took him away, and shortly afterward, in March 1969, Shawcross was honorably discharged from the Army. He and Linda settled in Clayton, New York, northwest of Watertown on the St. Lawrence River, where they rented a cottage behind Linda's family's house. By now, Linda Neary was three months pregnant.

Neary would drive Shawcross to various job interviews, but he wasn't too eager to go to work. He spent most of his time drinking and fishing off a dock near the cottage. Neary said, "He chattered constantly about death and dying and body bags. I got the idea he was afraid of death, but at the same time he was attracted to death himself. It was always on his mind."

Shawcross submitted a disability claim with the Veterans Administration, reporting that he had suffered shrapnel wounds and a cut thumb in May 1968 while in Vietnam. But there were no field commendations for a Purple Heart routinely awarded for injuries in Vietnam, nor was there any mention of combat service in his record. Shawcross was eventually awarded a disability pension amounting to seventy-three dollars per month for a minor injury he sustained while on duty in the United States.

At the same time, Shawcross began to rage more and throw violent temper tantrums while his drinking became heavier. In April, he found employment in a paper mill in Watertown. Three weeks later, he received a commendation for discovering and extinguishing a fire in the plant (which he had probably set himself). Neary recalls that Shawcross "lied about everything. No subject was too small for him to lie about."

In June, after Linda Neary returned late from her parents' house to serve Shawcross his dinner, he beat her unconscious in a rage. After regaining consciousness, Neary had to drag herself to the hospital, where she miscarried. Shawcross meanwhile cut his wrists in another suicide attempt, and Neary's father and brother had to take him to the hospital for stitches. Neary was hospitalized for two weeks and afterward demanded a divorce. When Shawcross refused to vacate the cottage, Neary's father waited until he went to work and then moved all his belongings out.

Shawcross moved in with a friend in nearby La Fargeville and went on a crazed crime spree. He burglarized a gas station, burned down a barn and then set fire to a milk plant. He was arrested, charged and eventually sentenced to five years in the notorious penitentiary Attica before being transferred to Auburn Correctional Facility. In October 1969, while he was in jail awaiting trial, Neary was granted her separation and eventual divorce from Arthur.

The Child Jeffrey Dahmer: The Last of the "Golden Agers"

May 22, 1960, was when the last of the "golden age" celebrity serial killers, Jeffrey Dahmer, was born into a middle-class Milwaukee, Wisconsin, family. His father, Lionel, a professor and research chemist, was born in 1936, himself of that generation of children I describe raised in the traumatic postwar and Cold War era. Jeffrey's mother, Joyce, worked as a teletype machine instructor. Joyce's pregnancy with Jeffrey was a particularly troubled one. She experienced excessive nausea, extreme nervousness, severe depression, hypersensitivity to noises and odors, lack of sleep and uncontrollable spasms that doctors could never diagnose. Lionel would later recall:

> At the time, her legs would lock tightly in place, and her whole body would begin to tremble. Her jaw would jerk and take on a similarly frightening rigidity. During these strange

seizures, her eyes would bulge like a frightened animal, and she would begin to salivate, literally frothing at the mouth.[49]

During the last months of her pregnancy, Jeffrey's mother was taking twenty-six pills a day including drugs such as morphine, barbiturates, and phenobarbital.[50]

Jeffrey's father admits to having problematic childhood fantasies of his own. He had an obsession with fires and remembers his own fantasies of murder from the age of eight to twenty. The father wrote:

> There were areas of my son's mind, tendencies and perversities which I had held within myself all my life. Certainly, Jeff had multiplied these tendencies exponentially, his sexual perversion generating acts that were beyond my understanding and far beyond my capability. Nonetheless, I could see their distant origins within myself, and slowly, over time, I began to see him truly as my son in far deeper ways than I had previously imagined.[51]

The marriage between Jeffrey's parents was a stormy and troubled one, filled with violent arguments. His mother on one occasion threatened his father with a knife. In school, Jeffrey was a lonely child and had difficulties forming friendships with others. His mother was frequently ill, and one of his teachers at school commented that Jeffrey appeared to be suffering from neglect at home. Once, little Jeffrey formed a rare attachment to a female teacher and presented her a gift of a bowl of tadpoles. The teacher eventually gave the tadpoles to another child, and Jeffrey was so enraged that he killed them by pouring motor oil into the bowl.

Dahmer is reported to have developed a fascination with dissecting animals at around the age of ten. He would dissect animals he found and attempt to reassemble their bones. He would often use acid to strip the meat off the carcasses. He appropriated a shed at the back of their house, where he kept his dissected animal specimens preserved in jars. There are no conclusive reports, however, of Dahmer killing animals for that purpose, and some of his playmates remember Dahmer hiking or riding his bike for miles in search of roadkill to bring back to his shed.

When 1970 arrived with its surge of serial killers, Jeffrey was ten, the youngest of the breed to come.

The Nest of Baby Snakes: "Killing Became the Same Thing as Having Sex"

Through the 1950s and into the 1960s, the future epidemic serial killers were being made, shaped and tutored as children and adolescents—like a nest of squirming baby snakes. Little Ted Bundy was wondering who his wartime soldier father was and mistaking his mother for his sister while sneaking under his young aunt's bedcovers with a knife in his hand as she slept. Henry Lee Lucas was growing up in Blacksburg, Virginia, watching his alcoholic mother, Viola, having sex with other men while beating his father. When Viola discovered that little Henry loved his pet mule, she forced him to watch as she shot it dead. Little Jerry Brudos watched his mom burn a pair of patent leather high heel pumps that Jerry brought back from the dump and loved as much as Henry Lee loved his mule. Lucas would later recall, "I've killed animals to have sex with them. Dogs, I've killed them to have sex with them—always killed before I had sex. I've had sex with them while they're still alive only sometimes. Then killing became the same thing as having sex."[52] In his little corner of the world, Jerry would eventually kill women in order to collect their severed foot along with the forbidden high heel shoe he desired. On his first day of school, Viola sent Henry Lee to class dressed as a girl, with his long hair set in curls and wearing a dress. Ironically, Ottis Toole, who would partner with Lucas in their crime spree, was also dressed as a girl by his mother. Carroll Edward Cole, who murdered thirteen victims, was dressed as "Mamma's little girl" by his mother and forced to serve drinks to her guests. At least seven male serial killers, including Charles Manson, are known to have been dressed as girls in their childhood.[53]

Other killers were adopted, including Kenneth Bianchi, one of the Hillside Stranglers, who killed twelve women from 1977 to 1979; Gerald

Stano, who killed twenty-two women between 1969 and 1980; Joel Rifkin, who killed from nine to seventeen sex workers between 1989 and 1993; David Berkowitz, "the Son of Sam," who shot six victims in 1976 and 1977; Lawrence Sigmund Bittaker, one of the two "Tool Box Killers" who tortured to death five teenage girls in 1979; and Joseph Kallinger, who killed three victims in 1975. They were all adopted from who knows what kind of hell; one theory holds that, as infants in institutional settings, they were not cuddled enough to form normal bonds and developed early-onset psychopathy as a defensive response to their infantile separation from their natural mother.

That poetic geometry of twisted trauma—the victim as victimizer; the child fathering the man—would become the universal theme for serial murder. Whenever we fail to understand something about a serial killer's motives, we can quickly mop it up from his dysfunctional childhood. The theory is sometimes painfully true and sometimes not true at all. Some serial killers had relatively banal and undramatic childhoods with well-meaning, stable families, like William Heirens, described above. Richard Cottingham, "the Times Square Torso Ripper," was brought up in an apparently ideal suburban middle-class family with three younger sisters who adored him and a dog named Gypsy. Cottingham's dad, William, was a successful vice president at Metropolitan Life in Manhattan. Yet scratch deep enough, the father had a dark side too. William was a scrappy Depression-era fifteen-year-old growing up in the Bronx with five brothers when his father was killed in a car accident, leaving his wife pregnant with their seventh son and the family to fend for itself. William enlisted in the Navy with a desire to serve in the warmth of the Pacific but ended up assigned to Alaska, where, according to his son Richard, "he bit the ear off a guy to take the fight out of him" and "shot a bear and made it into a fur coat for my mother." One day, William beat up an African American man in a bar because he had the same name as he had. Serial killer Richard Cottingham was the archetypical baby boomer, born on November 25, 1946, as was Ted Bundy, born the day before. Both on the surface appeared to have "normal," abuse-free childhoods, until one gazed deeper into their pasts.

The baby-boom generation of future serial killers was a nest of two thousand sick baby snakes, drinking their fathers' traumas, their mothers' neuroses, and sucking up the culture of rape and murder sold to them at the supermarket magazine rack, on TV and movies, and getting stepped on by bullies and rapists and life itself. That's how a surge of serial killers will be formed, simple and easy. You don't need a psych degree or a complex theory to figure it out; just peruse a men's adventure or true-detective magazine from the 1960s and ask your granddad, if he's still around, what he witnessed in the "last good war."

Climate Kill

The last of our 1950s innocence, which had lingered on into the 1960s even after the Cuban Missile Crisis in 1962 scared everyone shitless, finally died on Friday afternoon, November 22, 1963, when JFK was assassinated in Dallas. Those of us who were kids back then remember faithfully tuning in the next day to see our favorite cartoon friends on Saturday morning TV and being shocked to find them all preempted by coverage of the assassination. Nothing was for sure after that. We kids withdrew to our rooms to play with our sad toys while the adults gathered around the TV in collective shock. On the third day, TV broadcast live the accused assassin being shot dead. Then they replayed it over and over in slow motion. If the Cold War cartoon character Bert the Turtle warning us kids to "duck and cover" when the bomb fell hadn't gotten to us, then after the Kennedy assassination, the world definitely became spooky and twisted forever. The death of JFK defined for my generation the halfway point between Pearl Harbor and 9/11—when bad things stopped happening "over there" and began to occur "over here."

The crime statistics may indicate something else, but that is when it really started to *feel* bad and out of control: in November 1963. It was precisely around that time, on the second day after the assassination, that the Boston Strangler was raping and killing the twelfth victim of his eventual thirteen, a twenty-three-year-old Sunday school teacher. Twelve is a lot even by today's standards—academics studying serial homicide describe it as an "extreme" case: more than eight. (How did they come up with that number—why not seven or nine?)

The Boston Strangler stood out, as the press maintained a "score-keeping body count" of his murders, one by one, as they occurred—or allegedly occurred. There are reasons to believe that Albert DeSalvo did not commit all thirteen murders that he confessed to—if any. In fact, DeSalvo pleaded guilty to assault and armed robbery of four women in 1967, and his attorney F. Lee Bailey claimed his murder confession was entered into the record to support an insanity plea. Instead, DeSalvo was sentenced to life in prison without ever standing trial for a single murder.

Susan Kelly, in her book *The Boston Stranglers: The Public Conviction of Albert DeSalvo and the True Story of Eleven Shocking Murders*, and other critics, including Robert Ressler and John Douglas, argue persuasively that many of the Boston murders did not fit DeSalvo's profile, or the profile of any single murderer, including DeSalvo's last claimed murder of nineteen-year-old Mary Sullivan on January 4, 1964.

For decades, none of the Boston Strangler murders had been conclusively confirmed as DeSalvo's, until 2013. Boston, Suffolk County, and Massachusetts State law enforcement officials jointly announced that DNA testing confirmed that Albert DeSalvo was the source of seminal fluid recovered at the scene of Mary Sullivan's murder, the last in the canonical series of thirteen murders attributed to Albert DeSalvo.

While we were conscious of the Boston Strangler case as it was happening, at the end it melted away into the fog of the inclusive legal maneuvering behind DeSalvo's 1967 plea. And by then we were in a whirlpool of all kinds of new killers.

The times that followed the Boston Strangler and JFK assassination became unusually hyperviolent. People were being killed everywhere: in their homes, in church, at work, in the streets, in parks and schoolyards, overseas at war in rice paddies, in Third World missions, on college campuses at home, in Cotton Belt bayous, in shopping centers, in riots and cult killings. It was confusing. It was coming to and from all over, and out of it throughout the 1960s would spring forth an occasional new monstrous episode of murder and terror that captured people's paranoid imaginations as to how bad things can go.

In 1964, twenty-eight-year-old Kitty Genovese, a bar manager, was stabbed to death in the entryway of her apartment building in Kew Gardens, Queens, a relatively safe New York neighborhood. The story that was told by the newspapers was that thirty-eight witnesses heard Kitty screaming for help and none called the police, let alone intervened to help her, as the killer returned three times to continue stabbing her. One witness was described as raising the volume on his radio to drown out the sound of the girl's screaming. It would even become a theme in psychology textbooks and spawned a number of experiments and hypotheses on "bystander apathy."[54]

As a kid growing up in Toronto, Canada, in the 1960s, I was well versed in the Kitty Genovese case, and around the age of thirteen, my friend from across the street and I conducted our own psychological experiments on bystander apathy, covering ourselves in ketchup and staging assaults on each other in front of people passing in the street. Very few intervened. But that was a 1960s Toronto thing, an austerely inhibited Protestant city in those days. New York was nothing like that, and the Kitty Genovese story was bullshit. In fact, on my first day in New York in the 1970s, when I carelessly parked in the Bowery, people chased me down two blocks to tell me my car was being towed. Nobody would do that for you in my safe but coldhearted hometown, Toronto, even today. When Kitty Genovese was attacked, people did call the police, and some shouted at the perpetrator to leave the girl alone, and as the ambulance was coming, they cradled and comforted her as she bled to death, but we did not learn that until the 2000s.[55] Kitty Genovese was an urban myth spawned by bad reporting in the *New York Times* (according to the *New York Times* itself, reporting decades later).[56]

The Kitty Genovese story became a double parable in the early sixties: first, warning young single women that they are not safe alone and should stay close to home, and second, that nobody will "get involved" if something happens to them in the new apathy and anonymity of big urban life. Genovese was particularly pretty in that doe-eyed Audrey Hepburn way, and the press made sure to make no mention that she was apparently gay.[57] Who'd care to get involved if they knew *that*? was the thinking then. The stories focused on Kitty coming home alone late at night in a safe neighborhood and that she was murdered by a marauding African American male perpetrator from a "bad" neighborhood.

Then, in the summer of 1966, it was reported that in Chicago, an alcoholic pillhead skid row drifter, twenty-four year-old Richard Speck, killed eight student nurses in an amphetamine-fueled night of binding, strangling and stabbing.

Three weeks later, twenty-five-year-old Charles Whitman, an ex-Marine mechanical engineering student in Austin, Texas, stabbed his wife and mother to death in their homes, then climbed the University of Texas clock tower with a high-powered rifle and gunned down forty-five people, killing twelve victims on the campus and streets below (including an unborn child whose mother survived and a man who died in 2001 of long-term complications as a result of his wounds) and three victims in the tower observation deck.

Then Martin Luther King Jr. and Robert F. Kennedy were assassinated months apart in 1968, with more race riots in between.

And when our boys came home from My Lai as accused baby killers and pregnant actress Sharon Tate and her houseguests were hacked to death in her home in the Hollywood Hills by a howling tribe of Charlie Manson's apocalypse cult hippies, all the groovy summer of love flower power sixties choked in its own blood, in both the literal and the metaphorical senses.

After that, we could not imagine it getting any worse.

But it was already worse than we imagined.

We just did not quite pick out the serial killers around us from all the reports of other threats coming at us from all those directions and places.

The real story was that Kitty Genovese had been murdered by a necrophile serial killer, Winston Moseley, who had killed at least two other women in New York, but somehow the press did not latch on to this. Newspapers casually and skeptically reported that Moseley had confessed to two other murders. Moseley was married and had two children; his wife later said he just sat around staring off into space. Speaking for himself, Moseley said he just had an "urge to kill." (He died in prison in 2016.)

There was Jerome Henry "Jerry" Brudos, "the Shoe Fetish Murderer," a serial killer necrophile who murdered four women in Oregon between 1968 and 1969—a case I describe in detail in *Serial Killers: The Method and Madness of Monsters*. Brudos was Harvey Glatman and Ed Gein combined, except that like Moseley, he too was married and had two children. In the spring of 1969, when Brudos was arrested, the media did not report the horrific extent of his violence, in the way that newspapers did a decade earlier in the cases of Glatman and Gein. Brudos quickly pleaded guilty without a trial and was sentenced to life imprisonment and was soon forgotten. It was later that Ann Rule dug into the details of his case for her second true-crime book, *Lust Killer* (1983). In it she recounted the details of Brudos's fetish for female apparel going back to his childhood and described how he went over the edge in 1968 and began abducting women from the street or from his front door (an encyclopedia saleswoman) and strangling them, dressing up their bodies in his favorite items of clothing from his collection, photographing them and having sex with them before harvesting body parts like their feet and breasts. Brudos attempted to animate one corpse with jolts of electricity, he explained to police puzzled by two strange postmortem burn marks on each side of a victim's rib cage.

There were the six Ypsilanti Ripper or Michigan Murders of young women in Ann Arbor and Ypsilanti between 1967 and 1969. The female victims, who ranged from thirteen to twenty-one, were abducted, beaten, raped and murdered by stabbing or strangulation, and some mutilated. Eventually, twenty-two-year-old John Norman Collins was charged in one of the murders and convicted. Authorities were confident that he killed the other five victims (and one in California on a trip he took there). With only one conviction, he is not "officially" a serial killer, and to this day Collins claims innocence. He remains incarcerated in the Marquette Branch Prison in Michigan.

The Cincinnati Strangler raped and strangled seven mostly elderly women in Ohio between 1965 and 1966. Cabdriver Posteal Laskey Jr.

was charged in one of the murders in 1967 and convicted, and the murders stopped after that. Laskey died in prison in 2007.

And of course, always on the list of the most notorious unidentified serial killers, the Zodiac Killer murdered his five confirmed victims between December 1968 and October 1969.

Many other cases just slipped by without a lot of press, like Antone Charles "Tony" Costa, a carpenter accused of murdering and dismembering eight women in Massachusetts in 1968 and 1969; he was convicted and sentenced to life imprisonment in only two of the murders in May 1970 and hanged himself in his cell in 1974.

Lee Roy Martin in Gaffney, South Carolina, a thirty-year-old married textile mill worker with three children, was charged and convicted in 1969 in four strangulation murders of women in 1967 and 1968.

Some "epidemic" killers, like Ed Kemper, who began his killing precociously early in the 1960s, were interrupted by incarceration and then restarted their serial murders in the 1970s. Vaughn Orrin Greenwood, "the Skid Row Slasher" in Los Angeles, for example, killed two victims in 1964, spent six years in prison for an assault, and then killed nine more victims in 1974 and 1975. Kenneth McDuff, "the Broomstick Killer," abducted and murdered three victims, raping and strangling one with a broomstick forced across her throat, in 1966. He was sentenced to death, then had his sentence commuted and eventually was paroled in 1989 and went on to rape and kill an additional six women from 1989 to 1992. He was suspected in a total of fourteen murders.

Others began their killing in the 1960s but were not detected or apprehended until the 1970s, like Patrick Wayne Kearney, "the Freeway Killer" or "Trash Bag Killer," who between 1965 and 1977 was confirmed to have murdered twenty-one male victims, and was suspected in a total of forty-three murders. Kearney was a necrophile who would target young gay men hitchhiking or in gay clubs. As he drove his car with his left hand, he would use his right to shoot his victims in the passenger seat with a .22 derringer and then have sex with their corpses. Afterward, he would dismember the bodies and dump the pieces in industrial garbage bags.

Between 1963 and 1978, Rudy Bladel, a disgruntled, laid-off railway worker, ambushed and shot seven railway employees before he was indicted in 1979 for a triple murder of railway workers in a railway station in Jackson, Michigan, on December 31, 1978.

Richard Cottingham, "The Times Square Torso Ripper" or "The Times Square Torso Killer," 1967–1980

And then there was "my serial killer." This is the serial killer that started me writing about serial killers after my brief encounter with him on December 2, 1979, as he was fleeing the scene of a double murder. He had decapitated two female victims, severed their hands, set their mutilated torsos on fire and fled with their heads and hands in a valise. As he exited the elevator in the lobby, I entered it to go upstairs and we ended up bumping into each other, an encounter I described many times in detail in my previous books. The murders became known as the Times Square Torso Murders.

Richard Francis Cottingham, thirty-three years old, was arrested in May 1980. He was a computer console operator at an insurance company in New York and commuted daily from his home in New Jersey, where he lived with his wife and three children. He was eventually convicted in five murders in New Jersey and New York between 1977 and 1980, including the infamous torso killings. What nobody knew at the time was that Cottingham had started killing much earlier than 1977: at least since 1967, and I suspect perhaps as early as 1963 in his junior year of high school. Most people have not heard of Cottingham because he never gave any interviews and his victim count—five—wasn't spectacular enough to attract attention in the 1970s, when the "average" was eight or nine victims per serial killer.

In 2009, after thirty years of silence, Cottingham gave his first interview, telling Canadian journalist Nadia Fezzani that he had committed at least eighty to a hundred "perfect murders" of women in various regions of the United States. They were "perfect" because he was never linked to them.[58]

At first, nobody took Cottingham's claim seriously, but in 2010, he confessed and pleaded guilty to the murder of Nancy Vogel, the twenty-nine-year-old mother of two children whom he had killed in 1967—ten years before the known 1977 to 1980 series. This raised his total to six confirmed victims in thirteen years and suddenly extended his killing period by ten more years. In order to kill one hundred victims in that length of time, Cottingham would have had to kill one victim almost every seven weeks. An entirely plausible scenario, especially in the 1960s and 1970s when police were uneducated and naive in linking serial homicides.

Cottingham claims he methodically and intentionally "switched up" his MO, its geographical clustering and victimology. Throughout the 1960s and 1970s, Cottingham killed schoolgirls as young as thirteen, teenage street sex workers, a twenty-two-year-old upscale escort and every kind of woman in between, including the twenty-nine-year-old mother and homemaker Vogel and a twenty-seven-year-old X-ray technician. He alternately battered, strangled, asphyxiated, drowned and stabbed his victims. He transported the bodies of some victims to other locations where he would dump them, while others he left where he killed them. He left bodies outdoors, in victims' own cars, by roadsides, in parking lots, floating in rivers, or inside New Jersey motels and New York hotels. He decapitated at least two of his victims whose heads were never found and cut the breasts off a third. He set mattress fires under three of his victims' mutilated bodies. Some he handcuffed and gagged, tortured and raped, beat, burned with cigarettes; others he did not. He was unusually versatile and rapacious, and the various police jurisdictions in New Jersey and New York, and newspapers that rarely fail to jump to conclusions, mostly failed to link the string of murders to a single perpetrator. Of course, this was a time before profiling, before the term "serial killer" was even introduced into our vocabulary; we lacked the understanding that serial killers almost *always* change their MO because that's how they get to be serial. As in any successful undertaking, serial killing is a learning experience combined with dumb luck.

In 2018, I was contacted by Jennifer Weiss, the daughter of one of Cottingham's victims. She had been given up for adoption a year before the murder and beheading of her biological mother, sex worker Deedeh Goodarzi. Jennifer had been visiting Cottingham in prison in an attempt to get him to reveal where he'd put her mother's head. She was finding it challenging to assemble a coherent geographical and chronological narrative from what Cottingham was telling her. At her behest, Cottingham agreed to meet with me for a series of one-on-one prison interviews about his life and crimes that are still actively ongoing as I write this.

On December 30, 2019, I announced in a community meeting organized by a local citizen John Bandstra in Midland Park, New Jersey, that Richard Cottingham had confessed to police that he had committed three unsolved murders from fifty years ago and that the cold cases were now "exceptionally" closed:

- Jacalyn (Jackie) Harp, thirteen, who was randomly ambushed by Cottingham as she was walking home from a drum and bugle corps practice in Midland Park and strangled with the leather strap of her flag sling on July 17, 1968;

- Irene Blase, eighteen, who vanished on April 7, 1969, while shopping in Hackensack, and was found facedown in four feet of water in Saddle River, strangled with a wire, cord or perhaps the chain of a crucifix she was wearing, and stabbed once in the back;

- Denise Falasca, fifteen, abducted July 14, 1969, in Emerson/Westwood while walking to a friend's home and found the next morning in Saddle Brook by the side of a road next to a cemetery, strangled with a cord or the chain of her crucifix.

Robert Anzilloti, a detective and now chief of investigators in the Bergen County Prosecutor's Office, has been doggedly working the Cottingham cases since 2004 and elicited the three formal confessions in the cold case murders during his interviews with him, without the benefit of DNA evidence, which would not have been collected or preserved in the 1960s.

Midland Park, where Jackie Harp was murdered, was and still is a small, idyllic town north of Paterson, New Jersey. Jackie had gone to an evening practice of her drum and bugle corps—the Midland Park Imperial Knights—at the town's athletic field. In 1968, small towns like that were still considered safe from the crime and violence that afflicted big cities, but several parents offered her a lift home. She declined. All the kids were out and about on that warm summer evening, hanging out at the root beer joint on the main street, going on dates, visiting one another, buying ice cream, watching firemen putting out a practice fire and fishing in the creek that ran through town (near where Jackie's body would be found the next morning). Later, police pieced together her route, as she stopped and chatted with friends she encountered on her walk home. It was an enchanted midsummer's night in July, a gathering of innocent lambs when a wolf slipped in among them and killed Jackie as she strolled away from the gathered flock.

The kids of 1968 are Midland Park's elderly residents today, still haunted and traumatized more than fifty years later. Some of the girls who had been at practice that evening with her wondered for the rest of their lives how close they had come to sharing her fate. It was one of those "when people started locking their doors" and "keeping kids at home" moments for Midland Park.

And worse. For fifty years, accusations were directed at some boys in town, that they had gang-raped and strangled Jackie. (She had been sexually assaulted but not raped.) Those teenage boys are now in their sixties and seventies and have lived their entire lives under suspicion, fingers pointed at them and tongues wagging for fifty years.

These three murders were among the some fifty-eight unsolved sexual murders of teenage girls and women in New Jersey between 1963 and 1980; I've methodically cataloged and mapped them on my website www.newjerseygirlmurders.com in an attempt to determine which ones might belong to the "perfect murders" Cottingham claims he committed before he was apprehended literally "red-handed," torturing a teenage sex worker in a New Jersey motel where he had previously killed at least two other women. Cottingham commuted daily between New York and New Jersey, sometimes taking victims across the state line. He had uncles who lived in Long Island, New York. He was an avid gambler and occasionally flew to Las Vegas before gambling was legalized in

Atlantic City in 1978, and on occasion he drove to Florida through multiple states to visit his retired parents there. Pennsylvania was just across the state line from New Jersey. In the string of murders we know for sure he committed between 1967 and 1980, not once did Cottingham come to police attention as a suspect or was he connected by police in any way to any of the victims at the time of their murders. He remained entirely invisible for at least thirteen years until the day of his sudden arrest in May 1980, when his victim's desperate screams brought police to his motel room door. Today, cold case investigators in New Jersey and New York are sifting through two decades of unsolved sexual murders that might belong to Cottingham.

Cottingham is perhaps one of the more prolific serial killers in American history, and the one who succeeded killing the longest completely undetected and unconnected, not even as an anonymous "unsub"—unknown subject—in FBI profiler parlance. Of course, in the 1960s when he started and the 1970s when he wildly escalated, the FBI was not in the serial killer profiling business. Nobody was.

Even though Cottingham has been locked up for the last forty years, another part of him is still out there doing his control thing in the form of what he calls his "perfect murders"—the unseen and unsolved murders that have left open wounds among the living. These are the ones he was never linked to, the ones that cops don't "like him for." Or the murders that nobody even knew had happened, the ones hidden among the thousands of teenage girls and young women who simply vanished over the two decades. Or the thousands found by the side of the interstates from New Jersey all the way down to Tampa, Florida, dumped in bushy ravines or in shallow graves or floating in rivers, who were never identified, let alone the cause of death determined. Nobody even knows if anybody knows they are missing; the so-called missing missing.

The fifty-eight I counted are only the ones we knew happened in New Jersey. I rejoice that I can take three names off that list, Jackie Harp, Irene Blase and Denise Falasca, but there are so many more to go.

As I continue meeting with and questioning Cottingham, as I identify new victims that were never linked to him, I realize that "my serial killer" also comes with "my victims." Cold case investigations are excruciatingly difficult to describe let alone solve; it's like trying to catch up to the source of the distant light from a long-dead star. Evidence has been lost or expired, witnesses are mostly dead and gone and sometimes even the perpetrator is dead—but the pain just keeps shining on forever across the span of light-years. Cold case cops often talk of "truth" and "resolution" as opposed to "justice" and "closure." For families, there is *never* closure, only resolution at best. I have no idea if I am in the middle or at the end of this unfolding story, and sometimes in the middle of the night I suddenly awake in fear that perhaps I am only at its beginning.

The Planting Season, 1950–1969

From 1950 to 1969, some 225 serial killers appeared in the United States, but at the time, we were aware of only a handful, like Ed Gein, Harvey Glatman, Albert DeSalvo or Jerry Brudos.[59] Charles Manson was in a cult category of his own. None of them were called serial killers, and they were not recognized as belonging to a particular species or category of killer, although various terms had been suggested, like "multiple murderers," "pattern killers," "mass killers," "thrill killers," "recreational murderers" and "stranger-on-stranger murderers." None of these labels stuck because they could never quite fit case to case, and because nobody offered any kind of better definition of what they were. Each serial killer remained an individual "stand-alone" enigma—a monster all by himself. Amid the pervasive violence of the late 1960s, we were hardly aware of them and could not imagine anything worse than what we were already experiencing. But things were about to get worse.

As the decade closed, on December 18, 1969, Clarnell's boy, Edmund Kemper, turned twenty-one and was released from Atascadero, certified cured of whatever compulsions had driven him to kill his grandparents. Later, Kemper would recall that in Atascadero, "I found out that I really killed my grandmother because I wanted to kill my mother." Maybe that's true, or maybe that's Kemper's wishful thinking with hindsight. Six young women were going to be murdered before Kemper was ready to do what he says he found out he really wanted to do.

Two weeks after Kemper's release, the 1970s began.

CHAPTER 5

The Big Surge:
The Baby Boomer Serial Killers Come of Age
1970–1979

We serial killers are your sons,
we are your husbands,
we are everywhere.

Ted Bundy

In the next ten years during the 1970s, 605 serial killers were going to be identified, twice the number of the previous twenty years. In the 1980s, there would be 768 more, and in the 1990s, 669 more. A total of 2,042 new serial killers appeared in a thirty-year "epidemic" period: 88 percent of known American serial killers in the twentieth century. It would take a 2,042-page book to briefly summarize each case on a single page. It is beyond my scope here to even summarize some of the more "prominent" cases of the decade in the way I have been able to do so far for the 1930s to 1960s. How and when did it all go so virally epidemic?

When the steadily rising wave of serial killers finally crested, it came crashing in with a case that had a spectacularly unprecedented number of victims. There had been nothing like it in America since 1927, when the serial killing necrophile Earle Nelson, "the Dark Strangler" or "the Gorilla Man," was apprehended after murdering and raping twenty-two to twenty-five female victims in a two-year migratory murder trek across the United States and into Canada.*

---

*There were female serial killers with comparable victim numbers like Jane Toppan, "Jolly Jane," who had killed at least thirty-one victims in Massachusetts between 1895 and 1901. Clementine Barnabet, an eighteen-year-old African American woman, participated in thirty-five cult axe murders in Texas and Louisiana, wiping out entire families in 1911. H. H. Holmes in Chicago, in 1894 it was falsely reported in the news-

Juan Corona, "The Yuba City Peach Orchard Killer," Yuba City, California, 1971

On May 19, 1971, a peach farmer near Yuba City, California, led a Sutter County deputy sheriff to a large, mysterious filled-in hole on his orchard. Over the next few days, police would dig up an extraordinary twenty-four corpses, stabbed and hacked across their skulls with a machete, and a twenty-fifth with a gunshot wound. The case was very quickly closed within a week with the arrest of thirty-seven-year-old Juan Corona, a Mexican farm labor contractor in Northern California who had been providing laborers to the peach farmer. Witness statements and pocket litter recovered from the bodies linked Corona to the victims. If there was a "ground zero" in the "serial killer epidemic" to come, then Juan Corona fits the bill (with unfortunate irony these days).

Twenty-five was an astounding number of murders. It was immediately clear that they were not all killed at once. They were mostly killed one by one but in a short period of time from February to May 1971. Today we might describe Corona as a "spree serial killer" murdering in separate incidents but with an unusual rapidity, perhaps without a "cooling off" period between each murder, like, for example, Andrew Cunanan or the "DC Beltway Snipers," John Allen Muhammad and Lee Boyd Malvo.

The Corona story was shocking and perplexing for people in 1971. The enormity of that many murders. Unheard of. People asked naively if he killed them one by one; had nobody noticed when it was happening? Were they all buried in the same place? What do we call this kind of monstrosity? If he didn't kill them all at once, it's not "mass murder." This was something new, even if it really wasn't.

But once the body count was settled at twenty-five, we very quickly lost interest in the Juan Corona murders, and like the Kitty Genovese murder, there was a kind of spin and turn this story took in its parable telling. Firstly, the basic assumption was that the victims were Mexican

---

papers, killed twenty-seven victims but was conclusively confirmed to have murdered only four.

immigrant farm laborers—some perhaps even illegal. That immediately put a damper on any interest the newspaper-reading and TV-watching public might have had. Obviously. The victims were actually all white except for two: an African American and a Native American. None were Mexican.[1] They were mostly middle-aged—the youngest was forty, the oldest sixty-seven. Twenty-one victims were successfully identified. They were the last of the Depression-era generation of rail-riding migrant working tramps—"boomer hobos"—some coming annually like migratory birds all the way from northern states to work the California harvests. But had that been known, it wouldn't have changed anything as far as the general public was concerned; among "respectable" Americans, these tramps would have been as less-dead as Mexican migrants.

But there was even more to it.

"Homosexual Overkill"

It was alleged that a victim was found with gay pornography in his pocket, and the sheriff's office reported that some of the victims had their pants pulled down to their ankles or zipped open with their genitals exposed.[2] The victims appeared mostly to have been killed by one or two stab wounds, but their heads, throats and chests were subjected to multiple machete blows beyond what was needed to kill them. Excessive mutilation or multiple stabbing or repeated shooting is referred to by police as "overkill," and police considered it a frequent characteristic of gay interpersonal murders.[3]

Even today in policing, gay serial murder is categorized in its special deviant place, with overkill claimed as a "typical" characteristic of gay murder, serial or otherwise. As former NYPD homicide detective Vernon Geberth wrote in his often-used procedural textbook, *Practical Homicide Investigation* (now in its fifth edition published in 2015):

> It has been my experience that male homosexual homicides involving interpersonal violence often present patterns of injuries that can best be described as overkill. These injuries are often directed to the throat, chest, and abdomen of the victims. It has been suggested, but not empirically proven, that the as-

sault to the throat takes place because of the sexual significance of the mouth and throat in male homosexual "love-making." . . . The psychological significance in an attack to the throat in male homosexual homicides manifest the destruction of this "substitute sex organ" which engulfs the penis. Anal intercourse is often thought to be the most prevalent sexual behavior between men. However [a 1978 study] found that fellatio was the most common mode of sexual expression.[4]

The Sutter County Sheriff's Office treated the Yuba City murders as sex crimes, as psycho-homosexual murders. Juan Corona fit the bill perfectly because he had a history of both mental illness and issues with gays, including his own brother José Natividad Corona, who was gay. That would suit Corona's defense too, who pointed out that Juan was married and had four children and accused his gay brother, Natividad, as the "obvious" suspect for these pathologically homosexual murders.

Mex-Cal Border Story, 1940s–1960s

Juan Corona was born in 1934 in the Jalisco-Guadalajara region of Western Mexico.

His brother Natividad arrived in the United States in 1944 as a legal immigrant and settled in Marysville, across the Feather River from Yuba City. Juan entered the US legally in May 1953 to join Natividad and two other brothers as well in the Yuba-Marysville area. In December 1955, the region was hit by a catastrophic flood that killed over seventy people. Juan worked recovering and burying some of the dead and apparently became unbalanced, convinced that some type of apocalypse had killed everybody. Natividad had Juan committed to a psychiatric facility where he was diagnosed as suffering from "schizophrenic reaction, paranoid type" and given a series of twenty-four electroconvulsive treatments and then promptly deported back to Mexico.

Schizophrenic is often mistaken for the term "schizoid split personality." Schizophrenia is a debilitating organic mental illness that can be accompanied by paranoid delusions, hallucinations and other forms of disordered thought and perception. Sometimes its symptoms can come and go episodically. Schizophrenics are more frequently a danger to themselves rather than to other people.

Juan Corona's schizophrenic episode and deportation did not stop him from returning to the United States in 1962 with a green card. No further trouble was reported. He married, had four daughters and established a relatively successful and lucrative farm labor contracting business. He had no problem getting a bank mortgage in 1968 to purchase a family home in Yuba City, and most people did not think there was anything odd about him. While his workers complained that Corona didn't pay enough, about the cleanliness of his work camps and the condition of the big yellow school bus he transported them in, nobody accused him of mistreating or cheating his workers.[5]

There was one murky incident in 1970, however, when twenty-one-year-old José Romero Raya was found unconscious in a washroom in a tavern in Marysville owned by Juan's brother Natividad. Raya had been molested and disfigured by several machete wounds to his face and skull, similar to the ones that would be found later on the peach orchard bodies. Raya survived and successfully sued Natividad for $250,000 in personal injury and punitive damages as the owner of the premises, but Natividad himself was never charged criminally in the assault. Who committed the assault remained a mystery. There was gossip that Natividad had been covering up for his episodically schizophrenic younger brother, Juan. In any case, Natividad fled to Mexico after the judgment had been entered against him and died there in 1973 in the midst of the case, making it even more convenient for the defense to claim he was the real murderer of the twenty-five victims.

Corona offered little to no explanation as to where he had been when confronted in the courtroom with the chronology of the twenty-five murders. He was convicted on January 18, 1973, in all twenty-five murders and sentenced to life. His defense was so flawed that Corona was given a second trial but convicted again. Sutter County prosecutors believed that Corona had killed at least forty-three victims in total, some in other, surrounding counties, but stated that authorities there refused to cooperate because they did not want the "road show" in their jurisdiction.

Juan Corona died in prison at the age of eighty-five on March 4, 2019, without us ever coming to fully understand why he killed all those men, other than in madness.

Dean Corll, "The Candy Man," Houston, Texas, 1970–1973

No sooner had the public gotten their heads around the twenty-five Juan Corona murders than news broke in August 1973 of twenty-seven murders in Houston, Texas. The case was bizarre even by today's standards. Again, police were completely unaware that a serial killer had been on the loose for several years until they received a phone call from seventeen-year-old Elmer Wayne Henley Jr., reporting that he had just shot and killed thirty-three-year-old Dean Corll, a former vice president of a recently defunct family candy company, Corll Candies.

When police arrived, they found Corll curled up naked on the floor of his bungalow with six gunshot wounds. Wayne confessed that he and another boy, eighteen-year-old David Owen Brooks, had been helping Corll lure and abduct male youths who Corll would horrifically torture for days, rape and kill. He showed police an eight-by-two-foot plywood "torture board" with holes drilled into it to pass through chains and ligatures and a toolbox filled with torture implements and dildos. Wayne stated he would collect between $10 and $200 for each boy he brought to Corll, as did his friend Brooks. Wayne admitted to also participating in the abduction and killing of some of the boys and burying them and led police to a series of locations where within the week an astonishing twenty-seven bodies were unearthed of teenage boys and youths between the ages of thirteen and twenty, many of them neighborhood acquaintances and friends of Brooks and Henley.

The Houston Mass Murders, as it came to be known, with its twenty-seven victims, topped in numbers the Juan Corona and the Earle Nelson murders. It was now the largest number of confirmed victims in a serial killing case in recent modern American history. Again, the public was at first astonished as to how twenty-seven teenage boys, some as young as thirteen, could vanish in a community over a short period of several years without anybody raising the alarm. In fact, people had been look-ing for their missing sons and begging Houston Police to investigate their disappearances but were being ignored.

The Candy Factory and the Lost Boys of Houston Heights

Twenty of the disappearances occurred in Houston Heights, where the small Corll family candy factory was located and where Dean Corll lived and worked, or in the adjacent neighborhood. Eleven of the missing boys attended the same junior high school.[6]

The Heights was described at the time as Houston's "cast off com-munity."[7] Once a vibrant turn-of-the-century "streetcar suburb," it had declined significantly after World War II and by the 1970s was on the brink of becoming a slum. It was inhabited by mostly poor white, dis-possessed, often broken and dysfunctional families struggling to sur-vive in a transitioning economy, whose teenage sons began mysteriously disappearing in the 1970s, one by one. When families turned to the Houston Police for help, they were told, "we don't search for runaways." Since the 1950s when Houston had the highest murder rate in the United States, it had been nicknamed "Murder City," and the under-staffed Houston PD was very selective as to what murders they would allocate resources to investigate, let alone search for missing youths. Murders of less-dead African Americans or poor white trash victims were referred to inside the Houston PD as "misdemeanor murders," and very little effort was put into investigating these deaths. As for missing teenagers in the Heights, or anywhere in the United States for that mat-ter, male or female, they were not investigated unless there was conclu-sive evidence that an abduction had occurred. The vanishing teenage boys, some of them troubled, some deeply into drinking, smoking weed and huffing paint thinner, some with juvenile records, were automati-cally written off by police as "good riddance" runaways.[8]

Dean Corll was well-known in the Heights. Corll's Candy Kitchen once stood at 505 West 22nd Street behind the schoolyard of James F. Helms Elementary School. They produced divinity, pralines, pecan chewy and other types of candy popularly branded as "Mexican Candy." Some of the parents in the Heights would occasionally work in the candy factory as did their teenage sons. Dean Corll was known to frequently hand out free broken trims and leftovers from the candy production line to eager children who would flock to the factory facing the rear schoolyard. Rather than shooing them away, Corll installed a pool table in the back and invited the boys to come in and play. A few parents forbade their children to hang out at the candy factory, but most had no problem with it. Corll appeared to be an even-tempered, polite and well-spoken young Texan gentleman. Nothing about him was threatening.

One of the mothers who occasionally worked in the factory and whose sixteen-year-old son Gregory Malley Winkle would be identified among the twenty-seven unearthed bodies said of Corll:

> He was crazy about children; he'd let them walk all over him. Every afternoon that doorbell would ring and there'd be a gang of little kids from the Helms grammar school, beggin' for broken candy. Then Dean put a pool table in the back and the boys used to knock at all hours. "Can we play pool?" When I found out Malley was goin' there after work, I told him to cut it out. Not that I had any feelin' that Dean was doing wrong. I just felt that he shouldn't be disturbed. He worked awfully hard and I respected the man for it. . . .
>
> He was like a man that had nothin' on his mind but success. The lights were on many a night, all night. I got to feelin' sorry for him, that the job was too much for a poor kid like him maybe in his mid-twenties. His mother seemed to be involved in the business, but she really wasn't much help. . . . She'd want to know why he hadn't done this or done that.[9]

Dean became known to hundreds of elementary school kids growing up in the Heights as the Candy Man.

Dean Arnold Corll was born in 1939. His father, it was reported, had been strict, but his mother, Mary, lax and indulgent with her son according to some, overbearing and domineering according to others. She eventually divorced her husband, but then several years later remarried him, then divorced him again. She entered the candy-making business with a new husband but later divorced him and set up her own business in the early 1960s, Corll Candies, in which Dean became a vice president and his younger brother the secretary-treasurer. Dean grew up putting in long hours in the candy company and was its operational manager.

In 1964, twenty-four-year-old Dean was drafted into the US Army but after serving ten months was given an early "hardship" honorable discharge on the grounds his family's business needed him. His military record was apparently unblemished. Acquaintances of Dean would later state that he had realized that he was gay while serving in the Army and that his behavior changed upon returning home.

After Dean's return from military service, there had been complaints from some of the teenage male employees that Dean had attempted to molest them, but Mary responded by firing anybody who complained. Soon the complaints stopped.

The candy factory was liquidated in 1968 when Mary retired. Dean Corll took a job as a circuit board tester with the Houston Lighting and Power Company and eventually moved an hour away to the suburb of Pasadena, Texas, near the Gulf shore. But the Candy Man, a familiar figure to teenagers since their childhoods in elementary school, frequently visited the Heights driving a Plymouth GTX muscle car or a white van, inviting random teens to attend wild parties at his place, where fireworks, alcohol, solvents and weed were freely available.

Corll snared youths who passed out at his parties. They would regain consciousness finding themselves facedown and naked, shackled spread-eagle to his plywood torture board. Corll would torment and rape them sometimes for days in a sadistic frenzy. One of his favorite methods of torture was to take a thin glass tube and force it up the urethra of his bound victim's penis and shatter the glass with a fist-tight squeeze. Corll might have been inspired by James A. Michener's 1957 bestselling Cold War polemic, *The Bridge at Andau*, in which he described the Hungarian secret police using this torture method during the 1956 revolt.

The Bridge at Andau was a staple in public school libraries for decades, where with squeamish horror that lingers to this day, I read about the torture in my school library when I was eleven years old. I too am a juvenile product of the rape-and-kill-crazy culture of the 1950s and 1960s, not quite damaged enough to have become a serial killer myself, but by the age of eleven exposed and deadened to literary accounts and pulp adventure magazine and true-detective illustrations of torture, rape and murder to be able to contemplate and write about serial killing as an adult historian without waking in the middle of the night gasping for air from nightmares.

Afterward, Corll either strangled his victims or shot them in the head with a .22 handgun. Others he lured into his van, in which he installed a soundproofed wooden box fitted out with restraining hooks. The bodies of the victims were all buried either on remote Texas beaches, in woodlands or under a boat storage shed Corll had rented.

The Disciples

David Brooks, a longtime neighborhood acquaintance of Henley's, had been groomed by Corll in the candy factory since the age of twelve. He eventually began engaging in sex with Corll, was introduced to the abductions and killings, and was given a 1969 Corvette as a present and was paid for every victim he procured for Corll. Brooks had originally brought his friend Henley to Corll to sell as a potential victim, but for some reason Corll took a liking to Henley and, instead of raping and killing him, adopted him as a disciple too. In a 2010 prison interview, Henley would say, "Maybe Dean was considering me as one of his next victims. But we hit it off. He was this smart, clean-cut, nicely dressed man. He listened to me. He explained things to me.

"I'll be honest with you, it was important that Dean liked me. He was kind."[10]

Wayne Henley was also plied by Corll with lavish gifts of drink and drugs and cash payments for any boys he would bring him. Henley would later claim he didn't even know that Corll was gay, and when he did figure it out, he thought his friend Brooks was just "fag-hustling" Corll. Henley stated that he was told at first the boys he lured to Corll's place would be sold to a child slavery ring. Later, he began to witness what Corll was doing to them and assist him with the transport and burial of the bodies, and then he began helping him to abduct, subdue and murder some of the boys. Some of the victims were forced to write letters to their parents stating that they had run away and were well.

When asked why he didn't flee from Corll, Henley stated he tried joining the Navy but was rejected. He claimed, "I couldn't leave anyway. If I wasn't around, I knew Dean would go after one of my little brothers, who he always liked a little too much."[11]

While people in the Heights commented on how unusual it was for a man in his late twenties to be associating with teenage juveniles, nothing otherwise in Corll's behavior sparked any open suspicions that there was something sexual going on, let alone sadistic murder. At least nobody brought it up, even if they might have thought it.

"Is This for Real?"

In August 1973, fifteen-year-old Rhonda Williams, described as "a cherub with the face and figure of an early Brigitte Bardot," had reached a crossroads in her young and hard life.[12] Her mother had died from a thoracic aortic aneurysm when Rhonda was eighteen months old, leaving her and her two older sisters to be raised by her father, Ben. When Rhonda was seven, her father moved into a house on 23rd Street in the Heights and took up with a neighboring woman, Dorris, who did not get along with the girls. Her older sisters eventually married and moved out, leaving eleven-year-old Rhonda behind. Ben and Dorris could not manage the now-rebellious girl, and Rhonda was bounced between a children's home from which she escaped and stays with her grandmother or aunt, returning back to her father's place, where she was not welcomed nor wanted.

Rhonda was friends in school with Wayne Henley's younger brother and came to know Wayne very well. When Rhonda was thirteen years old, she developed a romantic relationship with a friend of Wayne's, eighteen-year-old Frank Aguirre. They fell in love and became engaged to be married when she turned fourteen. Frank was a hardworking and likable local boy who worked at a Long John Silver's seafood franchise. Even Rhonda's father liked Frank, who never failed to bring a bucket of food when he would visit Rhonda at her home. Frank worked diligently to build a stake so that he and Rhonda could be married if her father would give his consent.

On March 24, 1972, Frank was supposed to come over to Rhonda's after he finished work, but he never showed up. Rhonda went looking for him. She found his car in the Long John Silver's parking lot, but Frank was gone. She never heard from him again and became despondent. Her friends told her to move on, that he got a new girlfriend.

Her friendly neighbor Wayne Henley stepped into the vacuum as a big-brother figure. He told Rhonda that the Mafia killed Frank and that he was never coming back. She should really move on. Over the next year and a half, she would often turn to Wayne whenever she felt troubled or despondent.

Wayne of course knew exactly what happened to Frank on the day he disappeared. Wayne had lured him to Dean Corll's place. Frank's corpse was among the twenty-seven later dug up by police. The medical examiner concluded that Frank was killed by asphyxiation as the result of having a rag stuffed into his mouth and taped into place. When found, there was a noose tied around his neck.

Rhonda was arrested for possession of marijuana and put on probation. She was required to see a therapist and would often bike to his office accompanied by Wayne. Her father wanted her out of the house. The only advice the therapist gave her was "What you need to do is go home and cook dinner every night and every day, clean the house, and your dad will love you."[13]

One day, according to Rhonda's recent account, Wayne accompanied her on their bikes to the therapist's office. Wayne appeared troubled and asked Rhonda if perhaps her therapist could see him that day. The therapist refused. On their way back to the Heights, Rhonda's bike got a flat and they began trudging home, pushing their bikes on foot when Corll pulled up in his white van. They loaded their bikes into his van, and before driving away with Wayne, Corll gave Rhonda a ride home. She recalled sitting on a box in the back lined with soundproofing corkboard.

On the night of August 7 and 8, 1973, Rhonda had a huge argument with her father, enraging him to the point that she had to lock herself in a room of the house. Wayne showed up to console her with a nineteen-year-old friend, Tim Kerley. Rhonda did not want to stay at the house with her father in the state that he was in. Wayne told her she could come with him in Tim's car to Dean's place in Pasadena and spend the night hanging out with them there. When they arrived at about 3:00 a.m. at Corll's house, he became immediately upset to see Rhonda. He berated Wayne for "ruining everything" by bringing a girl. Wayne explained that Rhonda had no place to go. It appeared to Wayne that he had mollified Corll, who now generously offered the three youths some marijuana and a paper bag and rag with a can of solvent paint for a "huffing party." Within the hour, the three teens huffed themselves into a state of unconsciousness.

When Wayne awoke, he found himself with his hands handcuffed behind his back while Tim and Rhonda had been bound and gagged next to him on the carpeted floor. Corll dragged Wayne by his hand-cuffed wrists into the kitchen and thrust his .22 handgun in his stomach, accusing him again of "ruining everything" and threatening to kill him. Rhonda, in the meantime, still in a daze, thought that all this was some kind of party prank.

Wayne began desperately pleading with Corll not to hurt him and offered to help Corll torture and kill the two teens he had brought to his house; to do anything he wanted. Corll was not interested in Rhonda and ordered Wayne to rape and kill her himself.

Corll threw himself on Tim, ripping off his clothing. He dragged the naked boy to the torture board and shackled Tim facedown to one side while ordering Wayne to secure Rhonda faceup to the other side. Corll handed Wayne a knife and told him to cut away Rhonda's clothing and rape her. Corll then stripped naked, laid his handgun on a nightstand nearby, climbed up behind Tim and began raping him.

Wayne had removed Rhonda's gag and was cutting away her clothing, when she raised her head and asked him giddily, "Is this for real?"

Wayne responded, "Yes, this is for real."

"Well, are you going to do anything about it?"

Many years later, Wayne would say, "I would like to think that it was because she trusted me. The belief that she trusted me is what gave me the . . . push I needed to do something."

Wayne turned to Corll and said, "Hey, Dean, why don't you let me take the chick outta here? She don't wanna see that."

Corll ignored him.

Wayne scooped up Corll's handgun from the nightstand and pointed it at him, yelling, "Back off now! Stop."

Dean Corll then uttered many a murder victim's famous last words: "Go ahead shoot. You won't do it."[14]

Wayne fired six shots into Corll, who turned and ran out of the room, collapsed curled up naked on the hallway floor and died.

Wayne then untied Rhonda and Tim and called the police. They waited on the front porch for them to arrive.

Wayne confessed to everything, named David Brooks as his accomplice and led police to the graves. At the time, police recovered twenty-seven bodies but determined there was a twenty-eighth victim. Recently, a documentary filmmaker found a Polaroid amongst Wayne Henley's stored possessions showing an unidentified boy apparently restrained next to Corll's torture toolbox.[15]

Rhonda was charged with murder and held by the Harris County Juvenile Probation Department for weeks until everything was sorted out. Her father came by to visit and told her she had shamed the family and was never to return home. Eventually, her probation officer took Rhonda home to stay with her and her husband, and a juvenile court judge took interest in her case and ensured that she received counseling and other kinds of help.

David Brooks was found guilty in the murder of one victim and sentenced to life in prison. He died on May 28, 2020, in a Galveston prison hospital as a result of a COVID-19 infection.[16] Also dead from COVID-19 is serial killer Eddie Lee Mosley, "The Rape Man," connected to at least sixteen rape murders in south Florida of girls and women, and forty rapes between 1973 and 1987. With an IQ between 50 and 60, Mosley was found to have the mental capacity of an eight-year-old and did not stand trial on the grounds of mental incompetence. He died on May 29, 2020 while incarcerated in Sunland Center, a criminal psychiatric facility in Marianna, Florida. In the meantime, a number of serial killers have joined lawsuits filed by eager lawyers calling for "temporary release" of convicts over the age of fifty on the grounds that "Department of Corrections was unable to provide safe conditions amid the global pandemic." Gary Ridgway, "The Green River Killer," seventy-one-years-old and serving life for forty-nine murders was a party to such a motion in Washington State, but the courts dismissed it.[17]

Wayne Henley was charged with six counts of murder, found guilty and sentenced to six consecutive ninety-nine-year terms of imprisonment. The charges in the murder of Dean Corll were dismissed on the grounds of self-defense. Henley has been petitioning for parole since 1980 with no success. At this writing, his next eligible parole date is 2025, when he will be sixty-nine years old.

In a poignant article for the *Houston Press*, "The Girl on the Torture Board," journalist Craig Malisow chronicled the subsequent lives of Rhonda and Tim. Tim ended up a bitter, traumatized alcoholic and died in 2008 from a heart attack. Rhonda too was haunted and traumatized for the rest of her life. Today, she has mixed feelings about Wayne. On one hand, he had saved her life, but on the other hand, he had murdered her fiancé and brought her and Tim to Corll's house, knowing at least what awaited Tim.

In 2005, Rhonda visited Wayne in prison to find out for herself what Wayne Henley was about. She discovered he was a monster after all, Malisow reports. Rhonda said that Wayne told her during her visit with him that he had contemplated shooting her in the back of the head that night and saving his own skin and freedom.

But he didn't.

The Queering of Serial Murder

Like the Corona murders, the Candy Man murders also vanished from public view. The main perpetrator in this narrative, Dean Corll, having been shot dead, escaped the ritual trial so necessary to a true-crime narrative. To this day, we know very little about his past. He is but a shadowy figure, with only a few photographs of him in the public record. His disciples, Henley and Brooks, were fucked-up juveniles in fucked-up times in a fucked-up place, and that explained everything to everyone's satisfaction.

The homosexual dimensions of these two spectacular murder cases with a combined total of fifty-two male victims took on a sudden significance for conservatives. This carnage was dramatic evidence of the dangerous post-sixties creeping tolerance of all forms of "deviant" sexuality, especially homosexuality. In a way it foresaw "gay serial killers" in the manner AIDS was first characterized as an exclusively "gay disease" when it surged in the 1980s.

That many of the boys killed by Dean Corll were troubled juvenile delinquents residing in a poor inner-city neighborhood and that they had been lured with promises of marijuana and good-time parties, perhaps were even "male prostitutes" selling themselves, left a sense among staid conservative Americans that somehow the boys had "put themselves" at risk as drug users and/or as sex workers. Getting abducted, raped and murdered was an "occupational hazard" for prostitutes and young, poor weedheads as far as mainstream Americans were concerned, as was hitchhiking or running away from home, or many other things that made you one of the less-dead.

The superconservative mentality of the average police officer at the time further warped this perception. As one police officer explained it to the mother of one of the twenty-seven unearthed victims, "It looks like a homosexual thing."[18]

Both the Corona murders and the Corll murders confirmed for police their overkill theory and its connection to gay deviant sex. What Dean Corll did to his teenage victims was overkill; there was no denying that. True-crime literature also echoed this theme of exceptional violence in gay homicide. As Dennis McDougal asserted in his book on the gay serial killer Randy Kraft in California:

> Husbands and wives, boyfriends and girlfriends—they beat up on each other, shot each other, stabbed and strangled and slapped each other. But they rarely went in for torture and dismemberment and all of the other imaginative mutilation that

seemed to delight a small and perverse—but all too active—
segment of the gay community in southern California, particularly around Long Beach. They had their dungeons and
their whips and chains, all for fun. Just make believe, they said.
Heterosexuals did it too, of course: tying each other up and
going through crazy rituals of submission and punishment. . . .
But when it came to body dumps of nude young males, raped
and maimed at the hands of another, it could generally be
traced back to a lover whose anger or ecstasy—or both—got
out of hand. The results were almost always ghastly.[19]

Cops historically also added an extra flourish and flamboyant ego
twist to the motives of gay killers. In the case of Andrew Cunanan, for
example, Chicago police captain and serial killer specialist Tom Cronin
stated, "Down deep inside, the publicity is more sexual to him than
anything else. Right after one or two of these homicides, he probably
goes to a gay bar in the afternoon when the news comes on and his face
is on TV, and he's sitting there drinking a beer and loving it."[20]

David Schmid in *Natural Born Celebrities: Serial Killers in American
Culture* quotes Richard Tithecott's observations on the Jeffrey Dahmer
serial murder case: "For a heterosexual culture, the Dahmer case represents an opportunity to explain acts of savagery by referring to his putative homosexuality, to confuse homicidal with homosexual tendencies,
confuse 'sexual homicide' with homo sex."[21]

A whole host of gay serial killers would rack up huge victim counts
over the next three decades. In an era when homosexuality was just beginning to come out of the closet, an older generation of gay serial killers
was well versed in maintaining double lives since childhood. It was no
challenge to a gay serial killer with a lifelong history of deception and
concealment of their sexuality to have added to it another secret, an occasional two or three serial murders . . . or even thirty-three or more.

The 1978 case of John Wayne Gacy is horrifically familiar (and described in detail in *Serial Killers*). Gacy was ostensibly married, working in a "macho male" world of construction contracting, appeared so

straight that he was a Chicago Democratic Party precinct assistant captain and hosted First Lady Rosalynn Carter at the Polish Constitution Day Parade in May 1978, six months before he was apprehended in the thirty-three murders of teenage boys and young men between 1972 and 1978, twenty-six of whom were buried in the crawl space of his suburban house.

There were the three gay and independently nicknamed "Freeway Killers," Patrick Kearney (21 victims, 1965–1977), Randy Kraft (16 victims, 1971–1983) and William Bonin (14 victims, 1979–1980). These serial killers abducted and killed a confirmed 51 male victims between them and are suspected in a total of 146 victims. The cases were all characterized by overkill and, worse, horrific acts of prolonged torture and necrophilic possessive sex that in the case of Jeffrey Dahmer reached the epitome of taboo possessive deviance in the form of cannibalism.

For the conservative and religious bent, these "sodomite" serial murders fit well into their vision of post-sixties sexual liberation becoming the infernal "anything goes" hedonism that the 1970s became for almost everybody, gay or straight.

Sweet Little Mary

Vernon Geberth, whose current procedural textbook I quoted above, while a detective sergeant with the NYPD in the 1970s, zealously railed at sexual permissiveness. In 1974, twenty-five-year-old model and former airline hostess Brigitte Albrecht was found dead from an apparent "cocaine overdose" in the Travel Inn, the same notorious 42nd Street hotel where later in 1979 Cottingham would kill two sex workers and behead them. It was noted that Albrecht had been partying at the East Side singles bar and after-hours club scene and had checked into the hotel at 3:00 a.m. with an unidentified black male. Geberth told a *New York Times* reporter that the NYPD believes "there are hundreds of young women, from respectable, middle-class families, who are 'making it with street people' in a world defined by sex and drugs."[22]

Geberth explained:

Some of these young women come from very austere, religious backgrounds. Once they feel they've let their parents down, they feel they might as well do it again. Sweet little Mary who spends her weekends in the suburbs may be the wildest thing on the streets of New York City. It's absolutely amazing to see the Jekyll and Hyde personality that they develop.

The *New York Times* warned:

Young women who are exploring the perimeters of what they see as new-found freedoms—living alone in the city, going out with whom they please—are not fully cognizant of the danger involved in making choices, according to a young woman who lives in Queens with her boyfriend and two lesbians. "Young women are destroyed," she said, "by seeing liberation strictly in terms of sexual freedom." Even now, she said, "living with my boyfriend is just my way of fumbling around."

In the Big Apple

Calvin Jackson, "The House of Horrors Killer"

New York at first appeared to have been spared from "big number" serial murders, but then in 1973 and 1974, twenty-six-year-old petty ex-con serial killer necrophile Calvin Jackson strangled and suffocated and raped nine women. The case is probably vague and unfamiliar even to New Yorkers because the victims were not young, single women testing the limits of their sexual liberation, as the *New York Times* worried; they were all elderly female welfare indigents ranging in age between fifty-two and seventy-nine. Eight of Jackson's victims lived in a decrepit long-term hotel on the Upper West Side at 50 West 77th Street called the Park Plaza (not to be confused with the posh "Plaza" on Fifth Avenue and Central Park South). The ninth victim was murdered in a building two doors away.

Jackson lived with his twenty-five-year-old girlfriend in room 822 of the Park Plaza and was sometimes employed as a hotel caretaker and porter. He would gain access to the rooms, strangle or suffocate his elderly victims and rape and mutilate their corpses. He would then make sandwiches from food he found in the victims' fridges and linger over the corpses as he ate.

With access to the victims' rooms, Jackson would return to have sex with the corpses for another few days before the fly larvae eggs in their nostrils and dead eyes began to hatch maggots and neighbors would begin complaining about the smell. By then the bodies of the solitary, near-destitute victims were so badly decomposed that police did not recognize some of them as homicides and wrote off the deaths of the decayed, lonely elderly women as a result of alcoholism or natural causes.

On September 12, 1974, Jackson killed his ninth victim, but not in the Park Plaza. Pauline Spanierman, 69, was the widow of a prominent Manhattan art dealer. Like the other victims, she too had been strangled and raped, and her TV was gone. She lived in an upscale building a few steps away, at 40 West 77th Street and this time police put in a more thorough effort investigating.[23]

Jackson was arrested after he was seen by witnesses on a fire escape carrying the television set belonging to the victim and eventually he confessed to all the murders. Just to show how naive the world was to serial killing even as late as 1975, Calvin Jackson's primary motive was attributed to theft of property in supporting a drug habit while the murders and necrophiliac rapes were seen as secondary factors. The prosecutors could not understand why Jackson "had to" kill his victims and violate their corpses while committing the thefts!

Jackson's response was "I guess I kind of broke wild there, you know?"[24] Today we understand it was never about the thefts but always about the necrophiliac rape from the beginning. The TVs were the serial killer's trophies, entirely secondary to the commission of the postmortem rapes.

The district commander of the homicide squad was removed from his post when it was revealed that only five of the deaths were investigated as homicides. He blamed the medical examiner who had determined that the others had been natural deaths. The ME responded that the blame lay with the homicide squad that had failed "to detect a 'pattern of murder.'"[25]

Jackson had been arrested in 1973 for robbing a tenant in the building but plea-bargained himself into a short thirty-day sentence on a reduced charge. Nobody thought of evicting him from the building, nor had the building's management or police reviewed Jackson's criminal record once the deaths began. New York State attorney general Louis Lefkowitz demanded the closure of the "house of horrors" across the street from the American Museum of Natural History, declaring the Park Plaza "has become a repository of degradation and debauchery."[26]

Calvin Jackson was sentenced to hundreds of years in prison and is currently incarcerated in Elmira penitentiary in New York. The elderly $40-a-month welfare residents in the Park Plaza "house of horrors" were eventually evicted, the little hovel rooms gutted open, the corpse maggots swept out, and the building rebranded as "Parc 77 Apartments," where today a one-bedroom can rent for $4,500 a month.[27] The lonely old women subsisting on cat food were replaced by a trendy upscale Italian restaurant on the ground floor charging $19.50 for a shrimp cocktail until it was recently forced out when the landlord jacked up the rent beyond reason. According to the owners of the restaurant, "The landlords coveted a shinier, fancier model in our place."[28]

That's how serial murder comes to town and goes and gets forgotten. By the time Calvin Jackson's trial wove its way through the system, the Son of Sam killings had already begun. And that was the last people remembered of Calvin Jackson, despite the body count. Again, little old ladies on welfare get listed with the less-dead.

David Berkowitz, "The Son of Sam"

The Son of Sam was another of those seminal cases with a familiar "celebrity" serial killer: six murders in 1976 and 1977 in the Bronx, Queens and Brooklyn committed by twenty-four-year-old postal worker David Berkowitz, who used to sneak up on dating couples with a .44 Bulldog revolver and open up on them. Berkowitz was arrested in August 1977, in the "Summer of Sam," after a search of parking violations linked his car to the murder scenes.

What made the Son of Sam so big of course was his correspondence with police and with *Daily News* columnist Jimmy Breslin. Unlike the reputed self-naming by Jack the Ripper, Berkowitz actually did give himself the moniker in a letter he left near two victims addressed to an NYPD captain who in a press conference suggested that the serial killer had a hate for women. Berkowitz wrote in part:

> I am deeply hurt by your calling me a wemon [*sic*] hater. I am not. But I am a monster. I am the "Son of Sam." I am a little "brat". When father Sam gets drunk he gets mean. He beats his family. Sometimes he ties me up to the back of the house. Other times he locks me in the garage. Sam loves to drink blood. "Go out and kill" commands father Sam. . . . Police— Let me haunt you with these words; I'll be back! I'll be back! To be interrpreted [*sic*] as—bang, bang, bang, bank, bang—ugh!! Yours in murder Mr. Monster.

Until he was apprehended, his kooky messages and, again, the press's "scorekeeping victim count" kept the public fascinated and on edge. When Berkowitz was arrested, we were surprised by how mild mannered, soft, and pudgy the killer looked. Again, he seemed totally insane, claiming to receive orders from a black dog, and that was sufficient explanation for us.

Rodney Alcala, "The *Dating Game* Killer"

In the meantime, Rodney Alcala, "the *Dating Game* Killer," who would not be convicted until 2011 for his murders in New York, was posing in 1971 as an amiable East Village artist photographer, while he raped and murdered Cornelia Michel Crilley, a Trans World Airlines flight attendant, in her Upper East Side apartment. In the summer of 1977, he lured Ellen Jane Hover, an aspiring musician, to her death from her Midtown apartment. Alcala was originally from California and ended up in New York as a fugitive from charges in a brutal rape and attempted murder of an eight-year-old girl walking to school. He moved back and forth between the East and West Coasts, appearing infamously on the TV show *The Dating Game* as a bachelor contestant while he murdered another five females, including a twelve-year-old girl on her way to ballet practice.

Remarkably, in the early 1970s, Alcala worked in the same Blue Cross insurance office on Lexington Avenue that serial killer Richard Cottingham did, although Cottingham claims he has no memory of Alcala.

And then, of course, we have Richard Cottingham, who was wolfing down victims from an available flock of forty thousand sex workers on the streets and in the massage parlors of New York City in the 1970s. Nobody was aware of his existence until he killed two, decapitated them and set their torsos on fire in the Travel Inn in December 1979 and then killed another in May 1980 in the Seville Hotel on Madison Avenue, severing her breasts and leaving them on the headboard of the bed. Cottingham was captured "by accident" when the screams of one of his victims coming from a room in a New Jersey motel brought motel security to the door.

California Dreaming

California has always had a reputation as a dreamy mecca for the weird and occult. Strangely, its beautiful beaches, sunny days and palm trees became a backdrop to darker evil forces, madness and murder. A year before the Manson murders, Joan Didion described the murderous barometric Santa Ana winds blowing through the paradise:

> The Pacific turned ominously glossy during a Santa Ana period, and one woke in the night troubled not only by the peacocks screaming in the olive trees but by the eerie absence of surf. The heat was surreal. The sky had a yellow cast, the kind of light sometimes called "earthquake weather." My only neighbor would not come out of her house for days, and there

were no lights at night, and her husband roamed the place with a machete. One day he would tell me that he had heard a trespasser, the next a rattlesnake. "On nights like that," Raymond Chandler once wrote about the Santa Ana, "every booze party ends in a fight. Meek little wives feel the edge of the carving knife and study their husbands' necks. Anything can happen." That was the kind of wind it was.[29]

That was the kind of climate and terrain it was; the kind that Harvey Glatman and Charlie Manson and the unidentified Zodiac Killer would find themselves in. Driving. Driving like the three "Freeway Killers" Patrick Kearney, Randy Kraft and William Bonin. Driving like Edmund Kemper.

Unlike densely populated Eastern pedestrian cities like New York, Chicago or Boston, serial murder in California, and for that matter, most of the United States, was an automotive kind of thing. Serial murders occurred in automotive dimensions, like distant islands strung out in an archipelago of death. Throughout the United States, serial killers drove to find their victims, drove their victims to their deaths and drove their bodies to their dumping grounds. A 1980 study of serial homicides found that in 78 percent of serial murders, the killer used a vehicle directly or indirectly in the murder, and that 50 percent of the serial killers who did use a vehicle used it to offer their victims a ride.[30]

In California, serial killers were even teaming up to carpool. Serial killer cousins Angelo Buono and Kenneth Bianchi, "the Hillside Stranglers," in 1977 murdered ten girls and women between the ages of twelve and twenty-eight. They would pose as undercover police officers in Buono's car "arresting" women. They would drive their victims to Buono's car upholstery workshop, where they would torture, rape and strangle their victims before dumping them in the Hollywood Hills. Not realizing there were two serial killers, the murders were first ascribed to the Hillside Strangler. The case was solved only after Buono and Bianchi broke up and Bianchi went up to Bellingham, Washington, where he was arrested when he bungled a double murder there.

Lawrence Bittaker and Roy Norris, "the Tool Box Killers," met in prison and, with nothing to do, constructed a mutual fantasy to murder seven teenage girls, one of every age from thirteen to nineteen. Upon release they acquired a van with a sliding door on the side through which they could easily snatch up a victim in a parking lot or street. They nicknamed their van "Murder Mac" and installed a bed into it and outfitted it with a "toolbox" full of torture implements like pliers, ice picks and ball-peen hammers. In 1979, they lured five teenage girls into their van from beachside parking lots and shopping malls, brutally torturing them with the tools and raping and killing them while recording audio that eventually ended up being played in court during their trial.

Gerald Gallego and Charlene Gallego, "the Sex Slave Killers," a husband-and-wife team, murdered nine teenage girls in Sacramento from 1978 to 1980. (A tenth victim was a male date of one of their female victims.) Charlene afterward claimed to be an "abused spouse" forced into the murders and testified against her husband. The jury bought into her story even though at one point she nearly shot her husband dead in a rage when he began raping a victim in the back of their van while she was driving without waiting for her to join in. Gerald was sentenced to death while Charlene received a reduced sentence and was released in 1997, commenting, "There were victims who died, and there were victims who lived. It's taken me a hell of a long time to realize that I'm one of the ones who lived."[31] Coming from a wealthy family, Charlene returned to Sacramento, where for the last twenty years she has been doing "charity work."

Joseph James DeAngelo, "the Golden State Killer," a disgraced police officer, would begin in 1975 his series of thirteen murders and over fifty rapes in various regions of California. He wouldn't be identified and apprehended until 2018.

John Linley Frazier, "The Environmentalist Killer"

While a cluster of serial killers in a huge metropolis like New York or Los Angeles was not surprising, the cluster of emerging killers in a smaller city like Santa Cruz in California was much more puzzling and alarming because it was so out of scale to the region's population. The murders were "witchy" in that California-coast way, kind of like the way the Manson murders were in the summer of 1969.

The first in the series was actually a mass murder, when on October 19, 1970, twenty-four-year-old John Linley Frazier entered the home of a wealthy eye surgeon Victor Ohta and shot him dead with a .38 handgun along with his wife, two sons, Ohta's secretary and the family cat. He set their bodies floating in the home's swimming pool and typed a delusional note on a typewriter in Ohta's office before setting the house on fire. Similar to the recent environmentalist ATWA (Air Trees Water Animals) manifesto rants of Charlie Manson and the future correspondence of the Son of Sam, Frazier wrote:

> Halloween, 1970. Today World War III will begin, as bought to you by the People of the Free Universe. From this day forward, anyone and/or everyone or company of persons who misuses the natural environment or destroys same will suffer the penalty of death by the People of the Free Universe. I and my comrades from this day forth will fight until death or freedom against anyone who does not support natural life on this planet. Materialism must die, or Mankind will stop.
>
> KNIGHT OF WANDS
> KNIGHT OF CUPS
> KNIGHT OF PENTACLES
> KNIGHT OF SWORDS

Frazier had a history of petty crimes as a youngster but appeared to settle down after he dropped out of high school, married and found steady work as an auto mechanic. Then six months before the killings, he suddenly became delusional. Frazier had convinced himself that he was the John referred to in the New Testament's Book of Revelation and incorporated the occult and environmental agendas into his madness.

Frazier declared he had stopped driving, for example, on orders from the Almighty. An acquaintance later recalled, "He said God had told him that by driving his car he was polluting the environment and he would be killed if he drove anymore." (It is disconcerting reading today what was thought of as symptoms of madness in the 1970s.)

Frazier transformed into a Manson hippie / Ted Kaczynski Unabomber–like ecoterrorist persona, withdrawing to a small primitive cabin in the forest near the Ohtas' home. He became enraged at how many trees were cleared to make way for the Ohtas' luxury home, declaring that materialist people like that "should be snuffed."

Frazier was quickly tracked down to the nearby cabin and arrested a few days after the murders. Frazier's defense entered a plea of insanity, but by then, with dramatically rising murders, juries were reluctant to accept insanity pleas. Frazier was sentenced to death, and the sentence was later commuted to life. Frazier committed suicide in his cell in 2009 at the age of sixty-three.

Herbert Mullin, "The Die Song Killer"

Herbert Mullin was born in 1947 in Salinas, California, the son of a US Marine captain who had fought in the Pacific in the Solomon Islands campaign.[32] By most accounts he grew up in a stable and nurturing, but perhaps too strict, Roman Catholic household. In high school he was smallish—five feet seven, weighing in at 120 pounds—but he was popular with both boys and girls. He played offensive guard on the school football team, was unfailingly polite and well-mannered, got excellent grades and was voted "most likely to succeed" by fellow students. The first indication of some kind of instability in Mullin cropped up at age eighteen, when a friend of his was killed in a road accident. Mullin set up a shrine for him in his bedroom and began to obsess that he might be a homosexual.

Nonetheless, Mullin went on to graduate junior college with a two-year degree in road engineering in the summer of 1967 and was engaged to be married. But by the end of 1967 things began go wrong. Mullin began to hear distant voices—a classic symptom of paranoid schizophrenia—and his behavior became odd and erratic. He broke up with his fiancée. His condition perhaps was further aggravated by his consumption of marijuana and the hallucinogenic LSD.

In September 1972, Mullin began deeply contemplating the Bible. Mullin later stated that he discovered that killing was a biblical tradition, and that his father, the ex-Marine, had reinforced that in him. According to Mullin, his father used to urge, almost force, him to go deer hunting to develop his masculinity.

Mullin began to hear the disembodied voice of his father ordering him to sacrifice lives to stave off the natural disaster threatening California's coast. Mullin called it "the die song."

A psychiatrist asked Mullin, "What is the die song?"

"Just that. I'm telling you to die. I'm telling you to kill yourself, or be killed so that my continent will not fall off into the ocean."[33]

On October 13, 1972, Mullin was driving down a highway when he noticed Lawrence White, a fifty-five-year-old vagrant, walking along the roadside. Mullin stopped his vehicle ahead of him, and when White approached him, Mullin killed him with blows to the head with a baseball bat. He then dragged White's body into the bush and left it there.

Soon Mullin began to hear his father's voice explaining that pollution was coming from inside people's bodies. He had just been reading accounts of Michelangelo's dissections in Irving Stone's *The Agony and the Ecstasy* when on October 24 he picked up twenty-four-year-old Cabrillo College student Mary Guilfoyle, who was hitchhiking. When she climbed into his vehicle, he plunged a knife into her chest, killing her. He then dragged her body out into the woods and cut open her abdomen, taking out her organs and inspecting them for traces of pollution. So he could better inspect the intestines, he strung them across the branches of a tree. Her body would not be found for months.

Even today, with all the advances in profiling, it is hard to imagine investigators linking these two seemingly different crimes to the same perpetrator or understanding the motives behind the mutilation of Mary Guilfoyle. Most likely they were attributed to Jack the Ripper–type sexual lust, but in fact, these were not sexual fantasies driving Mullin—they were not really even fantasies, but hallucinations.

Still deeply linked to his Catholic faith, Mullin went in the afternoon of November 2 to St. Mary's Church in Los Gatos, a suburb of Santa Cruz, to seek help from a priest. Father Henri Tomei entered the confessional booth at random to listen to Mullin. Mullin began to hallucinate that Father Tomei was asking Mullin to kill him. Mullin recalls that he told the priest that his father had been telepathically ordering him to sacrifice people.

In Mullin's recollection of the conversation, the priest asked him, "Herbert, do you read the Bible?"

"Yes."

"The commandments, where it says to honor thy father and mother?"
"Yes."

"Then you know how important it is to do as your father says."
"Yes."

"I think it is so important that I want to volunteer to be your next sacrifice," the priest said, according to Mullin.[34] Mullin stepped over into the priest's compartment and beat and kicked him and stabbed him six times in the chest and back, leaving him to die in the confessional booth.

Mullin then acquired a handgun just as he became convinced that recreational drugs were poisoning his mind. On January 25, 1973, taking his handgun with him, Mullin went to find his former high school football teammate James Gianera, who had first shared a marijuana joint with him. Mistakenly, he arrived at a neighboring house instead. Kathy Francis was at home with her two children when Mullin knocked on her door. She knew Gianera and directed Mullin to his house. According to Mullin, she also told him that she and her children wanted to be sacrificed. She was found by police on the kitchen floor stabbed in the chest and shot through the head. Her two sons were found in their bunk bed, stabbed through the back and also shot in the head. The house appeared undisturbed.

Mullin then strolled over to James Gianera's house. After a brief conversation about old times and drug consumption, Mullin shot James dead. Gianera's wife, Joan, who was taking a shower upstairs, was shot dead as she tried to escape. Police identified the same weapon in all five murders. They also determined that the two families were jointly involved in a small-time marijuana-dealing business and classified their deaths as drug business related.

Mullin was what would be later classified as a rare "disorganized visionary mission" serial killer. His eight killings so far were mission driven but entirely unplanned and haphazard and rooted in organic paranoid schizophrenia. Mullin was simply mad. No connection would appear between the beating death of the vagrant, the mutilation of the college girl, the stabbing of the priest and the multiple shootings of the five recent victims. Each crime appeared different not only in the method but also in the apparent motive.

On February 10, 1973, Mullin came upon four teenagers camping in Cowell State Park, about two miles away from his parents' house. He shot all four dead, because, as he later explained, he believed they were disturbing the environment. Their bodies would not be found until a week after Mullin was already in custody.

On February 13, 1973, Mullin set out in his station wagon. Later there would be some speculation that Mullin was obsessed with the number thirteen, and indeed his first murder was committed on November 13, and his thirteenth victim would die on February 13.

Seventy-two-year-old Fred Perez was a former champion middleweight fighter in California in the 1920s (fighting under the name Freddie Bell) and a retired fish wholesaler.* Perez had four children, seven grandchildren, and five great-grandchildren. Around 8:00 a.m., he was gardening in his front yard when Mullin stopped his car about 150 feet away. Perez's niece and a neighbor saw Mullin lean out from his window, brace a .22 caliber rifle and squeeze off a single shot that hit Perez in the side of the chest. Mullin then calmly drove away as the neighbor phoned the police. The wound was so small that when a police officer arrived at the scene, he assumed that Perez was having a heart attack and assured him that he would be okay. But Perez died in his garden before paramedics could arrive.

With the description of the car on-air, police immediately apprehended Mullin and seized both the rifle and the handgun still in his car.

---

*He had not fought as a US Marine in the Boxer Rebellion in China, as I foolishly wrote in 2004 in *Serial Killers*, unless the Marines were enlisting one-year-olds.

Mullin refused to cooperate with the police, and at his arraignment he asserted his Fifth Amendment right not to incriminate himself. A week after his arrest, the bodies of the four teenagers were found and ballistics linked their deaths to Mullin.

Mullin was convinced that voices were directing him as the "savior of the world." Mullin explained, "Satan gets into people and makes them do things they don't want to do." By killing people (causing "small disasters"), Mullin believed that he was going to prevent the great disastrous earthquake and tidal wave that threatened California.

Mullin's insanity plea at trial was rejected by a jury for the same reasons that Frazier's insanity plea was, a fear that he would be later certified "cured" and released. Mullin is currently serving out life imprisonment in California for the thirteen murders he committed. Somebody maintains an Instagram account and a web page (herbertwilliammullin.org) where his current prison writings and photos are posted.

Edmund Kemper, "The Coed Killer," Santa Cruz, California, 1972–1973

Some newspapers reporting on the arrest of Herbert Mullin were reporting on the same page that students on the University of California, Santa Cruz (UCSC) campus were forming search parties to locate two missing coeds, Alice Liu and Rosalind Thorpe. The *San Francisco Examiner* reporting on Mullin's arrest for the murder of Perez unknowingly stated there had been no connection to his murder and the mutilation murder of Mary Guilfoyle, who "was the latest victim of the unknown killer or killers preying on girl students from UCSC and Cabrillo since last summer." It noted that Guilfoyle was the third coed from Santa Cruz murdered in recent months and described a string of similar recent mutilation murders and rapes: "Cynthia Ann Schall, 19, of San Rafael was identified from parts of her body that floated ashore here and in Monterey last month. . . . The head of Mary Ann Pesce, 19, a Fresno State University student, was found last August on Prieta Mountain. . . . Nine girls have reported being raped in the campus area in the last month by a man who picked them up while they were hitch-hiking."[35]

Edmund Emil Kemper III had come home to Mother.

Mother and Son Reunion: Clarnell's Boy Comes Home

In the six years that Edmund was away in Atascadero, Clarnell married and divorced for a third time and moved to Santa Cruz, where she found work as an administrative assistant on the UCSC campus. Anybody who has attended university knows how formidably competent and yet flamingly neurotic university department and faculty secretaries can be. Some hold graduate degrees and for various reasons bitterly grasp at university secretarial work as a "respectable" last resort after being unable to put their degree to work in some other professional career. They hold in their powerful hands not only the smooth career path of their boss, but the futures of thousands of students. It's a heady, powerful thing for an educated and competent woman—they are mostly women—who might feel she had not reached her potential. And that certainly was Clarnell, now going under the name Clarnell Strandberg.

The California parole board put the recently released Edmund into the custody of Clarnell, and in early 1970, he moved into her duplex in Santa Cruz. Immediately, the neighbors started hearing loud arguments and doors slamming.

"They paroled me right back to Mama," Kemper will tell anybody who listens. "Well, my mother and I started right in on horrendous battles, just horrible battles, violent and vicious."

Clarnell blamed her troubles on Ed, telling him, "Because of you, my murderous son, I haven't had sex with a man for five years."

By now Kemper was a six-feet-nine-inch, 280-pound giant. His ambition was to join the California Highway Patrol. His mother lobbied the psychiatrists to recommend his juvenile homicide record be sealed so that he could join the police, and eventually it was. But in the end, his application was rejected on the grounds of his being too tall.

Kemper found a job with the California Highway Department and moved out of his mother's place to a small apartment of his own. He complained that he still could not get away from his mother, that she constantly phoned him and paid him surprise visits. Kemper described using his "Atascadero learning" to "push her toward where she would be a nice motherly type and quit being such a damned manipulating, controlling beast."

During this period, Kemper faithfully made regular required visits to his probation psychiatrist. At the same time, he started rehearsing for his upcoming series of kills. He picked up dozens of young women hitchhiking in the Santa Cruz area, developing a nonthreatening "gentle giant" persona. Later, Kemper described how when he stopped in front of a female hitchhiker and she appeared unsure of getting into his car, he deliberately glanced at his watch. Kemper explained that this gesture subtly transmitted to the woman the message that he was a busy man and that she was of minor interest to him.

"Making Dolls"

On May 7, 1972, he acted out what he must have been fantasizing for years. He picked up two college girls, Mary Ann Pesce and Anita Luchessa, hitchhiking on a freeway ramp. Knowing the area well, Kemper managed to drive around without them realizing that he had changed directions from where they wanted to go. He then stopped his car in a remote area he was familiar with from his work with the highway department. Kemper first handcuffed Pesce in the back seat of the car. He later confessed, "I was really quite struck by her personality and her looks, and there was just almost a reverence there. . . . There was absolutely no contact with improper areas. In fact, I think once I accidentally—this bothers me too, personally—I brushed, I think the back of my hand when I was handcuffing her, against one of her breasts, and it embarrassed me. I even said, 'Whoops, I'm sorry' or something like that."

Kemper then took Luchessa out of the car and locked her in the trunk. Within thirty seconds of apologizing to Pesce for accidentally brushing against her breast, he threw a plastic bag over her head and wrapped a bathrobe belt around her neck. But as he pulled on the belt, it snapped; meanwhile, Pesce had bitten through the plastic bag. Kemper then drew his knife and began to stab Pesce in the back, but the blows did not seem to have any effect, and she began to twist around, facing Kemper. He then stabbed her in the side and in the stomach, and

Pesce twisted back the other way. He grabbed her by the chin, pulled back her head and slit her throat.

Kemper then went to the back of the car, opened the trunk, pulled Luchessa out and began to stab her repeatedly in the throat, eyes, heart and forearms. He recalled being surprised by how many heavy blows she took before losing consciousness.

Once the women were dead, he drove their corpses back to his apartment and carried them inside. In his apartment, he dissected their bodies, handled their various internal organs, snapped Polaroid photographs of them and cut their heads off. Kemper confessed, "I remember there was actually a sexual thrill. You hear that little 'pop' and pull their heads off and hold their heads up by the hair. Whipping their heads off, their body sitting there. That'd get me off!"

But Kemper insisted, "There was absolutely no contact with improper areas."

Kemper said, "I would sit there looking at the heads on an overstuffed chair, tripping on them on my bed, looking at them [when] one of them somehow becomes unsettled, comes rolling down the chair, very grisly. Tumbling down the chair, rolls across the cushion and hits the rug—'bonk.' The neighbor downstairs hates my guts. I'm always making noise late at night. He gets a broom and whacks on the ceiling. 'Buddy,' I say, 'I'm sorry for that, dropped my head, sorry.' That helped bring me out of the depression. I would trip on that."

One FBI behaviorist would later say that a serial killer like Kemper "has basically little or no contact with females, but is intrigued by them. [They] often times can act in a world like a five-year-old. They can be physically strong and everything like that and we used to liken them as much to the five-year-old taking a doll apart."[36]

Afterward, Kemper put what remained of the two women into plastic bags and buried them in the Santa Cruz hills, their torsos and limbs in one location, their hands in another, disguising the burial ground using techniques he had learned in the Boy Scouts. He kept the heads a few days longer before throwing them into a ravine. He returned to the grave where Pesce's headless body lay because, as he explained, he loved her and wanted to be near her.

Kemper acknowledged the duality of his psyche. Asked what he thought when he saw a pretty girl, he replied, "One side of me says, I'd like to talk to her, date her. The other side of me says, I wonder what her head would look like on a stick?"

Kemper said that just before he began killing, his fantasies of making love to women became dissatisfying because he came to believe he could never realize them. If he killed them, then they would not reject him as a man, he explained. He characterized his crimes as "making dolls" out of the women or as "evicting" them from their bodies in order to do what he wanted to do with them.

"No Psychiatric Reason to Consider Him to Be of Any Danger"

On September 14, 1972, Kemper picked up fifteen-year-old Aiko Koo hitchhiking to a dance class in San Francisco. He took her to another remote area, choked her into unconsciousness, raped her and then killed her. He placed her body in the trunk and on his way home stopped off for a beer. Emerging from the bar, Kemper said he opened the trunk of the car, "admiring my catch like a fisherman." He took the corpse back to his apartment, dissected it, had sex with it and cut off the head.

The next day, Ed Kemper had a scheduled appointment with his probation psychiatrists. In the morning before heading out to the appointment, Kemper buried Koo's body at one location and her hands at another but kept her head. He then drove to the psychiatrists' office with the head in the trunk of his car. Leaving his car in the parking lot, he went in for his interview. The psychiatric report resulting from that day's visit reads:

> If I were seeing this patient without having any history available or without getting the history from him, I would think that we're dealing with a very well adjusted young man who had initiative, intelligence and who was free of any psychiatric illness. . . . In effect, we are dealing with two different people when we talk of the 15 year old boy who committed the murder and of the 23 year old man we see before us now. . . . It is my opinion that he has made a very excellent response to the

years of treatment and rehabilitation and I would see no psychiatric reason to consider him to be of any danger to himself or to any member of society.

A second psychiatrist cheerfully chirped in:

> He appears to have made a good recovery from such a tragic and violent split within himself. He appears to be functioning in one piece now directing his feelings towards verbalization, work, sports and not allowing neurotic buildup with himself. Since it may allow him more freedom as an adult to develop his potential, I would consider it reasonable to have a permanent expunction of his juvenile records. I am glad he had recently "expunged" his motorcycle and I would hope that he would do that ("seal it") permanently since this seemed more a threat to his life and health than any threat he is presently to anyone else.

Instead of looking into Kemper's head and personality, the psychiatrists should have looked into the trunk of his car parked in their parking lot.

On November 29, 1972, Kemper's juvenile record was permanently sealed so that he could go on with his life as Clarnell had lobbied. In the meantime, not being able to work after an injury, he had moved back home with Clarnell.

On January 8, 1973, he picked up college student Cindy Schall.[37] He shot her in the head and then drove back with her body to his mother's house. While his mother wasn't looking, he put Schall's body in his bedroom closet and went to sleep. In the morning when his mother went to work, he took the corpse to bed with him and had sex with it. Afterward, he placed the cadaver in his mother's bathtub, drained it of blood, carved it up into pieces, bagged them in plastic and threw them off a cliff. He kept Schall's head for several days, often having sex with it. Afterward, Kemper buried her head in his mother's yard, facing up toward his mother's bedroom window because his mother always wanted people to "look up to her."

Warnings were issued to students in Santa Cruz not to accept rides from strangers. Kemper's mother had given him a university sticker for his car so that he could easily enter the campus to pick her up from work. This sticker gave women a sense of security when he offered them a ride.

On February 5, 1973, he shot two more women, twenty-three-year-old Rosalind Thorpe and twenty-year-old Allison Liu, and brought them back to his mother's house. He cut off one woman's head in the trunk of his car, and when his mother went to bed, he carried the headless corpse to his room and slept with it in his bed. Kemper explained, "The head trip fantasies were a bit like a trophy. You know, the head is where everything is at, the brain, eyes, mouth. That's the person. I remember being told as a kid, you cut off the head and the body dies. The body is nothing after the head is cut off. . . . Well, that's not quite true. With a girl, there is a lot left in the girl's body without the head. Of course, the personality is gone."[38]

Killing Mother

On Easter weekend, April 20, 1973, Kemper finally decided to face his lifelong nemesis.

At 5:15 a.m., he walked into his mother's bedroom while she slept and struck her head with a claw hammer. He then rolled her over and slit her throat. Upon killing his mother, Kemper said, he was shocked at how vulnerable and human she had been—that she had died just like his other victims. He said that before then he had always perceived his mother as foreboding, fierce and formidable, and whether he hated or loved her, she had always been a big influence in his life. Upon killing her, he felt relief. Kemper then decided, "What's good for my victims was good for my mother." He cut her head off and raped her headless corpse. He removed her larynx and fed it into the garbage disposal. "It seemed appropriate as much as she'd bitched and screamed and yelled at me over so many years," he later told the police. When he turned on the disposal, it jammed, throwing back up his mother's voice box. "Even when she was dead, she was still bitching at me. I couldn't get her to shut up," Kemper recalled bitterly.

Kemper then telephoned his mother's best friend, Sally Hallett, and invited her over for a "surprise" dinner party for his mother. He punched her, strangled her and cut her head off, placing it in his bed. He then spent the night sleeping in his mother's bed.

Kemper then drove to Colorado and from there called the Santa Cruz police to report the murders of his mother and Hallett. He waited in the phone booth for local police to pick him up. Kemper had cured himself, realizing that it was his mother that he had always wanted to kill in the first place. Now having done it, he was finished.

Years later, Kemper would be among the first serial killers to be visited by the "mindhunters" from the FBI, he was the subject of numerous television interviews and he has regained a new notoriety with the recent Netflix series *Mindhunter*.

Arthur Shawcross, "The Genesee River Killer," Part 2, Watertown, New York, 1972–1989

Mary Agnes Blake of Watertown, New York, came from a long line of poor, hardworking and hard-luck "North Country" folk. Mary had an alcoholic husband and nine children. They lived in a house set back from the road on 525 Water Street across from the Black River in Watertown near the huge Black-Clawson paper mill machinery plant around the corner on Pearl Street.

Jack Olsen in his magistral book on the Shawcross case *The Misbegotten Son* wrote that Mary "ran a salon of the poor" and "had been called 'Ma' since her early twenties."[39]

Her seventh child, Jack, was special. With blond hair, freckles, a pug nose and big ears, Jack seemed extra attached to his mom and his pet white cat. He would never go out to play without first hugging Mary and telling her he loved her. A good-natured child, Jack was ten years old, a good boy, looking out for his little brother, Pete, and kid sister,

Pam. Like many boys growing up in the region, he wandered the woods and river marshes, fishing on his own or with his little brother.

"The Fisherman"

One spring day in 1972 on their wanders, Jack and "Little Pete" came across a fisherman fishing near the Pearl Street Bridge over the Black River around the corner from their house. They were befriended by the amiable man in his mid-twenties whose name was Art and became familiar with seeing him fishing along the Black River. In late April, Jack came home and told his mother that a stranger named Art had taken him and Pete fishing. Mary immediately forbade Jack to go with "the fisherman" again. A few days later, the stranger appeared at their door, asking Mary and her husband for permission to take Jack fishing with him. There was something creepy about him, and when he asked Jack's father if he "minded" him taking Jack fishing, the father replied, "Yes, I do mind. Don't take my boys anywhere, I don't know you." The boys were warned by both their parents to stay away from "the fisherman."

Later that week, Jack and Pete saw Art walking across the Pearl Street Bridge near their home with his fishing rods. He immediately invited them to go fishing with him. When Jack told him that his parents had prohibited their going anywhere with him, he told them he'd "fix it" with them when they'd get back. The boys left with Art. They learned he lived a few blocks north of Water Street in the Cloverdale Apartments. He invited them to visit him there anytime they liked. Pete noticed that Art paid particular attention to his older brother Jack, speaking mostly to him and frequently reaching to stroke his blond hair. They wandered to various fishing spots with Art and stopped at a gravel pit where he built a small fire and cooked bacon in tinfoil. Art told them he had learned how to cook while a soldier in Vietnam. He told them that he had killed several infiltrators in Vietnam and discovered they were little girls. He then took out a picture of a naked woman and, showing it to them, commented, "Nice tits, eh." He told them how he "got" his wife and liked to make her moan, to which Jack, according to Little Pete, laughed.

They had spent several hours together when Art suggested they go out to a creek by the quarry and try their luck there. During the hike along the quarry edge, Jack ended up getting ahead of Shawcross and Pete, and at one point Art shouted out to Jack to wait up for them. When Jack did not, Art suddenly became enraged and grabbed Pete by the arm and hung him over the edge of a twenty-foot drop into the quarry. When Jack returned to them, Art set Pete back on his feet and laughed as if the whole thing was a joke. The two boys scurried off home. They did not tell their mother about the encounter with "Art the fisherman."

About a week later, on Sunday, May 7, 1972, the boys were scheduled to go fishing with their dad, but true to type, he got drunk by noon and the outing was canceled. Feeling sorry for the boys, Mary gave Jack a dollar to go buy cat food for his pet cat and told them they could go and play but to be back home for dinner. It was bingo night, and Mary planned to take Jack with her to play. Little Pete returned at dinnertime, but Jack had not come home, and Mary went to play bingo without him.

When Mary got home at 10:00 p.m., she was surprised to see that Jack was still out. This was alarming because Jack was afraid of the dark and never stayed out this late. She awoke Pete and began asking where his brother might be. Pete told her they played together for a while, but that Jack left to visit a friend who lived at the Cloverdale Apartments. Mary searched the neighborhood and called Jack's friends, but there was no trace of him.

At around midnight, Mary called the police and reported Jack missing. By then she recalled the strange "fisherman" named Art and his interest in her boys and that he lived at the Cloverdale Apartments, which she reported to the police officer. Mary felt that the officer did not seem to be overly interested or concerned. Again, this would have been typical for the 1960s and 1970s, especially when a young boy was missing without any obvious signs of an abduction. There was no legal stipulation that police could not investigate a missing person until twenty-four or forty-eight hours later; it was simply policy that various departments arbitrarily adopted. And indeed, very often missing kids would show up the next day, which seemed to justify this callous policy.

Mary decided to go to the Cloverdale Apartments and hunt down Art herself.

She located his apartment in the name of Arthur Shawcross.

Just then a police officer arrived anyway to call on Shawcross about Jack. Mary followed him and confronted Shawcross at the door. Shawcross immediately without hesitation told them that he had indeed seen Jack that afternoon playing in the park behind the apartment complex with another boy but that he did not see him after that. That was good enough for the cop. When Mary protested that Shawcross had been hanging around her missing son, the cop replied, "Lady, we can't arrest a guy for hanging around."

Again typically, the police assumed that ten-year-old Jack ran away, and no serious search or interview of Shawcross was done. It was left to Mary to return to the Cloverdale Apartments over the next few days and ascertain from other kids that indeed Jack had been playing there that Sunday but eventually left with Shawcross through the nearby woods to go fishing. When Mary informed the police of that, they just shrugged. No alarm was raised, and after a cursory search of the woods in the area, nothing further was done. One detective commented, "The boy don't want to be found."

On the fifth day of Jack's disappearance the *Watertown Daily Times* reported:

> Commenting on a report that the boy's mother said a man was seen leading the child into the woods, Chief Loftus called it "unfounded." "We have questioned the man, and there is nothing to the story. We've been doing everything we can, and have checked every possibility. We talked to friends of the boy, and have been told he left the area."[40]

And that was that. Nothing more was done.

That summer of 1972, as Jack Blake remained missing, Shawcross was complaining to his probation officer of marital woes and mental stress. He was sent for a psychiatric evaluation. The report stated that Shawcross showed "defective moral and social development" and that "when he becomes upset he acts impulsively. . . . He describes himself as always having felt that rules are to be broken and did everything in his power to break rules at home as a child and in school. . . . His mother had a very bad temper." Shawcross described her as "domineering" and derisive of him and his father.

Shawcross got himself a new ten-speed bike on which to pedal around on his fishing excursions: a beautiful white bicycle with distinctive brown-colored fenders.

In the meantime, Shawcross's former second wife, Linda Neary, as she read the story of the missing child in the newspapers, was wondering if the Watertown Police were aware that her ex-husband had killed a child in Vietnam according to his confession to her. Thinking about his irrational behavior, his violent outbursts culminating with the beating he gave her, resulting in a miscarriage, and his Vietnam atrocity stories, she thought of calling the police but in the end did not.

"I Must Have Done It"

Helene Hill, a divorced mother of four kids, lived in Rochester. She was dating a man from Watertown, and he invited her to visit his half sister and her husband with him in Watertown on the Labor Day long weekend. At the last minute, her daughter Karen, a blond eight-year-old girl, begged Helene to take her on the trip to Watertown.

Jack had been missing for four months when Helene and Karen arrived on Friday night in Watertown for the visit. Her boyfriend's half sister lived at 503 Pearl Street, a few hundred feet from where Jack had lived on Water Street and from the Pearl Street Bridge, where Jack had first encountered Shawcross.

Saturday, September 2, was a beautiful warm day. Helene dressed Karen in a matching red, white and blue top and shorts in a Labor Day theme and prepared herself to meet her new boyfriend's relatives later that day. That afternoon, Karen was anxious to play outside, and Helene let her out into the yard, warning her not to stray too far away. After checking on her daughter a few times to make sure she was staying close to the house, playing with a pet rabbit kept in the yard, Helene went to wash her hair. This was 1972 and Watertown was a peaceful little town and people in general were not very acutely afraid of child abduction or serial killers (the word did not even exist in popular usage). Although Helene was aware that her daughter Karen was sometimes disobedient and could boldly wander away, back home in Rochester she walked to school herself and was capable of finding her way home. Nor was Helene aware that a few hundred feet away from the house on Pearl Street was a bridge over a river.

A witness driving over the Pearl Street Bridge at around 2:00 p.m. recalled seeing a small blond girl climbing a low fence by the bridge and descending down to the stony embankment apparently in search of something. He recalled that a ten-speed bicycle was leaning against the bridge railing. Returning ten minutes later, the witness testified he no longer saw the girl but that the bike was still there.

Four teenage girls crossing the bridge a few minutes later would testify that they saw a man dressed in dark shorts, sandals and a white shirt climbing up from beneath the bridge onto the sidewalk. His bare legs were wet, and he attached two fishing rods to a white ten-speed bike with brown fenders.

A short time later, a sixteen-year-old boy having just crossed the Pearl Street Bridge carrying a shopping bag of clothes he had just bought spotted his weird neighbor from the Cloverdale Apartments pedaling his bike down the road. The boy rarely spoke with the man, but for some strange reason the man pulled his bike over to the youth and offered to buy him an ice-cream cone. Afterward, he offered to carry the shopping bag on the bike back to the apartment complex.

Even after Karen and the white rabbit had been missing for two hours, her mother still was not worried. Karen was a wanderer and the area seemed busy with people and the town seemed like a peaceful, friendly, quiet place. It wasn't until four hours later that Helene became worried enough to call the police. This time, the report of a missing eight-year-old girl visiting from another town spurred the police into quick action. They immediately began a search.

Karen's mother and search parties had walked back and forth across the Pearl Street Bridge several times, but it wasn't until after dark around 9:00 p.m. that Karen Hill's body was found under the bridge. The little girl was lying facedown near a cast-iron sewage pipe, her body covered by flat paving stones that had been tossed over the side of the bridge. She was naked from the waist down, and there were visible signs of bruising on her neck. Her Labor Day–themed red, white and blue shorts were tossed to the side and her blue underwear stuffed into a crevice. Both appeared to be crusted in blood. A preliminary examination that night would indicate that Karen had been punched in the face and stomach, strangled with her own shirt strings and viciously raped vaginally and anally. Her mouth and throat were plugged full with mud and sooty matter from the riverbank. The final cause of death was asphyxiation or suffocation. The white rabbit was never found.

Seeing mud and soot jammed into the little girl's mouth, one of the cops at the scene immediately thought of the man connected to the disappearance of Jack four months earlier. Hadn't he been recently fined for spanking and stuffing grass down a six-year-old boy's pants?

When the police arrived to pick up Shawcross for questioning, they noticed he had clumsily attempted to disguise his bike by attaching a baby carrier to the back. It only made their suspicion worse when he claimed he could not remember when he had bought and attached the carrier to his bike but under repeated questioning admitted it was a few hours after Karen's disappearance. With all the witnesses placing Shawcross on the bridge near the time of Karen's disappearance, police eventually squeezed out a vague confession in the murder of the girl. He said, "I must have done it." Then they began working on him for the disappearance of Jack.

Shawcross eventually had as much as confessed to killing Jack and was almost ready to take police to his body when a renewed and proper search by police located the little boy's body in the woods near train tracks about a mile north of the Cloverdale Apartments. His naked, decomposing body was found hidden beneath large strips of peeled tree bark. Thirty-five feet away from the body, police located his T-shirt, a green jacket with its arms tied together in a knot, his socks and running shoes. A hundred and twenty-six feet away police found the boy's jeans and underwear. Indications were that the boy was stripped of his clothing while still alive because the clothing had not been stained by decomposing body matter. Police found one of Jack's teeth knocked out on the ground. Cinders from the railway bed adhering to the bottom of the boy's feet indicated that he must have been stripped naked and chased through the bush and made it to the railway tracks before being sadistically dragged back into the woodland and murdered. It had been a violent, terrifying death for the child. The body was too decomposed to determine cause of death or whether he had been sexually assaulted. The medical examiner speculated that death was likely by strangulation or asphyxiation.

"Extreme Emotional Disturbance"

The prosecution of Shawcross would be as bungled as the investigation was. The semen samples taken from Karen's body were never tested for blood type (this was still in the pre-DNA era) and thus there was no evidence of a blood type match to Shawcross; potentially "reasonable doubt" in a jury's mind. His confession had been vague. The body of Jack had been found before Shawcross could lead police to it, and the evidence linking him to his murder was even more tenuous. Once the body had been found, Shawcross clammed up. There was no longer any advantage for him to lead police to the body in exchange for lighter charges. Without a confession and with such tenuous evidence linking him to Jack that day, Shawcross was not even charged for Jack's murder.

In his psychiatric examinations, after the child murders, and later after his arrest in the murder of twelve sex workers in Rochester, Shawcross claimed that he was suffering from Vietnam flashback experiences, garnering him potential sympathy as a suffering war veteran. Shawcross would tell his psychiatrists, "Vietnam turned [a] country boy into a crazy. . . . I tortured people over there, cut two heads off, took a lot of ears off. The Vietnamese ears, we'd always cut the left ear. We'd string 'em and dry 'em and cut their hair in a Mohawk. . . . And string bone, teeth, or ear on one of these little amulets. . . ."

His Vietnam war claims got crazier and crazier with time. In a written statement, Shawcross would claim:

> There is something in Vietnam that is still bothering me. It's got to be bad because as yet I am unable to bring it out. I was with some guys who took a whore and put a firehose inside her and turned the water on. She died almost instantly. Her neck jump [sic] about a foot from her body. Another time we took another prostitute and tied her to two small trees, legs to the trees, bent down. She had a razor blade inside her vagina. She was cut from her anus to her chin. Then the trees were let go. She split in half. Left her there hanging between the trees.

The things that Shawcross described were anatomically impossible, like firehose water making a victim's head "jump about a foot from her body" or splitting a person in half between two springing trees. His comic book cartoon descriptions of strapping a file cabinet packed with ammunition to his back and sauntering off all by himself into the jungle armed with multiple weapons and bandoliers of ammunition and grenades like Rambo were patently absurd to anyone with a minimal awareness of how the Vietnam War had been fought. Yet psychiatrists with PhDs in their pockets but dumb as sawdust in their heads were gobbling up the stories and still are today. During his first trial for murder, two very naive psychiatrists diagnosed him on the assumption that he was telling the truth about his experiences in Vietnam:

> Appears to have difficulty in discriminating between those activities that he was involved in when deep in combat in Vietnam and the types of activities that are acceptable when living freely among society outside the military. . . . The subject is often prone to compare his past warfare acts with the two killings he committed, as he attempts to minimize his present criminal predicament by informing that he has done much more heinous crimes during his stint in Vietnam.

The disorder PTSD had not yet been named in 1972, but by the time Shawcross would stand trial again in 1990 for his twelve murders in Rochester, the term PTSD—post-traumatic stress disorder—was well on its way to becoming a household term. Shawcross would milk it for all its worth.

In her recent book *Through the Eyes of Serial Killers: Interviews with Seven Murderers*, Canadian journalist Nadia Fezzani interviewed Shawcross shortly before his death from a heart attack in prison in 2008. Shawcross told her his same loony-tune tales from Vietnam, which Fezzani found difficult to swallow.

But in the end even the experienced journalist Fezzani seemed to buy into Shawcross's bullshit. She wrote, "Shawcross's years in the army appeared to have had a tremendous influence on his life. This was when he may have had his first experience with cannibalism." In her book, Fezzani quoted a story of cannibalism that Shawcross had told her:

> The most tender part of the body is the upper thigh of some-one fourteen to twenty-six years old. . . . I saw a young female placing a spring in one of our C-ration cans. She was making a personal bomb! . . . I tied her hands behind her with stovepipe wire and blindfolded her plus gagged her. Picked her up and carried her up the side of the hill into the trees and stood her up against a huge teak tree [near the first hut where the dead woman lay]. . . . When the girl saw me again and the body of the woman she did not flinch. But when I cut the body in half and cut off the right leg at the hip and knee she was shocked. She watched my every move too. I carried the body that was not wanted up next to a large anthill and I tapped the outer edge of the hill and the ants came out quickly and covered the body fast and started to tear it apart. I went back and dug a shallow hole in the dirt and placed a quarter size ball of C-4 plastic explosives there and lit it with a cigarette. It burns like a small sun, very hot and bright. I added sticks and larger pieces of wood. Then cut some bamboo and shoved two lengths into the ground at each side of the fire. I then fashioned a cross-bar and was about ready. I stripped the skin from the leg (which was about four inches across), then removed the cords and larger veins. Poured water over it and powder rock salt.

Placed it over the flames and it cooked down somewhat like a roast. I went up to the woman and asked her questions and she just looked at me. I knew she could understand me by the way she moved her eyes. When I went back and picked up the meat, I bit into and ripped off a chunk and started to chew. She urinated herself and passed out.[41]

When Shawcross first made his Vietnam War claims, inquiries were made into his military service, information that is on the public record. The response from the military was that for Private Arthur Shawcross, serial number 52967041 with the Fourth Infantry Division assigned to a Supply and Transport Company at Pleiku, there were no records indicating he ever saw any combat or was wounded as he claimed while in Vietnam. He worked in the air-conditioned comfort of a supply depot in the safety of a fortified Army base at Pleiku, and the closest Shawcross ever got to combat was perhaps ducking into a shelter when an occasional randomly aimed mortar round was lobbed into the base by the Vietcong. The only jungle Shawcross saw was in the pages of *National Geographic* magazine or in the John Wayne Vietnam war movie *The Green Berets* or in the lurid tales of his father's war in the Pacific told and garishly illustrated in men's adventure magazines on which he grew up.

Fezzani turned for advice to one of the psychiatrists who had evaluated Shawcross during his trial later in Rochester for his second series of murders, Dr. Dorothy Otnow Lewis, a Radcliffe College and Yale University School of Medicine graduate, a professor of psychiatry at Yale and New York Universities and the author of *Guilty by Reason of Insanity*. Lewis has made assessments and testified for the defense in several high-profile criminal cases, including Mark David Chapman, who murdered John Lennon, and serial killers Joel Rifkin, Joseph Paul Franklin, Ted Bundy, Washington Beltway Sniper John Allen Muhammad and Arthur Shawcross. When she visited Ted Bundy a few days before his execution, Lewis infamously returned his kiss on her cheek with a kiss and a hug of her own for the necrophile who confessed to murdering at least thirty women. Lewis would tell journalist Malcolm

Gladwell that she did not believe serial killers were evil. "To my mind, evil bespeaks conscious control over something. Serial murderers are not in that category. They are driven by forces beyond their control."[42]

Lewis insisted that Shawcross was truly suffering from PTSD from combat in Vietnam and much more. She claimed that there was something suspicious about the Army's statement that there were no records indicating that Shawcross ever saw combat. She told Fezzani:

> Curiously enough, many of Shawcross's records could not be found/obtained but we know that horrendous acts were witnessed and committed during the Vietnam War. Do not be too quick to dismiss his stories. Those particular ones have not changed over the years. We also do not know the nature of the training he received, but after World War II the army was determined to make their soldiers less squeamish and thus less reluctant to kill.[43]

We of course know exactly "the nature of the training" that Shawcross received. After basic training that every soldier receives, he was trained as a supply and parts specialist at Fort Benning, Georgia, before being assigned to a safe-and-sound supply depot in Vietnam.[44]

In Lewis's own book, couched in conspiratorial prose of innuendo that dangles questions but furnishes no answers, the "expert" defense psychiatrist claimed that "reports based on CIA documents indicate that during that period civilian and military prisoners, as well as ordinary citizens, were used in these mind-brain experiments." That the CIA conducted mind-brain experiments is true enough, but then Lewis follows with a kooky chain of *Alice in Wonderland* leaps of logic to suggest perhaps Shawcross was a subject of those experiments and that the prosecutor might be related to somebody who ran a CIA mind-control drug-testing safe house in New York State. She writes in prose tinged with paranoia:

> When I tried to get hold of Mr. Shawcross's army records, I was told that most of them, which were from the Vietnam era,

were missing, burned in a fire. Unfortunately Mr. Shawcross could remember almost nothing about his army experiences except for the name of Westmoreland. It was as though his memory had been erased. He had some wild recollections of slaughtering women in Vietnam and cooking and eating their parts. No one believed him. The prosecutor, who fought the insanity defense tooth and nail, dismissed these bizarre memories as the ravings of a sane man. Since then I have seen two other serial killers with similar memory impairment for their Vietnam years. One of them has only wild, grotesque recollections—half-dreams that no one believes. Their army records have also been destroyed. In my Shawcross workup, had I stumbled on something the Powers That Be were not too eager to reveal? Is that why I was made to look so incompetent, hung out to dry?

Funny thing. According to CIA records, a man of the same name as the prosecutor's, an uncommon name, ran a safe house in New York State in the 1960s where the CIA conducted experiments on mind control. It could, of course, be a coincidence, but I can't help wondering whether the prosecutor and the operator of the safe house are related to each other.[45]

The name of the New York Monroe County prosecutor leading the case against Shawcross to whom Lewis refers was Charles J. Siragusa, not an exceptionally rare Italian surname. He is a federal district judge today. Both his Italian immigrant grandfather and father worked their entire lives for the Prudential Insurance Company in Rochester.[46]

A Charles Siragusa of no known relation to the prosecutor was indeed accused in the 1970s of running a CIA safe house. That Charles Siragusa worked for the Federal Bureau of Narcotics (a predecessor of the Drug Enforcement Agency [DEA]) from 1935 to 1963 and rose to the rank of deputy commissioner. In 1977, he appeared as a witness before a Senate Hearing Subcommittee on Human Drug Testing by the CIA where he was asked by Senator Ted Kennedy whether he had set up a safe house in Greenwich Village for the CIA to run mind-control drug experiments. Siragusa responded that the Narcotics Bureau office in

New York and the CIA jointly operated a safe house on 13th Street off Sixth Avenue "to debrief informants, to work undercover operations," but denied knowledge of any drug experiments taking place there.[47]

The issue here is not the veracity of Siragusa's testimony, but the logic and quality of Dr. Lewis's "expertise" to assess a perpetrator like Arthur Shawcross. Maybe that's why, as she complains in her book, she "was made to look so incompetent, hung out to dry." With "expertise" like that, it's also the reason juries began rejecting insanity pleas from serial killers, even in cases like those of Frazier and Mullin despite the fact they were delusional to the point of legal insanity.

One of the psychiatric disorders that Shawcross clearly had was Munchausen syndrome, a disorder wherein those affected feign disease, illness or psychological trauma to draw attention, sympathy or reassurance to themselves. It is also known as hospital addiction syndrome, thick chart syndrome or hospital hopper syndrome. Karl Friedrich Hieronymous von Münchhausen was an eighteenth-century German baron and mercenary officer in the Russian cavalry. On his return from the Russo-Turkish wars, the baron entertained friends and neighbors with stories of his many exploits. Over time, his stories grew more and more expansive and finally quite outlandish. Münchhausen became somewhat famous after a collection of his tales was published. Almost a century later, an unusual behavioral pattern among young men gained recognition in the writings of nineteenth-century pioneering neurologist Jean-Martin Charcot. In 1877, he described adults who, through self-inflicted injuries or bogus medical documents, attempted to gain hospitalization and treatment. In 1951, psychiatrist Richard Asher coined the disorder Munchausen syndrome.[48]

Among certain mostly female serial killers, like mothers who murder their own children, or nurses, babysitters and caregivers who murder patients or children or the elderly in their care, the attention and sympathy is drawn through the deaths of others around them and is known as Munchausen syndrome by proxy. Shawcross was exhibiting ordinary Munchausen syndrome, not only in his tall tales of combat in Vietnam but as well during his childhood when he had unexplained bouts of paralysis and various seizures that could never be diagnosed.

How much it had to do with his homicidal psychopathology is entirely another issue.

Incompetence by police, the medical examiner and the prosecutor and a battery of defense psychiatrists and a smart lawyer got Arthur Shawcross a deal. In October 1972, a month after Karen Hill's murder, Shawcross pleaded guilty to two counts of first-degree manslaughter, which included a guilty plea in the death of Jack Blake so that authorities could close the case on his murder. A New York State prosecutor justified the reduction of charges to manslaughter citing Shawcross's "extreme emotional disturbance." The sexual elements of little Jack's death were brushed over. The story that went on the record was Shawcross's version.

> Jack Blake was following me about a couple hundred
> yards. . . . I walked down the railway track to see if I could lose
> him. . . . He was still coming down the track and I ducked into
> the woods. He followed me and he got up there, too, and I told
> him to go home and he said, "No." I got mad and belted him
> one with the back of my hand and hit him in the face and he
> hit a tree and fell down. I got scared then and I laid him down
> on the ground . . . stretched him out on the ground and put
> some bark on top of him, ran away from him.

The court was not made aware of the location of the clothing or that the boy had been disrobed prior to his death or the extent of the violence unleashed on him by Shawcross.

In the murder of Karen Hill, Shawcross claimed he was urinating under the bridge when the girl came down: "This girl pops up and I am on parole. I got scared after that, things went haywire. . . . I got scared and I grabbed her and, really, I didn't know what I was doing." Shawcross insisted he could not remember anything further and had no idea how the girl came to be raped and sodomized.

Shawcross was sentenced to an indeterminate sentence of up to twenty-five years but was technically eligible for parole after ten months. Nobody expected Shawcross to get parole anytime soon. He was packed off to the maximum-security Green Haven Correctional Facility just north of New York, where a battery of psychiatrists was waiting to "cure him" and get him out as fast as they could. At this point, the story of Shawcross is only in its beginnings. For the next fourteen years of incarceration, Shawcross would remain in so deep a state of "suspended animation" that when he was released and went on to murder twelve more victims, profilers famously underestimated his age by fifteen years.

Meanwhile Back in Kansas: Dennis Rader Metamorphosizes into the BTK

Dennis Rader, obsessed by the Harvey Glatman victim bondage photos he viewed in true-detective magazines as a fourteen-year-old, grew up often spying on female neighbors while dressed in women's clothing, including underwear that he had stolen, and masturbating with ropes or other bindings around his arms and neck. He would later take pictures of himself wearing women's clothes, a female wig and a mask while self-bound or suspended from a rafter. He admitted that he was pretending to be his own victims as part of a sexual fantasy.

After graduating high school, Rader served in the US Air Force from 1966 to 1970. He married in 1971 and fathered two children. Rader studied criminal justice administration at Wichita State University, graduating in 1979 with a BA while working at a Coleman factory as an assembler and later as an alarm installer for ADT Security. He was a member of his Lutheran church council and a Cub Scout leader. Eventually, he found work as a bylaw enforcement officer.

Dennis Rader, the BTK, "Bind-Torture-Kill," as he dubbed himself, first killed when he was twenty-eight, the typical statistical age at which serial killers first murder. In the morning hours of January 15, 1974, he entered the home of the Otero family as they were preparing their two younger children for school, nine-year-old Joseph and eleven-year-old Josephine. Armed with a handgun, he forced the father, Joe, to put the dog out into the yard, then strangled the mother, Julie, with a cord and suffocated the father and his son with plastic bags. He then turned on Josephine, the intended target of his sadistic fantasies. After asking the girl if her parents had a camera in the house (they did not), he took her down into the basement and hanged her by the neck from a water pipe. As she dangled suspended in the noose slowly strangling to death, he pulled down her clothing and fondled the dying girl and masturbated. The bodies would be found by the three older Otero children when they returned home from school later that afternoon.

The Otero family murders were an extremely savage and perverse case. It wasn't just Wichita police who had never seen anything forensically like it; this was unusual by any standard.

On April 4, 1974, Rader bungled his way through his second murder when his targeted victim, twenty-one-year-old Kathryn Bright, returned home unexpectedly with her nineteen-year-old brother, Kevin. Armed with a handgun, Rader attempted to subdue both victims, but they resisted. Kevin was shot twice in the head, but he still managed to escape into the street and get help. Rader panicked and quickly stabbed Kathryn multiple times and fled without an opportunity to act out his sadistic rituals. Kathryn subsequently died of her wounds. Police at first characterized the crime as a "burglary interrupted" and made no connection to the Otero murders.

In October 1974, the BTK phoned the *Wichita Eagle*, directing them to a letter stashed between the pages of an engineering textbook in the Wichita Public Library. In it he described the murder of the Otero family with enough detail to persuade police that the letter was genuine. It would be the first of a series of cryptic and taunting letters and poems sent to the Wichita news media and police for the next five years. Later, some of his letters were put into packages with victims' property, which he called "BTK Field Grams." They were placed inside empty cereal boxes ["cereal killer"] and left for police and media to find in various locations in Wichita.

In one of his letters, Rader wrote in broken grammar:

> And then hang the girl. God—oh God what a beautiful sexual relief that would been. Josephine, when I hung her really turn me on; her pleading for mercy then the rope took whole, she helpless; staring at me with wide terror full eyes the

rope getting tighter—tighter. You don't understand these things because your not under the influence of factor X. The same thing that made Son of Sam, Jack The Ripper, Harvey Glatman, Boston Strangler, Dr. H.H. Holmes, Panty Hose Strangler OF Florida, Hillside Strangler, Ted of The West Coast and many more infamous character kill. Which seems senseless, but we cannot help it. There is no help, no cure, except death, or being caught and put away. It a terrible nightmare but, you see I don't lose any sleep over it.[49]

By 1974, it was clear that Rader was self-aware of his place in both the myth and history of serial killers, without the term having yet been coined.

On March 17, 1977, while stalking another victim, on an impulse he feigned and forced his way into the home of twenty-four-year-old Shirley Vian and her three children. After securing the children in the bathroom, he sexually assaulted Vian, while asphyxiating her with a plastic garment bag secured around her head, and strangled her to death while her kids hammered on the door, screaming for their mother. Rader fled when the phone rang, without harming the children further.

On December 8, 1977, after weeks of stalking twenty-five-year-old Nancy Fox, he broke into her home while she was out and waited for her in the dark to return. When she did, he pounced on her, bound her hands and feet and strangled her to death with his belt; then he retied her corpse in one of his fantasy bondage positions and masturbated.

For the next two years, Rader sent police and news media messages claiming credit for the series of murders and enclosed poems mocking his victims with titles like "Oh death to Nancy" and "Shirley Locks."

In April 1979, after targeting and stalking sixty-three-year-old widow Anna Williams, he entered her premises and waited for her to come home. She was late. Frustrated, he stole several items and departed. In June, he sent Williams an obscene drawing of what he intended to do to her along with a sinister poem titled "Oh, Anna Why Didn't You Appear" and some of the items he had stolen from inside her home. He sent a similar package to a local TV station. Anna Williams fled Wichita.

And then Rader suddenly broke off contact. There were no more messages and no more murders for the time being. The unidentified serial killer was gradually forgotten.

When Rader committed another three murders (that we know of) in 1985, 1986 and 1991, the BTK was not linked to them. After that, Rader apparently retired. It is entirely possible that he could have gone the way of Jack the Ripper or the Zodiac Killer, leaving behind an unsolved series of murders. But in 2004, on the thirtieth anniversary of his first murders, of the Otero family, Rader began again communicating with the police and claiming responsibility for the three murders from 1985 to 1991. He was apprehended in February 2005 after police traced the metadata on a floppy disk Rader had included in one of his BTK messages to police to a computer at the Christ Lutheran Church in Wichita, where Rader was an elder.

First Kill: My Friend Dahmer, 1978

In his graphic nonfiction work *My Friend Dahmer*, Derf Backderf, who went to high school with him, gives a vivid and touchingly sad account of Dahmer's high school years. Dahmer was the school freak, the classroom clown, who nobody could quite figure out. He would bleat like a sheep in the classroom. He was that kid who would eat his own snot or take up any challenge to humiliate himself if it gave him some sense of belonging. Dahmer loved staging pranks, including falling into fake spasms in public places like the mall or a store, which became known among his peers at school as "doing a Dahmer." Dahmer began drinking heavily as an adolescent and might have been an alcoholic by the age of sixteen. He smuggled alcohol into school and reportedly was drunk almost every day. Nobody from the faculty noticed. He walked a fine line between hanging out with a circle of acquaintances and being ignored and ostracized.

But as Backderf writes, "Dahmer's descent was not just a straight line down." Sometimes Dahmer "rallied," according to Backderf, who describes a spectacular prank that Dahmer pulled on a high school trip to Washington, DC, in 1978. Dahmer phoned the White House and managed to talk the receptionist into connecting him with Jimmy Carter's vice president Walter Mondale's aide. Dahmer led the group of high schoolers into the White House for an unscheduled visit with Vice President Mondale.[50] (This was about the same time that the president's wife, First Lady Rosalynn Carter, was meeting John Wayne Gacy in Chicago.)

By the end of high school, Dahmer had a juvenile record for minor offenses: public drunkenness and indecent exposure. After graduating in June 1978, Dahmer dropped out of sight. Nobody missed him as graduates went their separate ways that summer.

That June, his parents separated, and his father moved out into a motel. His mother took Jeffrey's younger brother and moved out of state, leaving him behind all alone in the empty house. Although Jeffrey was no longer a minor, it was nonetheless a quintessential act of abandonment and rejection. It was at this point, on June 18, that Dahmer says he committed his first murder when he picked up eighteen-year-old Steven Mark Hicks, who was hitchhiking bare chested to a rock concert.

I had been having, for couple of years before that, fantasies of meeting a good-looking hitchhiker, and . . . sexually enjoying him. . . . [The fantasies] just came from within. . . . And that just happened to be the week when no one was home. Mom was off with David, and they had put up at a motel about five miles away; and I had the car, about five o'clock at night; and I was driving back home, after drinking; and I wasn't looking for anyone but, about a mile away from the house, there he was. Hitchhiking along the road. He wasn't wearing a shirt. He was attractive; I was attracted to him. I stopped then passed him and stopped the car and thought, "Well, should I pick him up or not?" And I asked him if he wanted to go back and smoke some pot, and he said, "Oh, Yeah." And we went into my bedroom, had some beer, and from the time I spent with him I could tell he wasn't gay. I didn't know how else to keep him there other than to get the barbell and to hit him, over the head, which I did, then strangled him with the same barbell.[51]

Dahmer said that he had no plans or fantasies to kill anybody—it just happened. He was at a stressful point in his life, and the homicide slipped out of him—what he really was fantasizing about was "having complete control." Like Kemper, however, he needed to "evict" the person of his desire from their body. Dahmer says, however, that from that homicide in June 1978, his fantasies became "locked-in" on possessing his subjects through acts of murder.

Dahmer claimed that had he not encountered the hitchhiker that night, he would not have later become a serial murderer. Perhaps. We do not know if there is such a thing as a "window of opportunity" for potential serial killers through which if they do not pass by a certain period in their lives they move on and never become killers. There are some serial killers whose first kill is fundamentally different from their subsequent series of murders. That would suggest that their first murder occurs in circumstances outside the direct context of their fantasies— unexpectedly. Only afterward is their murderous addiction awakened and articulated in a series of homicides that reflect a fatal signature. There are other serial killers, however, whose fantasies are so violent and murderous, before they even commit their first murder, that it becomes just a matter of time before they kill.

Former FBI profiler Robert Ressler, who interviewed Dahmer, dismisses his claim of fate in his crossing paths with the hitchhiker as "magical thinking." Ressler maintains that it was Dahmer's fantasies that led him to the hitchhiker and not fate.

Dahmer described to Ressler his actions after committing his first murder:

DAHMER: In the township where I was at, homosexuality was the ultimate taboo. It was never discussed, never. I had desires to be with someone, but never met anyone that was gay, that I know of; so that was sexually frustrating.

RESSLER: Okay. You say that the guy was going to leave, and you didn't particularly want him to leave, and that hitting him was a way of delaying him. You took the barbell and what, rendered him unconscious? And what transpired after that?

DAHMER: Then I took the barbell and strangled him.

RESSLER: And after that? Had there been sexual activity before then?

DAHMER: No. I was very frightened at what I had done. Paced the house for a while. Ends up I did masturbate.

RESSLER: Were you sexually aroused by the event? By having him there?

DAHMER: By the captivity.

RESSLER: Now he's unconscious, or he's dead, and you have him, and you know he's not going anywhere, and that was a turn-on?

DAHMER: Right. So later that night I take the body to the crawl space. And I'm down there and I can't get any sleep that night, so I go back up to the house. The next day, I have to figure out a way to dispose of the evidence. Buy a knife, a hunting knife. Go back the next night, slit the belly open, and masturbate again.

RESSLER: So you were aroused at just the physique?

DAHMER: The internal organs.

RESSLER: The internal organs? The act of evisceration? You were aroused by the cutting open of the body?

DAHMER: Yeah. And then I cut the arm off. Cut each piece. Bagged each piece. Triple-bagged it in large plastic trash bags. Put them in the back of the car. Then I'm driving to drop the evidence off a ravine, ten miles from my house. Did that at three o'clock in the morning. Halfway there, I'm at a deserted country road, and I get pulled over by the police. For driving left of center. Guy calls a backup squad. Two of 'em there. They do the drunk test. I pass that. Shine the flashlight on the back-seat, see the bags, ask me what it is. I tell them it's garbage that I hadn't gotten around to dropping off at the landfill. And they believe it, even though there's a smell. So they give me a ticket for driving left of center and I go back home.

RESSLER: Were you nervous when they stopped you?

DAHMER: That's an understatement.

RESSLER: Well, they apparently didn't perceive your nervousness, though, to the point of pursuing the bags, or anything like that. They just got into a routine.

DAHMER: Yeah.

RESSLER: And then you did what with the bags?

DAHMER: Put them back, under the crawl space. Took the head, washed it off, put it on the bathroom floor, masturbated and all that, then put the head back down with the rest of the bags. Next morning—we had a large buried drainage pipe, about ten feet long—put the bags in there, smash the front of it down, and leave it there for about two and a half years.[52]

Dahmer attended Ohio State University in the fall of 1978, planning to major in business. He spent most of his time drinking, failed all his courses (except for riflery) and dropped out at the end of the first semester. In January 1979, Dahmer enlisted in the US Army and began training as a military policeman. He washed out and instead was trained as a combat medic and then deployed to Germany. In 2010, two former soldiers stated that they had been raped by Dahmer while serving with him there.[53] (Dahmer claimed that he had no sexual encounters while in the military nor committed any rapes or other offenses in that period.) Although graded as "average," his performance in the Army deteriorated due to excessive drinking, and Dahmer was eventually found unsuitable for military service and given an honorable discharge in March 1981.

Dahmer settled in Miami, working in a sandwich shop for about six months before returning home to Ohio in September 1981. While his father, who had moved back into the house, was away at work, he opened up the drainage pipe, took the bones, smashed them into small pieces and scattered them in the underbrush.

It would be another six years before Dahmer would begin his series of sixteen additional murders in 1987.

Ted Bundy, All-American Boy Killing All-American Girls

Of the 605 serial killers who appeared in the 1970s, Ted Bundy was special. So special and well-known today that I hardly need to describe his crimes. Say "serial killer" and "Ted Bundy" is the first name that comes to mind. It would be Bundy who would define for us the new postmodern serial killer. As the *New York Times Magazine* commented in "All-American Boy" in 1978:

> The stereotype of mass killers with minds bedeviled by tumors or hallucinations is all too familiar to the American public. They were the drifters, the malcontents, the failures and the resenters. Ted Bundy, for all appearances, in no way resembled any of them. He had all the personal resources that are prized in America, that guarantee success and respect. He loved children, read poetry, showed courage by chasing down and capturing a purse snatcher on the streets of Seattle, rescued a child from drowning, loved the outdoors, respected his parents, was a college honor student, worked with desperate people at a crisis center and, in the words of one admirer, "Ted could be with any woman he wanted he was so magnetic!"[54]

Bundy was like so many of us can imagine ourselves being: an attractive college student with typical middle-class ambitions who drove a cute Volkswagen Bug. His outward persona was what many males identified with and what many females saw as qualities in a mate they desired. In other words, unlike serial killers of the past, he was not one of "them" but one of "us." He was our first postmodern serial killer.

His now well-known story first slowly trickled out of Utah and Colorado from 1975 to 1977, when he was linked to seventeen homicides of young women across multiple states, and then grew into a torrent everywhere after his two escapes and three subsequent murders in Florida. Eventually, Bundy would confess to at least thirty murders, with many more attributed to him but not conclusively proven.

Unlike the decade's murders of less-dead gays, transient "boomer hobos," troubled juvenile "throwaways," elderly welfare widows or street sex workers, many of Bundy's victims were the cream of America's crop: white, middle-class college girls. *Now* people became concerned. *Now* they started paying attention.

After Bundy was first arrested in 1975, the age-old problem of police "linkage blindness" took on a new urgency. Bundy not only crossed county lines in his killings, but state lines as well, murdering in Washington, Oregon, Idaho, Utah and Colorado and eventually in Florida. In several states, the police actually recognized a pattern in the killings in their respective jurisdictions but did not link the patterns to one another across state lines. Only now with Bundy under arrest did the several state agencies come together to compare notes. Everybody agreed that there should be a better centralized system, some kind of networked database like the one that LAPD detective Pierce Brooks had been proposing in California back in the late 1950s in the wake of the Glatman murders.

When Bundy escaped twice in Colorado in 1977, he was lionized as an outlaw, honored with T-shirts reading "Ted Bundy is a one-night stand" and restaurant menu items named for him. He became the first of the counterculture "good serial killers," the predecessor of the fictional sophisticated and cultured Dr. Hannibal "the Cannibal" Lecter, as played by Anthony Hopkins in *The Silence of the Lambs*, who became the *real* star of the movie, not Jodie Foster as FBI agent Starling. As Steven Egger writes:

> For many, the serial killer is a symbol of courage, individuality, and unique cleverness. Many will quickly transform the killer into a figure who allows them to fantasize rebellion or the lashing out at society's ills. For some, the serial killer may become a symbol of swift and effective justice, cleansing society of its crime-ridden vermin. The serial killer's skills in elud-

ing police for long periods of time transcends the very reason that he is being hunted. The killer's elusiveness overshadows his trail of grief and horror.[55]

Indeed, after his escape, Bundy committed three more horrific murders in Florida, the last the murder of twelve-year-old Kimberly Leach, whom he abducted from her school.

Bundy's trial in Florida was televised live, and the scope of his secret life began to be understood; the concept of a particular type of multiple murderer who kills serially began to take form in popular lore. Ann Rule's classic 1980 account of Bundy, *The Stranger Beside Me*, pioneered a whole new resurgence of true-crime literature with serial murder as its focus. It introduced the general public to the concept of serial murder, even though the term "serial killer" appeared nowhere in the text of her book. It still had not been coined.

Inevitably, as I wrote in 2004, "All roads in the empire of serial killers lead to Ted Bundy"; in 2019, Netflix premiered both *Conversations with a Killer: The Ted Bundy Tapes* and a Bundy biopic titled *Extremely Wicked, Shockingly Evil and Vile*, starring *High School Musical*'s Zac Efron. We are back to where we started, with the first of our postmodern serial killers being introduced to a whole new generation of consumers (and perhaps serial killers too), many of whom had not even been born when Bundy was put to death back in 1989.

Six hundred serial killers were going to seep into all corners of the United States, from Louisiana to New York, from California into the Pacific Northwest and everywhere in between. In Florida in 1970, thirty-year-old Samuel Little killed the first of his at least fifty victims (and perhaps ninety-three, as he currently claims). Over a period of forty years, he was arrested in eight states for crimes that included driving under the influence, fraud, shoplifting, solicitation, armed robbery, aggravated assault and rape. He was twice charged with murder in 1982. In one charge, a grand jury refused to indict him, while in the other charge, he was acquitted at trial. It wasn't until 2012 that Little was finally convicted of murder, and in 2019 he would make his widely reported confession; the FBI confirmed the veracity of his claims to at least fifty murders. If true, this makes Samuel Little the most prolific confirmed serial killer in American history, exceeding the forty-nine victims that Gary Ridgway, "the Green River Killer," was convicted for.

Journalists who were infants in the 1990s scratched their heads, asking how could Samuel Little commit all these murders over some thirty-five years without anybody noticing? Hopefully this book helps to answer that naive question.

After Bundy, the crimes of Corona, Corll and the Son of Sam began to take on a different perspective, and when people backtracked, they learned that there had been more serial killings recently than anybody had realized: there was an "epidemic" of serial murders among us. In the public and media's perception, local police agencies had failed to recognize the threat swelling over America's cities and towns, its highways and byways.

The question was what to do about it and who was going to do it. The time had come for the "Mindhunters" to take the stage.

CHAPTER 6

Mindhunters:
The Serial Killer Epidemic
1980–1990

People kill the way in which they live.

Patrick Mullany, FBI profiler

In the 1980s, we finally settled on a term for what has been described in these previous pages: "serial killers." According to the Radford/FGCU Serial Killer Database, there would be 768 serial killers that decade, an increase of 21 percent since the 1970s.

America's first serial killer of record, that is the first one to be labeled in the news media as a "serial killer" and "serial murderer," was Wayne Williams, "the Atlanta Child Murderer," described as such before his apprehension by reporter Myron A. Farber in the *New York Times* on May 3, 1981.[1] In the next ten years, the term "serial killer" would appear at least 80,038 times in US newspapers.

The irony is that twenty-three-year-old Wayne Williams, while suspected in twenty-three child murders from 1979 to 1981, was controversially convicted of only two murders, of adult male victims, and was technically not considered a serial killer until the San Antonio Serial Murder Symposium in 2005 updated the definition to "two or more murders." In addition, Williams continues to claim innocence. Recent DNA tests on trace evidence from the case do not exclude him from the small percentile of potential perpetrator DNA, but the tests do not definitively identify him as the *only* possible source of the DNA. Similarly, another set of DNA tests, on dog hairs found on some victims, did not *exclude* Williams's German shepherd, but again, did not establish definitive genetic links to the dog.

The Atlanta Child Murders are a gateway case in the history of serial murder in several ways. First, it was the case that introduced the public to the term "serial killer," along with the involvement of the FBI's Behavioral Science Unit and its profilers (the so-called Mindhunters).

Second, because the victims were African American children, there were rumors that a white Ku Klux Klansman was perpetrating "hate crime" killings. The FBI's conclusion that the unknown killer was probably black eased racial tensions to a certain degree and made the intervention of a federal agency more palatable.

Third, again because the child victims were all African American, the case highlighted the issue of race and poverty in murder investigations, of how "less-dead" (i.e., poor black) victims typically did not receive the kind of investigative effort they deserve.

Unfortunately, the case had another powerful effect: it advanced the idea that serial killers were an "epidemic" threatening America's children. There suddenly seemed to be one answer to the cases of thousands of missing children in the United States. This child-killing serial killer epidemic became a key to the FBI's claim on government financing as a national clearinghouse for serial murder that would be made in testimony before several much-publicized congressional committees.

There are two versions of the history of FBI profilers: the familiar canonical history as portrayed in the Netflix series *Mindhunter* and the books and reminiscences of former FBI profilers like Robert Ressler, John Douglas and Roy Hazelwood that inspired it; and the "anti-establishment serial killer as a social construct" version as argued by critics like Philip Jenkins and David Schmid, which I describe extensively in two of my previous books, *Serial Killers* and *Sons of Cain*.

As Oscar Wilde is reputed to have said, "History is what people think *should have* happened." So, here is a historian's familiar canonical version.

Come the Mindhunters

The FBI profilers of what used to be called the Behavioral Science Unit (BSU) are legendary, reputed to have an almost supernatural ability to

look at a murder scene and determine from its characteristics everything about the perpetrator, down to the likely color and condition
of the car they drove. The FBI did not invent criminal profiling, nor do
they claim to have. A police-employed physician, Dr. Thomas Bond,
attempted a psychological profile of Jack the Ripper in 1888; the OSS
intelligence service commissioned psychiatrist Walter C. Langer to profile Adolf Hitler; LAPD forensic psychiatrist Dr. J. Paul de River in the
1940s was the first to be permanently hired by a police department in
the United States to profile unknown perpetrators; and New York psychiatrist James Brussel famously profiled serial bomber George Metesky
with extraordinary accuracy in the 1950s (and the Boston Strangler in
the 1960s with a lot less).

Profilers were independent virtuosos hearing their own music in
their head; there was no system, no craft, no teaching it—you either
had the intuitive gift or you did not.

The BSU was founded in 1972, not as a response to serial killers, but
to a surge of hostage-taking incidents culminating in the massacre at
the Munich Olympics. Its objective was to psychologically profile
hostage-takers to assist a negotiator in persuading them to lay down
their weapons as an alternative to the use of force, which had led to the
deaths of hostages in Munich.

The BSU was housed at the newly opened FBI Academy on the US
Marine Corps Base at Quantico, Virginia, where FBI recruits were
trained and state and municipal police and other agency personnel took
advanced courses. Instructors at the academy were drawn from the
ranks of serving FBI special agents; like civilian university professors,
they were expected to balance a load of classroom teaching with research
work, while also consulting on active FBI investigations.

The attraction of Quantico was that the FBI instructors had a
relatively free hand in pursuing their research and developing curricu-
lums. This was not typical of the highly disciplined and neurotically
regimented white-shirt-and-dark-suit FBI of the J. Edgar Hoover years,
1924 to 1972.

Special Agents Patrick Mullany and Howard D. Teten were the found-
ing fathers of the priestly class of FBI criminal mindhunters and con-

fession collectors. Mullany was the theologian-inquisitor; Teten was its scholar-demonologist.

Pat Mullany declared, "It might sound very simple, but it's true, that people kill the way in which they live. It sounds so simple, people kill the way in which they live." Mullany believed in an intuitive approach to profiling: "If you have a dull sense of intuition you could get hit between the eyes and not realize what's going on, you're going to be useless as a profiler. I think it had a lot to do with the sensitivity . . . a person has in reading people."[2]

Mullany was from New York City and studied for the priesthood in a Catholic teaching order, the Congregation of Christian Brothers. He earned a BA in American history from the Catholic University in Washington, DC, and an MA in counseling and psychology from Manhattan College while teaching as a Christian Brother in New York. But in 1965, he left the order, and after an unhappy stint selling insurance at Metropolitan Life (where serial killer Richard Cottingham was also employed at the time in the computer department), he joined the FBI in 1966. After working in the FBI field offices in Jacksonville, Florida, and in Los Angeles, Mullany was sent to New York on a variety of specialized assignments in the FBI Training Division. That eventually brought him to the FBI Academy and the BSU, where Teten was already teaching and researching, in 1972.

Howard Teten was from Crofton, Nebraska, and joined the US Marines on the day he graduated high school in 1950. He served in an aerial photography unit in Korea during the war and then at the El Toro base in California until his discharge in 1954. Teten went to work part-time for the Orange County Sheriff's Department and then later for the San Leandro Police Department while studying criminology and criminalistics at UC Berkeley. Because of his background as a Marine photographer and the courses he was taking at Berkeley, Teten was assigned to the CSI unit, where he was able to compare what he was seeing at crime scenes with what he was learning in some of the abnormal and criminal psychology courses he was taking at Berkeley.

Teten joined the FBI in 1962 and during his service earned an MA in social psychology. By 1972, he was teaching a ten-hour course at the FBI Academy in applied criminal psychology, which introduced both FBI trainees and visiting police officers to basic psychological techniques for questioning suspects, facing a hostage-taker and other situations. The course was soon expanded to forty hours, and Teten partnered with the recently arrived Patrick Mullany to teach it.

Police officers attending the course would sometimes bring up their ongoing unsolved cases, with Teten and Mullany offering their observations on the possible psychology and character of the perpetrators. The course began to lean toward profiling unknown subjects, even though officially the FBI did not sanction the concept of profiling.

At some point, Teten went up to New York and met with retired psychiatrist James Brussel to gain insight into his profiling techniques. Teten found Brussel's approach helpful but rejected his "old school" Freudian interpretations as to what motivated the perpetrators. Teten believed that people were motivated more by their personality and daily life than by deep-seated subconscious impulses.

Teten was more heavily influenced by August Vollmer, the former marshal and later chief of police in Berkeley, California. Vollmer was one of the first American police chiefs to require his police officers to have university degrees and in 1916 persuaded Berkeley University to introduce a criminal justice program, which he headed. Teten said he learned from reading Vollmer that "the kind of crime a person commits is based on what kind of a person he is. Some kinds of people commit this crime. Other kinds commit their crime, you know."

Teten's approach fit well with Mullany's "people kill the way in which they live"; the two quickly teamed up, earning the nickname "Frick and Frack" among their FBI colleagues.[3]

The BSU in the early 1970s was divided into two factions—the "sociologists," who believed that environment dictated the behavior of criminals, and the "psychologists," like Teten and Mullany, who were convinced that personality trumped environment. As far as the FBI administrators were concerned, they couldn't care less, as long as the trainees received their classroom instructions and nobody from the

BSU embarrassed the agency. And so Teten and Mullany pursued their behavioral research while news of their profiling sessions at the FBI Academy began to spread throughout the law enforcement community.

Teten and Mullany were very different than academic forensic psychologists or psychiatrists and criminologists, who were researching *why* criminals did what they did, often after their subject was identified; Teten and Mullany were interested in the *who did it* and *how*. They profiled the personality and psychology of the perpetrator in order to identify and apprehend him—not explain him. The *why* was of little interest unless it helped to identify the unsub and secure his complete confession.

In the mid-1970s, a second generation of FBI agents, like Robert Ressler, Roy Hazelwood and Richard Ault, would arrive at the BSU and build on what Teten and Mullany started. All three had served in the military and had graduate degrees in psychology, or in Ressler's case, police administration. They would be followed by a third generation, led by the brash youngster with a psych degree, John Douglas, and somebody from outside the FBI to whip them into academic shape: Ann Burgess, a Boston University forensic nurse. But that came much later.

It was Teten, Mullany and Ressler who, back in 1974, would undertake the FBI's first operational profiling of an active unidentified serial killer in an ongoing investigation.

David Meirhofer, "Unsub Zero," Three Forks, Montana, 1967–1974

In 1973, Bill and Marietta Jaeger of Farmington, Michigan, spent months planning a family camping trip to Montana with their five children, three boys and two girls, thirteen-year-old Heidi and seven-year-old Susan. Their grandparents joined the trip as well. The adults would sleep in the trailer while the boys and girls slept in two separate tents set out next to it. The two tents had been set up in the Jaegers' backyard for two weeks before the trip, and all the neighborhood children took turns sleeping in them, roasting marshmallows and pretending they were on a camping trip.

On June 22, 1973, the family caravan arrived at a campground in the Missouri Headwaters State Park near Three Forks, Montana, in Gallatin County. The Jaegers had no way of knowing that the campground was the site of the unsolved mysterious murder of a twelve-year-old Boy Scout, Michael E. Raney, on May 7, 1968. Raney's tentmate had woken in the morning and found a slash cut through the side of the tent and Raney unconscious, covered in blood. He had been stabbed once, the wound puncturing his lung. Raney was rushed to the hospital, where he died. When an autopsy was completed, to everyone's surprise it was determined that Raney died of brain damage as a result of blunt-force trauma to his head, not the stab wound.

On the Jaegers' third night there, the adults went to sleep in the trailer while the kids turned in for the night in their two tents, just as they had before. Heidi awoke in the middle of the night, needing to go to the bathroom. She would later say that when she stepped out of the tent, she had a strange dread that something or somebody was watching them in the dark, but she just dismissed it as nighttime jitters. She rejoined her little sister in the tent and went to sleep. In the early morning, Heidi was awakened by a cold draft blowing into their tent. There was an arching hole slashed into the side of the tent next to where Susie had been sleeping, and Susie was gone.

Absent any ransom note or evidence that the victim had been taken across state lines, this was not an FBI case, but the Gallatin County Sheriff's Office requested the local FBI office's assistance. A number of suspects were questioned but no leads resulted. The FBI was no more successful than the sheriff's office in finding Susan, and within a few weeks the case stalled.

In the spring of 1974, about ten months after the abduction, the FBI agent assigned to the case, Pete Dunbar, came to the FBI Academy to take the applied criminal psychology course with Teten and Mullany. While there, he proffered the unsolved Susan Jaeger abduction case for the BSU to review, to see if perhaps he'd missed something in the investigation. Teten, Mullany and Ressler together reviewed the case files. There was no autopsy report, no extensive crime scene reports and no body. It was a difficult start for the FBI's first attempt to profile an unsub.

Mullany recalled in his self-published memoir, *Matador of Murder*:

> We felt that the suspect was a white male in his mid to late twenties, was unmarried and a loner, lived in the area, was well known in the area and regarded as odd, had military experience, was a repeat offender, had a dominant mother and no father or an absent father figure, was asocial, and had an impaired history of heterosexual relationships. We also felt that his work history would reflect a solitary position, not requiring interpersonal relationships. Perhaps most shocking to Dunbar was our certainty that if the suspect was apprehended and his house searched, body parts would very likely be found. We felt that the suspect had killed more than once.[4]

The BSU had one more thing to say in their profile: they predicted that when the suspect was arrested, he would attempt suicide.

Very early in the investigation, an anonymous informant had given the FBI the name of a suspect. By coincidence, Dunbar, who'd grown up in the area, was familiar with him—he had gone to school with his mother. The suspect was David Gail Meirhofer, a twenty-four-year-old handyman who lived alone. This is typical in serial killer investigations: when an arrest is made, it's quite often of someone on a list of suspects already identified and even interviewed. Gary Ridgway, "the Green River Killer," for example, had been interviewed at least four times as a suspect over a period of fifteen years before he was finally arrested and charged in 2001.

David Meirhofer fit the profile perfectly. He was a white male, single, a loner, a self-employed handyman and carpenter, lived in the area, was raised by his mother, had past difficulty in school, was ejected from the Boy Scouts when he had tried to stab a boy, intelligent, a Vietnam veteran, seldom dated, was asocial, and was regarded as somewhat strange.

Dunbar was at first skeptical of the profile furnished by the BSU. Despite a rocky juvenile history and a somewhat strange personality, Meirhofer was well-liked in the community; he was affable and helpful, and had a distinguished record in the Marines. Aside from the juvenile incidents, Meirhofer had no record of any trouble.

After the anonymous tip, Dunbar questioned Meirhofer, who had even submitted to sodium pentothal "truth serum" interviews. But Meirhofer had a lot of supporters in town, including the physician who had administrated the "truth serum." Meirhofer retained an attorney and claimed that he was being unfairly prosecuted. On the advice of the BSU, the FBI now polygraphed Meirhofer, who successfully passed the test when asked if he had any knowledge of Susan Jaeger's abduction.

One thing nagged Dunbar, however. Meirhofer had been acquainted with a recent murder victim, nineteen-year-old Sandra Mae Dykman Smallegan. She had disappeared in February 1974 after attending a local basketball game. Eventually, her car was found covered by a tarp and hay on the Lockhart ranch, an abandoned property. Inside the dilapidated house on the ranch, police discovered a bloodstained closet that had been once nailed shut. Some 1,200 charred bone fragments were recovered from the property, and Smallegan's remains were identified through dental records and an undergarment found at the site. While police conducted their search, a man approached the fence line and asked if anything had been found. It was David Meirhofer. But there was no evidence to charge him with anything or even serve a search warrant on his property. (Thirty years later, in 2005, construction workers would find Smallegan's wallet, identification and a small notebook bound in wire hidden inside a wall of a building on property that Meirhofer once owned.)[5]

"I Always Wanted a Little Girl of My Own"

Back at Quantico, the profilers now made a suggestion to Dunbar. Mullany recalls, "We felt the subject had a connection to the crime, much like an individual to a wedding anniversary. We felt there was a very high degree of probability that the subject would make an anniversary contact with Susan's parents. We convinced them that we had nothing to lose and everything to gain by having a tape recorder placed on the Jaeger residence phone in Farmington, Michigan. We also recommended that the phone call, if made, be traced."

Just as they predicted, on June 25, 1974, the one-year anniversary of Susan's abduction, her mother, Marietta, received a call from a man claiming that he had Susan. The FBI was standing by to record the call and trace it. Marietta kept the caller on the line for over an hour. When Marietta asked to talk to her daughter, the caller claimed he had "brainwashed" Susan's memory of her parents.

MJ: Have you been good to her?

C: Yes I have.

MJ: Why did you take her?

C: Well, it is kinda a long story. I always wanted a little girl myself [crying]. . . . I always wanted a little girl of my own.

MJ: Did you ever have a little girl of your own, your very own?

C: No.

MJ: Are you married?

C: Not now.

MJ: Has she been abused; have you hurt her?

C: No, just that first night—I had to choke her some.

MJ: When you took her out of the tent?

C: Yeah.

MJ: Did she wake up?

C: Not right away. I grabbed her around the throat.

MJ: How did you get away? No one could figure out how you possibly got away.[6]

Marietta eventually broke the caller down to tears, and he begged her to hang up the phone because he could not bear to do so himself. She recalled:

I was surprised at how calm I felt. Instead of feeling rage at him, I felt genuine compassion. . . . Without really knowing where the words came from, I asked him, "How are you? You must be very burdened by what you have done." I honestly felt concern for him, and he could tell this from my voice. I heard him gasp and then cry. He replied, "I wish this terrible burden could be lifted," and then the line went dead.[7]

Despite having over an hour to carry it out, the phone trace failed. In the predigital age of phone line switching, a trace had to be followed down wired relays physically from substation to substation. It was no easy task. The call vanished into a jungle of relays somewhere in a Florida substation. The only clue the FBI had was the sound of a passing train during the conversation. They began to look at houses around Three Forks in the vicinity of railway tracks, but none could be linked to Meirhofer or any other potential suspect. Nor was the FBI able to get anybody who knew Meirhofer to conclusively identify his voice as the one they recorded on tape.

A month later, a rancher in the area found an expensive long-distance call on his phone bill. When the phone company supplied him the name of the party called, it was the Jaegers in Michigan. The rancher immediately recognized the name from news reports and called the FBI. Dunbar and a sheriff's deputy walked the phone line along the rancher's property and, near a railway line, found vehicle tracks under a telephone pole. Meirhofer had not only done work on the rancher's property but in the Marines had been trained as a telephone technician. He had climbed the pole and made the call from there to confuse any tap that he presumed might be made on a call to the Jaeger family in Michigan. The problem, however, was proving it.

Again, on the advice of the BSU, the FBI and sheriff set up a meeting between Marietta Jaeger and Meirhofer in his attorney's office. The BSU argued that a strong female presence might intimidate Meirhofer and suggested a female agent be sent to pose as Marietta. Instead, Marietta volunteered to undertake the mission herself. The BSU advised that the room be carefully staged with Meirhofer seated in a position lower than Marietta to have her tower over him. Marietta would later recall:

> [Meirhofer] showed no signs of recognition as he entered the room. I stood up and walked towards him to shake his

hand. As I shook his hand, I thought how he was the last person to touch Susie. . . . We took our assigned seats, and I was
no more than three feet from him. He was very polite. He told
me how very sorry he was about what happened to my daughter. He told me that he would help me if he could but he didn't
kidnap Susie and didn't know where she was. He said that he
had been upset by news of the kidnapping and had taken part
in the search party. . . . This went on for about an hour, and
then his lawyer ended the interview, claiming that his client
had nothing further to say.

Before he left, I shook his hand again and looked firmly into
his eyes, but he looked away from me. One of the hardest things
I've done in my whole life was to let go of that hand. He was my
only connection to Susie, and I was desperate to find her.[8]

The next day, Marietta went over to a warehouse that Meirhofer
owned and confronted him again. Meirhofer again assured her that he
had no knowledge of Susan's abduction but was more hostile. He accused Marietta of carrying concealed recording devices.

"And Almost All Things Are by the Law Purged with Blood"

Marietta returned home to Michigan, feeling disappointed that the
confrontation failed. No sooner had she arrived than her phone rang.
The FBI was again standing by to do a trace. The caller identified himself as "Mr. Travis" and told Marietta that since she was talking to the
FBI, she would never see her daughter again. He berated her for accusing the wrong person of abducting her daughter and asked her if she
wanted to speak to her daughter. Marietta heard a small girl's voice say,
"He's a nice man, Mommy, I'm sitting on his lap right now." The voice
was obviously a recording. Marietta now called Meirhofer by his first
name, David, and that enraged him. He said angrily, "You'll never see
your little girl again," and hung up the phone.

This call was successfully traced to a hotel in Salt Lake City, Utah, four
hundred miles away from Gallatin County, Montana. Sheriff's deputies
were waiting for Meirhofer when he came home. In his pocket, they found

a receipt from the Salt Lake City hotel with the Jaegers' phone number written on it. A search warrant was now executed on his property.

Just as Teten, Mullany and Ressler had foreseen from their desks at Quantico, police in Montana found body parts stored in Meirhofer's home. In the freezer was meat labeled "Deerburger—SMDS" (Sandra Mae Dykman Smallegan). It was later confirmed as human remains. (Chillingly, two weeks before his arrest, Meirhofer had attended a church picnic to which he contributed a mystery meat casserole.) Also found in the freezer was one of Smallegan's severed hands. A sheriff's deputy presented it to Meirhofer's attorney, who had been avidly defending him for months and was at the house to ensure the police did not overstep their search warrant. The attorney ran out to vomit.[9]

On September 29, 1974, in exchange for the prosecutor declining to seek the death penalty, David Meirhofer confessed to a sniper shooting of a thirteen-year-old boy, Bernard L. Poelman, on March 19, 1967; the stabbing of Boy Scout Michael E. Raney on May 7, 1968; and abducting, strangling, dismembering and burning the bodies of Susan Jaeger in 1973 and Sandra Smallegan in 1974. Two of the four murders were committed prior to Meirhofer going to Vietnam, so war trauma was not going to be on his defense agenda.

Meirhofer's confession was cursory, and he refused to acknowledge several other suspected murders and attacks in the region. There were a great many bloodstained blankets found on his property, but Meirhofer denied knowing anything about them.

He described how he shot Bernard Poelman with a .22 rifle from across a river. He admitted to stabbing Michael Raney but denied bludgeoning him.

PD: OK, then what happened with Michael Raney?

DM: Well, I went to the park where the Boy Scouts were camped, and I was going to get somebody, and I opened this tent and saw this little boy, and I couldn't force myself to take him, so I stabbed him in the back.

PD: And then did you hit him with anything on the head or anything?

DM: No, I did not.

PD: This was just a stabbing; is that correct?

DM: Yes.

PD: You did not hit him with a club or your fist or anything?

DM: I did not.

[He described his abduction of Susan.]

PD: Being very blunt, very truthful, cutting this to the bare essentials, did you on June 25 take Susie from a tent? Susie Jaeger, in the Headwaters State Park at Three Forks.

DM: Yes.

PD: Did you cause Susan to be hurt, and if so, how?

DM: Yes, I had to choke her.

PD: Was she killed when you choked her?

DM: No.

PD: When was she killed?

DM: Uh, a little later.

PD: All right, let's start, David. I know this is difficult, but it's the only way I know to do it. When you took her from the tent and choked her, where did you take her?

DM: Uh, it was about one hundred yards north and then over to the highway and back down the highway fifty yards back across the highway up on top of the hill where the monument is, down the road on top of this hill about half a mile to my pickup, which was waiting alongside the river.

PD: Did you put her in the pickup?

DM: Yes.

PD: And then where did you take her?

DM: Went out to the ranch owned by Bill Bryant.

PD: The Lockhart ranch, right? Did you then nail her in the closet—I mean put her in the closet and nail the door shut?

DM: No.

PD: Well, what happened then?

DM: Well, I undressed her, and then, uh, well, uh, I proceeded to feel her body, and she got pretty wild, I guess, and I choked her. She died.

PD: She what?

DM: She died.

PD: OK, and then did you conceal her body?

DM: Yes.

PD: Where?

DM: Uh, I cut her up.

PD: And where is the body located?

DM: Well, not much left of it.

PD: What's left? Where, where did you put the pieces?

DM: I put her head in that outhouse behind the ranch, and all the rest of it was burned.

Police would recover Susan's skull from the outhouse. Meirhofer said that he had dismembered and decapitated Susan's body with his hunting knife before burning the pieces.

PD: OK, now, David, did uh, did you or will you tell us what happened to Sandra Smallegan?

DM: Yes.

PD: And in your own words, just the same way you did with Susie, go ahead.

DM: Well, I went up to her apartment about two o'clock in the morning of the tenth. . . . And, uh, I, she was sleeping, and I jumped on her and choked her and then tied her up and put a piece of tape around her mouth, and then I was gonna, while I was putting some of her clothes and stuff in the car, she evidently died. She couldn't get any air through the tape.[10]

Meirhofer then described how he drove Smallegan's corpse to the ranch and dismembered it with his hunting knife and a saw and afterward burned and disposed of the remains. The confession was terse.

At the end of the day, confession at least secured and signed off on, the sheriff locked Meirhofer in his cell for the night.

That night, just as the BSU had warned, Meirhofer used a towel to hang himself in his cell, taking any secrets and explanations to his grave.

A search of Meirhofer's house found no explanation either, no diaries, souvenirs or pornography—only a verse underlined in his Bible—Hebrews 9:22: "And almost all things are by the law purged with blood; and without shedding of blood there is no remission." According to Montana's *Great Falls Tribune*, a local clergyman said the passage had sometimes been a motivating force for demented and deranged people to justify heinous acts with religious overtones.[11]

That was the way FBI profiling worked the first time they tried it, and that's kind of how it still works today. Profiling works in tandem with a host of other investigative and forensic techniques combined with a policeman's tenacity and skill to take advantage of intuition along with random dumb luck, such as an anonymous tip, a rancher challenging his phone bill or a mother's steely nerve to bring her daughter's killer to justice with genuine compassion. Profilers are rarely at the actual crime scene; they rarely rush, weapons drawn, to a profiled suspect's location like in the movies or on TV, and while profiling is a valuable tool in narrowing down an already developed suspect list, there is no case on record of a serial killer being apprehended on a profile alone. Profiling is only one part of a complex mechanism that makes up a serial homicide investigation.

Mindhunters: The Third Generation

By the end of the 1970s, Teten and Mullany had risen higher in the ranks and moved on to other duties and assignments related to hostage-taking and the psychology of assassins and Americans spying for the Russians. Robert Ressler led profiling from its second into its third generation, recruiting FBI agent John Douglas and Boston University forensic nurse Ann Burgess into a new program of interviews with incarcerated serial killers, the subject of the recent Netflix series *Mindhunter*.

Ressler had been born in Chicago and served in the Army as a military policeman. He earned degrees in justice administration but had been fascinated with criminal psychology since the Chicago case of serial killer William Heirens (whom Ressler would eventually visit for a disappointing interview). In 1970, after leaving the Army, Ressler joined the FBI and was assigned to the BSU in 1976, where he taught and worked in the field of hostage negotiation.

Most historians agree that Ressler might not have first coined the term "serial killer" but that he at least introduced it into current usage. Ressler claims he was inspired by Saturday matinee movie "serial" cliff-hangers that left the audience wanting more and compelled them to return the next Saturday to see the next episode, very much in the way serial killers were left unsatisfied and wanting to kill again and again. In 1981, the term entered public usage.

In his recollections of the early days of the BSU, Patrick Mullany has only one thing to say about Ressler: "Bob was feisty. . . ."[12]

Ressler believed there were two kinds of FBI agents: those who ask permission for everything they do because they don't want to get in trouble with the hierarchy and "those who never ask permission to do anything because they want to get things accomplished." According to Ressler, he was influenced by seventy-one-year-old US Navy admiral Grace Hopper, who believed that once formal permission was put to paper and denied, a proposed project was dead and rarely could be revived in a command structure like the Navy. She would advise, "It's better to ask forgiveness than ask permission."

Ressler was interested in criminal psychology, but he was not a psychologist—his background was in administration, getting things done. It bothered him that most of the material that the BSU was collecting on criminal psychology was secondhand observations by either police officers or forensic psychologists or psychiatrists. What did the perpetrators have to say for themselves, he wanted to know. The FBI was sending Ressler around the country on a series of road courses to be delivered in various jurisdictions. Without telling anyone, without getting permission, Ressler started visiting prominent incarcerated killers and interviewing them; asking them what *they* thought they were doing. In those days, a prison visit could often be arranged merely by showing his FBI credentials.

Ressler began interviewing some of the prominent killers from the

1960s and 1970s, from the assassin of Robert Kennedy, Sirhan Sirhan, to the Son of Sam and Charles Manson. He carried on for about a year before he reported his visits to his supervisor at the BSU. Fortunately for Ressler, this was a moment when the FBI hierarchy was encouraging the BSU to undertake more research, and Ressler now got official backing to establish what would become the Criminal Personality Research Project.

Ressler now brought into his project thirty-three-year-old John Douglas, who had joined the FBI in 1970 after serving in the Air Force. He earned several graduate degrees in psychology and counseling and adult education and arrived at the BSU in 1977, like almost everybody there, teaching hostage negotiation. His first assignment in the FBI had been with a SWAT team in Detroit. A number of agents who had accompanied Ressler on the interviews had problems dealing with the horror stories some serial killers were telling them, or at least hiding their reactions from the serial killers. Ressler liked Douglas's affable and easygoing manner when interviewing serial killers. Douglas wore a nonjudgmental mask, was warmly encouraging and easily established a rapport with the psychopaths they were visiting, keeping them in a talkative frame of mind.

In order to secure funding for his project from the Justice Department, Ressler brought in forensic nurse and researcher Ann Burgess to help shape the grant application and the program protocols in a disciplined academic format.

The Criminal Personality Research Project ended up interviewing twenty-nine incarcerated sexual serial killers and seven solo sexual murderers, asking them about their childhoods, their fantasies and what they thought they were doing, as now fictionally portrayed on *Mindhunter*. These interviews, along with the work of Roy Hazelwood, who specialized in sexual crimes, and other behaviorists at the BSU, would lead to the FBI's controversial profiling system of organized/disorganized/mixed classifications of serial killers. After its use for nearly thirty years, in 2004, the FBI would conclude the system has "limited utility" in active serial killer investigations and it's no longer used in day-to-day case analysis.)[13]

In 1986, Ressler, Burgess and Douglas published their classic textbook based on their interviews, *Sexual Homicide: Patterns and Motives*, which is still considered an important text on the psychology of serial killers.

In 1981, Ressler put forth an initiative for what would become the National Center for the Analysis of Violent Crime (NCAVC), coordinating profiling and research in serial crime and housing the Violent Criminal Apprehension Program (ViCAP), a national database of violent crime incidents and their case characteristics—something that Pierce Brooks had first proposed back in the late 1950s and had revived in the late 1970s. Partnering with the Justice Department and the FBI, Brooks's proposal now secured major funding for his long-dreamt project, and eventually, he became the first director of ViCAP when it went operational in 1985.

John Douglas, in the meantime, affable, handsome, well-spoken, young, educated with a psychology degree, became the public face of the FBI's Behavioral Science Unit, especially when they became involved in the Atlanta Child Murders. The press loved him. And when Douglas later advised the prosecution on how to best goad Wayne Williams during his trial, the press loved him even more. Eventually, Douglas went on to change the unit designation to the Investigative Support Unit. He said he wanted to take the "BS" out of profiling and align it more with investigations and not behavioral science. Today it is called the Behavioral Analysis Unit (BAU). Douglas retired in 1996 to work as a private consultant and author of bestselling books.

There are many different forms of profiling developed outside of the FBI, and the effectiveness of FBI profiling, and that of ViCAP, is a matter of debate.

But this, at least, is the "official" history of the FBI's profiling system.

Making the Serial Killer Epidemic

At the exact same time as the term "serial killer" was entering our popular vocabulary, Congress was embracing the concept of a "serial killer epidemic." Coincidentally, the same guy who we think coined the term "serial killer" might have also coined "serial killer epidemic," when in the 1980s Ressler stated, "Serial killing—I think it's at an epidemic proportion. The type of crime we're seeing today did not really occur with any known frequency prior to the fifties. An individual taking ten, twelve, fifteen, twenty-five, thirty-five lives is a relatively new phenomenon in the crime picture of the U.S."[14]

There were three major committees on Capitol Hill from 1981 to 1983 that looked into the issues of increasing violence, linkage blindness, child abduction, child pornography and serial killers: the Attorney General's Task Force on Violent Crime, the House Committee on Civil and Constitutional Rights and Senator Arlen Specter's Juvenile Justice Subcommittee of the Judiciary Committee of the US Senate.

The start of these hearings in 1981 was punctuated by several dramatic cases of child abduction murder. In Atlanta, Wayne Williams was arrested in a series of thirty-one child murders; in New York, Etan Patz infamously vanished on his way to school (thirty-eight years later, in February 2017, the boy's killer was convicted);[15] and in Florida, six-year-old Adam Walsh vanished in a shopping mall. Adam's severed head was found floating in a canal; his body was never recovered. Adam's father, John Walsh, became a vocal advocate for victims and missing children, and the host of *America's Most Wanted*.

Testifying before the committees were an assortment of FBI officials, Pierce Brooks selling his database idea, which became ViCAP; John Walsh, now an advocate for abducted children; and true-crime author Ann Rule. The impression they left was that hundreds of migratory serial killers were roaming around the nation, abducting and murdering thousands of American children and young women every year.

Ann Rule told the senators on the Judiciary Committee looking into "Patterns of Murders Committed by One Person in Large Numbers with No Apparent Rhyme, Reason or Motivation":

> Several of the serial killers I have researched have put 200,000 miles a year on their cars. They move constantly. They may drive all night long. They are always looking for the random victim who may cross their path. . . . When we are talking

about a clean slate and a fresh start in this context, it is chilling because every time these men move to a new territory, maybe two States away, they are starting over. The police there do not recognize the pattern.[16]

Rule's claim was nonsense, but nobody questioned it. First, in order to drive 200,000 miles in a year, one would have to drive 547 miles every day. Rule never identified in her testimony the "several serial killers" she claimed drove those enormous distances. Moreover, statistically, the majority of serial killers stuck to their own region, their city or home state. Ted Bundy was atypical as a migratory serial killer ranging over multiple states.

When describing to the senators how Ted Bundy moved across state lines, Rule claimed, "I think ViCAP would have saved 14 to 15 young women's lives at the very least if we had ViCAP in operation."

Statistics were marshaled before Congress in a deceptive way to highlight an "epidemic" number of murders and child abductions. For example, the number of unsolved murders in a given year was combined with "motive unknown," "stranger" and "relationship unknown" murders to give the impression that nearly 25 percent of all murders in the US were perpetrated by anonymous serial killers. While some serial murders did fall into these categories, most did not.

As for the claims that thousands of children were being abducted by serial killing strangers, a study of 1,498 child murders in California between 1981 and 1990 determined that relatives, *predominately parents*, were the most frequent killers of children under the age of ten (in 44.8 percent of cases). Strangers, serial killers or otherwise, were involved in only 14.6 percent of the child murders.[17]

Further, the definition of "abduction" did not necessarily match the public's imagination. For example, in the California penal code at the time, abduction was defined as when a victim is lured or forcibly moved farther than twenty feet or held longer than half an hour if no movement occurs. Naturally, that inflated abduction statistics.[18]

As Joel Best put it in his analysis of the claims presented to Congress: "Three principles seem clear: Big numbers are better than small numbers; official numbers are better than unofficial numbers; and big, official numbers are best of all."[19]

Ressler himself admitted, "In feeding the frenzy we were using an old tactic in Washington, playing up the problem as a way of getting Congress and the higher-ups in the executive branch to pay attention to it."[20]

The frightening "big number" testimony did the trick. Millions in federal dollars now poured into ViCAP and NCAVC, and the FBI emerged as the only agency able to confront this "epidemic" of highly mobile serial killers crossing state lines.

Carrying on the Kitty Genovese discourse and that of Vernon Geberth's "Sweet Little Mary," the *New York Times* now spun the story in that direction. An article headlined "Officials Cite a Rise in Killers Who Roam U.S. for Victims" quoted officials who claimed that the rise in serial killings was "linked somehow to the sweeping changes in attitudes regarding sexuality that have occurred in the past 20 years."[21] Once again, female sexual promiscuity was blamed, rather than the repressively sick celebration of women's abduction, rape, mutilation and murder in mainstream men's adventure and true-detective magazines since the 1940s (and earlier) that the serial killers had consumed since childhood, long before "women's liberation" and the "sexual revolution."

Despite all the heavy profiling work in Quantico since the 1970s and the newly introduced ViCAP database, the 1980s brought us even more serial killers than before, although victim counts rarely surpassed the twenty to thirty plus accrued in the 1970s by killers like John Wayne Gacy, Ted Bundy, Juan Corona and Dean Corll. This suggests that serial killers were now being apprehended earlier in their "career," before they could amass the huge victim counts of the previous decade.

Psychological profiling—the FBI's and others (for a description of the array of different profiling systems, see *Serial Killers*)—gave homicide investigators on the front lines a better grasp of the difference between a changing MO and a static "signature." A change in MO or in the type of victim no longer automatically led to investigators dismissing the possibility of a serial killer. The average homicide investigator now had a more sophisticated understanding and awareness of serial perpetrators. Interjurisdictional communication and sharing of information improved throughout the 1980s as well.

Henry Lee Lucas, "The Confession Killer"

Henry Lee Lucas first hit the front pages in the early 1980s with spectacular claims of having murdered first 100, then 360, and then 3,000 people. Lucas was quickly labeled the "most prolific serial killer ever." The problem was that investigators from various jurisdictions rushed to Lucas eager to close cold cases on their books, and it turned out Lucas was known to be in other states at the times of the murders he claimed to have perpetrated. In 1986, the Texas attorney general concluded:

> Except for Lucas' original three confessions to the murders of his mother in Michigan in 1961 and Frieda Powell and Kate Rich in Texas in 1982, there is a notable lack of physical evidence linking Lucas to the crimes to which he confessed. Lucas did not lead authorities to any bodies of victims. Unfortunately, when Lucas was confessing to hundreds of murders, those with custody of Lucas did nothing to bring an end to his hoax. Even as evidence of the hoax mounted, they continued to insist that Lucas had murdered hundreds of persons. . . . We found information that would lead us to believe that some officials "clear cases" just to get them off the books.[22]

Lucas's uncanny ability to give details about some of the murders was the result of investigators sharing crime scene photos and reports to "help him" with his memory.

This resulted in Lucas being convicted by juries in eleven murders based on his confessions when he probably had murdered only two victims. (He had already been tried for the murder of his mother, had served the sentence and had been released.)

One of the eleven victims was the famous "Orange Socks"—an unidentified woman found in a Texas culvert in 1979, naked except for a pair of orange socks. Despite the fact that Lucas was at the time working in Florida, not Texas, the jury accepted his confession and sentenced him to death. (The sentence was later commuted by the governor.) In August 2019, based on a familial DNA match with her sister, "Orange Socks" was identified as twenty-three-year-old Debra Louise Jackson. Thanks to Lucas's false confession, her murderer escaped justice.

This kind of false and exaggerated serial killer confession became known as the "Henry Lee Lucas syndrome." Cold case departments have learned to be very wary of falling into this trap. One of the reasons that investigators in Bergen County, New Jersey, took so long to extract and process Richard Cottingham's confessions in the 1968 and 1969 schoolgirl murders had to do with their scrupulous review of his claims. A less discriminating jurisdiction might happily accept a confession at face value in order to take a cold case off their unsolved list.

Often these cold cases are declared as "exceptionally cleared," which means that they will not go to trial—either because the suspect is deceased, there is insufficient evidence other than the confession or an immunity deal was negotiated. The families of the victim are informed, but the press might not be advised of the "exceptional closure" or of the evidence behind the closure. The case just fades away, closed but perhaps not exactly "solved."

Serial killers are motivated to make false confessions by numerous factors, including competitive ego boosting and boasting, exercising control over police and media as they are sent scurrying around alleged burial sites with cadaver dogs and ground radar—sometimes it can be as simple as a day out of prison for a walk in the fresh country air to point out an alleged body site and a meal on the road instead of gray prison food.

The 1980s: "Lucifer Dwells Within All of Us! . . . See You in Disneyland"

With almost seven hundred serial killers identified in the 1980s and the Henry Lee Lucas story coming to a dead end, the media began to shift its focus away from victim numbers to the serial killer's novelty. It was no longer about numbers but style.

Right in the middle of the 1980s came Richard Ramirez, "the Night Stalker." He killed a "moderate" thirteen victims, but he had media flare. The murders happened in California in 1984 and 1985 and fit the bill perfectly for media attention. Ramirez's victims ranged from nine years old to seventy-nine years old, female and male. He committed some of his murders as part of home invasions and became known as the Walk-in Killer in addition to the Night Stalker. He gouged out one victim's eyes with a spoon and took them away with him. One night, he killed three victims; on other nights, he left them raped and battered but alive. (As Richard Cottingham explained to me, "Killing somebody does not make you God; it's knowing whether they will live or die that makes you that.")

The Night Stalker left occult symbols at some of his crime scenes, such as an inverted pentagram drawn on a victim's thigh in lipstick. Some crime scenes were signed "Jack the Knife." One victim who survived reported that as she was being raped, he forced her to recite, "I love Satan." When asked where they hid their valuables, victims were ordered to "swear on Satan" that they were telling the truth.

The victims seemed chosen completely at random, and the killer made unsuccessful attempts to disguise his fingerprints. His victims often saw his face, and he left them alive as often as he killed them. Outside the windows of the houses he entered, he left behind his shoe prints.

When the FBI's Behavioral Science Unit was asked to profile the crime scenes, they responded that the crimes were unique and did not conform to anything they had seen before.

With Los Angeles on the alert as these killings became more frequent and frenzied in the summer of 1985, a neighborhood volunteer safety patrol encountered the Night Stalker and nearly beat him to death before the LAPD arrived and rescued him.

At his trial, Ramirez flashed press photographers an inverted pentagram inked on his palm and chanted, "Evil, evil . . ." When he was convicted and sentenced to death, he growled at the court:

> "I don't believe in the hypocritical, moralistic dogma of this so-called civilized society. . . . I need not look beyond this room to see all the liars, haters, the killers, the crooks, the paranoid cowards; truly trematodes of the Earth, each one in his own legal profession. . . . You maggots make me sick; hypocrites one and all. . . . And no one knows that better than those who kill for policy, clandestinely or openly, as do the governments of the world, which kill in the name of god and country or for whatever reason they deem appropriate. . . . I don't need to hear all of society's rationalizations. I've heard them all before and the fact remains that what is, is. You don't understand me. You are not expected to. You are not capable of it. . . . I am beyond your experience. I am beyond good and evil, legions of the night—night breed—repeat not the errors of the Night Stalker and show no mercy. . . . I will be avenged. Lucifer dwells within all of us! . . . See you in Disneyland."

Entertainment Tonight had been on the air already for five years, airing right after the network news shows; while it used a newscast format, it focused exclusively on celebrity gossip. But as serial killers gained antihero celebrity status, their coverage in the hard newscast began to carry over into *ET* and similar shows like *Inside Edition* and *Hard Copy* that all followed the newscasts. With his inverted pentagram goat-head tattoo girls, who passionately pledged their deep, dark love for him, Richard Ramirez was a TV hit. He was hot. He was also in California, a state that permitted the televising of courtroom proceedings, like Florida, where Ted Bundy became the lead in his own televised trial (in which the judge sentencing him to death complimented him on his lawyerly skills).

Sometimes it was an extra twist in the headlines or moniker that brought them some measure of historical notoriety. The 1980s brought us serial killers like Douglas Clark, "the Sunset Strip Killer," and his girlfriend-accomplice, Carol Bundy, who infamously shampooed and set the hair and makeup of a severed head Clark brought home to have sex with; David Alan Gore, a Florida auxiliary sheriff's deputy and one of the Killing Cousins; Gary Michael Heidnik, a self-made millionaire who kept his enslaved victims chained in a basement pit in a squalid house in Philadelphia and would partly inspire the fictional Buffalo Bill in *The Silence of the Lambs* (along with Ed Gein); Robert Hansen, "the Butcher Baker," in Alaska, who would fly his female victims in his private plane to a remote cabin where he set them loose in the wild to hunt them down; Leonard Lake and Charles Ng in Calaveras County, in Northern California, who recorded video of themselves with their victims in a remote bunker they built; these were the few serial killers from that decade who came to some degree of prominence or fame while the rest of the seven hundred were barely mentioned in national news media and were not subjects of true-crime books.

Serial killers like Rodney Halbower and Harrison Graham—who has heard of them?

Halbower killed barely enough victims to make a Wikipedia list of serial killers, while Harrison Graham had a "respectable" number of victims, seven, but they were "less-dead": inner-city black sex workers. Typically, his case was reported for a few days and then forgotten.

That's how seven hundred serial killers tramped through the 1980s.

Arthur Shawcross, "The Genesee River Killer," Part 3, Rochester, New York, 1988–1989

Arthur Shawcross, whose story I have been telling since his father's return from the Pacific in 1945 to his first two murders in 1972, committed his fourteenth and last murder on December 28, 1989, closing out not only the decade but a strange, somnambulistic cycle with war trauma, which the father Roy Shawcross had suffered fighting in World War II in the Pacific, while his serial killer son, Arthur, fantasized his in a supply depot in Vietnam; Shawcross is a tale of two wars and one serial killer.

Shawcross certainly had the kind of twist the media loved; there were hints of cannibalism, which always gets press, and his claims to having perpetrated atrocities in Vietnam gave the story extra legs. Yet at the same time, there was something mediocre and average in his murder of desperate sex workers trying to survive in a rough city like Rochester. In his actual murders, he was like so many other serial killers, lurching about in the night, strangling in a rage vulnerable, drug-addicted sex workers. Take away his previous two child murders and his Vietnam stories, and Shawcross could stand in for every third serial killer there ever was. That's why of the nearly two thousand serial killers that made up the "golden age" between 1950 and 1999, his story is among those told here.

After murdering two children in 1972, Shawcross later said, "I was sent to prison for 0-25 years. The first 8 years were hard for me." Child murderers are targeted in prison by other inmates, and Shawcross had to be confined for his own safety in a segregation unit. He misbehaved, threw tantrums, malingered and faked seizures and frequently refused to cooperate with psychiatrists or to participate in therapy.

Between his mounting claims of child abuse at the hands of his domineering mother, incest with his sisters and an aunt, to his fantasies of the horrors of combat in Vietnam, Shawcross collected a babble of meaningless psychiatric evaluations and parole assessments and comments that included "dangerous schizophrenic pedophile suffering from 'intermittent explosive personality'; hears voices when he is depressed; engaged in fantasy as a source of satisfaction; oral-erotic fixation with a need for maternal protection; possible organic involvement; normal psychopathic individual; not much insight concerning maladaptive life dating back to early adolescence; less than complete sincerity in dealing with deep-seated intraphysic [sic] and interpersonal conflicts; antisocial personality disorder and schizoid personality disorder . . . psycho sexual conflicts; prone to be rather simplistic and childlike in his attitudes; remains to himself much of the time; appears unable to establish peer relations, but shows good deal of trust in authority figures; a release of this man to the community at this time, given his lack of change in behavior, might result in a murder of several more children; obviously he is quite dangerous and capable of horrible crimes; mother never let his father be the man in the house; for years his mother would swear at father, throw coffee at him; mother ran the house and the father just brought home the money; had a very unhappy childhood because his parents were constantly fighting. He was lonely. He felt unloved, unwanted by his parents; still denies memory of his actions toward the girl after he grabbed her; there are some uninformative psychiatric examinations in the inmate's file; do not feel that the inmate had any conscious desire . . . when his blood is cold to be a bad person or to hurt others. However the inmate has proved himself to be an extremely unusual person and one whose actual inner workings are probably completely beyond comprehension of any of us."

Shawcross's third wife, Penny Sherbino, remained loyal to him, convinced of his innocence. But after four or five years in prison, Shawcross became "engaged" to a pen pal, Rose Marie Walley, and he divorced Sherbino.

"Possibly the Most Dangerous Individual to Have Been Released"

In his eighth year of a prison sentence that could last twenty-five years, Shawcross began to feel motivated to get out. He set to work improving his image by enrolling in various therapy programs he had previously refused to participate in. It worked like a charm. His psychiatric reports immediately improved.

Psychiatrists wrote that Shawcross was:

> neat, clean, quiet, cooperative, attentive, and pleasant. No bizarre mannerisms. Normal facial appearance and posture. Self-esteem/self-image good. Tolerance for frustration within normal limits. Abstract thinking intact. No hallucination/delusions. Thought processes logical, rational. . . . Does not manifest any psychotic/neurotic symptoms. Positive attitude. Intelligence good, good reality contact, denies suicidal or homicidal ideation. Not depressed, not elated, mood neutral, affect

appropriate, motor activity normal, no bizarre gestures or mannerisms. Emotionally stable. Not mentally ill at present. No delusions, no morbid preoccupations. [Can] utilize psychotherapy to maintain his ability to control his emotional conflicts once he is placed on parole.

After fourteen years and six months in prison, the parole board decided to release Arthur Shawcross back into society and into his fiancée Rose Marie Walley's arms. Shawcross had gone into prison as a young, relatively good-looking, slim man of twenty-seven; he was coming out looking considerably older than his forty-one years. He was balding, his hair stringy and gray. His face was now puffy and bloated, and he had developed a potbelly. But along with all that aging tubby fat, Shawcross had powerful gorilla arms with hands that tightened with vise grip strength and a seething sexualized anger toward diminutive women. He hid it well behind an easygoing charm with an undertone of false vulnerability that he would turn on instinctually like a predator, in the way a chameleon takes on a color.

Not all psychiatrists and parole board officials were fooled by Shawcross. One psychiatrist had warned prior to Shawcross's release, "Though the psychiatric and psychological profession has apparently not as yet defined a diagnosis for this inmate's aberrant behavior or, even more pertinently, a cure, the society at large deserves protection until such is the case which would probably not be until well past this inmate's conditional release date."

After Shawcross's release was approved, a parole board official bluntly complained, "At the risk of being dramatic, the writer considers this man to be possibly the most dangerous individual to have been released to this community in many years."

Shawcross was released on April 28, 1987, and ordered to live in Binghamton, New York, in a Volunteers of America shelter under strict supervision. Shawcross was required to meet weekly with his parole officer, abstain from drugs and alcohol, abide by an 11:00 p.m. curfew, regularly attend a mental health clinic and stay away from children, playgrounds and anywhere else children routinely congregate.

Shawcross immediately breached all the terms of his parole. He routinely hung out in playgrounds and parks while fishing; he stayed out beyond his curfew; he did not seek employment and spent a lot of time on his bunk brooding in deep thought. After a few visits to required therapy, the psychiatrist concluded that Shawcross had "orgasmic and ejaculatory problems. No unusual sexual fantasies . . . [no insight into the child murders other than] having problems with anger and experiences in Vietnam."

The psychiatrist declared, "No mental disorder requiring any specific counseling or treatment at this time."

Shawcross now dropped out of therapy.

In the fifth week of his release, Shawcross came up behind a female volunteer at his shelter, seized her by her crotch and body-slammed her down on a bed. According to the parole board document reporting this incident, Shawcross did not go further after "she told him to let her alone, that she was not that type of a woman." The report further stated that Shawcross had stolen several hundred dollars' worth of property from the woman's residence. No action was taken.

While the parole board may have let the case fall between the cracks, Shawcross was hounded by police departments, citizens and the media. Reports of his crimes and his location were revealed to the public several times, and as a result, Shawcross and Rose Marie were shuffled around various communities in northern New York. Finally, after a huge public outcry, the parole board moved Shawcross to a new location and ensured that it was kept secret from the media and most authorities.

On June 29, 1987, Arthur Shawcross and Rose Marie arrived in New York State's third largest city, Rochester. Eight months later, in March 1988, Arthur Shawcross would begin killing anew and would not stop until he was caught two years later, munching away on a salad while admiring the frozen corpse of his twelfth female victim on January 3, 1990.

"What a Boy Would Want from Mama!"

In Rochester, Rose Marie was employed as a home care worker for elderly and disabled clients while Shawcross eventually landed a job chopping and preparing vegetables for a wholesale producer in Rochester's public market. He and Rose Marie moved into a creepy Tudor-style apartment building on 241 Alexander Street, in a neighborhood that was shabbier in 1987 than it is today. G. Jack Urso, who lived in the Normandie Apartments next door to Shawcross, blogged his recollections: "I would sometimes see Shawcross riding a little girl's bicycle. I didn't know him by name, but a large, overweight, middle-aged man riding around on a child's bike was an unforgettable, surreal vision. I can still see him in my mind all these years later, as clear as if it were yesterday, peddling past the Normandie with a stare fixed straight ahead, as oblivious to the world around him as the world was of him. 'My God, man,' I recall thinking to myself, 'have you no self-respect?'"[23]

Shawcross continued to drag his feet and avoid therapy. His psychiatrist in Rochester reported that Shawcross couldn't afford therapy: "As you know he has very limited income and the cost at this time, although on a sliding scale, still is quite difficult for him. When he does obtain fulltime work and possibly some health insurance, this may no longer present a difficulty for him. Shawcross reports extensive and what sounds like rather thorough counseling, both for his post-traumatic stress disorder while in Vietnam, as well as his sexual difficulties which led to his imprisonment. He does report extensive self-awareness and what sounds like very appropriate use of psychiatric and psychological resources while at Green Haven. . . ."

A parole officer optimistically reported, "His relationship with Rose appears to be a strong one and both appear to support each other. Once her divorce is finalized, they indicate they will be married and both hope to remain in the Rochester community where they can assume a quiet life."

Rose found life with Arthur a strange existence. On one hand he had a short temper and was demanding. He could be scary when he lost his temper, Rose learned. But on the other hand he was hardworking, helpful, sweet and protective. He did a lot of the household chores and he enjoyed cooking. True, he had some sexual hang-ups, but who doesn't? Rose would later comment. He had problems reaching a climax. He made lewd comments to Rose about women he saw on TV that were normally reserved for male conversation, like "Look at those tits!"

What maybe troubled Rose most were his silent, brooding "withdrawals." Ignoring her completely, he would sit blank faced, staring at the TV, moving his lips, or he would go off alone "fishing" or hang out at the Dunkin' Donuts a few blocks down, chatting up cops. He occasionally borrowed her car, but mostly he still got around on his bicycle. Neighbors had mixed reviews of Shawcross: he could be friendly and very helpful one day but unsmiling and cold the next, ignoring their greetings. Others noted that Shawcross could be speaking coherently and then blurt out something "inappropriate."

At work, Shawcross was reliable and punctual and mostly kept to himself, but there were some issues. He told graphic stories of atrocities he'd perpetrated in Vietnam, and once when a young fellow employee angered him, he grabbed the youth by the neck and slammed him up against a wall.

Then there was Loretta Neal, a young woman from West Virginia whom he pestered to the point that she complained. When Shawcross's boss told him to leave her alone, he was startled by Shawcross's aggressive response: "Everybody else in this joint is fucking her. I don't know why I can't."

Shawcross was warned that if he didn't stop harassing Loretta he would be fired. He backed off. Instead, he cozied up with Loretta's mother, Clara Neal, who was instantly smitten with him when she came by to pick up her daughter from work one day in late December 1987. In January, Shawcross began an affair with Clara.

Since their arrival in Rochester, Rose had seen a gradual degradation in her relationship with Arthur. The subject of his abuse and rejection by his mother was a constant refrain. His mother had refused to visit him during his incarceration, and there was no question of his returning to the scene of his two child murders in Watertown. Thus it was now fifteen years since he'd seen his mother. Shawcross repeatedly invited her to come visit him in Rochester; she never came. He spent a considerable amount of time, energy and money purchasing an antique silver plate for her as a gift, but she didn't like it, saying that he should buy only new things as gifts. Arthur grew even more sullen and withdrawn and began staying out longer and longer, returning with lame excuses about his absences. Claiming that Rose was hurting him while on top of him during sex, he forced her to go on a crash diet. When she didn't do what he wanted, he slapped her and grabbed her leg so hard she was bruised for days. She complained about the abuse to Shawcross's mother, who responded that Rose should tell his parole officer. Not wanting to lose Arthur because he "was still worth all the trouble," Rose instead concealed the deteriorating relationship from the parole officer in a deluded hope that when her divorce came through and she married Arthur, all would be well.

His mask of sanity peeling, Shawcross was openly seething at Rose, reserving his sweet and vulnerable mask for his new girlfriend, Clara Neal. As he raged and abused Rose, he purred and cuddled up to Clara. Clara told Jack Olsen:

> At first I think he appraised me more like a mother type than a lover or girlfriend. Even at forty-two, that's what he needed most. He'd scoot down the end of my couch, lay his head on my lap and go to sleep, me holding him jes' like you would a baby. He'd pull his shirt off and I'd take a hairbrush and rub his back gently. What a boy would want from Mama![24]

His visits to Clara were becoming regular, and he soon began borrowing her car, driving her to the nursing home where she worked and returning for her at the end of her shift. In between he would cruise the street hookers on Lyell Avenue.

One day in mid-March 1988, he picked up twenty-seven-year-old Dorothy Blackburn, who would become the first of his twelve victims in Rochester. He claimed that Dorothy bit him while they were engaged in "sixty-nine"—mutual oral sex—and that he bit her in retaliation. He confessed that he then stripped her, tied her arms, beat her and raped her and then when he was finished and told her to get dressed, she called him "little man," which so enraged him that he strangled her. He said afterward he "spent half the night with her" before dumping her body into a creek.

Around this time, both Rose and Clara noted a sudden change in his behavior. He became even more withdrawn and quiet. On March 24, the body of Dorothy Blackburn was found; the next day, as Shawcross was driving Clara and two of her grandkids in her car, a police car came up behind and signaled for them to pull over. Clara recalls he seemed panicked, and she had to persuade him to stop. It was a routine traffic stop, but his fear, he told Clara, was that his parole would be endangered because having Clara's grandkids near him was a violation. This episode must have been a wake-up call for Shawcross, especially if he was aware of Blackburn's body being found the day before.

After that, Shawcross stopped visiting Clara. He was acutely aware of his homicidal impulses and his behavioral disorders, and he now tightened up his mask of sanity. He refrained from killing for nearly eighteen months and broke off his relationship with Clara Neal, promising Rose he would marry her as soon as her divorce came through.

About a month after he had raped, mutilated and murdered Blackburn, he went in for a mental health assessment. The counselor happily chirped:

> For one thing he is engaged to be married to his fiancée and consort and he reports that their sexual relationship is greatly improved. She has lost a great deal of weight through dieting and feels more competent so they are no longer experiencing sexual difficulties.... Social adjust shows great improvement.... He has reestablished contact with his parents after eighteen years, has a pleasant apartment with his girlfriend and seems to have made friends.... There has been no recurrence according to his report of any impulses or inclination toward the sort of behavior which landed him in prison for a number of years.... I have left it with him that he can contact me on his own initiative should he feel the need for ongoing help with any personal problems. At this time I've scheduled no further visits and do not feel he should be compelled to come.

"This Motherfucker's Getting Weirder and Weirder"

After his first murder in Rochester, and the false alarm of being pulled over by the police, Shawcross kept his homicidal impulses under control for about a year and a half. Serial killers are often triggered by "stressors": a loss of employment, a breakup, or an impending marriage or birth of a child. In the spring of 1988, Shawcross's employers at the fruit and vegetable producer discovered his record as a child killer and harassed him into leaving his job despite his overall good work performance. When Shawcross found work with another grocer, his former employers warned them about the "child killer" but were told he was a "hell of a worker."

The one-year anniversary of Shawcross's arrival in Rochester was coming up on June 29, and the parole board requested another mental health assessment. After two meetings, the psychiatrist gave him a clean bill of health:

> I find that Art is a well controlled and fairly stable individual. Although he continues to exhibit some discomfort or flashes related to anger, he is able to manage these episodes very well.
>
> The one feature which continues to be present in his current functioning which was probably predominant in his past is his general inclination or personality style of dealing with guilt or bad feelings by becoming angry rather than becoming or experiencing serious discomfort, depression or low self-esteem.
>
> Given his history of childhood and early adult difficulties, traumas and anti-social behavior, it is logical that Art has developed elaborate and somewhat dysfunctional defenses in managing his feelings. However, this functioning style does not appear to present any current emotional or behavioral difficulties and Art does not have any particular motivation to pursue treatment at this time. Consequently I see no need for pursuing counseling with Art at this time.

But typical of psychopaths, all this time Shawcross was retreating into secret lives. He and Clara restarted their affair in the spring of 1989 despite his plans to marry Rose. Shawcross regularly borrowed her car to cruise Lyell Avenue for prostitutes while she was at work. In the meantime, Rose's divorce came through, and in August 1989, she became his fourth wife.

At the same time Shawcross was marrying Rose, he was going at it hot and heavy with Clara. He'd told her that he had been paroled into Rose's custody and that he would leave her when his parole expired in April 1990 and he and Clara would go live together somewhere warm. When her son warned her that Shawcross had been sent to prison for killing a little girl, Clara told him to shut up, she didn't want to know. She loved Shawcross and never brought it up, and neither did he. It was all in the past now, and he served his time in prison for it. He had the right to live in peace.

Clara's daughter Linda also did not like him at all. Shawcross pestered her whenever he saw her. He once threw her on a bed and she had to fight him off. Another time he pinched her nipple. When she complained to Clara, she laughed it off as only "joking around." Linda recalled that Shawcross was around little boys all the time, buying them presents and taking them places. It worried her that he took an interest in her young sons, watching cartoons with them and playing with them for hours. He liked to tussle with them roughly, once biting her fourteen-year-old on the nipple as he held him down on Clara's kitchen floor. Linda didn't like the bite marks she saw on her mother's breasts, upper arms and inner thighs. These weren't *love bites*, she observed; they were the bites of a vicious, angry animal.

Clara, on the other hand, maintained her rosy view of their relationship. Shawcross gave her a wedding ring that he said had belonged to one of his ex-wives. The ring was from one of his murder victims, Patty Ives, who had stubbornly refused to pawn or sell it even in the worst of times. Now Clara said the ring was so beautiful that it would make her cry and she hated it when police seized it from her. "They can tell me a thousand times," she said, "but I'll never believe it belonged to no dead whore."

Shawcross's neighbors got used to the middle-aged man riding a girl's bicycle and his odd comments, like asking one woman if she knew that pinching female breasts could cause cancer. He put his head into the lap of another woman and complained he hadn't had sex in months. The women he was acquainted with brushed him off as a harmless oddball but kept their distance from him.

In July 1989, the prospect of his wedding to Rose "triggered" Shawcross into murdering again, and now he would go on a serial killing rampage that would not end until his arrest some six months later. One after the other, Shawcross murdered women, mostly sex workers he picked up on Lyell Avenue:

- July 9—Anna Marie Steffen, 28
- July 29—Dorothy Keeler, 59
- September 29—Patricia "Patty" Ives, 25
- October 23—June Stott, 26
- November 5—Marie Welch, 22
- November 11—Frances "Franny" Brown, 22
- November 15—Kimberly Logan, 30
- November 25—Elizabeth "Liz" Gibson, 29
- December 15—Darlene Trippi, 32
- December 17—June Cicero, 33
- December 28—Felicia Stephens, 20

After his honeymoon with Rose, Shawcross's behavior escalated to the point that he was killing three to four victims a month. He was literally in a bloodlust frenzy by the end of 1989. He engaged in necrophiliac sex with the corpses of the women he had killed and mutilated some of them, cutting away their genitals, which he told police he ate. Shawcross claimed that after sawing out June Cicero's vagina from her frozen corpse, he sucked on it like a "meat Popsicle" while driving away from the scene. (In another version, Shawcross stated he warmed it with the car heater.)

Shawcross frequently covered his victims under concrete or asphalt debris, or brush and branches, as he'd done with his child victims. It could have been a sign of his remorse, or it could have been done simply to conceal the corpse. Shawcross later admitted that it served a practical purpose: to advance the decomposition of his victims in the hope that evidence would be destroyed, as it had been with his first victim, Jack Blake.

Many of the sex workers on Lyell Avenue were familiar with Shawcross as an amiable "john" they knew as "Mitch." He was seen as a goofy, harmless, easy date, at least for the girls he did not kill. Some even talked to him about the "strangler" stalking them, not realizing they were in his car. One veteran street worker, well into her forties, remembered getting picked up by "Mitch" and, as she later told police:

> Three minutes into the ride I caught the bad vibes. This guy was a nonstop talker. . . . His voice turns growly and he starts telling me about hoes that ripped him off. . . . I'm thinking, Something isn't right about this guy. Something doesn't hang together. . . . He said he could take my sons fishing. . . . I'm thinking, This motherfucker's getting weirder and weirder. . . . I did my little hoe's roll and got out and shuffled around to the backseat. . . . He joined me in the back. I asked him to use a rubber but he didn't want to hear about it. . . . I did an acrobat spread, feet against the back window, head propped on the passenger bucket seat. Then I went into a Georgia Buck, which is you push your chin tight against your chest bone so the john can't get at your neck—hard on the breathing but it may save your life.
>
> He says, "Wouldn't you be more comfortable with your head in between the seats?" Something told me, No, no, you gotta keep this sucker in sight. If I put my head between the seats, I wouldn't be able to see him and my neck would be in a blind-side position. . . . I thought, Maybe this guy is not strangling women, he's suffocating them. It would've been a cinch with my head between the seats. So I says, "No! I'm fine just like I am."
>
> He wasn't hard and he couldn't get it in, but he seemed cool enough. He talked all the time he was trying to fuck. His three favorite subjects were his wife is a bitch, hunting and fishing in the country, and all the shitty things the other hoes did to him.

I was being careful. I'm thinking, Could this goofy guy be the strangler?

. . . His hands keep fluttering toward my neck, and I'm telling him, "Don't *do* that! I have asthma." . . . He stops pushing and says, "What the fuck are you?" He looks me dead in the face and his voice turns mean: "*What the fuck are you, one of those bip bam thank you ma'am bitches?*"

He shoved at my chest. I went to myself, Fuck, this *is* the strangler and you're next! You better start playing this motherfucker right and let him know you can handle him. . . .

It went on like that for over an hour, a cat-and-mouse game as Shawcross kept attempting to get his hands around her throat. She had a knife with her ready to use if things went off the rails.

His hand went back up above my tits. I said, "Hey, I told you. *Don't* do that. I'm too ticklish." That was about the fifth time I had to tell him. I'm thinking, it's normal for a trick to reach up and grab my tits, but this guy was interested in my *neck*. See, my tits are so big they're over to the side. I don't wear a bra or underwear when I'm working. So his hands got no business up around my neck when my tits are over to the side, see what I'm saying?

Every time Shawcross sounded edgy, she would talk him down. And she let him know she had a knife in one of her hands near his rib cage. It was like that balance between war and diplomacy. She was very firm in her limits with Shawcross but without insulting or denigrating him ("Don't *do* that! I have asthma"; "Don't *do* that! I'm too ticklish"); at the same time, she kept a knife on hand and made sure Shawcross was aware she would use it on him. Eventually, Shawcross got tired of the whole thing and drove her home.

All the way home he's doing the motor mouth again. When I didn't respond, he said, "Why're you so quiet? Are you shy?"

Sounded kind of annoyed, like it was a social error if you didn't comment on every word. You see that in johns.

I had him drop me off, and when I went inside, I told my boyfriend, "I coulda' swore I was out with the fucking strangler tonight."

He said, "How could that be? You're still alive."[25]

That's what it took to survive a date with Arthur Shawcross and many others like him. Most women working the streets did not have the experience or focus that this veteran street sex worker had. The other ones that survived did so because they were lucky that Shawcross was not moody that night.

"Moments Thereafter His Hands Would Close Around the Necks of His Victims"

In November, as the victims began to pile up, the FBI's Behavioral Science Unit was asked to produce a profile. They were right in identifying most of Shawcross's characteristics, but wrong on one major one; starting with the serial killer's average age at the first murder and accounting for the arc of escalation, the profile estimated his age to be early thirties. What the FBI did not know was that while Shawcross was indeed twenty-seven when he killed his first two victims in Watertown, his killing "arc" was suspended by a fourteen-year prison term. It took Shawcross about ten months after his release from prison to pick up where he left off. He was killing like a thirty-year-old serial killer might.

FBI profiling is often criticized as ineffectual or "pseudoscience," but acting on the FBI's assessment that the serial killing unsub would return to the bodies, Rochester Police and New York State Police began flying helicopter patrols over areas where the serial killer liked to dump bodies.

On the morning of January 3, 1990, about four months before Shawcross's parole supervision was scheduled to end, the police helicopter spotted him eating a salad in the door of a car parked on a bridge above the body of June Cicero, a prostitute who had vanished a few days earlier right under the noses of a police surveillance team. After that it was simple: it took police a few days to squeeze a confession out of Shaw-cross in the deaths of eleven women. Shawcross led police to two victims who had not yet been discovered. In the end, Shawcross was charged in ten murders from the twelve he was suspected in. One murder, Eliza-beth "Liz" Gibson, was in a different jurisdiction, while another murder could not be conclusively linked to Shawcross. After being convicted of ten counts of second-degree murder in late November 1990, Shawcross was sentenced to twenty-five years imprisonment for each of the ten murders he was charged with; a total of 250 years. He later pleaded guilty in the murder of Elizabeth Gibson. There would be no hope for parole or early release for Shawcross this time.

In each case, Shawcross would later claim, the victim did something to anger or frighten him. He said he suffocated or strangled some vic-tims "by accident" while trying to keep them quiet because he was afraid of being discovered and having his parole revoked, or that he accidentally choked the victim with his penis during oral sex. He killed a woman for trying to steal his money, for hiding the fact that she was having her period or for mocking him when he was unable to have an erection. He said he unintentionally strangled another victim by closing an electric car window on her neck when she leaned into his car. In the case of an acquaintance, fifty-nine-year-old homeless woman Dorothy Keeler, whose head he later removed from her decomposing corpse, Shawcross claimed she tried to extort money from him by threatening to tell Rose they were having sex. It was a typical serial killer's propensity to blame the victim for instigating her own death at his hands.

To further distance himself from the sexual sadistic rage driving him, Shawcross claimed that he could not remember most of the mur-ders. He would describe an "aura" state of rage, where he would break out into a sweat and there would be bright light and then he would sud-denly return to consciousness, and oops, there is a dead woman next to him, golly gosh gee, how did that happen? And by the way, I might as well have sex with her warm corpse while I'm here, and maybe cut it up a little and take the vagina with me and eat it.

Now the corrections, judicial, medical and psychiatric communities came together to clean up the mess and try to figure out exactly what was wrong with Shawcross. Some of the diagnoses were the same as his early diagnoses: sadistic paraphilia, sociopathy, uninhibited aggression, sexual dysfunction, no impulse control, trauma-induced rage and the usual bogeyman of serial killing: psychopathy.

The defense psychiatrist Dr. Dorothy Otnow Lewis fell for Shawcross's Vietnam War tall tales, which by the time of his trial in 1990 were much more elaborate than the ones he first told in the early 1970s and now echoed the surrealistic Francis Ford Coppola movie *Apocalypse Now*. She argued, as quoted above, that Shawcross might have been a victim of CIA brainwashing experiments in Vietnam. She also suggested he had organic brain dysfunctions and believed his assertions that he could not remember his homicidal acts. She states:

> Arthur Shawcross had the classic signs and symptoms of temporal lobe seizures—the auras, the stereotyped behaviors for which memory was impaired, the subsequent deep sleep. For example, just prior to a homicidal episode, he would begin to sweat and his world would explode in bright, white light. Moments thereafter his hands would close around the necks of his victims. Then, amazingly, he would fall into a deep, post-seizure sleep. When he awakened, the memory of his murderous behavior would be hazy and distorted.[26]

There were certain physiological and biochemical explanations offered for his killing impulse. Shawcross had had multiple head injuries as a child and adolescent, which is common in serial killers. An EEG showed brain abnormality: "paroxysmal irritative patterns in bifrontotemporal areas—more in the right side."[27] A CT scan showed a slight asymmetry; an MRI showed a small subarachnoid cyst, a healed frontal lobe fracture and a slightly atrophied and foreshortened temporal lobe. The studies I cited above by Kent A. Kiehl do sustain a correlation between head injuries and "acquired psychopathy."

There were biochemical abnormalities that could lower the inhibition of aggression. Shawcross was diagnosed with pyroluria, an elevated level of kryptopyrrole in the urine; his number was 200, when 20 would be considered high. Pyrolurics have severe behavior problems, can't control their anger when provoked, have mood swings and tend to be night owls.

There were also genetic explanations advanced. Shawcross had a rare XYY chromosome combination. As we know, these are the sex chromosomes: XX in a woman, XY in a man. It is well known that atypical chromosomal combinations can result in atypical sexual development. For example, in Klinefelter syndrome, the combination XXY results in a male body with some female characteristics. Since an "extra X" appears to feminize men, some theorists speculated that an additional Y chromosome might "hyper masculinize" men who had it. Since men are more aggressive than women, it might be that men who have XYY chromosomes, the way Shawcross did, might be more aggressive than other men and hence more likely to commit violent crimes. However, while it was eventually established that XYY men *are* more common in the offender population, they tend to commit non-violent crimes, not violent crimes as the XYY hypothesis predicted.[28]

In the end, nobody could figure out Shawcross, not least because of his tendency to exaggerate and fantasize a range of traumas from childhood sexual abuse and parental abuse to aura states and PTSD. While it is very plausible that Shawcross endured some degree of trauma in his early life, the exact nature, extent and context of it forever remained cloaked by the constantly evolving fantasies he spun for anybody interested or needing to hear.

Finally, none of this may matter if Shawcross actually came to believe in his own lies and fantasies.

"Give Me Your Hand"

Confined in Sullivan Correctional Facility in Fallsburg, New York, Shawcross led a full and active life—perhaps the best and most fulfilling years of his life. He divorced Rose and in 1997 married his loyal mistress, Clara Neal, making her his fifth wife. He was fifty-two and she was sixty-six. Clara stated, "It was nice and all. It took 10 years to make the grade but I finally did it." Shawcross eventually divorced Clara and sought a sixth wife for himself from the hundreds of lonely serial killer groupies who wrote him in prison.

He developed a budding prison art career, painting canvases that were sold on eBay (a violation of prison rules) and were included in an annual inmate art show. The "Corrections on Canvas" show, which had been staged for thirty-five years, was discontinued in 2002, after the public protested that Shawcross was profiting from the sale of his paintings.

While in prison, Shawcross also developed a culinary career, compiling six hundred typed pages of recipes, which he would send one by one to "murderabilia" collectors; they trade today for about fifty dollars. To a journalist interviewing him about his recipes, Shawcross said he developed a taste for human flesh in Vietnam when South Korean soldiers fighting alongside American troops offered him pieces of cooked Vietnamese casualties. He said, "One of them says, 'Here, try it.' And I closed my eyes and I bit into it. And I said, 'This ain't bad.' It tasted like fresh ham. . . . Nobody eats my cooking. They might think there's a finger in there."[29]

He gave multiple interviews and sent out so many nail clippings and strands of his pubic hair to collectors that he created a glut in the "murderabilia" market. In several documentary and television shoots, looking like a nice, chubby grandfather with big eyeglasses, he told his usual Vietnam War fantasies, but the stories differed slightly with every telling.

One of the last people to interview Shawcross before his death was Canadian journalist Nadia Fezzani. She described meeting him in a prison interview room:

> His grey hair was combed back. Chest hair emerged from the top of his shirt. Only his eyebrows still revealed a little of the brown hair of his youth. He had a gentle, friendly looking face with a large nose and an easy smile on his thin lips. His misaligned teeth had yellowed over the years. His body lan-

guage clearly revealed his joy in seeing me. . . . Because of films about serial killers, often portrayed with physical features reflecting the monstrousness of their crimes, I had imagined a man with malevolent eyes. But Shawcross looked as gentle as a lamb. . . . I relaxed my vigilance a little, until I remembered that this paunchy sexagenarian had killed more than a dozen innocent victims.[30]

Fezzani had interviewed a number of serial killers and was experienced with their deceptive ways, but even she found herself needing to focus on resisting the cannibal strangler's amiable charm when interviewing him in prison.

> He looked at me through his big glasses and then said to me, "Give me your hand."
>
> My hand? Why did he want my hand? I hesitated for what felt like an eternity. If I chose not to obey him, he would say that I had no trust in him, and so why should he trust me? I held out my hand. He took it with both his hands and turned it over to read my palm.
>
> **AS:** You are going to live a long time, Nadia.[31]

"Arthur I Will Always Love You"

On November 10, 2008, Shawcross complained of a sudden pain in his leg and was rushed to Albany Medical Center, where he died several hours later of coronary failure at the age of sixty-three.

Dozens of his female pen pals would mourn his death, some posting last letters to him on the Internet:

> Well Arthur, we were writing to each other for a while, and although many might not have agreed with me, I'll still miss the letters we shared. Maybe you did change before the end, or maybe you were just the same as you were when you committed the horrendous acts, no one will ever no [sic], but you. I just hope you did. I hope you find some kind of peace

now, and I hope the families whose lives you tore apart also can find some peace, bye Art!

Kate

Arthur,

I have been wondering if you received my letter before you past away [sic]. In the past few letters that you wrote to me you said that you had been unwell, but was getting better! I can't believe that you are now gone. My boys have the pictures that you drew for them on the wall—thank you once again. I know we had some funny times and I know that you have changed from the person that you was—and i know the reason why you did what you did. I will miss you Arthur and the letters that we shared. May God take care of you and may you now rest in peace. I will never forget you:)

Rachael xxxx

Arthur, thanks for the countless emails, drawings, and 4 leaf clovers. We sure do miss hearing from you as we did look forward to every one of your letters . . . almost weekly.

Witter

Arthur I will always love you. I'm just sorry we didn't get to get married like we both talked about before you went into the hospital. I will cherish the ring that you sent me.

Courtney

Arthur and I were friends for 10+ years. I don't condone his killings but I felt he was a great individual deep down inside. He was always a cool person to me and I'll miss our visits and his letters.

Michigan Ghoul

Arthur I'm going to miss our communications, you truly were one of the good guys, misunderstood and punished for

acts you had no control over. You are now safely in the arms of
Jesus, away from the wicked and cruel world of satan who used
you as a tool for evil. Wait for me at the pearly gates my darling.

Julia

Shawcross's death was lamented and memorialized much more than
the deaths of his fourteen known victims. In her University of Rochester essay "The Tragic Death of Felicia Stephens," Katie Karp explored
the lamentable circumstances of Shawcross's last victim, one of the two
"less-dead" African American street prostitutes he had murdered. Karp
writes:

> Amongst cover photos and full page stories covering every
> aspect of the notorious serial killer's life, it was difficult to find
> as much as a small blurb mentioning Felicia. . . . Ms. Stephens
> was largely overshadowed by "the bigger story" and the only
> information available is her age and skin color. To this day she
> is often not even mentioned as a victim on many websites and
> video documentaries. . . . She is also the only woman without
> a picture of her to associate with her stories.[32]

Nor was Shawcross's first victim, the ten-year-old Jack Blake, memorialized. A statue of an angel erected on his grave shortly after his burial
was stolen by some souvenir-collecting asshole.

It was only forty-one years later, and five years *after* his killer's death,
that a former classmate of Jack's, Janet A. Fish, realized that Jack's grave
was unmarked and decided to do something about it, raising the funds
among Jack's former schoolmates to erect a headstone for the murdered
little boy. Jack's classmates had been traumatized by his murder in 1972.
Fish recalled, "It was a scary time for children in Watertown. Before
that, kids were allowed to go out on their own."

Another former schoolmate now in his fifties recalls, "He was the
first person who I knew who died. Jack was my friend. He was killed by
this monster. That was a lot for an 11-year-old to handle."[33] A headstone
was finally erected for Jack Blake on November 26, 2013.

Arthur Shawcross was but one of the 768 serial killers in the 1980s cataloged in the Radford University/FGCU Serial Killer Database. That was a horrific number. The good news was that the surge had ended; for the first time since the 1940s, the number of new serial killers was about to begin receding.

In the 1990s, there would be 669 serial killers, 13 percent *fewer* than in the 1980s.

CHAPTER 7

The Last Serial Killers:
Twilight of the Epidemic Era
1990–2000

We bury our dead and walk away.

Danny Rolling, serial killer

You might as well call Elizabeth Taylor a serial bride.

Dennis Nilsen, serial killer

The 1990s started off looking a lot like the 1970s and 1980s, with new and increasingly crazy serial killers coming at us with every year, just as before. While the average number of victims per serial killer began to decline, the serial killer scripts continued to push the envelope further and further into the realm of unimaginable horror as we slipped out of the 1980s into the 1990s.

The decade opened with a series of shocking unsolved murders in the college town of Gainesville, Florida. The murders garnered national attention and eventually inspired Wes Craven's 1996 slasher black-comedy movie *Scream*. But there was nothing funny about what was happening in Gainesville.

Danny Rolling, "The Gainesville Ripper," Gainesville, Florida, 1990

Gainesville, the capital of Alachua County, is located in the middle of the northern part of the state, and the University of Florida has a large campus there. In August 1990, Gainesville was a frenzy of activity as students arrived to begin the fall semester. Many students choose the University of Florida as a place of study because of its sunny climate and party-time reputation. Students from all parts of the country were un-packing their belongings and moving into various dormitories and off-campus apartments and houses.

On August 24, two female freshman students, eighteen-year-old Sonja Larson and seventeen-year-old Christina Powell, were found bru-tally stabbed to death in their apartment. The killer had apparently walked in through an unlocked door during the night. Powell was found nude on the carpet of the living room floor near the couch, with a tight grouping of five stab wounds to her upper back. One stab wound was driven into her back with such force that it traversed her torso, the tip of the knife emerging below her right breast. She had been raped. Her nip-ples had been cut away, leaving behind circular wounds about two and a half inches in diameter. The absence of hemorrhaging indicated that this occurred postmortem. Her head was turned toward her right shoul-der, and her hair fanned out from the right side of her head, deliberately placed in that position by her killer. Both of her arms extended above her head, and both legs were spread wide apart, bent at the knees, fully ex-posing her pubic area. A half-empty bottle of green Dawn dishwashing soap had been left between her knees on top of a damp towel. The soap coated her vaginal area and left a layer of foam around her vulva. Her cotton bra had been cut and ripped off her and tossed nearby, but her semen-stained underwear was neatly folded next to her left foot.

The room was strewn with crumpled paper towels that the killer must have used to clean himself up. The contents of Powell's purse were spilled out on the floor and devoid of paper cash; police would find none in the apartment. A photo from the purse of a young man and woman was cut in half, the woman's part missing.

Her roommate, Larson, was found in her bedroom upstairs wearing only a T-shirt pulled up past her breasts, revealing multiple stab wounds to her arm, thigh and both of her breasts. Five knife wounds were tightly clustered just around the nipple of her right breast, and a deep slash was inflicted on her left breast. The interior of her right arm had been punctured with eleven wounds. All the wounds had been inflicted while she was alive. Her arms stretched upward past her head, while her legs extended off the end of the bed, spread apart with both feet touching the floor. There was a tight cluster of stab wounds around her right breast.[1]

From the traces of adhesive, police determined that both victims had been gagged and restrained with duct tape, but the tape was later removed by the killer. The type of knife used was identified by the distinct wounds made by its uniquely designed blood groove: a foot-long fighting knife issued by the US Marine Corps, known as the Ka-Bar and available at any sporting goods store. Its seven-inch clip-point blade was forged in "1095 Cro-Van" (chromium and vanadium) hypereutectoid carbon steel alloy that allowed its edge to be honed razor-sharp with a microscopically subtle "toothy" bite. The name "Ka-Bar" was adopted by the manufacturer in 1923 after they received a torn and crumpled letter from a fur trapper attesting to how he "killed a bear" with the knife with only "k a b ar" legible. It is a formidable killing knife and utility tool first issued to Marines in the Pacific in 1942 and is still in service today.

As horrific as this crime was, it hardly made a ripple in the press outside of Florida. A double-stabbing homicide was not particularly big news by the 1990s. Nonetheless, the killings were a haunting reminder of Ted Bundy's murders of two college girls in a sorority house in Tallahassee, Florida, twelve years earlier.

Then on August 26, another student, eighteen-year-old Christa Hoyt, was found raped and murdered in her apartment. The killer had pried open a glass door while she was out and waited in the dark apartment for the victim to come home.

Hoyt was found on her bed, headless, sitting hunched forward midway between the foot of the bed and the headboard. Her hands drooped beside her thighs, which were spread wide apart. Her abdomen was cut open from her breastbone to her pubic bone, exposing her intestines, abdomen lining and colon. The cut demonstrated a hunter's "dressing" skill in that it exposed the intestines but did not cut into them.

A single knife entry wound at her back traversed her body seven and a half inches through her aorta, heart, lung, exiting between her ribs through the tissue of her left breast. Her nipples were removed and tossed into the bedding next to her.

Her severed head was on a bookshelf that the killer had carried into the bedroom and carefully positioned to face the bedroom door. The head was cut off neatly, again demonstrating a hunter's experience. Except for two small scratches on the cheek, her face appeared serene and her eyes were closed. The head was propped up by a wooden jewelry box and carefully positioned to be looking down at her own decapitated body and toward anybody entering the room.

Detectives immediately noted the presence of lividity on her back, a postmortem phenomenon where blood is drawn down by gravity and pools at the lowest points in a corpse, leaving a distinct purplish bruising. It helps police to determine whether a body has been moved or manipulated postmortem from its original position. Hoyt had to have been moved from her back into the sitting pose hours *after* her death. The ME would later note that had not rigor mortis set in, it would have been impossible to position her in that pose. Rigor mortis, the temporary stiffening of muscle due to chemical changes after death, begins approximately four hours after death and peaks at about thirteen hours. Was the perpetrator so brazen as to linger in the apartment so long?

Again the murder weapon was identified as a Ka-Bar, and traces of adhesive on the victim's wrists and mouth indicated that she had been bound with duct tape.

Coming so quickly on the heels of the previous murders, the horrific murder garnered national press attention. And of course, there was now a moniker: the Gainesville Ripper.

University students are cocky and confident, and while the murders frightened them, at the same time they provided grist for collegiate humor—the campus was nicknamed "Murder U." Daughters phoned home every night and morning, assuring their parents they had locked the doors and windows and survived the night. Young men suddenly found that young women were more willing to spend the night in their company. As it often is in cases like this, while the women trembled in fear, the men felt safe and secure.

All that changed on the morning of August 27, when the Gainesville Ripper forced open a locked aluminum door and slipped into an apartment platonically shared by a strong athletic male and a female, twenty-three-year-old Manny Taboada and Tracy Paules. Tracy had made a conscious choice to take a male roommate to feel safer.

Taboada was attacked as he slept in his bed but managed to struggle before he succumbed to a flurry of knife blows and slashes to his chest, abdomen and arms. His intestines protruded from a particularly deep and powerful knife wound in his abdomen. He was lying on his back on the bed in a pool of blood.

Awakened by the noise of the struggle, Tracy Paules must have attempted to lock her bedroom door. From the blood drops and bloody footprints, police surmised that the killer, covered in blood, kicked open her bedroom door. Paules had been anally and vaginally raped and then rolled over on her stomach and stabbed in the back three times. Liquid soap was found in her genitals. The killer dragged her body from the bedroom into the entry hallway, leaving behind a smeared trail of blood. She was placed with her legs open toward the front door, a folded towel propping up her buttocks, posed to shock whoever first entered the premises. This time, however, there was no gross mutilation: the blood was washed away from her face by the killer and her hair neatly rearranged. (Reminiscent of the victims of the 1940s serial killer William Heirens.) Profilers interpreted it as a sign of remorse.

Gainesville now resembled a disaster area as desperate parents drove cross-country to get their children and take them home. The streets of the student neighborhoods were jammed by columns of cars with hastily piled luggage tied to their roofs trying to make their way out of Gainesville through a gauntlet of network television news satellite trucks. By the Labor Day weekend on August 31, Gainesville was almost deserted of students. More than seven hundred students never returned to the university at all.

In September, the police and newspapers identified a suspect in their custody, a University of Florida freshman with a history of mental illness and behavioral issues who had recently been threatening to stab people. On August 30, he had been arrested when he assaulted his grandmother. He had a Ka-Bar in his possession, and when questioned by police, he admitted to the Gainesville murders. After his arrest, no further murders occurred. Relieved by the news of the arrest, students and parents calmed down. Several weeks later, disturbing news was announced: the suspect had been cleared and released. Despite the fact that the Gainesville Ripper had not been identified after all, the killings had ceased, and things returned to normal.

Judging by the washing of the last victim's face instead of the signature mutilation, some profilers ventured that the Gainesville Ripper had come to the end of his cycle of murders—like Albert DeSalvo or Edmund Kemper had. Other investigators suspected he had committed suicide or otherwise died. The majority, however, believed that it was most likely the Gainesville Ripper was in custody on another charge. The police carefully inspected their arrest records for any recently detained criminals with a history of sex crimes. They found none that fit.

More than a year would pass before thirty-nine-year-old Danny Rolling was charged with the Gainesville murders. As police suspected, he was already in their custody, but his criminal record wasn't typical of a serial sex murderer. Rolling, a boyishly attractive, intelligent man sporting designer-frame glasses, was in prison for a series of dramatic armed robberies, involving car chases and shoot-outs with police, not the sexual offenses that serial killers often accrue. His preferred weapon was a handgun, not a knife. Rolling had been arrested in Ocala, some one hundred kilometers south of Gainesville, on September 7, 1990, ten days after the last of the murders in Gainesville. A few days earlier, in Tampa, he had robbed a store and exchanged gunfire with police before managing to escape in a high-speed chase. In Ocala, Rolling robbed a supermarket, was again chased by police but this time he crashed his stolen car. He fled on foot through an office building and out into a flea market, where he was finally boxed in and captured.

Since then he had been sitting in jail awaiting trial for the armed robberies.

"Don't Ever Forget That My Grandfather Cut My Grandmother's Throat While She Was Eating"

Danny Harold Rolling was born on May 26, 1954, in Shreveport, Louisiana, to Claudia and James Harold "Baby Dumpling" Rolling.[2] James had recently returned from the Korean War, one of the most decorated servicemen in his home state. He joined the Shreveport Police, where he served twenty-one years. James was fucked-up long before he went to Korea. According to Danny and his mother, Claudia, when his father was five years old in 1936, he was sitting at the kitchen table with his maternal grandparents when his grandfather Robert Elmer "Elmo" Phelps got into an argument with Sarah, his wife of twenty-seven years and the mother of their nine children.[3] As James watched, grandpa Elmer stood up from the table, picked up a butcher knife and slit Sarah's throat at the table as she sat soaking her feet in a big pan of water.[4] James would recall how the water turned red with her blood. Whether this was how James remembered it, or how he perhaps told and spun the story, we will never know for sure. According to the newspaper reports, Elmer stabbed Sarah in the heart with an ice pick and strangled her.[5] No further details were reported. Elmer's death sentence was commuted to life, and he was stabbed to death in prison in 1948. His grandson James, however, was never quite right after that.

There was madness in the family, according to Claudia's testimony: "He has an uncle who laid down on the couch, put a shotgun in his mouth and pulled the trigger and blew his head off. He had another uncle that died in a mental institute. He has a brother that lives in California that is [sic] the only way he functions is on medication."

Whatever disorder emerged in James after witnessing the murder of his grandmother, it worked for him in the Korean War, where he earned many decorations for killing North Koreans and Chinese, and it even worked in the Shreveport PD after he returned from the war; he successfully rose in police ranks to lieutenant. It didn't work so well at home with his family. On at least one occasion, James woke in the middle of the night with a war "flashback" and nearly choked Claudia to death. She complained that he slept with a knife under his pillow.

In a sense, this is the quintessential genesis of so many serial killers: a violent heritage that passes from one generation to another, each crippling its young, leaving behind, at best, a crop of abused and maladjusted individuals, or at worst, a series of raped and dead murder victims.

Claudia became pregnant two weeks after their marriage. James did not want the child. It was a difficult pregnancy for Claudia right from the beginning. James was a violent, short-tempered husband who bullied, choked and pushed Claudia down a flight of stairs while she was pregnant.

Danny's mother wrote to the court during his sentencing, "Danny was abused from the day he was born. My husband was jealous of him. He was told from the time he could understand that he would be dead or in jail before he reached the age of fifteen."

Claudia's sister recalled that James did not want to bring the baby home from the hospital and would kick him, the baby sliding halfway across the room. When she threatened to call authorities, James drew his police revolver and warned her off. Claudia recalled that James would hit the baby when it attempted to crawl: "He sat on his little backside and put one leg underneath and pushed with the other leg and James didn't like that. To him I think it looked crippling or something, and with my husband, everything has to be perfect."

A year later, a second son, Kevin, was born. James Rolling was violent and frighteningly moody—at one moment he could be friendly; at the next he could break out into vile rages. He had compulsive obsessions—a fear of germs that required that every member of the family wash their hands prior to entering the kitchen, that shoes be taken off and placed in a certain way when entering the house. Any breach in these strict rules was punished by vicious beatings, often with James's heavy police-issue belt. He kicked their puppy to death when it soiled the floor. He forced them to come to the dinner table blindfolded or made them walk around with paper bags or pots over their heads as punishment. He handcuffed his sons to kitchen chairs. He whipped Kevin so hard that he wet himself.

Perfection was expected of the children. When Danny was ten and Kevin nine, James decided it was time for them to learn how to drive a car. Their feet could not reach the pedals, but that did not stop James from screaming at and hitting his sons when they failed to start the car as he instructed.

James Harold controlled every aspect of his sons' lives: until they were sixteen, they were not allowed to date or choose the clothing they wore. He strictly supervised their haircuts, and they were prohibited from sitting on the couch in the living room—they might infect it with germs from the outside.

Danny was a witness to extraordinary violent fights between his mother and father, with the father on several occasions threatening to shoot his mother with his revolver or cut her with a knife. Once, James pointed a handgun at his wife and said, "Don't ever forget that my grandfather cut my grandmother's throat while she was eating."

Gemini

Around the age of thirteen or fourteen, Danny Rolling began window-peeping, an obsession that stayed with him all his life. Danny was caught several times by neighbors, which was humiliating to James, and he beat Danny mercilessly. Danny developed a reputation as a window-peeper in the neighborhood and at school, and girls laughed at him. Rolling would write:

> Voyeurism for me began as a mere curiosity. The female form was a beautiful mystery and very exciting to look on. At the first stage of adolescence, I made the connection by peering in windows and masturbating while watching lovely ladies do their thing. Eventually, the pretty butterfly that fluttered across my genitals metamorphosed into a dominant beast of lust. As I developed into a man, the secret behavior developed into a personality with an identity all its own, that finally took on the face of murder.[6]

Rolling later gave these "personalities" their own names—the armed robber personality, the professional criminal, was called "Ennad" (Danne backward), while the raging homicidal personality was named "Gemini." Danny was the good and gentle boy, while "Ennad" and "Gemini" struggled to dominate Danny's psyche. But this was not a multiple personality syndrome. According to Rolling, these were external entities that possessed him at various points in his life, which did not *make* him do things, but *caused* him to do things.

A psychiatrist who assessed him reported:

It has become compartmentalized or disassociated. It's out there, it's somebody else, it's not Danny, it's Gemini. So he will say it's Danny that is the voyeur, it's Danny that robbed, it's Danny that raped, but it's Gemini that killed. Because that's what he cannot accept. And I don't mean he's saying the devil made him do it or he's not responsible.

But that was exactly what Danny was saying. The devil made him do it. And he meant it.

A clue lurks in Rolling's strict fundamentalist Christian discipline and later his Pentecostal zeal. The intensity of Rolling's adolescent rage and trauma, combined with his Christian upbringing, which condemned that very rage he was feeling compulsions to act upon, in the conventional beliefs of fundamental Christianity, was readily recognized as a "possession" by evil forces. God and Satan were coexistent entities, each with legions of angels, prophets and servant-soldiers. In fundamental Christianity, when it comes to God and Satan, you cannot believe in one without believing in the other.

In the context of dogmatic Christianity, there is really nothing "psychiatric" about Rolling's belief in Gemini—what explanation could he possibly have, other than a relationship with evil forces? Perhaps here at last we have a precise definition of evil—it is the thing that drove Rolling to rape and kill. The psychiatrists can call it "a variety of dissociative disorders"; the priest will call it "Satan"; Danny Rolling called it Gemini. I think it's still a little too early for us, even in our age of science, to conclusively write off old-time biblical Evil. We are still too puppy blind on our trip down Evolutionary Road.

But when it comes to Gemini, we will see that there was a secular source behind Danny Rolling's vision. As it frequently is, the source was Hollywood.

"Any Weapon Just Takes Up Space, Until the Human Hand Finds Work for It"

Of course, the fact that Danny Rolling consumed inordinate amounts of liquor and later extensive amounts of LSD certainly did not help. At the age of sixteen, Rolling began to drink. The conflicts with his father increased, and his father "arrested" him and locked him in the station house jail one night. When Rolling was seventeen, he left home and joined the US Air Force, where he was trained as a military policeman (following the same military career path that Albert DeSalvo and Jeffrey Dahmer did with various degrees of success). This was 1971 in the last years of the Vietnam War, yet another story of a father and son, two wars and one serial killer.

On the eve of being deployed to Vietnam, Rolling was arrested for possession of marijuana and ended up with a dishonorable discharge, coming home to the contempt of his father. Upon returning to Shreveport, Danny became involved with the Pentecostal Church, going to services Wednesday, Thursday, Friday, Saturday and Sunday. There he met his wife and married in 1974. A year later, the couple had a baby girl, Kiley Danielle.

Rolling claims that his wife was frigid and that caused him to roam the streets at night, peeking into windows. The police caught him one day, but because they knew he was James Rolling's son, they did not charge him. But they did tell his wife. It was during this period that Rolling says evil spirits first began to make their presence known to him. He recalls that he would chant, "Jesus . . . Jesus . . . Jesus," to make them leave. They would come as he slept in bed with his wife.

Around this time, Danny was driving a truck and crashed it into a van that had stopped at a blind corner. A woman was flung out the back door of the van by the impact and hit the pavement, split her skull open and died. Although entirely accidental, for Danny Rolling, this event might have served as his "first kill."

After several years of marriage, Danny's wife left him for another man, taking their daughter with him. Danny raged, planning to kill his wife and her lover, but never went through with it. The day after Rolling was served with his divorce papers, he raped a woman whom he spotted while window-peeping. He went on to commit a string of similar rapes before he began killing. The classic escalating pattern had begun.

In 1979, Rolling stole his father's service revolver and went on a spree of armed robberies across the Southern states until he was caught in

Georgia and sentenced to six years imprisonment. He was released in 1984, but by 1986 was back in prison, this time in Mississippi, on new convictions of armed robbery. He was sentenced to four years this time. Rolling claimed that Gemini became a fully formed identity for him while he was in prison.

In July 1988, Rolling was paroled on the condition he return and live at home in Shreveport. He moved back home with his parents, a sure formula for trouble.

Danny was good-looking and had this innocent, vulnerable, boyish vibe that many women found attractive. His mother described him as permanently an eleven-year-old. Rolling dated an older woman, a country song writer who doted on him and encouraged his singing and guitar playing.

Rolling took on sporadic employment. He claims that he was a good worker but that when his employers would find out he had a criminal record, he would get fired. Eventually, he got a job at Pancho's Mexican restaurant.

He began carrying a Ka-Bar knife around this time. He wrote later:

> Any weapon just takes up space, until the human hand finds work for it. Then it becomes as deadly as its master's intent. . . . A Ka-Bar is a foot-long fighting knife, but it was comfortable hidden under a light jacket. I made an improvised shoulder holster from a black leather belt that I threaded through the Ka-Bar's holster and carried it under my left armpit.[7]

On November 4, 1989, Rolling was fired from Pancho's for missing work three days in a row. He exploded in a fit of rage and threatened to kill the manager and cook. Rolling claims that he was fired because the manager was jealous of the attention he received from the waitresses.

Grissom Family Murders: "He Was like a Werewolf"
Two days later, on November 6, Rolling committed a triple homicide: fifty-five-year-old William Grissom, his twenty-four-year-old daughter, Julie, and his eight-year-old grandson, Sean. The family was attacked in

their home as they prepared for dinner. Julie Grissom's body was mutilated and posed on her bed faceup, her legs spread apart. The victims had been bound with duct tape, but the killer removed the tape and took it away with him. Julie's underwear was also placed in the washing machine and the cycle started, and the killer douched her genitals with vinegar in an attempt to destroy biological trace evidence. This was a "forensically aware" perpetrator.

According to a jailhouse informant, Rolling said:

> The old man was outside doing some barbecuing or watering the yard or something. He went and put a knife to him, took him in the house and tied him up. Taped up the old man, the girl and the kid, then he took the old man into a utility room and killed him first. Came back into the living room and took the little kid, rolled the kid onto his stomach and killed him. Stabbed him in the back through the heart. Took the girl into the bedroom, raped her and killed her, did all kinds of stuff to her. . . . He was like a werewolf. He had all the power over everybody to kill them or do whatever he wanted with them.[8]

Rolling's pastor said that he came to the church on the night of the murders seeming very incoherent: "He wanted to stay around the church a bit and pray. I got the impression he was really high on something."

At home, things were getting extremely tense between the raging son and the obsessive, violent, now-retired policeman father. Danny's aunt would testify, "I was always greeted with James Harold yelling, 'He's no good, he's not going to live here, I hate him. One of these days, he's going to cross me just a little bit, and I'm going to hurt him, I'm going to hurt him bad, I want him out of here!'"

On Friday evening, May 18, 1990, both father and son finally crossed the line. Danny came home after a drinking session at a bar. The father told Danny to roll up the windows of his car because it was going to rain. Danny ignored him. James started to fume. Then Danny put his foot on a bench in the hallway to tie his shoe, something his father had told him many times not to do. An argument began, and James finally lost his temper beyond all control. He drew his revolver and chased Danny down the driveway, firing multiple shots that were either, depending on the account, fired into the air or aimed at Danny but missed. James went back into the house and locked Danny out. Danny went into the toolshed, where he kept a hidden .38 revolver, returned to the house with it and kicked in the back door, shouting, "I've got something for you this time, Pop!"

James was in the kitchen when Rolling came through the door and opened fire. One shot hit James in the stomach while the second shot hit him in the face. Rolling stood over his father, kicking him and screaming, "Die, motherfucker. *Die!*"

Danny then jumped into his car and drove off.

James Howard Rolling survived his gunshot wounds but lost the sight in one eye and hearing in an ear.

For the next three months, Danny Rolling remained on the run, robbing supermarkets and stores. He stayed in motels, using a stolen identification card. He restlessly moved from town to town, state to state, eventually arriving in Florida. On his way to Sarasota, where he would spend several weeks, he passed through Gainesville, noting all the pretty college girls walking around town.

Danny maintained his boyish good looks. While on the run he had his hair styled and bought jewelry. He frequently picked up women and had brief relationships with two women in Sarasota, whom he wined and dined and serenaded on his guitar. He was reasonably talented, they said. He told them he was a trucking company owner on vacation. He told others he was a successful country music songwriter. Yet, at the same time, when the compulsion struck him, he would foray from his motels at night, peeking into windows and committing sporadic rapes when an opportunity arose. The rapes were highly organized: Danny would dress in black and carry a small bag at his waist with duct tape, handcuffs, mask, gloves and a Ka-Bar knife.

Constantly on the move, the fugitive Danny Rolling was difficult to apprehend—not that there was an intensive manhunt looking for him.

Wounding his father did not exactly make him one of America's "most-wanted." His armed robberies were not linked to him or to each other, nor were the rapes, or the three murders in Shreveport the previous year. Rolling was the kind of fugitive that the police wait for to make a mistake, rather than actively hunt and pursue.

Gainesville: The Exorcist III

On August 18, 1990, Danny Rolling arrived in Gainesville—death on a Greyhound bus.

He said:

> It was destiny—I was driven to Gainesville. God as my judge, I was driven there. Spirits can control and put thoughts in your mind. They can even possess you. The Intruder, the Dark One calls. And if you answer, you will be driven like the restless wind. The Darkness called and I answered.
>
> I could have easily gone to any other place in Florida with the cash I had left back then. Gemini wanted it to be Gainesville. The only reason I can think of would be the obvious—because Gainesville is a college town filled with beautiful girls. I suppose it was there in my subconscious all along. The eight souls for every year I was abused by the prison system had something to do with it, and Gemini became the catalyst.[9]

For the next five days, Rolling stayed at the University Inn, a seedy and run-down hotel on Southwest 13th Street. He reconnoitered the various neighborhoods for apartment complexes where students lived. He drifted into the "Porters," at the time a blighted African American neighborhood where he bought crack cocaine and hired for forty dollars thirty-one-year-old sex worker Denise Taylor, whom he took back to his motel room.[10] According to her testimony, they smoked the crack and then he had her undress and lie down on her back on the bed. He grabbed her by the ankles and pulled her to the edge of the bed, positioning her with her legs spread and dangling over the edge. Assuring her he would not hurt her, he opened a small box with an assortment of knives and medical instruments and selected a scalpel, which he lightly ran along her arms, legs and torso. He then instructed her to turn over and stand on the floor with her hands resting on the bed. He sat down on the floor beneath her, positioning a mirror in which he could see the reflection of her genitals as he masturbated with his other hand.

Rolling was building up toward something bad.*

On August 23, he began running short of money and checked out of the motel. He staked out a spot for himself in a large, dense patch of woods frequented by homeless people in the vicinity of Butler Plaza near the corners of Archer Road and Southwest 34th Street.

Later that day, Rolling paid cash for a tent at a Walmart and stole a black-handled screwdriver and a pair of tightly fitting black leather athletic gloves. At the exact same time, at a cash register a few rows away, Sonja Larson and Christina Powell, college freshmen just out of high school, put a purchase on a credit card for their new apartment. Police later speculated that Rolling had seen and targeted his victims in the store, but he vehemently denied it. He said he never even noticed the two girls.

Rolling pitched his tent in the secluded woods and strolled over to the Butler Plaza movie theater to see *The Exorcist III*.[11] Unlike the 1977 sequel *The Exorcist II*, considered not only the worst of the *Exorcist* franchise but among the worst movies ever, *The Exorcist III* was a critical and popular success. Written by William Peter Blatty, author of the novel *The Exorcist*, the film features the character of police lieutenant William F. Kinderman from the original movie, now investigating a series of demonic serial murders perpetrated by a character that Blatty loosely based on the unidentified real-life Zodiac Killer. Blatty named him Gemini.

In September 1990, as the Gainesville murders were being reported, long before Rolling was identified and claimed that Gemini had possessed him, Florida newspapers reported there were rumors that the murders were connected to *The Exorcist III*.[12] We will see that the

---

*In his autobiography, Rolling vehemently denied the entire account, stating he never had any medical instruments and writing, "I did not—repeat, did NOT—and have not EVER—had sex with ANY black woman, least of all this Denise Taylor."

Gainesville killings are not the only case of serial murder in which *The Exorcist III* comes up.

"I'll Come Back for You After You're Dead"

On August 24, Rolling made a tape recording in his tent. On the audio tape he greets his mother and hopes his father is doing well after the shooting. He sings "every song I ever wrote." He spends an inordinate amount of time telling his brother how to hunt down deer with a bow and arrow—how to shoot them through the lungs and wait for them to bleed to death. The tape concludes with Rolling saying to his father, "You know, Pop, I don't think you was ever really concerned about the way I felt anyway. Nope, I really don't. You never would take time to listen to me. You never cared about what I thought or felt. I never had a Daddy I could go to and confide in with my problems. You just pushed me away at a young age, Pop. I guess you and I, we both missed out on a lot. I wanted to make you proud of me. But I let you down. I'm sorry for that. Whelp! I'm gonna sign off for a little bit. I got something I gotta do. I love you. Bye."

Like a nocturnal predatory animal, he slept in the day and emerged from the woods in the night. The murders he committed were all within a foraging range of his campsite. He silently rode on a stolen bicycle, scouting out student housing complexes, wearing a ninja-black outfit and carrying the tools of his rage in his bag: a roll of duct tape, recently acquired handgun, screwdriver, Mini-Mag penlight, mask, gloves and the Ka-Bar knife. Once he located a promising cluster of apartment buildings, he would don his mask and gloves and proceed on foot, searching out potential victims. Several times he was spotted peering at women through windows and was chased away.

According to Rolling's confession, he came upon the apartment of Sonja Larson and Christina Powell completely at random at about 3:00 a.m. When he tried to force their door with his screwdriver, he found it was already invitingly open. He tore off several strips of duct tape and stuck them to his arm just above the elbow, ready for use. He found Christina Powell sleeping on a couch in the living room and did not disturb her. Rolling slipped upstairs into Sonja Larson's bedroom, holding his penlight in his mouth to keep his hands free. As she slept, he clapped a strip of tape over her mouth and at the same time stabbed her in the upper chest. She attempted to struggle, but he unleashed a flurry of knife thrusts to her upper torso. Eleven thrusts struck her in the arm as she attempted to ward off the blows. As the girl faded into death, Rolling said he whispered in her ear, "I'll come back for you after you're dead."[13]

Rolling then went back downstairs and woke up Christina Powell. As he taped her hands, he sadistically told her that he intended to rape and kill her. Rolling walked her around different parts of the apartment, repeatedly raping her for about two hours, telling her, "Take the pain, bitch, take the pain."[14] Finally, he laid her down on her stomach on the floor and drove the Ka-Bar through her back five times.

Rolling returned upstairs and peeled the tape away from the mouth of the dead Sonja Larson. He recalled removing her teddy bear print underwear and spreading her legs, dangling them over the edge of the bed in an obscene pose. He had been in the house so long that rigor mortis had already set in, and Rolling said that Larson's legs "yielded like old boards." She was too bloody to rape, he said.

Danny Rolling then returned to the corpse of Christina Powell and raped her again, "chewing on her nipples like a mad dog gnaws a bone," he said. After he was finished, he took some dishwashing detergent and paper towels and cleaned and douched her genitals. This act was later instrumental in linking his murders, yet it is unclear whether this was some kind of pathological "signature"—a "cleansing" of his act—or whether it was part of his MO to destroy evidence. If it was an MO, Rolling was not thorough. He left Powell's underwear soaked in his semen, neatly folded next to her body.

Next, Rolling carefully excised her nipples, again unclear whether he was concealing the bite marks he left around her nipples or acting out some pathological "signature." He dropped them into a plastic sandwich baggie, which he pocketed.

Afterward, he went to the refrigerator and calmly ate some fruit.

By then it was daylight. Saturday morning. Taking all the duct tape with him so as not to leave evidence, Rolling then slipped out of the house and biked back toward his tent. On the way, he passed a news-paper boy on his bike making early-morning deliveries and commented to himself on the irony of two bicyclists on separate ways, "the boy to deliver his papers, the man to his destiny."

Prior to reaching his tent, he found the baggie with the severed nip-ples. He stated he did not recall taking it and was sickened at the sight of the bag. He tossed it through a sewer grate and returned to his tent to sleep.

"Apartment Murder"

That evening of August 25, as the sun began to set, he rose from his tent, hungry for more. He knew exactly whom he wanted and where to find her. She lived but eight hundred yards away from his wooded campsite on the other side of the road. He had spotted her the previous night while prowling and looking into windows. He watched her undressing just as he did when he was a teen. And more. She looked *a lot* like his ex-wife. He noted her location in the complex—apartment M. He made the short bike ride over to "Apartment Murder," as he called it, to rape and kill her.

Eighteen-year-old Christa Hoyt was out playing racquetball when Rolling broke into her apartment by forcing with the screwdriver the lock of a glass door leading to a garden out back. Once inside, Rolling moved a bookshelf into her bedroom from an alcove near the door, in order that he could hide in the space to ambush her as she entered. He patiently waited in the dark for about an hour for Christa to come home. At around 10:00 p.m., he watched her through the window as she walked across the parking lot toward her apartment, carrying her rac-quet. He positioned himself in the dark of the alcove and waited. Christa entered her apartment, locked the door securely behind her and placed her keys, racquet and balls on the table by the door. According to Rolling, she had sensed there was somebody in the room, but before she could flee, he burst out of the alcove and overpowered her. He duct-taped her mouth and hands and forced her into the bedroom, where he raped her. Then Rolling turned Christa on her stomach and drove his knife through her back once, almost instantly killing her. He then turned her over and cut her abdomen open and excised her nipples. Rolling says that he then felt the dead girl's eyes watching him, so he closed them.

Rolling rode his bike toward his tent site. On the way, he stopped and defecated, using a roll of toilet paper he carried with him on these nocturnal missions; then he stopped off at a convenience store to purchase a soda, where he discovered that he had lost his wallet. Fearing that he might have left it at the scene of the murder, Rolling bicycled back to Christa's apartment and reentered it. Using his penlight, he searched for his wallet. Possessed by Gemini or not, Danny Rolling was making sure that no evidence was going to expose him as the murderer. He didn't find the wallet, but while there he went to look at Christa's corpse and was shocked to discover that her eyes had opened. He then decapitated her with his Ka-Bar knife and placed her head on the shelf he had moved into the bedroom. He took Christa's headless body and sat it upright at the edge of her bed, posing her in the stance of Rodin's *The Thinker*, Rolling said. He wrote, "It was like molding a block of Playdoh—just a lifeless lump of clay."

He left the apartment drained and exhausted and slept most of the day in his tent.

"You're Him, *Aren't You?"*

On the night of August 26 and 27, Rolling rode out on his bike again, trolling through the archipelago of student apartment complexes. He watched twenty-three-year-old Tracy Paules for hours through a window as she spoke on the phone, waiting for her to go to sleep. At around 2:30 a.m., her male roommate, Manuel Taboada, who worked nights as a barman, came home and went to bed. Only then did Tracy feel safe to go to bed herself. Shortly after 3:00 a.m., Rolling silently forced the door with his screwdriver and slipped into the apartment. He stabbed and struggled with Manuel, killing him.

The noise coming from Taboada's room awakened Tracy. She cautiously made her way to Taboada's room, hopelessly brandishing a curling iron to defend herself, and caught a glimpse of a hooded black figure standing with a large knife over Taboada, who lay in an expanding pool of blood bubbling out of his wounds. Tracy dashed back into her room, screaming, and locked her bedroom door. Rolling effortlessly kicked open her door and overpowered Tracy.

"You're *him*, aren't you?" Rolling recalled her blurting out.

After warning her not to scream, Rolling chose not to tape her mouth. Tracy did what survivors of *some* serial killers did: she engaged the killer in conversation, attempting to de-objectify herself in his perception. When she asked him what happened to her roommate, Manuel, Rolling replied that he was an ex–Green Beret skilled in the martial arts and that he had knocked him out.

"My brother was a soldier too," she said, doing her best to establish a sympathetic rapport. "He was killed in Vietnam."

It might have worked had Rolling actually been in Vietnam.

"Really? Vietnam was a bitch! I'm tempted to let you go. But then again? I guess not," Rolling said as he proceeded to rape her.

When he was done, he turned her over on her stomach, forced her face into a pillow and stabbed her three times in the back, the seven-inch blade of the Ka-Bar fatally cleaving her lung and drowning her in her own blood.

Rolling then dragged Tracy's body into the hallway, stopping at the bathroom door. Taking a wet washcloth, he wiped the blood from her face and combed her hair into place. Not as a sign of remorse, as some thought, but to make her presentable to him. Then he raped her again, postmortem, on the hallway floor, before he douched her with dishwashing soap. Afterward, he dragged her body by the ankles out toward the entryway of the apartment, where he posed her at the door to greet the first person who came through it.

"You Look Like You Could Use a Friend"

Later that day, about a kilometer away from the murder scene, Rolling robbed a bank and was seen by a witness slipping back into the woods where he had his tent. The police descended on the woods and found the tent—along with Rolling's handgun, money, mask, gloves and screwdriver—but Rolling escaped. The evidence was bagged and locked away in storage. No connection was made to the murders.

Rolling fled Gainesville and went to Tampa, where he committed a series of burglaries and robberies to sustain himself. There over the Labor Day weekend he came upon a young woman, Diana, sitting on a park bench sketching portraits in pastels. He said, "You look like you could use a friend." He gave her a hundred dollars to sketch his portrait. He was kind. He was gentle. He was boyishly vulnerable and sweet. Afterward, he took her to a nearby arcade where he won a teddy bear for her. She invited him home to her apartment, where they spent the evening pleasantly talking. He took a shower and laundered his clothes in her washer. They ordered in Chinese food and watched *Good Morning, Vietnam* on her VCR. He slept the night on her couch while she slept in her bedroom. When he left the next morning, she gave him directions on how to find his way back to her apartment, but he never returned.

Diana would be one of the dozens of women who had nothing but fond memories of their encounter with sweet, angelic Danny. Luckily for her, the angel Gemini had been dormant when gentle Danny crossed her path. Or maybe Diana herself was the better angel of them all.

"You Are Not Going to Be Satisfied with My Answer Here"

On September 7, Rolling was finally arrested in Ocala while attempting to rob a supermarket. Both the Shreveport and Gainesville investigators almost immediately invited FBI profilers from the BSU to assist in the investigations. The profiles the FBI furnished were a reasonable fit for a number of suspects, including Danny Rolling, as well as the freshman suspect Gainesville PD had arrested.

Police in Shreveport got wind of the similarities between their still unsolved Grissom murders and the Gainesville murders, in particular the use of liquid soap or vinegar to douche evidence from the victims' genitals and the removal of the duct tape bindings by the perpetrator. The crimes had been cataloged with ViCAP, which had been launched specifically to link multijurisdictional crimes, but typically, nobody bothered to query ViCAP for possible links to other cases. (See the next chapter for more on the failures of ViCAP.)

On November 5, Shreveport PD called the Gainesville PD task force, alerting them to the similarities between the Grissom and Gainesville murders.

Detectives in Ocala in the meantime also called the task force to report that they had a suspect by the name of Rolling, whom they arrested driving a car stolen in Gainesville at the time of the murders. And guess what; Rolling was from Shreveport, the site of the Grissom murders.

Everybody was suddenly "liking" Rolling, as cops say. The hunt for the hunter was on.

Now, for the first time in my accounts of the epidemic era, DNA takes the stage. The DNA age had arrived and would take a big bite out of the serial killer surge. The first serial killer to be convicted using DNA evidence was Timothy Wilson Spencer, "the Southside Strangler," who murdered five women in Virginia between 1984 and 1988. DNA quickly became a huge game changer in serial murder investigations and prosecutions and remains even more so today.

On January 11, police ran a preliminary enzyme test comparing Rolling's blood samples with the blood and body fluids collected at the scene of the crimes. The test was not as accurate as a DNA test, but it narrowed down Rolling to a small 0.3 percent of the population that had the same type of blood.

Despite all his concerted attempts to eliminate biological evidence from the crime scenes, Rolling's douching and cleaning were not entirely successful, and now the law was closing in on him.

On January 21, police surreptitiously acquired a sample of his blood when Rolling had a tooth extracted by the prison dentist. His DNA came back as an unequivocal positive match to all three crime scenes in Gainesville. To ensure that the surreptitious search would not be thrown out in court, police obtained a search warrant in February to take DNA swabs and hair samples, and other biological and material evidence, from Rolling's person and his cell.

The DNA results from that search reaffirmed a positive match to that found at all three murder crime scenes.

As police were working up the evidence against him for the Gainesville murders, Rolling stood separate trials in September and October 1991 for the series of armed robberies and burglaries he had committed in Tampa and Ocala. As a habitual offender, he was sentenced to four terms of life imprisonment. He wasn't going anywhere now.

On November 15, 1991, Rolling was indicted by an Alachua County grand jury on five counts of first-degree murder, sexual assault and burglary in the Gainesville slayings.

Throughout 1992, the Alachua County prosecutors worked on building their case. Rolling had blabbed and bragged about his murders to numerous fellow inmates whose testimony was now collected by investigators.

On June 7, 1992, at his arraignment, Rolling pleaded not guilty to the charges.

Meanwhile, Rolling had begun corresponding with true-crime author Sondra London, to whom he eventually became engaged. Throughout 1993, London orchestrated a blitz of media coverage for Rolling and herself, writing about his pending trial in the *National Enquirer*, in a five-part series for the *Globe* and participating with him in interviews on *A Current Affair*.

The two of them cowrote Rolling's autobiography, *The Making of a Serial Killer*, an insightful psychological memoir revealing the depths of a serial killer's mind, memory and imagination.

As this was happening, Rolling was confessing to investigators through a cellmate informant, who would participate in the confessionals speaking for Rolling, who claimed he could not bear to hear himself vocalize the horrific confessions and would only affirm or negate the cellmate's responses to questions. Rolling claimed that his fundamentalist Pentecostal beliefs drove him to confess because his conscience troubled him too much.

His murder trial was in its first day on February 15, 1994, when to everyone's surprise Rolling suddenly changed his plea to guilty on all five counts of murder. After a mandatory sentencing trial before a jury, he was formally sentenced to death on April 20.

Louisiana declined the cost of extraditing and putting him on trial for the Grissom murders despite positive DNA matches to those murders. On the eve of his execution in 2006, Rolling confessed in writing to the three Grissom family murders in Shreveport.

———

Other than Gemini, Rolling never gave any lucid explanations as to why he committed any of his brutal crimes. How could there be any?

In the end, Rolling wrote:

> We bury our dead and walk away. And the circle of insanity is complete . . .
>
> You are not going to be satisfied with my answer here. I really don't have a message. It's a tragedy—a terrible, terrible, TRAGEDY. I regret it. I wish it never happened.[15]

He was right about one thing—we are not going to be satisfied with his answers.

Danny Rolling was executed by lethal injection on October 25, 2006.

"The Kings of Follow-Up": FBI Profilers and The Silence of the Lambs

Shortly after the Gainesville murders, *The Silence of the Lambs* was released in February 1991 and would become the fifth-highest-grossing film that year. If any film defined the cultural "state of the union" in American serial murder during the 1990s and beyond, then it was the Jonathan Demme movie based on Thomas Harris's book. It elevated both serial killers and FBI profilers to a "high-concept" status in popular culture and entertainment not unlike dinosaurs, baseball or aliens. It was not the first movie about serial killers, nor the first to feature profilers: there had been movies like the 1986 *Manhunter*, also based on a Thomas Harris novel, *Red Dragon*, but for various reasons the movies did not catch on.

The Silence of the Lambs was produced with FBI cooperation and starred Jodie Foster as FBI trainee agent Clarice Starling; Scott Glenn as a veteran profiler like Robert Ressler or John Douglas; and Anthony Hopkins as Hannibal "the Cannibal" Lecter, whom Clarice is sent to interview in the hope of gaining insight into an unidentified serial killer nicknamed "Buffalo Bill," loosely based on a composite of Ed Gein and

Gary Heidnik. The FBI hosted Foster and Glenn at Quantico, where they met behaviorists, and the production was even allowed to film scenes at Quantico. This FBI collaboration with Hollywood was not something new. Since J. Edgar Hoover, the FBI has collaborated with movie and TV studios on productions that laud the agency and promote its worth to the American public.

As *The Silence of the Lambs* went into production, the FBI's profilers were under a siege of bad publicity. On April 19, 1989, a gun turret mysteriously exploded, killing forty-seven crewmen on board the battleship USS *Iowa*. Navy investigators decided that Clayton Hartwig, one of the sailors who perished in the turret, deliberately caused the explosion. It was alleged that he was motivated by a frustrated homosexual fixation on a fellow crewman. The problem was proving it. The Naval Investigative Service (NIS) asked the FBI to conduct an "equivocal death analysis"—a type of psychological autopsy intended to determine a cause of death: Was the death accidental, suicide or murder? The FBI profilers concluded that Hartwig committed suicide "in a place and manner designed to give him the recognition and respect that he felt was denied him."[16]

While it was not the fault of the FBI that their assessment was treated by the Navy as hard evidence, the fact of the matter was that there was no conclusive evidence that Hartwig had deliberately caused the explosion. A congressional Armed Services subcommittee hearing was held, and unlike the "serial killer epidemic" hearings the decade before, this one resulted in a very hostile and dismissive assessment of the FBI's profiling system. In its report, the Armed Services congressional subcommittee concluded:

> Just as the FBI psychological analysis was key to the Navy investigation, so it was to the subcommittee inquiry. As a result, the subcommittee, using the professional services of the American Psychological Association, sought the opinions of 11 independent clinical licensed psychologists and one psychiatrist. Additionally, the subcommittee consulted independently with a psychiatrist and a psychologist who had some previous

knowledge of this case. Ten of the 14 experts consulted considered the FBI analysis invalid. And even those who believed the analysis to be somewhat credible were critical of procedures, methodology, and the lack of a statement of the limitations of a retrospective analysis of this nature.

The FBI psychological analysis procedures are of doubtful professionalism. The false air of certainty generated by the FBI analysis was probably the single major factor inducing the Navy to single out Clayton Hartwig as the likely guilty party.... The procedures the FBI used in preparing the Equivocal Death Analysis were inadequate and unprofessional.[17]

Profilers working for other agencies rushed to disassociate themselves from the bungling of the BSU. They pointed out that murder is rarely in the jurisdiction of the FBI and few of their agents had any actual homicide investigation experience. The late Robert Keppel, who worked on the Atlanta Child Murders, Ted Bundy and the Green River murders and is considered one of the leading profilers outside the FBI, dismissively recalled his experience with the FBI in the Atlanta case:

We couldn't wait to hear what gems of wisdom would come from the BSU's agents, most of whom were only self-proclaimed experts in murder investigations and had never investigated one lead in an actual murder case. The FBI were the kings of follow-up but couldn't solve a crime in progress. Most local homicide detectives knew this.[18]

In defense of the FBI profilers, they never claimed that they could solve a case alone, nor definitively identify a perpetrator. The way the US Navy used the FBI's profile is not the way the FBI intended it to be used. A BSU profile is intended to narrow the focus from a list of suspects developed by local homicide investigators, help lure an unsub out into the open and assist in the psychological approach to the suspect during the interview once identified. It is supposed to work the way it did the first time the BSU tested their system in the field, during the

1974 investigation of serial killer David Meirhofer in Montana as described earlier in these pages.

When the FBI's public affairs people read the script of *The Silence of the Lambs* with the ridiculous scenes of the FBI dashing about the country in military transport aircraft to arrest suspected serial killers and Clarice Starling coming to the rescue and engaging in a gun battle with Buffalo Bill, they knew it was just the Hollywood whitewash that the FBI needed at that moment. They opened their doors at Quantico to the film production.

Good Serial Killers Rising

What nobody calculated was the resulting promotion of serial killers to the kind of cult status that Anthony Hopkins's Hannibal Lecter would achieve. FBI agent Clarice became the naive straight man [woman] to Lecter's leading man genius and charm. By the time Lecter rips the face off one of his guards and wears it as a mask to escape captivity, the audience is cheering *him* on instead of Clarice. In fact, Lecter escapes to make sequels, while Clarice goes after Buffalo Bill and is retired from the screen with no sequel.

In the public's perception, the Chianti-sipping Lecter became a "good" serial killer, while the sexually confused, poverty-ridden, rural shack–dwelling, nipple-pierced pseudo-transsexual Buffalo Bill, who kept his victims in a stinking pit and skinned them, was the "bad" serial killer. Buffalo Bill was himself "less-alive." Many movie viewers could imagine themselves enjoying the company of Dr. Lecter at a dinner party (as long as they weren't on the menu), but none would want to even be seen in public with Buffalo Bill.

Steven Egger argues that such post–*Silence of the Lambs* demarcation in popular culture between "good" and "bad" serial killers paved the way further, since the first adulation for Ted Bundy, for raising serial killers in status above "ordinary" killers:

> For many, the serial killer is a symbol of courage, individuality, and unique cleverness. Many will quickly transform the

killer into a figure who allows them to fantasize rebellion or the lashing out at society's ills. For some, the serial killer may become a symbol of swift and effective justice, cleansing society of its crime-ridden vermin. The serial killer's skills in eluding police for long periods of time transcends the very reason that he is being hunted. The killer's elusiveness overshadows his trail of grief and horror.[19]

Social critic Mark Seltzer also argues a similar viewpoint. According to him, serial killing in the United States had supplanted an earlier, uniquely American cultural institution:

> Serial murder and its representations have by now largely replaced the Western as the most popular genre-fiction of the body and of bodily violence in our culture. . . . The Western was really about serial killing all along.[20]

Even serial killers criticized the character of Lecter. Dennis Nilsen, convicted in the murder of twelve men in Britain, thought that Lecter was a fraudulent character and said, "He is shown as a potent figure, which is pure myth. It is his power and manipulation which please the public. But it's not at all like that. My offenses arose from a feeling of inadequacy, not potency. I never had any power in my life."[21]

From there it was but a short road to serial killer collectible murderabilia, trading cards, calendars, art, cookbooks, lunch boxes and action figures and the ultimate obscenity, Dexter, the good serial killer who serially kills bad serial killers.

I've lost count of how many radio and podcast interviews I have done where I am asked, "Who is your favorite serial killer?" or "If you were a serial killer, what kind would *you* be?" My response is usually, "The kind who eats podcast hosts who ask stupid questions."

Jeffrey Dahmer, "The Milwaukee Cannibal," Milwaukee, Wisconsin, 1987–1991

In July 1991, as police in Gainesville and Shreveport were still piecing together the evidence in their cases, police in Milwaukee, Wisconsin, were removing the pieces of human remains from eleven victims found in Jeffrey Dahmer's apartment.

Tracy Edwards, the victim who escaped Dahmer's apartment on July 22 and flagged down a police car, was brought to the police station and recounted his story. Edwards stated that he had been hanging out with two other friends on the street when Dahmer approached them and invited them to come to his place to drink beer and keep him company. He offered one hundred dollars to any of them who would also pose for nude photos. Edward agreed to pose for the photos, but only if his two friends would accompany him to Dahmer's place. The other two agreed but had an errand to run first. Edwards did not hear Dahmer give them a false address.

Upon entering Dahmer's apartment, Edwards immediately noted the foul smell. Dahmer told him there were problems with the sewer pipes. Otherwise, Edwards did not notice anything unusual about the apartment or its decor. A large aquarium quietly gurgled as its filter pumped water to fish swimming inside. It was soothing. Dahmer offered Edwards an alcoholic drink that Edwards did not know was drugged. But he was not a big drinker and only sipped at it slowly. As they sat chatting, Edwards was growing anxious that his friends had not arrived while Dahmer was getting anxious that Edwards was not drinking enough to sedate him. When Edwards began to prepare to leave, Dahmer became agitated. Dahmer contrived to show Edwards the fish in his aquarium, and as his attention was drawn to the fish, Dahmer suddenly drew a pair of handcuffs from behind his back and snapped them around Edwards's left wrist. Before he could close the other cuff around his right wrist, Edwards twisted his free arm out of the way. Dahmer produced a knife, which he held at Edwards's side, warning him to do as he ordered or else he would kill him. Dahmer now led Edwards by his handcuffed left wrist into the bedroom. Edwards was immediately overwhelmed by a powerful smell of chemicals and decay emanating from a large blue plastic chemical drum in the corner of Dahmer's bedroom.

Edwards played along with Dahmer, carefully trying not to provoke him. Dahmer sat down on the bed with Edwards and turned on the TV and VCR with the remote. The movie in the VCR had already been cued up to play. Dahmer told Edwards he wanted him to watch the movie with him very carefully. He liked it so much that he had spent one hundred dollars to purchase a videocassette copy of it.

It was *The Exorcist III.** The same movie that apparently moved Danny Rolling.

As Edwards and Dahmer sat watching Gemini in *The Exorcist III* committing his serial murders, Dahmer appeared to be chanting to himself under his breath. He would enter and exit into what appeared to Edwards as a trance, especially around the scenes of demonic possession in the movie. After his arrest, Dahmer was asked by police about his fascination with *The Exorcist III*.

> He stated he was unsure, but he knows that he felt a tremendous amount of guilt, because of his actions. He felt evil and thoroughly corrupted, body and soul, because of the horrible crimes he had committed against people. Every time he would try to overcome his feelings of wanting to kill and dismember people, they would haunt him and overcome him, almost like an addiction. He felt that he could not fight that feeling and wondered if in fact the devil had anything to do with his evil thoughts. Because of this he watched the movie Exorcist [III] almost on a weekly basis, for approximately 6 mos., and sometimes 2 and 3 times a week. In the movie he could tell that the devil was angry for being condemned and that he could relate with the devil, because he felt that his life on earth was condemned. He went on to state that the main character in the movie appeared to be driven by evil and that he could relate to

---

*Police reports mistakenly reported that it was *Exorcist II*.

this character as he felt that his life was driven by evil.[22] [repetitive police prose "He stated that . . ." edited out]

At one point, Dahmer laid his head on Edwards's chest and listened to his heartbeat. He then told Edwards he was going to eat his heart. Edwards kept a cool head, constantly trying to talk Dahmer down from his trancelike state. At Dahmer's trial, Edwards described how Dahmer's face appeared to physically transform into a demonic mask as he slipped in and out of these trances.

Eventually, Edwards gained enough of Dahmer's trust to allow him to use the washroom without Dahmer holding the knife to his chest. As he left the washroom, Edwards sucker punched Dahmer, knocking him down, and dashed out the door of the apartment into the street where he managed to flag down the approaching police car.

The Dahmer Confessions

Once the police secured Dahmer's apartment and brought him in, the confessions began . . . and went on for weeks. Dahmer occasionally forgot some of his victims' names or the exact chronology, but he had a clear memory of most of the seventeen murders he had committed between his first murder in 1978 of Steven Mark Hicks in Ohio and his sixteen in Milwaukee from 1987 to 1991.

In his confessions, Dahmer appeared to be very self-aware as to what motivated him. According to the Milwaukee PD detectives' interview notes:

He remembers his early family life as being one of extreme tension. Tension came from the relationship that existed at that time between his mother and his father. Although he was not physically or sexually abused and he did not witness any physical abuse from his parents, he stated that they were "constantly at each others throats" and arguing. His mother appeared to have some psychiatric problems and had in fact suffered a nervous breakdown at one time during his early childhood. She was on medication and had been seeing a doctor much of the time. He was advised by relatives that his mother suffered severe Post-Partum Depression after he was born, and he took that as an indication that he was at least partially the problem for his parents' bad marital state.

He believes his mother became depressed after his birth and never quite fully recovered, and thereby he states he felt a certain amount of guilt in regard to the bad marriage of his parents.

When he was approximately 18-yoa [years of age] is when a divorce occurred between his mother and his father, and at this time his mother moved to Chippewa Falls, WI., and his father had been court ordered to stay out of the house and had moved to a motel which was several miles from the house. At this time his mother took his younger brother, who was approximately 6-years younger than him when she moved out and that he was left all alone at the house in Richfield, Ohio.

It was at this time when he started to have strong feelings of being left all alone, and that it was at this time that he remembers having strong desires of not wanting to have people leave him. He stated it was also at this time that he began hating to sleep alone at night.

He began having fantasies of killing people at the early age of 17 or 18. He states although these fantasies were fleeting, he feels that he had the fantasies to overcome the feelings he had of frustration, and emptiness which he felt were in his life. . . .

As a teenager of 15 or 16, he realized that he was a homosexual. He stated that he has never been interested in women, and he had no idea why he was a homosexual, but that he distinctly remembers that in high school, and during his teenage years, he became acutely aware of the fact that he was only attracted to men.

It was at this time that he began to have fantasies of killing human beings. He also began picking up animals which he had found on the road, which had been killed apparently by vehicles, and he would bring them home to his house, and he would use a knife in order to cut them up, and cut them open to see what was on the inside of them and what they looked like. Several of the animals that he cut up, he would completely strip down the flesh and meaty areas, and then use bleach and various other liquids which he found around his household, and experiment to see which ones would clean the bones the best.

He found a large dog that had been hit by a car and that he brought this dog home, cut it up, looked at its insides, completely cleaned it, and then soaked the bones in a bleach solution, and that he eventually planned to reconstruct the bones and mount the skeleton, much the way a taxidermist would do it. He stated, however, that he never got around to doing this.

During this time that he was cutting up animals, he would fantasize what it would be like to cut up a human being. He realized at this early age that his homosexual fantasies and his fantasies of killing and dismembering human beings were interlocked, and that he received gratification from these fantasies, and they occurred many times. Whenever he had fantasies of homosexual activity, he also had fantasies of killing and dismembering. He felt that the retrieving of road killed animals and the cutting of them up, satisfied his urges and his fantasies of killing and dismembering human beings. . . .

After leaving home in Bath, to join the Armed Forces, while in the Army, he was stationed in Germany. He believes the reason he did not kill or dismember anyone while he was serving his tour of duty in Germany, was because he enjoyed the structure of the Army. During the entire tour of duty, he lived on base and was in a dorm with three other men. Although he did not have any homosexual or heterosexual relationships while he was in Germany, or in the Army, he did satisfy his urge for sexual excitement by masturbation. He stated that he enjoyed the Army and wished that he could have finished his entire tour of duty; however, his abuse of alcohol made that impossible as the Army decided to let him go six months before his tour of duty was up.

After he moved to Milwaukee in 1981, the fantasies of killing people began to excite him and became more frequent. Regarding his victims, he states that he received physical pleasure from being with the victims when they were alive and he would have preferred that the victims remained alive; however, that it was better to have them with him dead than to have them leave. He states that when he felt when they were to leave, that is when he would decide to kill them.[23]

Killing for Company

Dahmer might have been inspired to offer that explanation by the accounts of Dennis Nilsen's serial murders in England. Between 1978 and 1983, Nilsen killed twelve (perhaps fifteen) male victims in his apartment, keeping their bodies to have necrophilic sex with. After they began to decay, he would cut them up into little pieces and flush them down the toilet. Eventually, the severed body parts, hair and clumps of human fat blocked the pipes, and after plumbers found the human remains, police came calling at Nilsen's door. Nilsen, like Dahmer, had severe alcohol problems, served in the military (although more successfully and longer than Dahmer) and was later a police constable in London. Nilsen stated that he was lonely and killed male victims to keep them near him. Brian Masters wrote a book on the Nilsen case appropriately titled *Killing for Company*, published in 1985. Perhaps Dahmer recognized himself in the book or learned from it.

Dahmer said after being discharged from the Army, his attempt to move to Florida was unsuccessful. He could not make ends meet and eventually was forced to move in with his paternal grandmother in a basement apartment of her house in West Allis, near Milwaukee. His grandmother always had a soft spot for him. Dahmer told detectives that while living with her:

He decided to make a concentrated effort to find some direction in his life. He constantly felt lonely and empty without direction, and that there was no meaning in life for him. His grandmother was a religious woman, a protestant, and a regular church goer and talked to him several times about religion and how it could turn his life around. He had continual fantasies again about homosexuality, and that along with the homosexual fantasies, came the urges to want to dominate, to kill, and to dismember other men. He stated that he constantly fought this urge by attending church with his grandmother, by reading the Bible, and by trying to live his life in an orderly fashion. "To walk the straight and narrow" are the words in which he used. He constantly had the interlocked feelings and fantasies of homosexual behavior, killing and dismembering and that they finally overcame him as he was finding it more and more impossible to continue with the lifestyle of "church going and right living" as he put it.[24]

It is frustrating that we don't have Jeffrey Dahmer's actual words in his initial interviews, only the paraphrasing of the detectives who interviewed him. When they write that "his homosexual fantasies and his fantasies of killing and dismembering human beings were interlocked," was this Dahmer speaking, or is this how Milwaukee PD detectives interpreted his statements in the police culture of the time? See again my earlier references to David Schmid and Richard Tithecott: "For a heterosexual culture, the Dahmer case represents an opportunity to explain acts of savagery by referring to his putative homosexuality, to confuse homicidal with homosexual tendencies, confuse 'sexual homicide' with homo sex."[25]

Of course, heterosexual serial killers also "interlock" their heterosexual fantasies with fantasies of murder, domination and rape. I don't think there was homophobia at work in the Dahmer case so much as a police culture that disapproved of unbridled sexual behavior of any kind—and that applied not only to the perpetrators but to victims as well, who were seen as contributing to their own murders by their sexual promiscuity.

In Grandma's House

Upon settling into his grandmother's house, Dahmer was the dutiful grandson, tending to her yard and attending church with her. With his military medical training, he found work as a phlebotomist, drawing blood at a blood bank. He said he took home a vial of blood and drank from it, just out of curiosity, but that he did not like the taste and spat it out. He also toyed with satanism, purchasing Anton LaVey's *Satanic Bible*, but found it wasn't for him.

Dahmer lost his job at the blood bank after nine months, and his grandmother supported him while he sporadically took on casual jobs until he found steady work at the Ambrosia Chocolate factory as a mixer.

Dahmer accumulated an escalating number of encounters with police. In 1981, he was charged with disturbing the peace, resisting police and possession of an open container of alcohol in a Ramada Inn lobby. In 1982, he exposed himself to a crowd of women and children at the Wisconsin State Fair but was charged with only drunk and disorderly behavior. He was arrested for lewd and lascivious behavior after masturbating in front of two twelve-year-old boys in a park. The charges were reduced to disorderly conduct, and he was sentenced to one year of probation. In 1985, he was cautioned for making obscene gestures toward police officers, and in another incident he became belligerent when a bartender refused to further serve him. Nothing in the minor charges he accumulated hinted at the depth of depravity into which he would sink.

It was while living in Milwaukee in his grandmother's basement that Dahmer says he discovered gay bars and baths and began engaging frequently in casual sex. There were accounts after his arrest that Dahmer's father reported that Jeffrey had been raped by a neighborhood boy when he was an adolescent. There is no evidence that this had occurred, and his father would later withdraw the allegation of rape. But there is this entry made by a detective in his interview notes with Dahmer:

> I then informed him that we had just spoken with his father, and we had received information that he may have had a sexual experience when he was 14 or 15 years old with a person who lived across the street. Mr. DAHMER stated that this did oc-

cur, and this person and him had gotten undressed and did some body rubbing and kissing. . . . He stated he did not consider this a homosexual experience at the time, but stated, "But I guess it was."

Other than this incident and the pickup of Hicks, his first murder victim, he does not appear to have had any actual sexual contact until his mid-twenties when he settled in Milwaukee. (Although there would later be accusations that he drugged and raped fellow soldiers while serving in the military, they were never proven.)

In 1985, Dahmer hid himself inside a department store after closing hours and stole a male mannequin, which he brought home. He told a forensic psychiatrist, "I just went through various sexual fantasies with it, pretending it was a real person, pretending that I was having sex with it, masturbating, and undressing it."[26] Dahmer's grandmother was disturbed when she found the mannequin in Jeffrey's bedroom and prevailed on him to get rid of it. He smashed it into little pieces with a hammer and put them into the trash, the way he soon would his human victims. Dahmer later commented, "It would have been better if I'd just stuck to the mannequins. Much, much better."

"He Is Definitely SPOOKY!"

Dahmer was not left alone to stew in his impulses and twisted fantasies. His grandmother remained in constant touch with Dahmer's father, Lionel, who would come to Milwaukee to see his son. He suggested to Jeffrey a plan of action to put some direction back in his life. Dahmer passively agreed to everything his father proposed. Lionel enrolled him in some college courses and paid the tuition. A few weeks later, he learned that Jeffrey was not attending the classes. Jeffrey told him he couldn't attend because he'd found some temporary work. Lionel would later write, "In that regard he had told the truth, something that, when I learned of it, actually surprised me. He had become the most artful of all deceivers, one who mixes falsehood with just a pinch of truth. Still his lies seemed relatively harmless. His life for all its disorder and lack of purpose, still seemed essentially harmless. For all Jeff had done, at least as far as I knew of what he had done, he had harmed no one but himself. I had no reason to believe that he would ever do otherwise."[27]

In June 1987, Dahmer was drugging and raping victims in a private room in the Club Baths. One of his victims could not be revived and had to be rushed to the hospital; Dahmer was banned from the bathhouse.

Dahmer claims that all these years he had agonized with guilt and remorse over his spontaneous murder of Steven Hicks in 1978. He attempted to reform himself by adopting a disciplined life like service in the Army or attending church on Sundays with his grandmother. For nine years, Dahmer killed nobody, as far as we know. He managed to keep his demons and his fantasies under control.

But Dahmer's self-control was slipping. On September 8, 1986, he was arrested for exposing himself in front of two boys in a Milwaukee park.

A condition of his bail was that he undergo psychological counseling for sexual deviance and impulse control, and the court referred him to clinical psychologists, one of whom concluded that Dahmer "could become a psychopathic deviate (sociopath) with schizoid tendencies. His deviant behavior will at least continue in some form if not be exacerbated. . . . Without some type of intervention which is supportive, his defences will probably be inadequate and he could gravitate toward further substance abuse with possible subsequent increased masochism or sadistic tendencies and behaviors." The other wrote in her report, "No doubt at this time that he is a Schizoid Personality Disorder who may show marked paranoid tendencies. He is definitely *SPOOKY*!"[28]

Schizoid personality disorder (SPD) is a diagnosis that has often appeared in assessments of serial killers since the 1940s. The symptoms of SPD are said to be a lack of interest in social relationships, a tendency toward a solitary or sheltered lifestyle, secretiveness, emotional coldness, detachment and apathy. Affected individuals may be unable to form intimate attachments to others and simultaneously possess a rich and elaborate but exclusively internal fantasy world.[29]

Second Murder

On November 21, 1987, everything changed for Dahmer; again. Dahmer went out cruising gay bars, having booked a hotel room, as he had done several times before, to bring a pickup back for a night of sex. He had no luck at the bars, but after closing time, he met twenty-five-year-old Steven Tuomi waiting for a bus. Tuomi agreed to go with Dahmer to his room in the Ambassador Hotel. According to the police interview report:

> Both DAHMER and TUOMI got undressed and laid on the bed. At that time they had what DAHMER called "light sex." He described this as hugging, kissing, and mutual masturbation. After about an hour or two, DAHMER made a drink for TUOMI in which he put the sleeping pills. TUOMI drank this and fell asleep. DAHMER kept drinking and eventually fell asleep himself. DAHMER related that when he woke up he was lying on top of TUOMI and DAHMER's forearms were visibly bruised. He then saw that TUOMI was obviously dead. He was bleeding from the head and his chest was crushed in and some of the bones were broken. DAHMER then carried TUOMI and placed him in a closet in the hotel room. DAHMER sat around the hotel room for a couple of hours, trying to figure out what to do.
>
> At about noon he went to the Grand Avenue Mall. He bought a large suitcase with wheels on it and returned to the Ambassador Hotel. During that time he may have had some beers and he left the hotel room to get a bite to eat. At about 5:00 PM he returned to the hotel room and placed TUOMI into the large suitcase. DAHMER related that it was a very tight fit, but he was able to get him into the suitcase. DAHMER related that he had purchased the room for another night and he remained in the room that night until 1:00 AM.
>
> At that time he left the room with the suitcase, taking an elevator to the ground floor. He got a cab and upon approach-

ing the cab, had the cab driver help him place the suitcase in the backseat of the cab. He then took the cab to his grandmother's house.[30]

Dahmer's second murder, like his first nine years earlier, occurred spontaneously without much planning in advance. Moreover, Dahmer claimed he had no memory of the murder or what sparked it, strange considering how much force and fury it would take to kill a victim in that way with one's bare hands. On the other hand, Dahmer kept in shape, lifting weights and working out. We will never know the whole story because Tuomi's body would never be recovered.

Dahmer kept Tuomi's corpse in his grandmother's cold fruit cellar for a week. His family came by for Thanksgiving dinner while the corpse lay in the basement. After everybody left and his grandmother went to bed, Dahmer stripped himself naked and then severed Tuomi's head with a kitchen knife and slit open his abdomen, extracting the intestines and organs, and emptied the torso of blood into the basement drain. He filleted the flesh from the body and cut it into small pieces that he collected into plastic trash bags. He wrapped the bones in an old sheet and then pulverized them into small fragments with a sledgehammer, the sheet preventing bone fragments from flying about the cellar.

Dahmer was in territory that even veteran homicide investigators rarely go. Dahmer assured them that there was nothing sexual in his being naked while dismembering his victims.

He stated that whenever he dismembered his victims, he was always completely naked, that he wore no shoes, socks, or any clothing of any type. He stated this was not in fact done because of sexual gratification, but simply for necessity because the job of cutting and dismembering his victims was quite messy and he did not wish to get blood and body fluids about his clothing.[31]

Dahmer put the bags of flesh out with the trash the next day but kept Tuomi's head.

Dahmer called the Ace Hardware store asking for advice on how to remove flesh from a rabbit skull. The hardware store recommended boiling it in Soilax, a popular non-suds wall, floor, tile and woodwork cleaner first introduced in 1934. (In their reports, police misspelled it as "Soilex"—a different product, a detergent produced in Kenya, which confuses true-crime writers to this day. But crime scene photographs confirm boxes of Soilax. The product was discontinued in 2005.)

According to the police interview notes:

> He states that this solution would help to turn the brain matter into a mushy substance and that after approximately 1 hr of boiling, the upper vertebra, located in the neck area, would become loose and he could dislodge them. At this time he would use a large serving spoon or utensil to dig into the back part of the skull and scoop out the brain matter which had turned into mush. After scooping out the brain matter and discarding it in the toilet, he would again place the skull into the boiling water and boil it thoroughly until it was completely clear of any flesh, hair, mucus, or brain matter.[32]

Afterward, Dahmer would masturbate with the skull. He had over-cooked Tuomi's head in the Soilax solution, and the skull eventually became too brittle and he was forced to destroy it. Without any physical evidence, police chose not to charge Dahmer with Tuomi's murder.

The Psychic Abolition of Redemption

Two months later, on Saturday, January 16, 1988, Dahmer lured his third victim, fourteen-year-old James Edward Doxtator, to his grandmother's house on the pretext of fifty dollars for posing for photographs and watching videos. After having sex, Doxtator told Dahmer he needed to go home. That sealed his fate. Dahmer prepared a cup of coffee with Baileys Irish Cream into which he crushed some Halcion sleeping pills. Doxtator drank the concoction and soon fell asleep in Dahmer's lap as Dahmer listened to his heartbeat. Later, Dahmer explained he had "an incessant and never-ending desire to have someone at whatever cost, someone good looking, really nice looking, and it just filled my thoughts all day long, increasing in intensity throughout the years when I was living with Grandma. Very overpowering, just relentless. . . . I knew my grandma would be waking up and I still wanted him to stay with me so I strangled him."

He stored Doxtator's body in the fruit cellar. The next day while his grandmother was at church, Dahmer carried the body into his bedroom and caressed and kissed it and had anal sex with the corpse. Every day after work he would cuddle and have sex with the corpse. By the end of the week, his grandmother began complaining of a foul odor from the cellar, and Dahmer told her it was the cat litter box and that he would take care of it. The next Sunday while his grandmother was at church, Dahmer destroyed Doxtator's body in the same way he had Tuomi's. He boiled Doxtator's head in Soilax and kept the skull for a few more weeks to masturbate with. Again, he overcooked the skull and it became brittle, and Dahmer was forced to dispose of it after a few weeks.

Having killed three victims, Dahmer was now a serial killer by anybody's definition.

Serial killer Ian Brady, who with his female partner, Myra Hindley, "the Moors Murderers," killed five children and youths in Great Britain in the 1960s, would later write about the significance of a serial killer's first three murders.

> The first killing experience will not only hold the strongest element of existential novelty and curiosity, but also the greatest element of danger and trepidation conjured by the unknown. Usually the incipient serial killer is too immersed in the psychological and legal challenges of the initial homicide, not to mention immediate logistics—the physical labour that the killing and disposal involve. He is therefore not in a condition to form a detached appreciation of the traumatic complexities bombarding his senses.
>
> You could, in many instances, describe the experience as an effective state of shock. He is, after all, storming pell-mell the

defensive social conditioning of a lifetime, as well as declaring war upon all the organized, regulatory forces of society. In extinguishing someone's life he is also committing his own, and has no time to stop and stare in the hazardous, psychological battlefield.

In another very significant sense, he is killing his long-accepted self as well as the victim, and simultaneously giving birth to a new persona, decisively cutting the umbilical connection between himself and ordinary mankind.

Having fought his former self and won, the fledgling serial killer flexes his newfound powers with more confidence. The second killing will hold all the same disadvantages, distracting elements of the first, but to a lesser degree. This allows a more objective assimilation of the experience. It also fosters an expanding sense of omnipotence, a wide-angle view of the metaphysical chessboard.

In many cases, the element of elevated aestheticism in the second murder will exert a more formative impression than the first and probably of any in the future. It not only represents the rite of confirmation, a revelational leap of lack of faith in humanity, but also the onset of addiction to hedonistic nihilism.

The psychic abolition of redemption.[33]

On March 24, 1988, Dahmer took twenty-two-year-old Richard Guerrero to his grandmother's home, where the two had sex and afterward Dahmer drugged and strangled him and quickly disposed of his body before his grandmother complained of the smell. She complained anyway, about the smell of the acidic chemicals in the garage and the basement that Dahmer was using to soften the flesh for easier removal. He did not keep any parts of Guerrero. Dahmer made one last attempt to resist his "psychic abolition of redemption." He managed to refrain from killing for a year after murdering Guerrero. It could have been an intellectual and moral choice to resist killing or it could have simply been the problem of having his grandmother around, complaining of the smell coming from the basement. His father brought it up with Jeffrey, who said he was experimenting with dissolving animals in various chemicals. Accustomed to his son's "chemical experiments" since childhood, Dahmer's father did not become alarmed. But his grandmother had another complaint: Jeffrey was bringing people home to her house late at night and it disturbed her. On September 25, 1988, Jeffrey moved out into an apartment of his own in the Villages Apartments on 808 North 24th Street, a block away from the Oxford Apartments, the scene of his last series of murders.

"Must Be Considered Impulsive and Dangerous"

The next afternoon, Dahmer encountered thirteen-year-old Milwaukee High School of the Arts student Somsack Sinthasomphone on the street. Somsack came from a large family of Laotian refugees. Dahmer offered Somsack fifty dollars to pose nude for some photographs. They returned to his new apartment where Dahmer gave Somsack a cup of coffee with Baileys Irish Cream and Halcion mixed in. Afterward, Somsack posed without a shirt on Dahmer's bed for some photographs. When Dahmer attempted to fondle the boy, he leapt up, put his shirt back on and told Dahmer it was time for him to leave. Dahmer asked Somsack to sit with him for a few more minutes so that he could "listen to his stomach." Dahmer was probably trying to stall Somsack long enough for the drugs to take effect. Somsack complied, but when Dahmer began kissing and licking his stomach from his navel down to his groin, Somsack got up, grabbed his school bag and left. Dahmer reminded him to take his fifty dollars and not tell anyone about their encounter. By the time Somsack arrived home, he was feeling sick from the effects of the drugs. As he began to have difficulty maintaining consciousness, his family took him to a hospital where Somsack revealed the encounter he just had with Dahmer.

Dahmer was charged with second-degree sexual assault and enticement of a child for immoral purposes. Compared to his previous charges, this was a serious charge. One of the court-appointed psychiatrists concluded that Dahmer was a "very psychologically problemed man. . . . There is no question that Mr. Dahmer is in need of long-term psychological treatment." Jeffrey's father hired a lawyer who retained a psychiatrist for a second opinion. The defense psychiatrist's conclusion was even more severe than the prosecution's: "would not show others the depth, severity or extent of his pathology. . . . Others may not take his behaviours as seriously as they should. . . . A seriously disturbed young man. . . . The pressure he perceives seems to be increasing. . . . He must be considered impulsive and dangerous."

Apparently, this was the first time that Jeffrey and his father acknowledged that he was gay, his father insisting that he had no idea. In the meantime, Dahmer moved back into his grandmother's house.

On January 30, 1989, Dahmer pleaded guilty and was sentenced to eight years' imprisonment, but as this was his first serious conviction and he expressed remorse, the sentence was reduced to one year's overnight detentions and five years' probation. This meant he could keep his job at the chocolate factory and return to the jail at night. He was also to receive psychological treatment to deal with his sexual confusion and his dependence upon alcohol.

"Him I Like Especially Well"

Almost exactly a year to the day that Dahmer had murdered Guerrero, on March 25, 1989, Dahmer met twenty-four-year-old Anthony Lee Sears, an African American man. Dahmer told the detectives interviewing him that he had not killed anyone for over a year. He went out that night for a few drinks with no plans of meeting anybody or having any sexual encounters. He said that Sears had aggressively cruised him as Dahmer was leaving a bar. The two hit it off. Sears had beautiful curly hair and a short ponytail secured by a rubber band, which Dahmer found very hip and attractive. Dahmer told Sears he was visiting from Chicago and staying with his grandmother. Sears suggested they go to his grandmother's house for a night of sex.

A friend of Sears's drove the couple to grandma's house, with Sears in the back seat serving Dahmer oral sex. Even Dahmer was taken aback by how horny Sears was for him. He said it was "a surprise. I didn't think he was *that* anxious."[34]

It was Sunday morning, 3:00 a.m., when Dahmer and Sears quietly slipped into the house and fumbled and tongued and groped each other in the kitchen before Dahmer took Sears into his bedroom, where he now went down on Sears. It was wonderful. Dahmer *really liked* Sears; he was smitten. He could do this all night and all day forever. Would Sears stay or come back later? he asked him. No, he had to go and he was not planning on coming back either, Sears replied.

Dahmer gave him a sweet kiss and said he'd make him a nice warm nightcap for the road. Quietly, as not to awake his grandmother, Dahmer padded down to the kitchen and prepared his usual coffee and Baileys Irish Cream drink for his guest. He crushed seven Halcion pills into it.

Sears gratefully drank the bracingly warm nightcap as Dahmer gave him a lingering goodbye hug, laying his head on Sears's chest and listening to his heartbeat as he slipped into unconsciousness. Dahmer snuggled and smooched with Sears and fondled him, and then strangled him as his grandmother slept soundly with her Bible. It was Easter Sunday morning.

Dahmer knew she was going to be away at church much longer than usual.

When she got up to make breakfast, Dahmer joined his grandmother at the table, and after he saw her leave for church, he returned for another lovemaking session with Sears's corpse, which was still mildly warm. (After death, a corpse loses 1.5 degrees Fahrenheit [0.83 degrees centigrade] every hour, but the body was under the bedcovers.) When he was finished, Dahmer carried the body into the bathroom and began butchering it in the tub, draining the blood, disarticulating and dismembering the limbs, flaying the flesh from the bones and cutting it all down into manageable morsels to put into garbage bags, separate from the bones, which were going to be later crushed and broken with his grandma's sledgehammer.

Dahmer severed the head and the genitals and tossed them into a separate plastic bag.

Sears was Dahmer's fifth victim since 1978, but he was the first whose body parts Dahmer would harvest and keep with him. This might have been Dahmer's first true necro-love. Dahmer said, "Him I like *especially* well." Sears was going to be his forever; at least his head and genitals were. The problem was how to preserve the flesh from decaying.

The next morning, Dahmer called the helpful folks at Ace Hardware for advice on how best to preserve flesh with bone for taxidermy. With acetone, he was told. Dahmer purchased a ten-gallon plastic drum with a sealable lid, dropped the head and genitals into it, filled it with acetone and put the sealed drum in the back of his bedroom closet for a week.

When he opened and drained the drum, the head and genitals were preserved in their fleshy self. For extra life, Dahmer used makeup to powder and paint some flesh color back into the body parts. He would copulate with the head and hold and stroke it as he masturbated. But after a few weeks, the skin around the head started to shrink and slip. Dahmer was scheduled to start serving nights in prison detention, and he worried about leaving the head in his grandmother's house. He put it and the genitals into a cosmetic case and stored it in his locker at the chocolate factory. After his release from night detention, Dahmer recovered the case from his locker but discovered that the head was beginning to mold. Before Dahmer Soilaxed the decayed flesh from the skull, he scalped the skull around the ponytail that Sears had sported and kept it as a sacred totem of his eternal love. Police would find Sears's skull and genitals in Dahmer's black filing cabinet in his bedroom. He later told a psychiatrist, "If I could have kept him longer, all of him, I would have." True love hath no bounds.

"It Was Just All Slush, Black Slush"

After he completed his sentence, his grandmother fed up with the chemical smells, on May 14, 1990, Dahmer moved into the Oxford Apartments, bringing Sears's skull and painted genitals with him. Having killed five men, now secure in his own private abattoir, in the next fourteen months Dahmer would murder and mutilate twelve more victims in an escalating bloodbath.

On May 20, 1990, Dahmer lured thirty-two-year-old sex worker Raymond Smith, nicknamed Cash-D, to his apartment, drugged and strangled him in the usual way. Smith was the first of several victims that Dahmer would cannibalize. The police interview memo laconically reads, "Jeff DAHMER went on to relate that he had originally told us that he had only eaten a bicep of one of his victims. He related that there were other times in which he had eaten part of the victim. The first time was the person he identified as CASH D (Raymond SMITH—Victim #5 [in Milwaukee]). He related that he eat [sic] this victim's heart. He related that it tasted kind of spongy."[35]

Dahmer had recently bought a black table that he intended to convert into an altar to his victims, which he planned to decorate with their body parts. (Later, he would put his aquarium on it.) He bought a Polaroid camera, which he now used to capture images of his victims in various poses and states of dismemberment. In his account of the Dahmer case, Brian Masters writes:

> He was, in a way, virtually creating his own pornography, as if the picture of beauty was more alluring than beauty itself. This is tantamount to saying that fantasy—solid, sculpted, manageable, unthreatening—has finally become more deeply important than reality. It is also more stimulating; whereas Dahmer had found it impossible to reach orgasm with the partners he met at the Unicorn Bathhouse in Chicago, he was able to stand over the dead body of Cash D and masturbate to ejaculation. The camera translated reality into fantasy, and the orgasm celebrated it.[36]

This time, Dahmer did something new with the victim's skull after boiling off the flesh. At an art supply store, Dahmer purchased some enamel simulated granite spray paint in order to give the skulls an artificial look, in case someone saw them. Police found three such painted skulls in his apartment and indeed at first thought they were plastic decorative prop skulls. Dahmer told police "he wanted to keep the skulls of his victims, because to him the skull represented the true essence of his victims. He states that he felt by at least keeping the heads, the death of his victims would not be a total loss, because the heads would be with him."[37]

Dahmer had wanted to preserve some of Smith's body parts, and the next day he bought a freezer to preserve them in. He decapitated and dismembered Smith's body in the bathtub. The parts he did not want to keep, he boiled for an hour in a huge steel kettle in a water and Soilax solution. Afterward, he scraped the remains of the soft boiled flesh from the bones in the kitchen sink. He couldn't sledgehammer the bones in his apartment the way he did in his grandmother's house. He bought a trash container with a sealable lid and put the bones into it with a solution of acid. Dahmer said, "I waited a week or two and they had all turned to slush at that time, which I scooped out with a smaller trash thing and poured it into the toilet and flushed it down. It was just all slush, black slush."

Again, I wonder whether Dahmer had read about Nilsen and how the raw fat from body parts he flushed down the toilet blocked the pipes and eventually led to his arrest. Reducing them in acid to a flushable sludge would be a solution to that problem.

"It Tasted Like Beef or a Filet Mignon"

Dahmer lurched his way through his next eleven murders from May 1990 until his arrest in July 1991. On June 14, 1990, he murdered twenty-seven-year-old Edward Warren Smith, but Dahmer overbaked his skull while drying it in an oven and had to throw it out. No traces of Eddie Smith's body were found.

On September 2, Dahmer met another victim he found himself in awe of, a twenty-two-year-old dance student, Ernest Marquez Miller. Dahmer fell for the dancer's tightly corded muscular physique. Miller agreed to go back to Dahmer's apartment for fifty dollars. Dahmer drugged Miller into unconsciousness and then sexually assaulted him. But Dahmer was running out of money for pills and had only two to slip into Miller's drink. (Unable to afford a refill of sleeping pills, Dahmer attempted to render a victim unconscious with a blow from a rubber mallet, but it did not work. The victim left enraged but alive.) Dahmer played with Miller's body as if he were a sex doll, but he became concerned that he would not be able to control the muscular youth if he awoke. Using his Army medic's training, Dahmer carefully located Miller's carotid artery at his neck and slit it open with a paring knife, showering his bed and wall with arterial blood. Dahmer said he could never properly clean the blood off the wall and mattress. A year later, police would note the smears of dried blood on the wall behind Dahmer's bed and his mattress still saturated with crusty, dry gore.

Dahmer posed Miller's body in various positions and shot multiple Polaroid pictures as he dismembered and decapitated his corpse in the bathtub. According to the Milwaukee PD interview memorandum, "He related that this was a person he really liked. He indicated that he had filleted his heart and had kept it in the freezer and also kept his bicep. He indicated that he had eaten the thigh muscle of this subject, but it was so tough he could hardly chew it. He then purchased a meat tenderizer and used it on the bicep. He stated that it tasted like beef or a filet mignon."

On September 24, 1990, Dahmer killed twenty-two-year-old David Courtney Thomas. Dahmer would later say he wasn't "his type," but just the same, he took Polaroid photos of his corpse as he dismembered it. He didn't like Thomas, and police found no trace of his remains in Dahmer's collection of victims he liked.

On February 18, 1991, Dahmer lured seventeen-year-old Curtis Durrell Straughter to his apartment. Dahmer now incorporated handcuffs into his fantasy play, despite the fact that his unconscious victims did not need to be restrained. He also changed the way in which he killed. Previously, Dahmer had strangled his victims with his hands, but now he acquired a leather strap with which he would kill until the strap became so soaked in saliva, vomit and blood that he had to throw it away.

He harvested Straughter's skull, his severed hands and his genitals, which police found in his apartment.

"Drilling Technique"

Having now killed an even ten victims, Dahmer perhaps was again having moral qualms; or perhaps they were simply practical concerns. He began to seek a way to keep his loves without killing them. On April 7, 1991, Dahmer for the first time attempted what he called his "drilling technique." He lured nineteen-year-old Errol Lindsey to his place and as usual drugged him into unconsciousness. Then he drilled a small hole in Lindsey's skull using a power drill with sixteenth-inch and three-eighth-inch bits and injected hydrochloric acid into his brain with a giant turkey baster he purchased at Lechters Kitchen Supply. The purpose was to transform Lindsey into a sex zombie. Dahmer explained, "I didn't want to keep killing people and have nothing left but the skull."

It did not work. When Lindsey regained consciousness, he complained of a headache. Dahmer drugged him again and strangled him. Dahmer decided he would skin Lindsey's severed head. According to the police notes:

> DAHMER related that the skin of the human being was easily detached; he states much the way you would detach skin from a chicken which you are planning to cook. After the initial incision, he could pull on the skin and it would pull off the muscle tissue of the body easily. The only time it was difficult was when he was pulling the skin off around the joints and at this time he would use a small paring knife to carefully cut the skin around the joint portion of the body. Regarding the fact that the skin was completely taken off the head of the subject, DAHMER related that he would start an incision in the lower portion of the back of the neck and slice up to the top (or crown of the head). At this time he could pull on either side of the skin from the incision and it would completely pull right off the skull of the individual. The only time he needed to do any real cutting would be around the facial features, that being the eyes, nose, lips and mouth. The entire skull portion of the skin came off in one complete piece and while it was off it actually looked somewhat like a mask you can buy at a party store. He kept the skin and the mask-like facial features of this subject and planned to treat them with a solution he made up of salt and borax. He soaked them in a salt, borax and water solution for several weeks and then planned to take them out and dry them

to preserve them. He wanted to keep the skin and the mask-like portion of the individual's head, however he underestimated the powerful mixture, of borax and salt. After several weeks in the solution, the skin turned to a mushy-like substance and was unable to be kept and it had to be thrown out.[38]

Lindsey's painted skull was found in Dahmer's apartment.

Dahmer had clearly gone off the dark deep end, somewhere between the Stone Age and Ed Gein's cornholed madness. In the last two months, Dahmer went into a killing machinelike frenzy in which he killed six victims, the last three of which he would kill over fourteen days in July.

On May 24, Dahmer lured thirty-one-year-old Anthony Hughes, a deaf-mute. Dahmer and Hughes wrote notes to each other as Dahmer persuaded him to return to his apartment for fifty dollars. Friends of Hughes drove the two to Dahmer's apartment as they exchanged notes in the back of the car. After Dahmer drugged and killed Hughes, he kept his body in his bedroom for days without dismembering it.

Just when you think this narrative can't get any more twisted than it already is, it takes another sick turn. Hughes was still lying dead in Dahmer's bedroom when he brought his next victim home to the apartment.

"I Can't Do Anything About Somebody's Sexual Preferences in Life"

On May 27, three days after killing Hughes, Dahmer completely by co-incidence encountered fourteen-year-old Konerak Sinthasomphone. This was the younger brother of the Laotian refugee Somsack Sintha-somphone, who survived Dahmer's assault. Konerak agreed to pose for photographs at Dahmer's apartment. The two returned to the apart-ment, and Konerak posed on the couch, unaware that there was a three-day-old dead body in the bedroom. Konerak downed the drugged drink and lost consciousness as Dahmer sexually assaulted him. Then Dah-mer drilled a hole into Konerak's cranium three-quarters of the way to the rear of his skull, slanted forward. The intention was to access behind the frontal lobe, but Dahmer did not quite get the cerebral anatomy. He then inserted the turkey baster about two inches deep into the skull and injected Konerak's head with hydrochloric acid. Konerak slept through the entire "procedure."

With Konerak unconscious, Dahmer now waited for him to regain consciousness, hopefully in a compliant zombie state. Dahmer discovered he was out of beer and decided that Konerak would be out for a while longer and left to go get a beer at a local bar. Konerak in the meantime awoke in a daze with a brain full of hydrochloric acid and stumbled out naked into the street, babbling incoherently.

Three young black women saw Konerak and called the police. One of the women had recognized him because they picked dew worms together and she was sure he was a minor. Unfortunately, in her call to 911, she described him as a "young man."

Before the police arrived, Dahmer returned from his beer run and saw Konerak sitting on the curb with the three women hovering around him protectively. Dahmer tried to take Konerak back to his apartment, but the women stopped him.

What exactly happened next is a matter of dispute. The women claimed that Konerak had a stream of blood running down his leg from his rectum. Dahmer later claimed he'd only had oral sex with Konerak at this point. Nobody noticed beneath his long hair the hole that Dahmer had drilled in his head. A police patrol car and a fire truck arrived at the scene and wrapped Konerak in a blanket.

The two police officers responding to the call interviewed Dahmer, who presented his Ambrosia Chocolate work ID and assured them that the man was his twenty-year-old boyfriend and had drunk too much and they had quarreled. He gave them a false name for Konerak. As the women insisted that Konerak was obviously a child, they were brusquely warned off by the officers to go home and not to interfere in their investigation.

Later, detectives would say of Dahmer:

> He was extremely nervous during the time of the questioning by police, he put on a very calm attitude and felt he was able

to convince the police that it was a lovers' problem between two homosexuals. He related that due to the fact that he was able to convince all these people, in positions of authority, his parents and neighbors who questioned him regarding his activities, it gave him a feeling that he could get away with his crimes. He felt that he had the ability to make people see a phase of him that only he wished them to see and that this encouraged him to continue on with his crimes, feeling that he would never be caught.[39]

The two officers now escorted Dahmer and the incoherent Konerak back to Dahmer's apartment, where they saw Konerak's clothing neatly folded on the couch. Dahmer showed them the Polaroids he shot of Konerak willingly posing for him and assured them he was an adult and they were in an intimate relationship. Konerak sat passively on Dahmer's couch in a stupor. All this while Hughes's body lay dead on the bedroom floor and the apartment smelled of decaying body parts. One of the officers peeked through the door into the dark bedroom but did not go in or see anything.

The officers told Dahmer to take good care of Konerak and left. As they drove off they radioed the dispatcher, chuckling, "The intoxicated Asian naked male was returned to his sober boyfriend and we're 10-8. . . . My partner's going to get deloused at the station."[40]

The aunt of one of the three women who called the police followed up later that night with the dispatcher, who patched her through directly to the police officers who had responded to the call. The 911 transcript was later released:

WOMAN: What happened? I mean my daughter and my niece witnessed what was going on. Was anything done about the situation? Do you need the names or information or anything from them?

OFFICER: No, not at all.

WOMAN: You don't?

OFFICER: No, it was an intoxicated boyfriend of another boyfriend.

WOMAN: Well how old was this child?

OFFICER: It wasn't a child. It was an adult.

WOMAN: Are you sure?

OFFICER: Yep.

WOMAN: Are you positive? Because this child doesn't even speak English. My daughter had, you know, dealt with him before, seen him on the street, you know, catching earthworms.

OFFICER: Yeah, no, no, he's—it's all taken care of, ma'am.

WOMAN: Are you sure?

OFFICER: Ma'am, I can't make it any more clear. It's all taken care of. He's with his boyfriend in his boyfriend's apartment, where he's got his belongings also. I mean, that's where it's released.

WOMAN: But I mean isn't this, I mean what if he's a child and not an adult. I mean are you positive this is an adult?

OFFICER: Ma'am, like I explained to you, it's all taken care of. It's as positive as I can be. I can't do anything about somebody's sexual preferences in life.

WOMAN: Well no, I'm not saying anything about that, but it appeared to be a child. This is my concern.

OFFICER: No, he's not.

WOMAN: He's not a child?

OFFICER: No, he's not. OK? It's a boyfriend-boyfriend thing and he's got belongings at the house where he came from. He's got pictures of himself and his boyfriend, and so forth.

WOMAN: Oh, I see.

OFFICER: OK?

WOMAN: OK, I'm just, you know, it appears to have been a child, that was my concern.

OFFICER: I understand. No, he's not.[41]

The optics of this encounter are obviously not great for the Milwaukee PD. In their defense, they claimed that there was no "probable cause" at the time to search Dahmer's bedroom without a warrant and that out of respect to the gay community, police were responding to the incident as a "domestic dispute" as they would with a heterosexual couple. They claimed no particular racial discrimination against the black women who reported Dahmer, a white man, nor discrimination against the Laotian Konerak, other than claiming that it was difficult for them to estimate the age of a young Asian male. The "delousing" comment was said to be par for the course, that police officers frequently have to delouse themselves after having physical contact with street people. While that might be true, the officer did not actually go in for delousing. It was apparently a wisecrack. The bottom line is that the police officers did not make the time to confirm Konerak's identity or age and handed the fourteen-year-old boy back into the hands of a serial killer. Nor did they radio in Dahmer's name for a criminal record check, which would have revealed the recent sexual assault and enticement of a child convictions—and that the victim was Konerak's brother. Not only could they have saved Konerak, but four more victims would not have been murdered had Dahmer been apprehended that night.

As soon as the police left his apartment, Dahmer injected another syringe full of acid into Konerak's head, but instead of making him more compliant, it killed him. Dahmer proceeded to dismember and "process" Konerak's and Hughes's bodies, taking a day off from work at Ambrosia Chocolate. Police found Konerak's head preserved in the freezer, while Hughes's boiled skull was found in the filing cabinet.

After this close encounter with the police, Dahmer paused for a month.

On June 30, Dahmer attended the Gay Pride Parade in Chicago, where he met twenty-year-old Matt Cleveland Turner. He persuaded Turner to return with him to Milwaukee. He drugged and strangled Turner and dismembered and decapitated him, putting some of his remains into the freezer.

On July 5, Dahmer returned to Chicago, where he encountered in a gay bar twenty-three-year-old art school student Jeremiah B. Weinberger, a half–Puerto Rican, half-Jewish man. Weinberger actually liked Dahmer and readily agreed to return with him to Milwaukee.

They made out on the one-and-a-half-hour bus ride from Chicago. But by now, Dahmer was oblivious to whether his victims wanted to leave or not. He was keeping them all. After drugging Weinberger, he drilled a hole into his cranium, but instead of acid, he injected boiling water in an attempt to "cook off" his free will. At first it seemed to work. Dahmer said, "He woke up at the end of the day, the next morning, and he was sort of groggy and everything. He talked, it was like he was dazed and I thought I would be able to keep him that way." Dahmer said there was no bleeding or effusion from the hole drilled into his cranium. "He was walking around, going to the bathroom, but I had to go to work the second night, at the end of the second day, and he was still walking around so I gave him another dose of pills and another shot of boiling water in the same hole."

When Dahmer came home from work, he found Weinberger was dead. He took photographs as he decapitated Weinberger and put his head into the freezer. He then filled the bathtub with cold water and bleach and put Weinberger's headless torso into the water, where it soaked for a week. Dahmer continued showering next to the torso floating at his feet.

"He Stated That He Ate Only the People That He Really Liked"

On July 12, with his freezer jammed with heads and body parts and a torso floating in the bathtub, Dahmer purchased the fifty-seven-gallon plastic chemical drum, which he rolled into his bedroom. He brewed and brined three torsos and other remains in a chemical concoction, a process he'd been mastering since he was a ten-year-old collecting roadkill.

Dahmer's life was beginning to unravel beyond the gravitational pull of his ability to appear entirely harmless.

And yet what does he do? He kills two more.

On July 15, Dahmer encountered another big love. Twenty-four-year-old Oliver Joseph Lacy was a bodybuilder and had that perfect body that Dahmer lusted for. Dahmer lured him to his apartment with the photo-posing gambit. He promised to pay Lacy more if he'd let him rub and massage his body. He eventually drugged him and strangled him with the leather strap. Then he butchered Lacy and ate parts of him, wrapping other parts in plastic bags and putting them in the freezer for later.

According to the police interview notes:

> He states that the victim, whose right bicep he had eaten, was one that he cared for and the individual had big biceps. He stated that he put Crisco on the bicep, softened it up with a meat tenderizer, and then fried it in a skillet. He states he also saved this individual's heart in the freezer, and a portion of an arm from the black male that he had met at a bookstore about one year ago. He states he did intend to consume these parts. . . .
>
> We asked him if he had eaten the body parts, just plain. He stated that he would use salt, pepper and A-1 Steak sauce on them. He stated that the reason he ate these parts was because he was curious but then it was because he wanted to make them a part of him. He stated that this way he could keep these people with him. He stated that he ate only the people that he really liked and wanted them to be a part of him or with him all the time. . . .
>
> We asked him why he had not informed us of eating the various body parts when he first stated that he only ate the bicep. He stated that he did not want to talk about it, because it was not very appealing and he did not want us to think less of him.[42]

Dahmer was so engrossed in butchering and eating Lacy that he never made it to work that day.

Again.

Ambrosia Chocolate suspended him for absenteeism, pending a final decision.

The next day, July 18, Dahmer went to see his probation officer to complain about everything going wrong in his life. She sent him to see a doctor, who prescribed antidepressants. Dahmer was contemplating suicide. Building management was getting complaints about the foul odors emanating from Dahmer's apartment, and he was warned that he would be evicted before the end of July. Where was he to go with his cache of heads, torsos and severed penises?

Dahmer was only thirty-one, but he had traveled an old man's measure of madness. His unraveling secret life was finally bankrupted in those two ways that Hemingway had described how bankruptcy happens: gradually and then suddenly.

I can do no better than Brian Masters in describing the end:

> The scene at Apartment 213 in that week from 12 to 19 July was more lurid than Giotto's vision of hell on the wall of the Scrovegni chapel in Padua, which depicts devils munching on the intestines of the fallen. When Oliver Lacy was being massaged in one room, the headless body of Jeremiah Weinberger was floating in a bath of cold water and bleach next door. Dahmer was obliged to take a shower with two corpses in the tub. He took one photograph of Matt Turner in a standing position after death, because rigor mortis had set in and he was able to position the body properly. Other pictures show a headless Oliver Lacy hanging by a strap from the bar of the shower curtain, and the same mutilated corpse, also with the rib-cage exposed, lying on top of the decapitated body of Weinberger. Both heads were separately preserved in the fridge and freezer, along with two others. A bag containing internal organs was stuck to the bottom of the freezer. Hearts were in the fridge, and a whole bicep, large enough to cover a plate, had been fried and eaten. The drum in the bedroom contained the remains of three people.[43]

On July 19, Ambrosia Chocolate formally fired Dahmer. It was the end. Later that same day, Dahmer picked up Joseph Arthur Bradehoft, a twenty-five-year-old father of three kids from Minnesota trying to eke out a living in Milwaukee. He accepted Dahmer's offer to pose for photographs back at his apartment. Dahmer strangled him and kept his corpse in bed with him, sleeping and cuddling with it for two days. It was extra hot that July, and the air-conditioning did not work well in his bedroom. Dahmer woke up on the morning of July 21 and pulled back the blanket to find Bradehoft's head crawling with maggots. Dahmer decapitated him in the bathtub and scraped the maggots off into the toilet. He put the decaying head into the freezer compartment, where police would later find it. His dismembered torso was put into the blue chemical drum with the other two torsos and severed heads.

Serial killer Dennis Nilsen later commented on Dahmer's final frenzy of killing, "Each one seemed to be its own last time." Nilsen argues that the term "serial killer" is inaccurate because it implies an intention to repeat. "You might as well call Elizabeth Taylor a serial bride," he wrote.[44]

Three days later, Dahmer brought Tracy Edwards to his apartment, and after Edwards escaped into the street with handcuffs dangling off one wrist, it was over for Dahmer—his secret life bankrupted that very night—with police trooping through his charnel house of an apartment.

The Last Serial Killer?

Dahmer pleaded guilty to fifteen counts of murder in Wisconsin in January 1992. The only outstanding courtroom matter was whether Dahmer was sane. The hearings were covered on TV "gavel-to-gavel," the biggest crime story in Wisconsin since Ed Gein, the biggest story in the United States since . . . well, since them all, since Albert DeSalvo, Ed Kemper, Juan Corona, Ted Bundy, David Berkowitz, John Wayne Gacy, Arthur Shawcross, Richard Ramirez and Henry Lee Lucas. What we did not know was that Jeffrey Dahmer would be the last of that generation of serial killers as viral celebrities.

By now we were familiar enough with the serial killer insanity hearing to know that the frontiers of grotesque horror were not the measure of insanity. Dahmer was crazy, perhaps, but not insane. He was aware of what he was doing at all times. In February, Dahmer was sentenced to life in prison for fifteen murders. In May, he pleaded guilty in Ohio to the 1978 murder of Steve Hicks.

In a strange way, Dahmer was a pitiful sight. He did not show the arrogance of Bundy or the unrepentant gall of Gacy, nor did he spin excuses in the way Shawcross did. He appeared to be apologetic and remorseful. Although the victims' families were devastated by what Dahmer had done, somehow he lacked a veneer of evil, in almost the same way old Ed Gein seemed to be beyond evil. There was something tragic and sad about Dahmer, like one of those medieval lost-love were-wolves. Dahmer was a strange brew of horror and pity; Derf Backderf captured perfectly his pathos in his graphic nonfiction book *My Friend Dahmer*. Dahmer just wanted somebody to be with him forever. What bride doesn't dream the same?

In the world of serial homicide, it was hard to imagine anything worse than the extreme depravity of the Dahmer case. Where was there left to go? As hard as it would be for anyone to top Dahmer's depravity, those of us who paid attention to this kind of thing stood poised just the same for the next serial killer to come.

In January 1992, as Dahmer was making his courtroom appearances, forty-one-year-old William Lester Suff, a mild-mannered warehouse clerk in Riverside County, California, was arrested and accused of raping, torturing, stabbing and strangling twenty-two women between 1989 and 1991. Some of Suff's victims were drug-addicted sex workers, whose bodies Suff would pose in obscene positions by dumpsters in fast-food parking lots; he allegedly severed the breast of one of his victims and served it at the Riverside County Employee Chili Cook-off. Suff delivered furniture to the police task force assigned to investigate his series of murders and often posed as a police officer.

Then in Long Island on June 28, 1993, a New York State trooper saw a Mazda pickup truck missing a rear license plate and tried to pull it over. The vehicle sped away, and during the high-speed chase the driver lost control and crashed it into a pole. As the troopers approached the vehicle, they could smell the distinct odor of death wafting from the truck's covered rear bed. The driver, thirty-four-year-old landscaper Joel Rifkin, was unhurt. When troopers pulled him out from the truck, they noticed he had a layer of Vicks VapoRub smeared under his nose. When they lifted the blue plastic tarpaulin in the rear, they uncovered the decaying corpse of twenty-two-year-old sex worker Tiffany Bresciani. The smear of VapoRub was a trick Rifkin saw in *The Silence of the*

Lambs, which portrayed FBI agents smearing it under their noses when attending the autopsy of a decayed corpse.

Rifkin matter-of-factly told the officer, "She was a prostitute. I picked her up on Allen Street in Manhattan. I had sex with her, then things went bad and I strangled her. Do you think I need a lawyer?" This routine traffic stop would uncover the murders of seventeen women at Rifkin's hands.

The trials of Suff and of Rifkin would be some time in coming, and press and true-crime writers went into standby mode for the next big serial killer story. But it was slow in arriving with all the usual pretrial preparation and maneuvering.

In the case of Joel Rifkin, New York prosecutors prepared to try him in separate cases, victim by victim, which was disappointing to the media. Single murder trials lacked the drama of the checkerboard of victims' faces that accompanied serial murder trials. This was when the Internet was dawning and network television news divisions were being put under the supervision of television *entertainment* executives. And serial killers had certainly been "entertaining." In 1994, newspaper columnist Dave Rossie lamented:

> It's no secret that newspapers and television are locked in a struggle for the hearts and minds of the American public. . . . New Age journalism as practiced by the *Daily News*, reads like what might happen if one of those TV shows such as "Hard Copy" or "Current Affair" decided to put out a newspaper. . . . Recently, the *News* ran a two-part piece on alleged serial killer Joel Rifkin, who has been transformed by the *News* into "Joel the Ripper Rifkin." God knows what the *News* will call him if and when he's convicted.[45]

In May 1994, Rifkin was convicted in the murder of Bresciani, his last victim, in what was supposed to be the first of the slayings to come to trial.

Then came June 17, 1994.

PFFFFFFFFFFFT.

Somebody suddenly changed the channel.

Ninety-five million people that day were transfixed by a live image on their television screens of a white Ford Bronco slowly driving down the Santa Ana Freeway trailed by a phalanx of police cars.

Everything and everybody turned to the O. J. Simpson case.

By the time Joel Rifkin stood his next trial and Lester Suff went on trial in Riverside, old-school serial killers like them were yesterday's monsters, tired old news. Has-beens. Their trials were barely noted in the press. The 1995 O. J. Simpson trial media circus turned us on to a new source for our true-crime thrill-kill fix-of-the-month: celebrity defendants. O. J. would be followed by Robert Blake, Snoop Dogg, Phil Spector, Ray Lewis, Michael Skakel, and Lillo Brancato Jr.

After O. J., the only thing that brought Jeffrey Dahmer's name back into the news briefly was his murder in prison on November 28, 1994. The epidemic era of celebrity serial killers had run its course. The Golden Age of Serial Murders, as Harold Schechter had tongue in cheek coined the era, was over. Thank God.

Jeffrey Dahmer became the last of the celebrity "epidemic" generation of serial killers, just in time, because God only knows what could have been worse than Dahmer.

After Jeffrey Dahmer, there were still many serial killers to come, 669 of them in the 1990s, which was still a lot but a 13 percent decline since the 1980s. They had names like John Eric Armstrong, Anthony Balaam, Lucious Boyd, Robert Eugene Brashers, Rory Enrique Conde, Andre Crawford, Richard Evonitz, Wayne Adam Ford, Alfred Gaynor, Hubert Geralds, Orville Lynn Majors, Glen Edward Rogers, Paul Runge, Heriberto Seda, Robert Shulman, Jack Owen Spillman, Henry Louis Wallace, and Nathaniel White. If you haven't heard of them, you are not the only one. Some didn't even have monikers. The few that came to prominence—like Keith Jesperson, "the Happy Face Killer," and David Parker Ray, "the Toy Box Killer"—were few and far between, and they were "B-listers" just the same.*

---

*Some might argue Andrew Cunanan in 1997 was the last prominent serial killer of the decade, but he, like John Allen Muhammad and Lee Boyd Malvo later—the Beltway Snipers in 2002—was a rarer subset of serial killer, a so-called lethargic "spree serial

"Real" celebrity defendants like Snoop Dogg and Robert Blake now outclassed them, even if they were acquitted. The emergent Internet and a plethora of cable TV channels fragmented the former collective gathering of Americans around a single horror story. The horrors were now packaged into different morsels for different tastes on different channels and media platforms, and serial killers began to lose that monopoly on monstrosity they once held. Once video could be streamed over the Internet, the fragmentation was complete.

---

killer" rampaging over a period of weeks or months, never returning to the conventional "normalcy" of his life, to a so-called "cooling-off" period, as "traditional" serial killers do. Cunanan's infamy was linked to the celebrity of his final victim, fashion designer Gianni Versace. Cunanan was perhaps the last of the "queering" of serial murder in the US, his murders inseparably linked to his sexuality.

The Post-Epidemic Era 2000–2020

The next big-news serial killer after Jeffrey Dahmer was the Green River Killer, fifty-two-year-old Gary Ridgway, who was arrested on November 30, 2001, after his DNA was successfully linked to some of his victims. Ridgway wasn't a new serial killer per se—he had begun killing in 1982 but apparently "retired" in 1998. For nearly two decades as the Green River Killer he had the legendary status of unidentified serial killers like the Zodiac and BTK, perhaps even Jack the Ripper.

Shortly after his arrest, I wrote about him in my book *Serial Killers*, describing him as "typical," but looking at him now with twenty years' hindsight, I can place him better in the historical pantheon. Ridgway was a creature who came crawling out at us from a pool of DNA collected in the vanished past of the big-number epidemic years. He killed an extraordinary forty-nine women (and maybe more) between 1982 and 1998. He remains at this writing the American sexual serial killer with the highest number of murder convictions. (Samuel Little, it was revealed in 2019, is suspected to have killed between fifty and ninety-three victims but has not gone to trial on most of them, and might not.)

Despite Ridgway's huge victim count, and even though he was a cold case throwback of that epidemic era and everything it represented, once caught and identified, he was a yawn. He had none of that "celebrity heat" and colorful personality of the "golden age" superstars. He was a banality in evil—an Adolf Eichmann of serial killers—high in victim numbers, low in charisma. Ridgway was a monotone, mealymouthed, gnat-stupid, Bible-beating necrophile with an IQ tested in the low eighties. He earned perfect-attendance awards at work, where he labored as a truck painter for thirty years. He would bring his young son along with him to visit his secret stash of corpses in the forest, leaving him sleeping in the cab of his truck, as he would go off into the woods to have sex with his most recent victims before they completely decayed.

But Ridgway was gifted with natural-born serial killer instinct and cunning. He was a savant of "forensic awareness." He compulsively bought new tires every time he thought he might have left tracks, donned gloves when killing and, if any of his victims scratched him as he raped and strangled them, he'd clip their fingernails afterward. He randomly collected chewed gum and discarded cigarette butts on the street and seeded them at some of his crime scenes to mislead investigators sampling for DNA.

Over a period of sixteen years, as the Green River Killer, Gary Ridgway somehow managed to sleepwalk his way unapprehended through at least forty-nine (he claimed seventy-one) manual and ligature strangulations of predominately marginalized runaways and street sex workers. In 1998, he appeared to retire from killing, as some serial killers do once they burn out on the realization that they can never satisfactorily transform their fantasies into reality, no matter how many times they try. He could have gone the way of Jack the Ripper and the Zodiac Killer, a mystery forever that only became bigger with every year it remained unsolved.

But once identified and arrested, the Green River Killer made for boring news fodder. In the climate of the 2000s, he no longer fascinated us. He was a serial killing Wizard of Oz: when the curtain was pulled back, there was nothing there but a dumb-dog mediocrity called Gary.

After pleading guilty, Ridgway was quietly sentenced to life imprisonment in December 2003 and has not been heard from or of since. The two decades that followed saw a significant decline in the number of serial killers being apprehended: 371 in 2000 to 2009, a decline of nearly 50 percent from the 1990s, and an estimated 117 serial killers in 2010 to 2019, again a decline of more than 50 percent from the previous decade. Not only were serial killers figuring less in the news stream; there actually were fewer of them, just like there were fewer murders overall.

In the argument about whether serial killers have become better at evading law enforcement or law enforcement has become more effective in detecting and apprehending serial killers, the general consensus is that the latter is the case, with advances in DNA technology, the ubiquitous carrying of cell phones by both offenders and victims and ever-present video surveillance cameras becoming major game changers in the investigation of serial murder.

Indeed between 2000 and 2020, the serial killers who attracted national press attention were often confessed or recently arrested serial killers "left over" from the epidemic years of the 1970s to 1990s, such as Dennis Rader, the BTK, in 2005; Lonnie Franklin Jr., "the Grim Sleeper," in 2010; Rodney Alcala, "the *Dating Game* Killer," who was finally convicted in 2010; Joseph James DeAngelo, "the Golden State Killer," in 2018; and Samuel Little and Richard Cottingham, "the Times Square Torso Killer," who both made spectacular confessions in 2019.

If any one thing symbolized the end of the epidemic era, it is probably the FBI's new definition of what constitutes serial murder as "the unlawful killing of *two or more* victims by the same offender(s) in separate events" *for any reason*, including "anger, thrill, financial gain, and attention seeking." People joked that the FBI was running out of serial killers and lowered the threshold from three to two to "stay in business." Which brings us to the FBI's crown jewel from that era: ViCAP.

The Failures of ViCAP

FBI profiling, especially its simplistic organized/disorganized/mixed trinity of categories, is sometimes unfairly criticized without taking into account how the BSU intended it to be used. In any regard, NCAVC has not embraced the organized/disorganized dichotomy since 2004 and no longer uses it when reviewing cases in day to day operations. In 2014 the FBI admitted "Applying the organized/disorganized dichotomy to active serial murder cases has limited utility in serial investigations."[1]

The other product of the "serial killer epidemic" era congressional hearings, the Violent Criminal Apprehension Program (ViCAP) database, has come under scrutiny too. All is not well at ViCAP.

When it was implemented in 1985 after years of lobbying by Pierce Brooks, the objective of ViCAP was to create a central national database at the FBI containing details of all homicides and rapes and other violent crimes committed in the United States. Various police agencies could submit to it detailed descriptions of unsolved murders in their own jurisdiction, which would hopefully result in a computer match to similar crimes in other jurisdictions. The problem was that it required *a substantial amount of paperwork*. Need I say more? Overworked cops and paperwork don't mix well. The ViCAP form was fifteen pages long, with 189 detailed questions, many of them multipart.[2] It was as painstaking as an income tax form, if not worse . . . and then it had to be put in the mail! Computers were still a rare commodity, and the postal service or courier was the only way to send a document as long as a ViCAP form.

To derive any benefit from ViCAP, a police agency not only had to fill out and submit the form; it also had to make a formal request to the FBI to process it through their database and report back the results, if any.

By 1990, things improved a little bit: police agencies were able to fax their forms rather than rely on snail mail. By 1995, everybody had a PC, and the FBI distributed ViCAP packages as computer software, where at least a police officer could digitally fill out the form and e-mail it to the FBI as an attached electronic file. The 189 questions were reduced to 95 in the hope of encouraging police departments to submit data. But again, to derive any result from ViCAP, a police agency had to file an official request for the FBI to search their database and report back to them on possible "hits" in their system. There was no way for a police agency to log on directly to conduct a search of their own. As a result, police departments ignored ViCAP.

In 1997, out of 18,209 murders and 96,122 forcible rapes, ViCAP received only 1,500 case data submissions. That was a record high, but still only a minuscule fraction (0.013 percent) of annual reported murders and rapes in the United States. In the first twelve years that ViCAP had been in operation, it had successfully linked only 33 cases, none of which led to the apprehension of any serial killers.[3]

By the mid-2000s, a lot of police departments had lost touch with ViCAP's existence. Many police officers who were first introduced to ViCAP in the 1980s had retired, while police departments were constantly swamped with updates, bulletins and info packages in which the

FBI's reminders of ViCAP were easily overlooked by a new generation of overworked officers on the force.

After twenty-two years in operation, in 2007 ViCAP for the first time successfully made a link in a serial murder case, but only after the serial killer was captured by the parents of a victim when he entered their daughter's bedroom as she slept and attempted to kill her. Truck driver Adam Leroy Lane committed two murders and a number of attempted murders along his truck route through Pennsylvania, New Jersey, Connecticut and Massachusetts. Two Massachusetts State Troopers who were not directly involved in the investigation had recently attended a seminar reintroducing ViCAP to a new generation of police officers. They suggested to a neighboring police department to make a submission to ViCAP, and it successfully linked Lane to a number of incidents for which he was eventually prosecuted.[4]

Finally, in 2008, the FBI announced a major upgrade to ViCAP that made it directly accessible for online queries by authorized police agencies. In its press release, the FBI claimed it had a database of 150,000 closed and open cases, submitted over the years by some 3,000 agencies, including unsolved homicides going back as far as the 1950s.[5] A ProPublica investigation in 2015, however, found that patently untrue, reporting that "only about 1,400 police agencies in the U.S., out of roughly 18,000, participate in the system. The database receives reports from far less than 1 percent of the violent crimes committed annually. FBI has about 89,000 cases on file."[6]

In the same 2008 press release, the FBI claimed that reports are "continually compared" for matches as new cases are entered into ViCAP. But according to ProPublica, "In an interview, program officials said that does not happen. 'We have plans for that in the future,' said Nathan Graham, a crime analyst for the program. The agency said it would update the information on its website." At this writing, twelve years later, the web page remains uncorrected.

ViCAP is all smoke and mirrors. In its entire thirty-five year history, the FBI reports it has led to no apprehensions of serial killers at large and has been instrumental in only four cases of serial killers who were all already identified and under arrest: Adam Leroy Lane in 2007; Bruce Mendenhall, a trucker arrested in 2007 who was linked to the murder of four women; Israel Keyes, a serial killer who committed suicide after his arrest in 2012 and who was linked to eleven killings; and in 2019, Samuel Little, whose helpful confessions were entered into ViCAP for confirmation. Hardly a resounding success.

Just how hollow ViCAP is becomes evident when one compares it to a similar system used in Canada, where the population is about one tenth of the US's and the violent crime rate a fraction of that. The Canadian system, called ViCLAS—Violent Criminal Linkage Analysis System—is run by their equivalent to the FBI, the Royal Canadian Mounted Police (RCMP). Compared to ViCAP's current annual $800,000 budget and staff of twelve, the Canadian federal ViCLAS system currently has a budget in the range of $10 million a year and a staff of one hundred officers and analysts.[7] Moreover, municipal and provincial police departments each have a huge ViCLAS budget of their own for the purposes of collecting, compiling and submitting data to the national database, including pay for police officers when liaising with ViCLAS. The ViCLAS budget in 2017 for the Toronto Police Service, just one city, albeit Canada's largest, was an astounding $218,000![8] That's just for a city of 2.9 million people but equivalent to 25 percent of the entire total of ViCAP's $800,000 budget, serving 328 million Americans.

As a result, Canada's ViCLAS maintains a database containing more than 500,000 criminal case profiles and has linked together some 7,000 unsolved crimes since 1995.

By 2013, submission to ViCAP had declined significantly from the high of 1,500 cases in 1997. Local and state police departments submitted only 232 homicide cases out of 14,196 murders and 240 cases of sexual assault out of 79,770 forcible rape incidents. In 2014, ViCAP provided analytical assistance to local cops just 220 times.

Hardly any law enforcement agency in the United States uses it. ViCAP is a joke.

Golden Ager Nostalgia

The few hundred "freshman" serial killers (as opposed to "epidemic era" Golden Age carryovers) apprehended over the last twenty years are just as anonymous as those arrested in the 1990s following Jeffrey Dahmer. Who has heard of Terry A. Blair, Joseph E. Duncan III, Paul Durousseau, Walter E. Ellis, Ronald Dominique, Sean Vincent Gillis, Lorenzo Jerome Gilyard Jr., Mark Goudeau, William Devin Howell or Darren Deon Vann?

The recent surge of television shows like *Mindhunter* and highly watched documentaries and dramas on epidemic years serial killers like Ted Bundy, Henry Lee Lucas and Ted Kaczynski confirm that few new narratives of any interest are emerging, and the serial killer true-crime genre is falling back into nostalgia for the old reliable and familiar epidemic era "celebrity serial killers" of twenty and thirty years ago, to which this book is itself a testament. A whole bunch of Ted Bundy movies and documentaries in recent years have introduced him to a new generation that had not even been born when Bundy first came to infamy.

Serial killers are still out there in the United States. Conservative estimates suggest there might be as many as thirty-five unidentified serial killers on average any given year. Leading in coverage of ongoing unsolved serial killings at this writing is probably the Long Island Serial Killer (LISK, also known as "the Gilgo Beach Killer" or "the Craigslist Ripper"), suspected in as many as sixteen murders between 1996 and 2013. Other unsolved cases include the Bone Collector, linked to eleven female victims found buried together in West Mesa, New Mexico; the Seven Bridges Road Killer in North Carolina linked to the murder of eleven African American prostitutes; the Jeff Davis 8 Killer in Jennings, Jefferson Davis Parish, Louisiana, suspected in eight murders; the Daytona Beach Killer in Florida with four murders; the February 9 Killer, who has killed at least two women in Salt Lake City on the same date in different years; and the Eastbound Strangler Killer near Atlantic City, who left his four strangled female victims behind a dilapidated motel carefully posed facing east, fully clothed but stripped of their shoes and socks, and who some suspect might be the same person as the LISK.

The ditches and roadsides of the American interstate freeway system alone are the scene of so many unsolved homicides—almost five hundred over thirty years—that the FBI in 2009 to 2011 launched a special

Highway Serial Killings Initiative (HSKI) targeting serial killers suspected to be working as truckers. At least 25 truckers have been convicted in serial homicide cases, while the HSKI is investigating a suspect list with more than 275 names, almost all long-haul truckers.

While the overall decline in American serial killers since the 1990s might be bad news for sensation-seeking media and true-crime authors, it is good news for the rest of humanity.

For now.

If I am right that the serial killer "epidemic era" was a result of a "perfect storm" *diabolus in cultura* of Great Depression and World War II parental traumas plus true-detective / men's adventure "sweats" rape culture that twisted a generation of male children in the 1940s to 1960s into the surge of serial killers of the 1970s to 1990s, then we're in for nasty weather.

I dread what will come from the familial traumas of the financial crisis of 2008, the unspeakable secrets of a War on Terror fought by not only the warrior fathers of the current generation of kids, but now their warrior mothers too, and finally the catastrophic COVID-19 pandemic we are in the midst of today. In World War II that brought on the American Noir at home, 405,000 American GIs were killed over a period of *forty-five months* of brutal combat; in 2020 at this writing in early November, in just *nine months*, 236,000 Americans have been killed—more than half of the World War II deaths. You do the math if COVID lasts as long as World War II did.

Unlike our scattered dead that Ernie Pyle saw on distant foreign hillsides, we are collectively seeing ours here at home. We are looking into the abyss of a new American Noir like the one in 1940s but worse. This time there will be no solemn homecoming flotillas of the dead in flag-draped coffins from overseas; they are already here with us in mass graves like New York's Hart Island and in refrigerator trucks in hospital and funeral home parking lots.

Throw into that mix of *diabolus in cultura* the current unfettered availability of absolutely anything on the Internet, including those old images from the true detectives and the "sweats" and far more graphic and explicit material, and see what happens next with the generation of children we are raising today.

If books had soundtracks, this one would close with John C. Fogerty.[9]

I see a bad moon a-rising
I see trouble on the way

Notes

Introduction: The "Golden Age" of Serial Murderers

1. http://www.slate.com/articles/news_and_politics/crime/2011/01/blood_loss.html.
2. Eric W. Hickey, *Serial Murderers and Their Victims*, 7th ed. (Boston: Cengage Learning, 2016), 241; "FBI Seeking Assistance Connecting Victims to Samuel Little's Confessions," US Department of Justice, FBI, October 6, 2019, https://www.fbi.gov/news/stories/samuel-little-most-prolific-serial-killer-in-us-history-100619.
3. Hickey, *Serial Murderers and Their Victims*, 239.
4. M. G. Aamodt, "Serial Killer Statistics," September 4, 2016, retrieved July 28, 2019, http://maamodt.asp.radford.edu/serial killer information center/project description.htm.
5. US Department of Justice, FBI, Behavioral Analysis Unit, National Center for the Analysis of Violent Crime, *Serial Murder: Multidisciplinary Perspectives for Investigators* (Washington, DC, 2008), 10; https://www.fbi.gov/stats-services/publications/serial-murder.

Chapter 1. Sons of Cain: A Brief History of Serial Murder from the Stone Age to 1930

1. Peter Vronsky, *Sons of Cain: A History of Serial Killers from the Stone Age to the Present* (New York: Berkley Books, 2018).
2. For example: Owen D. Jones, "Sex, Culture, and the Biology of Rape: Toward Explanation and Prevention," *California Law Review* 87, no. 4 (July 1999): 827–39; Jared Diamond, *The Third Chimpanzee: The Evolution and Future of the Human Animal* (New York: HarperCollins, 1992), 45; João Ricardo Faria, "What Happened to the Neanderthals?—The Survival Trap," *KYKLOS* 53, no. 2 (2000): 161–72; Kwang Hyun Ko, "Hominin Interbreeding and the Evolution of Human Variation," *Journal of Biological Research-Thessaloniki* 23, no. 17 (December 2016); Grant S. McCall and Nancy Shields, "Examining the Evidence from Small-Scale Societies and Early Prehistory and Implications for Modern Theories of Aggression and Violence," *Aggression and Violent Behavior* 13, no. 1 (2008): 1–9.
3. Christoph P. E. Zollikofer, Marcia S. Ponce De León, Bernard Vandermeersch, and François Lévêque, "Evidence for Interpersonal Violence in the St. Césaire Neanderthal," *Proceedings of the National Academy of Sciences of the United States of America* 99, no. 9 (2002): 6444–48.
4. Richard Stephen Charnock, "Cannibalism in Europe," *Journal of the Anthropological Society of London* 4 (1866): xxii–xxxi; Elizabeth Pennisi, "Cannibalism and Prion Disease May Have Been Rampant in Ancient Humans," *Science, n.s.*, 300, no. 5617 (April 11, 2003): 227–28; Elizabeth Culotta, "Neanderthals Were Cannibals, Bones Show," *Science, n.s.*, 286, no. 5437 (October 1, 1999): 18–19.

5. Robert Eisler, *Man into Wolf: An Anthropological Interpretation of Sadism, Masochism, and Lycanthropy* (London: Routledge and Kegan Paul, 1951), 36–42.

6. Eisler, *Man into Wolf*, 78n10.

7. Vronsky, *Sons of Cain*, 46–47.

8. Ann W. Burgess, John E. Douglas, and Robert K. Ressler, *Sexual Homicide* (New York: Free Press, 1992), loc. 1281–82, Kindle.

9. Robert J. Morton, Jennifer M. Tillman, and Stephanie J. Gaines, US Department of Justice, FBI, Behavioral Analysis Unit, National Center for the Analysis of Violent Crime, *Serial Murder: Pathways for Investigation* (Washington, DC, 2014), 43–47.

10. Lee Mellor, Anil Aggrawal, and Eric Hickey, eds., *Understanding Necrophilia: A Global Multidisciplinary Approach* (Cognella Academic Publishing, 2017).

11. https://en.wiktionary.org/wiki/monstrum.

12. Willem de Blécourt, "The Werewolf, the Witch, and the Warlock: Aspects of Gender in the Early Modern Period," in *Witchcraft and Masculinities in Modern Europe*, ed. Alison Rowlands (New York: Palgrave Macmillan, 2009), 207.

13. John Philip Jenkins, "H.H. Holmes: American Serial Killer," in Encyclopaedia Britannica, https://www.britannica.com/biography/H-H-Holmes.

14. See Peter Vronsky, *Female Serial Killers: How and Why Women Become Monsters* (New York: Berkley Books, 2007).

15. Adam Selzer, *H. H. Holmes: The True History of the White City Devil* (New York: Skyhorse, 2017).

16. Aamodt, "Serial Killer Statistics."

17. *Times and Democrat*, June 28, 1906; *St. John Daily Sun*, May 1, 1906; *Home Daily Sentinel*, June 16, 1906; *Queanbeyan Age*, September 6, 1907.

18. Aamodt, Radford/FGCU Serial Killer Database.

19. Philip Jenkins, *Using Murder: The Social Construction of Serial Homicide* (New York: Aldine de Gruyter, 1994); "Serial Murder in the United States 1900–1940: A Historical Perspective," *Journal of Criminal Justice* 17, no. 5 (1989): 377–92.

20. Eric Godtland and Dian Hanson, *True Crime Detective Magazines 1924–1969* (Cologne: Taschen, 2013), 65.

21. Kent A. Kiehl, *The Psychopath Whisperer: Inside the Minds of Those Without a Conscience* (New York: Crown/Archetype, 2015), 170–1, Kindle.

22. Kent A. Kiehl, "A Cognitive Neuroscience Perspective on Psychopathy: Evidence for Paralimbic System Dysfunction," *Psychiatry Research* 142, nos. 2–3 (June 15, 2006): 107–28.

23. Harold Schechter, *Bestial: The Savage Trail of a True American Monster* (New York: Gallery Books, 1999); Michael Newton, *The Dark Strangler: Serial Killer Earle Leonard Nelson* (St. John's, NL, 2016).

24. Henry Lesser, "Panzram Papers," Special Collections & University Archives, Carl Panzram Papers, 1928–1980, box 1, folder 3: typescript of Panzram Manuscript: part I, section 1, c. 1928–1930, San Diego State University.

25. Harold Schechter, *Deranged: The Shocking True Story of America's Most Fiendish Killer* (New York: Simon & Schuster, 1990); Mel Heimer, *The Cannibal: The Case of Albert Fish* (New York: Lyle Stuart, 1971).

26. http://stuffnobodycaresabout.com/2014/05/24/notorious-crime-scene-property-is-for-sale/.

Chapter 2. American *Monstrum*: The Rise of Sexual Signature Killers 1930–1945

1. Michael Hall, "Two Barmaids, Five Alligators, and the Butcher of Elmendorf," *Texas Monthly*, July 2002, https://www.texasmonthly.com/articles/two-barmaids-five-alligators-and-the-butcher-of-elmendorf/.

2. See Colin Wilson, "The Rise of Sex Crime," in *A Criminal History of Mankind* (London: Grafton Books, 1985).

3. Eric W. Hickey, *Serial Murderers and Their Victims,* 6th ed. (Belmont, CA: Wadworth, 2013), 226.

4. J. Paul de River, *The Sexual Criminal: A Psychoanalytical Study,* ed. Brian King (Burbank, CA: Bloat Books, 2000), xxvi.

5. De River, *The Sexual Criminal,* 96.

6. De River, *The Sexual Criminal,* 164–65.

7. *Dayton Daily News* (Dayton, OH), January 26, 1936, 62.

8. *Herald-Press* (Saint Joseph, MI), January 3, 1936, 8.

9. *Star Tribune* (Minneapolis, MN), December 9, 1934, 66.

10. Cindy Gueli, "World War II Edition—Part 1: A Serial Killer on the Loose," *Scandalous Washington,* https://scandalouswashington.com/2015/08/20/scandalous-washington-world-war-ii-edition-part-1/.

11. *Daily News* (New York, NY), June 17, 1941, 4.

12. Mary-Elizabeth B. Murphy, *Jim Crow Capital: Women and Black Freedom Struggles in Washington, D.C., 1920–1945* (Chapel Hill: University of North Carolina Press, 2018), 203–4.

13. Murphy, *Jim Crow Capital,* 203.

14. *Daily News* (New York, NY), June 18, 1941, 4.

15. *Times* (Shreveport, LA), July 13, 1941, 2.

16. See the *Afro-American* newspaper archive online at https://www.afro.com/archives/.

17. *Knoxville Journal* (Knoxville, TN), September 19, 1943, 2.

18. *Time,* September 8, 1941.

19. *Washington Post,* August 30, 1941, 14.

20. *Washington Post,* September 3, 1941, 17.

21. *Washington Post,* January 9, 1943, B1.

22. *Washington Post,* August 30, 1941, 3.

23. Lucy Freeman, *Catch Me Before I Kill More* (New York: Crown Publishers, 1955), 200.

24. *Life,* December 6, 1968.

25. Paul Friswold, "William Heirens, Chicago's Lipstick Killer, Dies in Prison," *Riverfront Times,* March 6, 2012, https://www.riverfronttimes.com/newsblog/2012/03/06/william-heirens-chicagos-lipstick-killer-dies-in-prison.

26. Amended Petition for Executive Clemency, To the Honorable George H. Ryan, Governor of the State of Illinois, April 2002 Docket, 5.

27. Amended Petition for Executive Clemency, 5–6.

28. http://home.earthlink.net/~chicago1946/p21.html.

29. Foster Kennedy, Harry B. Hoffman, and William H Haines, Court Directed Psychiatric Report, in Freeman, *Catch Me Before I Kill More,* 337.

30. Kennedy, Hoffman, and Haines, Court Directed Psychiatric Report, 339.

31. Louis-Alexandre Marcoux, Pierre-Emmanuel Michon, Sophie Lemelin, Julien I. A. Voisin, Etienne Vachon-Presseau, Philip L. Jackson, "Feeling but Not Caring: Empathic Alteration in Narcissistic Men with High Psychopathic Traits," *Psychiatry Research: Neuroimaging,* October 2014.

32. Katie Heaney, "My Life As a Psychopath," *The Cut,* August 10, 2018, https://www.thecut.com/2018/08/my-life-as-a-psychopath.html.

33. Colin Wilson, *Manhunters: Criminal Profilers and Their Search for the World's Most Wanted Serial Killers* (New York: Skyhorse Publishing, 2007), 52.

34. https://en.wikipedia.org/wiki/List_of_longest_prison_sentences_served.

Chapter 3. American Noir: Raising Cain Through the Trauma Years 1930–1950

1. See, for example, Vernon J. Geberth, *Sex-Related Homicide and Death Investigation: Practical and Clinical Perspectives* (Boca Raton, FL: CRC Press, 2003); Michael H. Stone and Gary Brucato, *The New Evil: Understanding the Emergence of Modern Violent Crime* (New York: Prometheus Books, 2019).

2. Simon Harrison, *Dark Trophies: Hunting and the Enemy Body in Modern War* (New York: Berghahn Books, 2012), loc. 4297–98, Kindle.

3. Steven A. Egger, *The Killers Among Us: An Examination of Serial Murder and Its Investigation* (Upper Saddle River, NJ: Prentice Hall, 1998), 74–75.

4. Angus McLaren, *A Prescription for Murder: The Victorian Serial Killings of Dr. Thomas Neill Cream* (Chicago: University of Chicago Press, 1993), xiii.

5. Mark Seltzer, *Serial Killers: Death and Life in America's Wound Culture* (New York: Routledge, 1998), 1.

6. Robert Kennedy, in statement by Attorney General Robert F. Kennedy to the Permanent Subcommittee on Investigations of the Senate Government Operations Committee, Washington, DC, September 25, 1963.

7. H. W. Brands, *Traitor to His Class: The Privileged Life and Radical Presidency of Franklin Delano Roosevelt* (New York: Doubleday, 2008), 134.

8. Paul Avrich, *Sacco and Vanzetti: The Anarchist Background* (Princeton, NJ: Princeton University Press, 1991), 140–43.

9. Mike Davis, *Buda's Wagon: A Brief History of the Car Bomb* (New York: Verso, 2007).

10. Cameron McWhirter, *Red Summer: The Summer of 1919 and the Awakening of Black America* (New York: Henry Holt and Company, 2011), 31–32.

11. Arkansas State Assembly, Senate Concurrent Resolution to Commemorate the Ninety-Fourth Anniversary of the United States Supreme Court Ruling in Moore v. Dempsey, State of Arkansas, 91st General Assembly, Regular Session (2017).

12. Brendan Livingston, "Murder and the Black Market: Prohibition's Impact on Homicide Rates in American Cities" (Rowan University, American Economic Association Conference, 2014), https://www.aeaweb.org/conference/2014/retrieve.php?pdfid=801.

13. Joseph Swanson and Samuel Williamson, "Estimates of National Product and Income for the United States Economy, 1919–1941," *Explorations in Economic History*, no. 10 (1972): 53–73.

14. Victor Davis Hanson, *An Autumn of War: What America Learned from September 11 and the War on Terrorism* (New York: Knopf Doubleday, 2007), 44.

15. Vronsky, *Sons of Cain*, pp. 319–324, citing J. Robert Lilly. *Taken by Force: Rape and American GIs in Europe During World War II*. New York: Palgrave Macmillan, 2007. and Miriam Gebhardt. *Als die Soldaten kamen (When the Soldiers Came)*. Munich: DVA/Random House, 2015; [English version] *Crimes Unspoken: The Rape of German Women at the End of the Second World War*, Malden, MA: Polity Press, 2017.

16. Dave Grossman. *On Killing: The Psychological Cost of Learning to Kill in War and Society.* New York: Open Road Media. Kindle ed., pp. 135–36.

17. Vronsky, *Sons of Cain*, 319–30.

18. *The Perilous Fight*, "The Mental Toll," PBS, http://www.pbs.org/perilousfight/psychology/the_mental_toll/.

19. Bernard Rostker, *Providing for the Casualties of War: The American Experience Through World War II* (Santa Monica, CA: RAND Corporation National Defense Research Institute, 2013), 214.

20. *Time*, May 24, 1943.

21. Tom Brokaw, *The Greatest Generation*, (New York: Random House, 2004), Xxxviii.

22. Edgar L. Jones, "One War Is Enough," *Atlantic Monthly*, February 1946, https://www.theatlantic.com/past/docs/unbound/bookauth/battle/jones.htm.

23. Ernie Pyle, "On Victory in Europe," unpublished, © by Scripps Howard Foundation, https://sites.mediaschool.indiana.edu/erniepyle/wartime-columns/4/.

24. "Vote to Support Overtime Pay Bill," *Independent Record* (Helena, MT), July 9, 1942, 5.

25. "Local Brush Artist Turns to Writing," *North Hollywood Valley Times,* September 20, 1946, 14.

26. Ted Kemp, *A Commemorative History: First Special Service Force* (Dallas: Taylor Publishing, 1995), 21.

27. "Quentin Tarantino: One Helluva BASTERD," *Fangoria*, August 22, 2009.

28. "Mrs. E.E. Kemper, Jr., and Children Spending Vacation at Jung Home," *Independent Record* (Helena, MT), August 26, 1951, 10.

29. Margaret Cheney, *Why: The Serial Killer in America* (Lincoln, NE: Back Imprint Books, 2000), 7–8.

30. Jack Olsen, *The Misbegotten Son: The True Story of Arthur J. Shawcross* (New York: Island Books, 1993), 179.

31. Katherine Ramsland, *Confession of a Serial Killer: The Untold Story of Dennis Rader, the BTK Killer* (Lebanon, NH: University Press of New England, 2016), loc. 710–11, Kindle.

32. Ann W. Burgess, John E. Douglas, and Robert K. Ressler, *Sexual Homicide: Patterns and Motives* (Lexington, MA: Lexington Books, 1988), loc. 547, Kindle.

33. Richard Lingeman, *The Noir Forties: The American People from Victory to Cold War* (New York: Bold Type Books, 2012), 132–33.

34. Rostker, *Providing for the Casualties of War,* 202.

35. Lingeman, *The Noir Forties,* 53.

36. Lloyd Shearer, "Crime Certainly Pays on the Screen: The Growing Crop of Homicidal Films," *New York Times*, August 5, 1945, 77.

37. Victor Dallaire, "The American Woman? Not for This GI," *New York Times,* March 10, 1946, SM8.

38. Max Allan Collins, George Hagenauer, and Steven Heller, *Men's Adventure Magazines in Postwar America* (Cologne: Taschen, 2004), 285–364.

39. Collins, Hagenauer, and Heller, *Men's Adventure Magazines in Postwar America,* 470.

40. See, for example, Collins, Hagenauer, and Heller, *Men's Adventure Magazines in Postwar America*; Adam Parfrey, ed., *It's A Man's World: Men's Adventure Magazines, The Postwar Pulps* (Los Angeles: Feral House, 2003); Tom Brinkmann, *Bad Mags 2* (London: Headpress, 2009); David Saunders, *Norman Saunders* (St. Louis, MO: Illustrated Press, 2008); Godtland and Hanson, *True Crime Detective Magazines 1924–1969*; Google Images: "pulp adventure magazines" https://www.google.ca/search?q=pulp+adventure+magazines&biw=1164&bih=569&source=lnms&tbm=isch&sa=X&ved=0ahUKEwi38-PCg8vLAhVFnoMKHYlgC88Q_AUIBigB or Google Images: "true detective magazines" https://www.google.ca/search?q=true+detective+magazines&biw=1164&bih=569&source=lnms&tbm=isch&sa=X&ved=0ahUKEwiXh9vXg8vLAhXrkYMKHV9JBx8Q_AUIBigB.

41. Collins, Hagenauer, and Heller, *Men's Adventure Magazines in Postwar America,* 470.

42. Collins, Hagenauer, and Heller, *Men's Adventure Magazines in Postwar America,* 9; Godtland and Hanson, *True Crime Detective Magazines 1924–1969,* 234.

43. Mark Pettit, *A Need to Kill* (New York: Ballantine Books, 1990); Robert K. Ressler and Tom Shachtman, *Whoever Fights Monsters: My Twenty Years Tracking Serial Killers for the FBI* (New York: St. Martin's Press, 1992).

44. Ramsland, *Confession of a Serial Killer,* loc. 1292–93, 1458–59, 3289–91, Kindle.

45. P. E. Dietz, B. Harry, and R. R. Hazelwood, "Detective Magazines: Pornography for the Sexual Sadist?" *Journal of Forensic Sciences* 31, no. 1 (January 1986): 197–211.

46. De River, *The Sexual Criminal*, 65.

Chapter 4. Pulp True Horror: The Rise of the New Serial Killers 1950–1969

1. *Oshkosh Northwestern* (Oshkosh, WI), November 21, 1957, 13.

2. George W. Arndt, "Gein Humor," in Robert H. Gollmar, *Edward Gein* (New York: Pinnacle Books, 1981), 203–5.

3. *Life*, May 22, 1944, 35, accessed March 30, 2016, http://time.com/3880997/young -woman-with-jap-skull-portrait-of-a-grisly-wwii-memento/.

4. http://www.gettyimages.ca/detail/news-photo/filthy-cluttered-kitchen-of-alleged -mass-murderer-ed-gein-newsphoto/50425931.

5. The definitive book, although sometimes flawed, on Harvey Glatman is Michael Newton, *Rope: The Twisted Life and Crimes of Harvey Glatman* (New York: Pocket Books, 1998). Also helpful is the e-book by Edward S. Sullivan, *Hellbound: The Sadistic Sex Murders of Harvey Glatman* (Elektron Ebooks, 2013).

6. Stephen G. Michaud with Roy Hazelwood, *The Evil That Men Do* (New York: St. Martin's, 1998), 24.

7. Newton, *Rope*, 45.

8. Silvia Pettem, *Someone's Daughter: In Search of Justice for Jane Doe* (Lanham, MD: Taylor Trade Publishing, 2009), loc. 2898, Kindle.

9. Ressler and Shachtman, *Whoever Fights Monsters*, loc. 3526–38, Kindle.

10. Newton, *Rope*, 192–96.

11. Sheila O'Hare and Andrew Smith, "Gifts Nobody Wants: The State of the Art in Dealing with Unwanted Donations," *Kansas Library Association College and University Libraries Section Proceedings* 1, no. 1 (2011): 10; Pettem, *Someone's Daughter*, loc. 3131, Kindle.

12. Pettem, *Someone's Daughter*, loc. 4476, Kindle.

13. Ginger Strand, *Killer on the Road: Violence and the American Interstate* (Austin: University of Texas Press, 2012), Kindle.

14. Strand, *Killer on the Road*, loc. 892–94, Kindle.

15. Strand, *Killer on the Road*, loc. 939, Kindle.

16. Strand, *Killer on the Road*, loc. 927–28, Kindle.

17. Janet McClellan, *Erotophonophilia: Investigating Lust Murder* (Amherst, NY: Cambria Press, 2010), loc. 2442, Kindle.

18. Ramsland, *Confession of a Serial Killer*, loc. 1084–1115, Kindle.

19. https://www.pinterest.ca/pin/567735096754029516/?lp=true.

20. Morton, Tillman, and Gaines, *Serial Murder*, 47.

21. Katherine Ramsland, *The Sex Beast* (Crimescape, Rosetta Books, 2013), Kindle.

22. *Charlotte Observer* (Charlotte, NC), June 17, 1956, 2.

23. *News* (Frederick, MD), June 11, 1956, 1.

24. Ramsland, *The Sex Beast*, loc. 225–30, Kindle.

25. *Salisbury Times* (Salisbury, MD), June 27, 1957, 1 and 8.

26. *Evening Sun* (Baltimore, MD), June 28, 1957, 2.

27. *Greenville News* (Greenville, SC), February 2, 1959, 11.

28. *News Leader* (Staunton, VA), March 5, 1959, 1.

29. *Times-Dispatch* (Richmond, VA), March 7, 1959, 4.

30. *Times-Dispatch* (Richmond, VA), March 5, 1959, 1.

31. United States of America v. Melvin Davis Rees, Jr., 193 F. Supp. 849 (D. Md. 1961), Cr. No. 5300, March 22, 1961.

32. Ressler and Shachtman, *Whoever Fights Monsters*, loc. 646, Kindle.

33. *Daily News* (New York, NY), March 5, 1961, 74.

34. *Honolulu Advertiser* (Honolulu, HI), June 3, 1962, 2.

35. *News Leader* (Staunton, VA), April 24, 1953, 14.

36. *Daily Press* (Newport News, VA), January 22, 1961, 24.

37. https://www.stoppingpoints.com/north-carolina/sights.cgi?marker=Pineland+ College-+Edwards+Military+Institute&cnty=Sampson.

38. *The Honolulu Advertiser* (Honolulu HI), June 3, 1962, 2.

39. *Daily News* (New York, NY), May 20, 1962, 371.

40. *Daily Press* (Newport News, VA), February 17, 1961, 9.

41. https://en.wikipedia.org/wiki/Pat_Barrington (accessed January 19, 2020).

42. *Daily News* (New York, NY), April 8, 2001, 46.

43. https://www.scotusblog.com/2013/01/opinion-recap-rees-clarified-after-forty-six -years/.

44. Craig Whitlock and April Witt, "Deathbed Tale Offers a Solution to 1955 Slayings," *Washington Post*, June 15, 2000, A1, https://www.washingtonpost.com/wp-srv/WP cap/2000-06/15/089r-061500-idx.html.

45. *San Antonio Express* (San Antonio, TX), August 29, 1964, 7.

46. Cheney, *Why: The Serial Killer in America*, 30.

47. Olsen, *The Misbegotten Son*, 189.

48. Tom Williams, *Post-Traumatic Stress Disorders of the Vietnam Veteran* (Cincinnati, OH: Disabled American Veterans, 1980).

49. Lionel Dahmer, *A Father's Story* (New York: William Morrow, 1994), 33–34.

50. Stephen J. Giannangelo, *The Psychopathology of Serial Murder: A Theory of Violence* (London: Praeger, 1996), 68.

51. Dahmer, *A Father's Story*, 212.

52. Joel Norris, *Henry Lee Lucas* (New York: Zebra Books, 1991), 42.

53. Michael Newton, *Serial Slaughter: What's Behind America's Murder Epidemic?* (Port Townsend, WA: Loompanics, 1992), 64.

54. Rachel Manning, Mark Levine, and Alan Collins, "The Kitty Genovese Murder and the Social Psychology of Helping: The Parable of the 38 Witnesses," *American Psychologist* 62, no. 6 (2007): 555–62.

55. Nicholas Lemann, "A Call For Help: What the Kitty Genovese Story Really Means," *New Yorker*, March 10, 2014, https://www.newyorker.com/magazine/2014/03/10/a -call-for-help.

56. Robert D. McFadden, "Winston Moseley, Who Killed Kitty Genovese, Dies in Prison at 81," *New York Times*, April 4, 2016.

57. Jeff Pearlman, "Infamous '64 Murder Lives in Heart of Woman's 'Friend,'" *Chicago Tribune*, March 12, 2004.

58. Nadia Fezzani, *Through the Eyes of Serial Killers: Interviews with Seven Murderers* (Toronto: Dundurn Press, 2015), loc. 3598–99, Kindle.

59. Aamodt, "Serial Killer Statistics."

Chapter 5. The Big Surge: The Baby Boomer Serial Killers Come of Age 1970–1979

1. John B. Dickson, *Twenty-Five Murders [and Probably More]: Looking for a Reason: The Juan Corona Trials and Confessions* (Xlibris, 2012), 19.

2. Ed Cray, *Burden of Proof: The Case of Juan Corona* (New York: Macmillan, 1973), 196–202.

3. Vernon J. Geberth, *Practical Homicide Investigation: Tactics, Procedures, and Forensic Techniques*, 4th ed. (Boca Raton, FL: CRC Press, 2006), 501, citing Bell and

     Weinber (1978) in R. Crooks and K. Baur, *Our Sexuality,* 4th ed. (Redwood City, CA: Benjamin/Cummings Publishing, 1990), 317, 324, 332–33, 340.

4. Geberth, *Practical Homicide Investigation,* 501.

5. Tracy Kidder, *The Road to Yuba City: A Journey into the Juan Corona Murders* (New York: Doubleday, 1974).

6. Skip Hollandsworth, "The Lost Boys," *Texas Monthly,* April 2011, https://www.tex asmonthly.com/articles/the-lost-boys/.

7. *Pampa Daily News* (Pampa, TX), August 20, 1973, 8.

8. Jack Olsen, *The Man with the Candy: The Story of the Houston Mass Murders* (New York: Simon & Schuster, 1974), 32, Kindle.

9. Olsen, *The Man with the Candy,* 51–52, Kindle.

10. Hollandsworth, "The Lost Boys."

11. Hollandsworth, "The Lost Boys."

12. Olsen, *The Man with the Candy,* 59, Kindle.

13. Craig Malisow, "The Girl on the Torture Board," *Houston Press,* October 15, 2014, https://www.houstonpress.com/news/the-girl-on-the-torture-board-rhonda -williams-opens-up-about-being-attacked-by-dean-corll-6736780.

14. Malisow, "The Girl on the Torture Board."

15. Alyssa Newcomb, "New Victim Discovered in Decades-Old Candyman Serial Kill- ing Case," *ABC News,* February 8, 2012, https://abcnews.go.com/blogs/headlines /2012/02/new-victim-discovered-in-decades-old-serial-killing-case.

16. https://beyondthedash.com/obituary/david-owen-brooks-1079355835.

17. Fred Grimm, "Florida Serial Killer Eluded Conviction but not COVID-19", *South Florida Sun Sentinel,* June 12, 2020; Gina Tron, "Green River Killer Gary Ridgway Denied Release Amid Coronavirus Concerns, *Oxygen.com,* April 24, 2020.

18. Olsen, *The Man with the Candy,* 139, Kindle.

19. Dennis McDougal, *Angel of Darkness* (New York: Warner Books, 1991), loc. 1405, Kindle.

20. Vronsky, *Serial Killers,* 234.

21. David Schmid, *Natural Born Celebrities: Serial Killers in American Culture* (Chi- cago: University of Chicago Press, 2005), 221, Kindle, citing Richard Tithecott, *Of Men and Monsters: Jeffrey Dahmer and the Construction of the Serial Killer* (Madi- son: University of Wisconsin Press, 1997), 73.

22. Leslie Maitland, "For Singles, Scene Has Sordid Side," *New York Times,* November 1, 1974, 41.

23. David J. Krajicek, "NYPD slow to make the connection in Park Plaza Hotel slay- ings," *Daily News* (New York, NY), March 1, 2014, https://www.nydailynews.com /news/justice-story/doom-service-upper-west-side-flophouse-article-1.1707471.

24. https://murderpedia.org/male.J/j/jackson-calvin.htm.

25. "Shift Sleuth for Not Seeing Murder Pattern at Hotel," *Daily News* (New York, NY), September 24, 1974, 5.

26. Donald Flynn, "Jury Given the Key to Park Plaza Hotel," *Daily News* (New York, NY) March 11, 1975, 115.

27. https://www.apartmentratings.com/ny/manhattan/parc-77_10024/ (accessed Feb- ruary 5, 2020).

28. https://foursquare.com/v/scaletta-ristorante/4ad914d4f964a520ec1721e3/menu; https://www.westsiderag.com/2018/03/23/scaletta-ristorante-to-close-after-30-years -saying-landlord-pushed-them-out; https://patch.com/new-york/upper-west-side-nyc /uws-italian-restaurant-scaletta-close-after-30-years-report (accessed February 5, 2020).

29. Joan Didion, "Los Angeles Notebook," in *We Tell Ourselves Stories in Order to Live: Collected Nonfiction* (New York: Alfred A. Knopf, 2006), 162. (First published in *Slouching Toward Bethlehem*, 1968.)

30. Earl James, *Catching Serial Killers: Learning from Past Serial Murder Investigations* (Lansing, MI: International Forensic Services, 1991), 297.

31. *Reno Gazette-Journal*, October 29, 1997, 13.

32. Donald T. Lunde and Jefferson Morgan, *The Die Song: A Journey into the Mind of a Mass Murderer* (New York: W. W. Norton, 1980), 165.

33. Lunde and Morgan, *The Die Song* 207.

34. Ressler and Shachtman, *Whoever Fights Monsters*, 148.

35. Don West, "Students Hunt Missing Coeds," *San Francisco Examiner*, February 14, 1973, 3.

36. Michael M. O'Brien, "Interview of Former Special Agent of the FBI Patrick J. Mullany (1966–1986)," FBI Oral History Project, Society of Former Special Agents of the FBI, Inc., August 29, 2005, 29.

37. "Body is Identified—SC Girl", *Santa Cruz Sentinel*, January 24, 1973, 1

38. Donald T. Lunde, *Murder and Madness* (New York: W. W. Norton, 1979), 199.

39. Olsen, *The Misbegotten Son*, 3.

40. *Watertown Daily Times*, May 12, 1972.

41. Fezzani, *Through the Eyes of Serial Killers*, loc. 866–83, Kindle.

42. Malcolm Gladwell, "The Criminal Brain," *Independent*, May 3, 1997, https://www.independent.co.uk/life-style/the-criminal-brain-1259436.html.

43. Fezzani, *Through the Eyes of Serial Killers*, loc. 1041–44, Kindle.

44. Olsen, *The Misbegotten Son*, 209.

45. Dorothy Otnow Lewis, *Guilty by Reason of Insanity: A Psychiatrist Explores the Minds of Killers* (New York: Random House, 2009), loc. 288–89, Kindle.

46. Will Astor, "Hard Work Is This Judge's Chief Conviction," *Rochester Business Journal*, October 25, 2002, https://rbj.net/2002/10/25/hard-work-is-this-judges-chief-conviction/.

47. Human Drug Testing by the CIA, 1977: Hearings Before the Subcommittee on Health and Scientific Research of the Committee on Human Resources, 95th Cong. 117–18 (1977).

48. Vronsky, *Female Serial Killers*, 277.

49. Aly Vander Hayden and Benjamin H. Smith, "These Are the Crime Scene Photos from the BTK Killer's Twisted Murders," Oxygen.com, August 31, 2018, https://www.oxygen.com/snapped/crime-time/crime-scene-photos-btk-killer-murders.

50. Derf Backderf, *My Friend Dahmer* (New York: Abrams, 2012), 96–97.

51. http://www.robertkressler.com/ex_lived.html (Archived November 20, 1997).

52. Robert K. Ressler and Tom Shachtman, *I Have Lived in the Monster: A Report from the Abyss* (New York: St. Martin's, 1997), 116–18.

53. David Usborne, "Soldiers, Sexual Abuse—and the Serial Killer: The US Military's Secret Sexual Assaults," *Independent*, June 28, 2013, https://www.independent.co.uk/news/world/americas/soldiers-sexual-abuse-and-the-serial-killer-the-us-military-s-secret-sexual-assaults-8679271.html.

54. Jon Nordheimer, "All-American Boy on Trial," *New York Times Magazine*, December 10, 1978.

55. Egger, *The Killers Among Us*, 75.

Chapter 6. Mindhunters: The Serial Killer Epidemic 1980–1990

1. M. A. Farber, "Leading the Hunt in Atlanta's Murders," *New York Times*, May 3, 1981, ProQuest.

2. O'Brien, "Interview of Former Special Agent of the FBI Patrick J. Mullany (1966–1986)," 29, 31.

3. Stanley Pimentel, "Interview of Former Special Agent of the FBI Howard D. Teten (1962–1986)," FBI Oral History Project, Society of Former Special Agents of the FBI, Inc., November 19, 2004.

4. Patrick Mullany, *Matador of Murder: An FBI Agent's Journey in Understanding the Criminal Mind* (self-pub., 2015), 63–64, Kindle.

5. Becky Shay, "Items Owned by '74 Murder Victim Found," *Billings Gazette*, October 12, 2005, https://billingsgazette.com/news/state-and-regional/montana/items -owned-by-murder-victim-found/article_bc5dae98-5e27-5094-be3d-5b8769d 84122.html.

6. Mullany, *Matador of Murder*, 68, Kindle.

7. Rachel King, *Don't Kill in Our Names: Families of Murder Victims Speak Out Against the Death Penalty* (New Brunswick, NJ: Rutgers University Press, 2003), 17.

8. King, *Don't Kill in Our Names*, 21–22.

9. Mullany, *Matador of Murder*, 73, Kindle.

10. Gallatin County Prosecutor's Office, Interview with David Meirhofer, September 29, 1974.

11. *Great Falls Tribune* (Great Falls, MT), October 4, 1974, 4.

12. O'Brien, "Interview of Former Special Agent of the FBI Patrick J. Mullany (1966–1986)," 28.

13. Morton, US Department of Justice. 2014. p. 5

14. Ressler quoted in Philip Jenkins, *Using Murder*, 67.

15. *New York Times*, February 2, 2017, https://www.nytimes.com/2017/02/14/nyregion /etan-patz-pedro-hernandez-guilty.html.

16. *Hearing Before the Subcommittee on Juvenile Justice of the Committee on the Judiciary, United States Senate on Patterns of Murders Committed by One Person, in Large Numbers with No Apparent Rhyme, Reason or Motivation*, 95th Cong, 14–16 (1983).

17. Kenneth Chew, Richard McCleary, Maricres Lew, and Johnson Wang, "The Epidemiology of Child Homicide in California, 1981 Through 1990," *Homicide Studies* 3, no. 2 (May 1999): 151–69.

18. David Finkelhor, Gerald Hotaling, and Andrea Sedlak, "The Abduction of Children by Strangers and Nonfamily Members: Estimating the Incidence Using Multiple Methods," *Journal of Interpersonal Violence* 7, no. 2 (June 1992): 226–43.

19. Joel Best, "Missing Children: Misleading Statistics," *Public Interest* 92 (1988), 92.

20. Ressler and Shachtman, *Whoever Fights Monsters*, 229–30.

21. Robert Lindsey, "Officials Cite a Rise in Killers Who Roam U.S. for Victims," *New York Times*, January 21, 1984.

22. Jim Mattox, Attorney General of Texas, *Henry Lee Lucas Report*, April 1986.

23. G. Jack Urso, http://www.aeolus13umbra.com/2012/04/arthur-john-shawcross -monster-on.html.

24. Olsen, *The Misbegotten Son*, 274, Kindle.

25. Olsen, *The Misbegotten Son*, 360, Kindle.

26. Lewis, *Guilty by Reason of Insanity*, loc. 272, Kindle.

27. Mike Aamodt, http://maamodt.asp.radford.edu/Psyc%20405/Shawcross%20Pre sentation.pdf.

28. Aidan Sammons, *Criminological Psychology*, "Physiological Theories of Offending," psychlotron.org.uk.

29. Jamie Schram, "Cannibal Recipes for Discerning Diners," *Weekly World News*, February 3, 2004, 34.

30. Fezzani, *Through the Eyes of Serial Killers*, loc. 581–91, Kindle.

31. Fezzani, *Through the Eyes of Serial Killers*, loc. 895–903, Kindle.

32. Katie Karp, "The Tragic Death of Felicia Stephens," https://urresearch.roch ester.edu/fileDownloadForInstitutionalItem.action?itemId=28271&itemFileId =143265.

33. Craig Fox, "41 years later: Shawcross victim receives a headstone," *Watertown Daily Times*, November 27, 2013. https://web.archive.org/web/20180704033422/http://www.watertowndailytimes.com/article/20131127/NEWS07/711279992.

Chapter 7. The Last Serial Killers: Twilight of the Epidemic Era 1990–2000

1. JT Hunter, *A Monster of All Time: The True Story of Danny Rolling, The Gainesville Ripper* (RJ Parker Publishing, 2018), 11, Kindle.

2. https://www.geni.com/people/James-Rolling/6000000034217057430.

3. Robbie Cavis Rolling (Phelps), https://www.geni.com/people/Robbie-Rolling /6000000034217259306.

4. Claudia Rolling, transcript of videotaped deposition, May 8, 1992.

5. *Phenix-Girard Journal* (Girard, AL), September 4, 1936, 1. See also: http://files.us gwarchives.net/al/pike/newspapers/gnw233robertel.txt.

6. Danny Rolling and Sondra London, *The Making of a Serial Killer* (Portland, OR: Feral House, 1996), 34.

7. Rolling and London, *The Making of a Serial Killer*, 102.

8. *Tallahassee Democrat*, February 26, 1994, 33.

9. Rolling and London, *The Making of a Serial Killer*, 137.

10. *Tampa Tribune*, September 15, 1993, 6.

11. "Expert: 'Exorcist III' May Have Influenced Rolling," *Florida Today*, March 18, 1994, 24.

12. "For Some, Fear Will Never Go Away," *Palm Beach Post*, September 2, 1990, 11.

13. Rolling and London, *The Making of a Serial Killer*, 17.

14. James Fox and Jack Levin, *Killer on Campus: The Terrifying True Story of the Gainesville Ripper* (New York: Avon Books, 1996), 171.

15. Rolling and London, *The Making of a Serial Killer*, 153–54.

16. Quoted in Richard L. Schwoebel, *Explosion Aboard the Iowa* (Annapolis: Naval Institute Press, 1999), 254.

17. House of Representatives, *U.S.S. Iowa Tragedy: An Investigative Failure*, report of the Investigations Subcommittee and Defense Policy Panel of the Committee on Armed Services, March 5, 1990.

18. Robert Keppel, *The Riverman: Ted Bundy and I Hunt for the Green River Killer* (New York: Simon & Schuster, 1995), 102.

19. Egger, *The Killers Among Us*, 75.

20. Seltzer, *Serial Killers*, 1.

21. Brian Masters, "Dahmer's Inferno," *Vanity Fair*, November 1991, https://www.van ityfair.com/style/1991/11/jeffrey-dahmer-dennis-nilsen-serial-killer.

22. Milwaukee Police Department, Supplement Reports, 08-08-91, 131.

23. Milwaukee Police Department, Supplement Reports, 07-24-91, 20–21; 07-23-91, 34–35.

24. Milwaukee Police Department, Supplement Reports, 07-25-91, 37.

25. Schmid, *Natural Born Celebrities*, 221, Kindle, citing Tithecott, *Of Men and Monsters*, 73.

26. Brian Masters, *The Shrine of Jeffrey Dahmer* (London: Coronet Books, 1993), 85, Archive.org PDF edition.

27. Dahmer, *A Father's Story*, 122.

28. Masters, *The Shrine of Jeffrey Dahmer*, 107.
29. Arthur S. Reber, *The Penguin Dictionary of Psychology*, 4th ed. (London: Penguin Books, 2009), 706.
30. Milwaukee Police Department, Supplement Reports, 08-05-91, 126–27.
31. Milwaukee Police Department, Supplement Reports, 07-30-91, 68.
32. Milwaukee Police Department, Supplement Reports, 08-08-91, 132.
33. Ian Brady, *The Gates of Janus: Serial Killing and Its Analysis* (Los Angeles: Feral House, 2001), 87–88.
34. Masters, *The Shrine of Jeffrey Dahmer*, 123.
35. Milwaukee Police Department, Supplement Reports, 08-22-91, 151.
36. Masters, *The Shrine of Jeffrey Dahmer*, 128.
37. Milwaukee Police Department, Supplement Reports, 08-08-91, 132.
38. Milwaukee Police Department, Supplement Reports, 08-22-91, 157–58.
39. Milwaukee Police Department, Supplement Reports, 08-22-91, 157.
40. Tobin Beck, "Tape: Police Thought Boy Was Dahmer's Adult Lover," UPI, August 1, 1991, https://www.upi.com/Archives/1991/08/01/Tape-Police-thought-boy-was-Dahmers-adult-lover/4451681019200/ (accessed March 6, 2020).
41. Beck, "Tape: Police Thought Boy Was Dahmer's Adult Lover."
42. Milwaukee Police Department, *Supplement Reports*, 07-24-91, 24.
43. Masters, *The Shrine of Jeffrey Dahmer*, 165.
44. Masters, "Dahmer's Inferno."
45. Dave Rossie, "A 'Ripping' Tale, New Age Style," *Star-Gazette* (Elmira, NY), April 5, 1994, 4.

Epilogue: The Post-Epidemic Era 2000–2020

1. Morton, US Department of Justice. 2014. p. 5
2. US Department of Justice, Federal Bureau of Investigation, ViCAP Crime Analysis Report, FD-676 (Rev. 3-11-86), OMB No. 1110-0011, Quantico, VA, 1986.
3. T. Christian Miller, "The FBI Built a Database That Can Catch Rapists—Almost Nobody Uses It," ProPublica, July 30, 2015, https://www.propublica.org/article/the-fbi-built-a-database-that-can-catch-rapists-almost-nobody-uses-it.
4. Peter Vronsky, "The Hunting Humans 'Ninja' Truck Driver," in *Serial Killers True Crime Anthology 2015* (RJ Parker Publishing, 2015), 288–89.
5. http://www.fbi.gov/news/stories/2008/august/vicap_080408.
6. Miller, "The FBI Built a Database That Can Catch Rapists—Almost Nobody Uses It."
7. Government of Canada Budgets and Expenditures, https://www.canada.ca/en/treasury-board-secretariat/services/planned-government-spending/budgets-expenditures/actual-expenditure-program-organization-2016-17.html.
8. Toronto Police Service, "2017 Preliminary Operating Budget Program Breakdown," http://www.tpsb.ca/images/TPS_2017_Budget_Information_Public_rev.pdf.
9. John C. Fogerty, "Bad Moon Rising" lyrics © The Bicycle Music Company.

Index